Desperate Measures

Desperate Measures

The Life and Music of Antonia Padoani Bembo

Claire Fontijn

OXFORD
UNIVERSITY PRESS

2006

OXFORD
UNIVERSITY PRESS

Oxford University Press, Inc., publishes works that further
Oxford University's objective of excellence
in research, scholarship, and education.

Oxford New York

Auckland Cape Town Dar es Salaam Hong Kong Karachi
Kuala Lumpur Madrid Melbourne Mexico City Nairobi
New Delhi Shanghai Taipei Toronto

With offices in

Argentina Austria Brazil Chile Czech Republic France Greece
Guatemala Hungary Italy Japan Poland Portugal Singapore
South Korea Switzerland Thailand Turkey Ukraine Vietnam

Copyright © 2006 by Claire Fontijn

Published by Oxford University Press, Inc.
198 Madison Avenue, New York, New York 10016

www.oup.com

Oxford is a registered trademark of Oxford University Press

Library of Congress Cataloging-in-Publication Data
Fontijn, Claire Anne, 1960–
Desperate measures : the life and music of Antonia Padoani Bembo /
Claire Fontijn.
p.   cm.
ISBN 978-0-19-513538-1

1. Bembo, Antonia, fl. 1643–1715. 2. Bembo, Antonia, fl. 1643–1715—
Criticism and interpretation. 3. Composers—France—17th century—Biography.
4. Women composers—France—17th century—Biography.   I. Title.
ML410.B4475F66 2006
782.0092—dc22   2005033125

3 5 7 9 8 6 4 2

Printed in the United States of America
on acid-free paper

For Amica
figlia scorta e fonte

In the conventual buildings attached to this church [Santa Maria dei Frari] are the state archives of Venice . . . they are said to number millions of documents. "They are the records of centuries of the most watchful, observant, and suspicious government that ever existed—in which everything was written down and nothing spoken out." They fill nearly three hundred rooms. Among them are manuscripts from the archives of nearly two thousand families, monasteries, and convents. The secret history of Venice for a thousand years is here—its plots, its hidden trials, its assassinations, its commissions of hireling spies and masked bravoes—food, ready to hand, for a world of dark and mysterious romances.

—Mark Twain, *The Innocents Abroad*

ACKNOWLEDGMENTS

Many people and institutions have contributed over a rather long period of time to the nascence of this book. I am indebted to the generosity of Welles-ley College for all it has supplied in research support over the past decade of my professorship, for providing a substantial publication subvention, and for its libraries and Interlibrary Loan service. By now several members of the Wellesley community are familiar with the name of Bembo and have con-tributed to this project in ways great and small. In the Music Department, I thank Tamar Barzel, Pamela Bristah, Martin Brody, John Diggins, Marion Dry, Charles Fisk, Emily Kennedy, Julia Pollock, Elise Yun, and Arlene Zall-man for their unflagging support and encouragement. I am grateful to the music majors who have helped over the years with the research, musical ex-amples, and proofreading: Rebecca Soderman, Heather Burnett, Joanna Wulfsberg, Alex Swartsel, Brooke Bryant, Krista Kateneva, and Stephanie Kacoyanis. In the Feminist Reading Group, comments offered by Vicki Mistacco, Lidwien Kapteijns, Susan Reverby, Geeta Patel, and Elena Tajima Creef have proven to be most useful. Wellesley colleagues Margaret Cézair-Thompson, Rachel Jacoff, Eleanor De Lorme, Bill Joseph, Steve Harris, and Jamie Goodbinder all offered critical assistance along the way.

I am grateful to the Publications Committee of the American Musicolog-ical Society whose Dragan Plamenac Fund supported the production of the musical examples as they evolved from manuscripts to modern editions. I ac-knowledge the Gladys Krieble Delmas Foundation for Research in Venice, which provided funding to support three separate research trips as well as a generous publication subvention. I am obliged to Princeton University, and particularly to Scott Burnham and Paul Lansky, for having welcomed me as a Visiting Scholar during the 1997–1998 year when I began writing up the research.

The greater scholarly community of musicologists and Venetianists has inspired much of my work, and I owe a debt of thanks in particular to Adrienne Fried Block, Patricia Fortini Brown, Ersie Burke, Mauro Calcagno, Tim Carter, Catherine Gordon-Seifert, John Hajdu Heyer, Holly Hurlburt, Frederick Ilchman, Anna-Kerstin Källman, Robert Kendrick, Jean-Paul Montagnier, Ardal Powell, Joshua Rifkin, Alexander Silbiger, Judith Tick, Steven Zohn, and the members of the CUNY Music Biography Seminar. John Mayrose of Duke University typeset the musical examples found here.

The warm hospitality of Marinella Laini and Stefano Polizzi in Venice and of Philippe Suzanne and Nicole Joyé in Paris contributed in many ways to the joys of research. While in Europe, I benefited from the interest and talent of the following people: in Paris, Catherine Massip of the Bibliothèque Nationale and Fabienne Queyroux of the Institut de France; in Venice, Eduardo Giuffrida, Alessandra Sambo, Claudia Salmini, and Michela dal Borgo of the Archivio di Stato; in Padua, Giovanni Zanovello, Rea Caseracciu, and Emilia Veronese; in Mantua, Anna Maria Lorenzoni and Claudio Gallico; in Trieste, Ivano Cavallini; and, in Bologna, the late Oscar Mischiati.

A project such as this one—which deals with music that has long lain forgotten in manuscripts—relies heavily on performers who are willing to experiment with making editions and trying out first-time performances. It has also made a great deal of difference to a scholar working in relative isolation to learn of others' love of Bembo's music. I am thankful for the opportunity to work with Laury Gutiérrez and La Donna Musicale—particularly Lydia Heather Knutson, Laura Gulley, Na'ama Lion, Ruth McKay, and Daniela Tosič—on a decade of performances of Bembo's psalms, portions of the opera, and arias. A collaboration with Maria Jonas helped deepen my familiarity with the gargantuan compilation of *Produzioni armoniche.* I am grateful to Wolfgang Fürlinger, Conrad Misch, Dorota Cybulska, Ralf Dahler, and the Radio Suisse Romande for sharing with me recordings of their performances of Bembo's music. It has been a recent delight to work closely with Elena Russo of Bizzarrie Armoniche, Milan, and to discover the magnificent results achieved by singer Roberta Invernizzi. Toby Mountain of Northeastern Digital mastered the accompanying CD.

At Oxford University Press, I am grateful for the assiduous production work of Assistant Editor Norm Hirschy, Editor Suzanne Ryan, Senior Production Editor Bob Milks, and also, in the early stages, the assistance of Maribeth Anderson Payne, Maureen Buja, and Ellen Welch.

Giovanna Roz, Sergio Parussa, Denis Grélé, Massimo Ossi, Giovanni Zanovello, and Michael Talbot all offered invaluable help with the translations found throughout the book. Indeed my greatest debt of gratitude goes to Professor Talbot, whom I first met in 1992 at the Biennial Conference on Baroque Music in Durham, the month after Antonia Bembo had surfaced at the Archivio di Stato di Venezia. From the start, he could see the project's inherent worth and understood the cross-cultural issues and feminist challenges that accompanied it. His comments on the book's chapters have been indispensable over the course of their developing narrative. It is rare to find a reader at once so encouraging and so discriminating, and surely no one reads more thoroughly and quickly than he.

No musicologist in Venice should undertake any project without at some point consulting Beth Glixon and Jonathan Glixon. Their methodology and meticulous knowledge of the Archivio di Stato and the Biblioteca Marciana has provided much of the basis for this biography. I cannot thank them enough for their unstinting gifts of time, documents, and friendly collegiality over the course of the past decade.

Finally, I would like to acknowledge the help offered by my friends and family. Effie Papanikolaou, Karen van Dyck, Nelson Moe, Palliath George Mathew, Lenard Milich, and K. V. Lakshmi have all offered intellectual and moral support at crucial times. I am grateful for the interest shown in this project by Francophiles Herbert Fontijn and Annet Fontijn-Davidson as well as by Marie-Louise Desbarats Schönbaum and the late Eduard Schönbaum. From the start of this project, my parents, Sylvia Elvin and Arthur Fontijn, have patiently listened to the "bare bones of research" and have consistently offered intelligent comments testifying to their acute attention. This book is dedicated with profound affection to my daughter, Amica, light of my life and hope for the future.

This book has been typeset in the Bembo font.

EDITORIAL POLICY

The goal throughout this book has been to normalize and modernize the notation found in the manuscripts. Likewise, the text has been normalized and modernized in the intercalated musical examples and in appendix 2, and orthographic mistakes tacitly corrected. By contrast, the texts found in appendix 1 represent transcriptions that have remained as faithful as possible to the original documents.

For the labeling of instrumental and vocal parts, see the abbreviations list. The instruments in use during Bembo's time were quite different from those found in the modern orchestra. While the violin roughly corresponds to the instrument she called the "violon," the inner and bass parts contrast with the standard string family of today. The first and second violins are usually called first "dessus" and second "dessus" to indicate their treble range; the same term is employed for the first and second soprano parts. The inner parts correspond to the modern viola in their alto range, but in French performance practice Baroque violas were named variously "haute contre de violon" or "taille de violon." The vocal parts correspond to the instrumental parts, with "haute contre"—male or female—as a designation referring to the alto or high tenor range. The basso continuo part could be played by the harpsichord, organ, and/or theorbo, along with the viola da gamba, violoncello, and/or bassoon. Bembo called for flutes at several junctures; the final chapters consider to which instruments she may have been referring.

For the meaning of abbreviations used in references to documents in the text and notes, see the bibliography.

CONTENTS

List of Documents (Appendix 1)   xv

List of Longer Musical Examples (Appendix 2)   xvii

Abbreviations   xix

Introduction: Uncovering Her Story   3

PART I. THE LIFE

Chapter 1.   The Girl Who Sings   13

Chapter 2.   Our Lady of Good News   42

PART II. THE MUSIC

Chapter 3.   Harmonic Productions   85

Chapter 4.   Ties That Bind   133

Chapter 5.   The United Tastes   181

Chapter 6.   Penitence   213

Chapter 7.   *Hercules in Love*   241

Postscript: Sunset   273

Appendix 1.   Documents   277

Appendix 2.   Longer Musical Examples   299

List of Compact Disc Tracks   339

Bibliography   341

Index   361

LIST OF DOCUMENTS
(APPENDIX I)

1. F-Pn, Rés.Vm^{1}117, *Produzioni armoniche,* Dedication, ff. 4r–5r

2. I-MAa, Archivio Gonzaga, *Carteggi esteri,* Carteggi ad inviati (Venezia), Busta 1571

3. I-MAa, Archivio Gonzaga, *Lettere ai Gonzaga Mantova e Paesi* (1654), Busta 2796/VII, carta 269

4. I-MAa, Archivio Gonzaga, *Lettere ai Gonzaga Mantova e Paesi* (1654), Busta 2796/VII, carta 271

5. I-MAa, Archivio Gonzaga, *Carteggi esteri,* Carteggi ad inviati (Venezia), Busta 1571, Bosso Residente 1654

6. I-MAa, Archivio Gonzaga, *Carteggi esteri,* Carteggi ad inviati (Venezia), Busta 1571, Bosso Residente 1654

7. I-MAa, Archivio Gonzaga, *Carteggi esteri,* Carteggi ad inviati (Venezia), Busta 1571, Diversi 1652

8. I-MAa, Archivio Gonzaga, *Carteggi esteri,* Carteggi ad inviati (Venezia), Busta 1571, Bosso Residente 1654

9. I-Vas, Notarile, *Atti,* Pietro Bracchi e Girolamo Brinis, Busta 884, ff. 194v–196

10. I-Vas, Notarile, *Atti,* Camillo Lion, Busta 8022, f. 176

11. I-Vas, Notarile, *Atti,* Camillo Lion, Busta 8022, f. 178

12. I-Vas, Notarile, *Testamenti,* Camillo Lion, Busta 591, no. 87 (13 March 1662)

13. S. Romanin, *Storia documentata di Venezia* (Venice: Pietro Naratovich, 1858), 7: 453–454

14. I-Vasp, Curia Patriarcale, *Sezione antica: Filciae causarum,* Busta 68 (1672–1673), f. 3

15. I-Vas, Notarile, *Atti,* Giovanni Antonio Mora, Busta 8651 bis, ff. 208–208v

16. I-Vas, Corporazioni religiose, *San Bernardo di Murano,* Busta 18, Mazzo Q, Plica D
17. I-Vas, Corporazioni religiose, *San Bernardo di Murano,* Busta 18, Mazzo Q, Plica D
18. I-Vas, Corporazioni religiose, *San Bernardo di Murano,* Busta 18, Mazzo Q, Plica D
19. I-Vas, Notarile, *Atti,* Vincenzo Vincenti, Busta 13852 (protocollo, 1683), ff. 141 r–v
20. I-Vas, Corporazioni religiose, *San Bernardo di Murano,* Busta 18, Mazzo Q, Plica D
21. I-Vas, Corporazioni religiose, *San Bernardo di Murano,* Busta 18, Mazzo Q, Plica D
22. I-Vas, Capi del Consiglio de' Dieci, *Notatorio,* Filza 38 (1681–1700), ff. 1r–v
23. I-Vas, Consiglio de' Dieci, *Parti Criminali,* Filza 119, f. 1
24. I-Vas, Notarile, *Atti,* Pietro Antonio Ciola, Busta 4032 (minute), 20 August 1704
25. F-Pn, Rés.Vm¹112–113, *Te Deum* and *Divertimento,* Dedication, ff. 3–3v
26. F-Pn, Rés.Vm¹114–115, *Te Deum* and *Exaudiat te, Dominus,* Dedication, ff. 3–3v
27. F-Pn, Rés. Vm¹116, *Les sept Pseaumes, de David,* Dedication, ff. 2v–3
28. F-Pn, Rés. Vm¹116, *Les sept Pseaumes, de David,* Dedicatory poem, ff. 3v–4
29. F-Pn, Rés. Vm⁴9, *L'Ercole amante,* Title page, f. 2
30. F-Pn, Rés. Vm⁴10, *L'Ercole amante,* Dedicatory Madrigal, opp. p. 243

LIST OF LONGER MUSICAL
EXAMPLES (APPENDIX 2)

Ex. A.1.   F-Pn, Rés. Vm¹117, *Produzioni armoniche,* no. 22, pp. 181–184

Ex. A.2.   F-Pn, Rés. Vm¹117, *Produzioni armoniche,* no. 18, pp. 163–165

Ex. A.3.   F-Pn, Rés. Vm¹117, *Produzioni armoniche,* no. 19, pp. 166-169

Ex. A.4.   F-Pn, Vm⁷546, Ballard, *Recueil* (1713), p. 215

Ex. A.5.   François Couperin, *Concert instrumental sous le Titre d'Apotheose,*
p. 15

Ex. A.6.   F-Pn, Rés. Vm¹113, "Menuet," mm. 337–358

Ex. A.7.   Lully, *Ballet de la Raillerie,* LWV 11, "Dialogue de la musique
italienne et de la musique française"

Ex. A.8.   F-Pn, Rés. Vm¹114, pp. 50–51, mm. 195 bis–204 bis

Ex. A.9.   F-Pn, Rés. Vm¹114, pp. 77–82, mm. 282 bis–332 bis

Ex. A.10. F-Pn, Rés. Vm⁴9, pp. 34–42, Juno (I, iii)

Ex. A.11. F-Pn, Rés. Vm⁴9, pp. 103–113, Pasithea (II, vi)

ABBREVIATIONS

A.1	a longer musical example found in appendix 2
anti.	antiphonal passage
B	bass
b. bb.	*busta*—a large folder in an Italian archive
b.c.	basso continuo
bis	measures appearing in the manuscript and not in the modern edition
Bsn.	bassoon
CD tr.	tracks on the accompanying compact disc
Chorus	"chœur de voix" (S^1, S^2, HC, T, B, b.c. with figures)
d.c.	da capo
doc.	appendix 1, documents 1–30
doux	soft (piano)
ff.	plural of folio (f.), or of what follows (m. 34 ff. means the measures after m. 34)
Fl.	flute
fort	loud (forte)
HC	*haute-contre* (male or female singer in the alto range)
HCV^1	*haute-contre* or *taille de violon* 1, corresponding to the modern viola
HCV^2	*haute-contre* or *taille de violon* 2, corresponding to the modern viola
m., mm.	measure, measures
m.v.	*more veneto:* the Venetian calendar year starts in March (e.g. January 2005 m.v. = January 2006)
Ps.	Psalm
rit.	ritornello

S^1	soprano 1
S^2	soprano 2
Symph.	"chœur de symphonie" (V^1, V^2, HCV^1, HCV^2, b.c. unfigured)
sync.	syncopated passage
T	tenor
Tutti	the full complement of voices and instruments
V^1	*premier dessus de violon* (or top treble line) corresponding to violin 1
V^2	*deuxième dessus de violon* (or second treble line) corresponding to violin 2
Vdg.	viola da gamba
Vm^1	library shelf number for Parisian sources

Desperate Measures

INTRODUCTION:
UNCOVERING HER STORY

Sire,

The immortal fame of Your Majesty's most glorious name, instilled in my heart since childhood, made me decide to leave my country, family, and friends to come and bow down before so great a monarch. I arrived at this royal court already many years ago where, by my fate, it was presented to Your Majesty that I had some talent in singing and you were willing to listen to me; learning that I had been abandoned by the person who took me away from Venice, Your Majesty was so kind as to reward me with a pension, with which I could stay in the community of Notre Dame de Bonne Nouvelle, until the occasion arose to put me in a more suitable place. Now in this holy refuge, obtained through the magnificence of Your Majesty, I have made some compositions in music; I come to deliver them at your royal feet as a most reverent tribute of my immense obligation. I beg you most humbly to accept them with your customary royal kindness and to you I make my deepest bow.

Your Majesty's humblest and most obedient servant,
Antonia Bembo, Noble Venetian[1]

The composer's dedicatory letter to King Louis XIV introduces her first collection of vocal pieces, *Produzioni armoniche*.[2] It also provides intriguing autobiographical information. Why would she leave Venice? How had she gained admiration for the king so early in life, and under which circumstances did he deem her a singer worthy of a pension? How was she abandoned and what was "the community of Notre Dame de Bonne Nouvelle" ("Our Lady of Good News")? When did she move to the "holy

---

[1] For a complete transcription of the document, see appendix 1, document 1; hereinafter, doc. 1.

[2] F-Pn, Rés. Vm¹117, ff. 4–5.

3

refuge," and where was it? How did she learn to compose all of this music? This book takes on these questions, as well as others that sustained a decade-long search for details about her career. Bembo's letter begs as much for biographical as for musical attention; the tale of her life has remained even more obscure than her œuvre.

In late January 1990, I read that Yvonne Rokseth in 1937 had relegated the composer's identity to the "enigmas of music history."[3] It appeared that, even decades after Rokseth's statement, no one had matched a person with the manuscripts of *Produzioni armoniche* (now in the Bibliothèque Nationale in Paris) signed "Antonia Bembo." Thanks to fellow French Baroque music scholar Antonia Banducci, who sent me microfilms of the music manuscripts, my quest could begin immediately. In Paris that summer, I determined that Bembo's "holy refuge" referred to the community of the Petite Union Chrétienne des Dames de Saint Chaumond. In Venice at the start of the 1991–1992 academic year, I developed a working hypothesis that the composer had not been born a "Bembo," but had married into the family. I gathered information about the family of the only "Antonia" who matched that criterion in the pertinent years, mostly having to do with her father, Dr. Giacomo Padoani. From October through April I combed Paris for any mention of her, but there was none. To date, her name appears in no source in France beyond her own music manuscripts.

Shelf browsing one morning in the Reading Room of the Marciana Library during the last week of a second research trip to Venice in May, I opened a book mentioning a collection of papers concerning "Antonia Padoani who had gone to Paris." Quickly crossing the city from San Marco to the Frari, I inquired about the papers at the Archivio di Stato, where I learned that they were preserved somewhere inside the archive's 22 large folders (*buste*) containing the records of the former convent of San Bernardo di Murano. Working backward from *busta* 22 to *busta* 20, and then forward from *busta* 1 to *busta* 17, by the week's end I was still empty handed, exhausted from working at top speed, grimy from documents covered in centuries of accumulated matter, and heavy hearted as a *tempesta di mare* brewed outside the apartment where I was staying with my colleague Marinella Laini. On my last working day in Venice, a morning made crystal clear by the storm, I ordered *busta* 18. Within minutes, I held the envelope with the papers pertaining to Antonia—at last making contact with the heretofore hypothetical composer. *Busta* 19 brought still more treasure: the Parisian address of "la Bemba" written in a small journal kept by one of her friends at the convent on the island of Murano.

The following summer, I examined the documents at a more normal pace, finding an abundance of information about the branch of the Bembo fam-

[3] Yvonne Rokseth, "Antonia Bembo, Composer to Louis XIV," *Musical Quarterly* 23 (1937): 169.

ily into which Antonia had married. With a crucial lead from Beth Glixon, further digging in the Archivio di Stato of Mantua revealed Antonia's encounters with composers Francesco Cavalli and Francesco Corbetta during the 1650s. The "Corbetta Hypothesis"—that the musician escorted her to Paris some two decades later—has become an increasingly plausible explanation of her definitive departure from Venice, and of how she came to live among other Italian expatriates in Paris, apparently, before moving to the Petite Union Chrétienne.

Produzioni armoniche does not stand alone; the Bibliothèque Nationale in Paris preserves five other manuscripts by Bembo. In the 1930s, the library had acquired her two-volume opera *L'Ercole amante* (table I.1b), which joined the four other manuscripts that had belonged to the former Bibliothèque Royale (table I.1a).[4] The acquisition led Rokseth to write a far-ranging article about Bembo, whose music had neither been published nor copied into other exemplars. Rokseth effectively offered the first study of the *Gesamtausgabe* of a rather prolific composer.

Rokseth's article served as the source of information for all other writings on Bembo until the work of Marinella Laini and my own.[5] Those included reference works, catalogues, and books that address specific issues related to women in music, as well as general music histories.[6] Since I began my research, further references to the composer have appeared in several studies of musical culture.[7]

---

[4] Previous to the acquisition of the opera, Michel Brenet had noted the four manuscripts in her dictionary entry, "Bembo, La signora Antonia," in Robert Eitner, *Biographisch-Bibliographisches Quellen-Lexikon der Musiker und Musikgelehrten* (Leipzig: Breitkopf und Härtel, 1900), 1: 429.

[5] Mine include: "In Honour of the Duchess of Burgundy: Antonia Bembo's Compositions for Marie-Adélaïde of Savoy," *Cahiers de l'Institut de recherches et d'histoire musicale des états de Savoie* 3 (1995): 45–89; "Antonia Bembo," in *Women Composers: Music through the Ages,* ed. Martha Furman Schleifer and Sylvia Glickman (New York: G. K. Hall, 1996), 2: 201–216; "Baroque Women 5: Antonia Bembo," *Goldberg Early Music Magazine* 6 (1999): 110–113; and "Le armoniose relazioni," *Amadeus* 175 (June 2004): 28–30. Laini published findings in "Le 'Produzioni Armoniche' di Antonia Bembo" (Laureate Thesis, Università degli studi di Pavia, 1987); "La musica di Antonia Bembo: Un significativo apporto femminile alle relazioni musicali tra Venezia e Parigi," *Studi Musicali* 25 (1996): 255–281; and "Antonia e le altre: percorsi musicali femminili nella Venezia del Sei-Settecento," in *Ecco mormorar l'onde: la musica nel Barocco,* ed. C. de Incontrera and A. Sanini (Monfalcone, 1995), 138–169. In addition, we collaborated on two dictionary entries: "Bembo, Antonia," in *The Norton/Grove Dictionary of Women Composers,* ed. Julie Anne Sadie and Rhian Samuel (London: Macmillan, 1994), 56–57, and "Bembo, Antonia" in the *New Grove Dictionary of Music and Musicians,* 2nd ed., ed. Stanley Sadie and John Tyrrell (London: Macmillan, 2001), 3: 220–221.

[6] For a literature survey, 1937–1994, see Fontijn, "Antonia Bembo: 'Les goûts réunis,' Royal Patronage, and the Role of the Woman Composer during the Reign of Louis XIV" (Ph.D. diss., Duke University, 1994), 2.

[7] Such studies include those by Jane L. Baldauf-Berdes, *Women Musicians of Venice: Musical Foundations 1525–1855* (Oxford: Clarendon Press, 1993; rev. ed., Elsie Arnold, 1996), 237; Barbara Garvey Jackson, "Musical Women of the Seventeenth and Eighteenth Centuries," in *Women and*

TABLE I.I Bembo's Music Manuscripts at F-Pn (Paris, Bibliothèque Nationale)

	Shelf number	Date[a]
a. Manuscripts from the Bibliothèque Royale		
Produzioni armoniche	Rés. Vm¹117	1697–1701
Tè Deum and *Divertimento*	Rés. Vm¹112–113	1704
Tè Deum and *Exaudiat te, Dominus*	Rés. Vm¹114–115	1708
Les sept Pseaumes, de David	Rés. Vm¹116	1710
b. Manuscripts acquired, mid-1930s		
L'Ercole amante, in two volumes	Rés. Vm⁴9–10	1707

[a]Date is putative for manuscripts from the Bibliothèque Royale. The date for *L'Ercole amante* is on the title page.

The groundwork laid by Rokseth and Laini oriented my initial study of the manuscripts. Rokseth dated and ordered them, discussed their bindings and their royal dedicatees, and noted the occasions for which they may have been composed. She identified the authors of several of the texts, considered the subject of female education in France and in Italy relevant to the composer, transcribed and provided facsimiles of representative works, and identified the characteristics of Bembo's musical style. Laini transcribed the texts of *Produzioni armoniche*, evaluated their quality, enumerated the pieces in the compilation, and edited an aria and a cantata from it.[8]

The absence of information or eyewitness accounts in chronicles from the period remains a challenge in writing about Bembo's musical career. Yet the numerous documents that have now surfaced regarding her relations with the Padoani and Bembo families permit a reconstruction of her biography in part I. As the only daughter of Venetian *cittadini*—members of Venice's professional middle class—she followed for some time the path that her parents set out for her. Part of her father's ambition almost certainly concerned making connections to musical circles. He wrote that he and his wife had worked hard to "nourish her soul in order to make her succeed in 'virtù' to the astonishment of the world" (doc. 12). Chapter 1, "The Girl Who Sings," confirms Antonia's studies with Cavalli, the renowned composer and *maestro di cappella* of St. Mark's, and examines the implication that she was something of a child prodigy.

Recent scholarly inquiry into the lives and works of long-ignored women composers has led to new information about them and to new recordings of

---

Music: A History, 2nd ed., ed. Karin Pendle (Bloomington: Indiana University Press, 2001), 120–123; Julie Anne Sadie, "Paris and Versailles," in *The Late Baroque Era: From the 1680s to 1740,* ed. George J. Buelow, Music and Society Series (Englewood Cliffs, NJ: Prentice Hall, 1993), 137; and Marcia Citron, *Gender and the Musical Canon* (Cambridge: Cambridge University Press, 1993), 248, n. 1.

[8] Laini, "Le 'Produzioni Armoniche'," 31–75.

their music, as is the case for Bembo's two most important contemporaries, Barbara Strozzi in Venice and Élisabeth-Claude Jacquet de La Guerre in Paris. For several reasons, Bembo's story has remained far more obscure than theirs. Unlike Strozzi, who had a significant place in the musical life of her father's academy in Venice, or La Guerre, who came from a musical dynasty and enjoyed both royal and public support for her work as a musician, Bembo had no family connection to music. Her tale therefore can only be pieced together from archival evidence, with only the rare document linked to the musical world. Her compositions must be interpreted entirely from manuscripts rather than from the printed editions that her female contemporaries managed to have had published. Now, supplied with specific details of her life excavated from the archives and with several editions of her music,[9] this study offers a comprehensive biography and an analysis of representative pieces that together establish her place in the musical culture of Venice (1640–1677) and Paris (1677–1720).

Similar research projects—on Strozzi and La Guerre, but also on Francesca Caccini and on music in Italian women's convents—reveal that many women enjoyed significant musical careers in seventeenth-century France and Italy.[10] Evidently Bembo had little public presence, given that her name appears in no contemporary chronicles; yet preserved correspondence, her manuscript dedications, and several song texts reveal her proximity not just to Cavalli and Corbetta but to the private circles of Carlo II Gonzaga, Duke of Mantua; the Italians in Paris; Marie-Adélaïde of Savoy, Duchess of Burgundy; and Louis XIV. Having escaped from Venice, Bembo needed to be sure she would not be found in Paris and forced to return. Apparently she concealed her whereabouts until she reached the safety of the semi-cloistered Petite Union Chrétienne. If indeed no mention of her exists in Paris, perhaps

---

[9] Five edited works are available from *Produzioni armoniche:* John Glenn Paton, ed., *Italian Arias of the Baroque and Classical Eras* (Van Nuys, CA: Alfred, 1994), 56–59; three pieces in Fontijn, "Antonia Bembo," and Fontijn, ed., *Per il Natale* (Fayetteville, AR: Clar-Nan, 1999). Also see Wolfgang Fürlinger, ed., *Te Deum* (F-Pn, Rés. Vm^{1}114) (Altötting: Coppenrath, 1999), Conrad Misch, ed., *Les Sept Psaumes de David,* vols. 1–7 (Kassel: Furore Verlag, 2003), Conrad Misch, ed., *Te Deum* (F-Pn, Rés. Vm^{1}112) (Kassel: Furore Verlag, 2003), and Conrad Misch, ed., *Exaudiat te Dominus* (Kassel: Furore Verlag, 2003).

[10] On Caccini, see Suzanne Cusick, *A Romanesca of One's Own: Voice, Subjectivity, and Power in Francesca Caccini's Florence* (Chicago: University of Chicago Press, forthcoming). Beth Glixon's articles—"New Light on the Life and Career of Barbara Strozzi," *Musical Quarterly* 81 (1997): 311–335, and "More on the Life and Death of Barbara Strozzi," *Musical Quarterly* 83 (1999): 134–141—reveal astounding new facts about Strozzi's life in Venice and that she lived until 1677—well past 1664, the publication date of her last work. On La Guerre, see Catherine Cessac, *Élisabeth Jacquet de la Guerre—Une femme compositeur sous le règne de Louis XIV* (Arles: Actes Sud, 1995). For information about women and musical life in convents, see especially Robert L. Kendrick, *Celestial Sirens: Nuns and their Music in Early Modern Milan* (Oxford: Clarendon Press, 1996) and Craig A. Monson, *Disembodied Voices: Music and Culture in an Early Modern Italian Convent* (Berkeley: University of California Press, 1995).

it was of her own doing, in order to protect her precarious existence abroad. She now emerges, joining La Guerre as one of the two most prolific women composers active in France during the Sun King's reign.[11]

Bembo's further musical career would wait until well after the years she lived as a Venetian nobleman's wife.[12] Chapter 2, "Our Lady of Good News," notes a shift in focus from singing to composition after she obtained the king's support (doc. 1). Like many recent historical projects, this study examines one of the common people, one of the good but not "great" musicians.[13] In this sense, this project diverges from most life and works studies of composers in that so little of Bembo's documented life has anything to do with music making. It seems quite unlikely at this point that more substantive documentation about her career will surface, but her pieces provide vibrant testimony to the milieux in which she worked. Her music navigates smoothly between two cultures and between her worldly and religious environments.

Part II examines each manuscript (table I.1), the products of a mature musician composing music between her fifties and her seventies. Her music presents nothing less than a retrospective sweep through the predominant styles of vocal music, chamber music, and opera found in Venice and Paris in the 1650–1710 period. In chapter 3, "Harmonic Productions," the autobiographical details of the dedication to *Produzioni armoniche* guide an analysis of the narrative unfolding throughout its contents. Bembo wrote the majority of its pieces for her own voice, a high soprano, with the accompaniment of the basso continuo (b.c.). Most notable are the solo songs, sacred and secular, delivered in the subjective voice of a woman asserting an incontrovertibly feminine force. In all likelihood several represent her long-standing repertory as a singer, only here committed to paper. Harking back to Monteverdi (with an allusion to *L'Orfeo*), Cavalli (with a new setting of *L'Ercole amante*), and Strozzi (with amorous song and clever madrigalism), some of the Italian pieces suggest that they were conceived, if not composed, in Venice. Music for the

---

[11] Citron named Bembo and La Guerre as early examples of professionals. Although they do share other characteristics (such as precocious talent, the composition of an opera, and royal patronage), the concept applies only to the latter. See *Gender,* chapter 4, "Professionalism," 81. For details about the two dozen or so women actively pursuing composition during the reign of Louis XIV, see my "Antonia Bembo: 'Les goûts réunis,'" 115–214.

[12] For a description of the restrictive life of Venetian noblewomen, see Alexandre Toussaint de Limojon, Sieur de Saint Disdier, "Des Gentils Donnes venitiennes," 355–363 in *La Ville et la République de Venise* (Paris: Louis Billaine, 1680).

[13] See Carlo Ginzburg, *The Cheese and the Worms: The Cosmos of a Sixteenth-Century Miller,* trans. John and Anne Tedeschi (Harmondsworth: Penguin, 1982; orig. *Il formaggio e i vermi: Il cosmo di un mugnaio del '500* [Turin: Giulio Einaudi Editore, 1976]). Ginzburg cited Brecht as the inspiration: "In the past historians could be accused of wanting to know only about 'the great deeds of kings,' but today this is certainly no longer true. More and more they are turning toward what their predecessors passed over in silence, discarded, or simply ignored. 'Who built Thebes of the seven gates?' Bertolt Brecht's 'literate worker' was already asking" (xiii).

French royal family represents new encomiastic song. The pieces espousing the French styles of the Lullian *petit motet* and the airs of the urban salons demonstrate remarkable acculturation. The core of the compilation reflects the *poesie per musica,* comedic play, and music produced by Bembo's compatriots in Paris.

The set of wedding pieces in *Produzioni armoniche*—in which Bembo made her Monteverdian allusion—may have won her the patronage of a fellow Italian-speaker at court: Marie-Adélaïde of Savoy, Duchess of Burgundy. First honored with three of Bembo's pieces when she arrived in France, she received a much larger composition for the occasion of the birth of her first child and heir to the French throne, the Duke of Brittany. The boy's mixed Italian and French heritage offered the perfect vehicle for Bembo to blend the two national repertories with which she was familiar: a French-style *Te Deum* in Latin and a *Divertimento* in Italian. Chapter 4, "Ties That Bind," takes particular note of the fact that Bembo focused on the duchess's heroic role as peace-maker and mother, rather than on the more customary consideration of a foreign bride as a pawn in a peace treaty.

In keeping with the pious final years of the reign of Louis XIV, Bembo turned her attention to offering him two large-scale pieces of sacred music, the subject of chapter 5, "The United Tastes." Bembo emulated the practice of the Chapelle Royale by scoring a second setting of the *Te Deum* as a *grand motet* for soloists, chorus, and orchestra. Drawing on the models of Charpentier and Lalande but ultimately enjoying the freedom to adopt her own manner, she found here an optimal site for vital interplay between the French and the Italian styles. "Les goûts réunis," a phrase coined by François Couperin in 1724 to describe a burgeoning mixture of the French and Italian styles, refers here to Bembo's particular way of synthesizing them. As a language belonging to both nationalities, Latin offered neutral ground for uniting the tastes. Expanding on the Lullian *petits motets* of *Produzioni armoniche* and employing the same scoring as the *Te Deum* for Marie-Adélaïde, *Exaudiat te, Dominus* effectively paved the way for her next project: a complete setting of the penitential psalms.

Chapter 6, "Penitence," furthers the notion that Bembo sought ways to give voice to women's experience. Taking on French paraphrases of the seven penitential psalms, she championed the work of the extraordinary Parisian poet, painter, engraver, sculptor, academician, musician, and teacher: Élisabeth-Sophie Chéron. It may have been Chéron's salon at Saint Sulpice that offered a venue for the performance of Bembo's settings of her poetry, intimate music for an assortment of voices with an instrumental trio. The Parisian salon offered a forum for artistic and intellectual exchange among the many gifted women who prospered during the reign of Louis XIV. *Les sept Pseaumes, de David* represents Bembo's most Gallic moment; in its dedication she styled herself "Antoinette" and likened her patron to the king of the psalms.

Chapter 7, "*Hercules in Love,*" treats Bembo's greatest achievement: a new setting of Buti's libretto for *L'Ercole amante.* The operatic medium brought together all her skills in vivid text painting, character depiction, chamber and orchestral instrumental music, and choral writing. It has been argued that Cavalli left no successors.[14] It is the contention of this study that a good part of his legacy resides in these manuscripts, but the process involved in judging the truth of the claim—editing, performing, and recording the music—has only just begun.

[14] Jane Glover, *Cavalli* (New York: St. Martin's Press, 1978), 151.

Part I

The Life

Chapter 1

THE GIRL WHO SINGS

In the dedication to her first compilation of pieces, the composer identified herself as a noble Venetian brought by an unnamed person to Paris, as a pensioner supported by Louis XIV to live at Notre Dame de Bonne Nouvelle, and as a singer with some talent (doc. 1). Effectively serving as an autobiography gleaned from her six manuscripts of music, these details long remained the sole source of information about her; apparently no further testimony survives in France. In 1992, the discovery of a packet of documents at the Archivio di Stato in Venice corroborated her words and launched the biography of the person now known by her full name, Antonia Padoani Bembo (c. 1640–c. 1720).[1] Thanks to the careful preservation of further documents held in several more Italian institutions, dozens of new archival findings have since surfaced. The vital interplay between the emergence of her story and the analysis of her compositions makes possible a reconstruction of her extraordinary career.

Doctor Padoani's Daughter

In September 1634 "Jacobus Padoani Vicentinus" received his medical degree from the University of Padua.[2] In more than one instance, Giacomo Padoani (1603–1666) described himself as belonging to a family of modest means from the province of Vicenza and emphasized that it had been through hard work in his profession that he had gained status as a Venetian *cittadino,* a mem-

---

[1] Fontijn, "Antonia Bembo," 3.
[2] I-Paau, Dottori licenziati in chirurgia del 1629 al 1640, Codex 275, ff. 90–90v.

ber of Venice's professional middle class.[3] His degree was awarded by the Collegio Veneto of the University of Padua.[4] By comparison with the noble Paduan Count Girolamo Frigimelica Roberti (1611–1683), who received his degree at age 18, Padoani became a professional quite late in life.[5] Antonia's father nevertheless enjoyed a successful career, known as one of the chief physicians of Venice.[6]

Padoani's skill in oratory also earned him recognition in several publications. The eighteenth-century bibliographer Cinelli Calvoli noted his epigram and sonnet published in Padua in 1632.[7] The next year, the doctor was invited to deliver a speech at the convocation of his last year of university studies.[8] In 1640 he published a valedictory oration for Girolamo Bembo, who from 1637 to 1639 served as *Podestà* (mayor) of the Istrian city of Montona (Motovun), a town then belonging to the Venetian Republic.[9] The title page describes Padoani as "medico ordinario di detta terra," an indication that he was the official physician of Montona.[10] The oration represents an initial link between the Bembo and Padoani families.

[3] In his first will of 1651, Padoani specified that all of his earnings "acquired through his labors in medicine" ("aquistato con le . . . fatiche della medicina"), as well as his inheritance from his mother's dowry, should go to his daughter and wife but not to any other family members (I-Vas, Notarile, *Testamenti chiusi*, Girolamo Brinis, b. 642, f. 1v).

[4] Private communication with Dr. Emilia Veronese and Dr. Rea Caseracciu at the Archivio Antico dell'Università di Padova, who identified Padoani's diploma in that list.

[5] Charles Patin, *Lyceum Patavinum* (Padua: Frambotti, 1682), 12–13. Frigimelica Roberti received his medical degree in 1629 and taught in the Collegio Veneto beginning in 1633; he served as witness to the birth of Antonia's first-born son in 1665.

[6] Francesco Sansovino, *Venetia città nobilissima et singolare, descritta in XIIII libri, con aggiunta da D. Giustiniano Martinioni* (Venice: Steffano Curti, 1663; facs. repr., Venice: Filippi, 1968), 2: Terzo Catalogo, 16–17.

[7] I-Vnm, Misc. 207/5 preserves the original print. See the reference to this booklet in Giovanni Cinelli Calvoli, *Biblioteca volante* (Venice: Albrizzi, 1734–1735; facs. repr., Bologna: Arnaldo Forni, 1979): "de' PADOVANI (Giacomo) Oratio Illustriss[imo] & Excellentiss[imo] viro Aloysio Valaresso Equiti, cum Praefectura Patavii summa cum laude & applausu administrata abiret dicta a *Jacobo de Patavinis* Vicentino anno reparatae salutis 1632. die 16. Mensis Decembris. Patavii ex Typographia Bartolomae Caretoni 1632. in 4. ★ nel fine v'è un Epigramma e Sonetto dello stesso Padovani" (4: 3). Emmanuele Antonio Cicogna, *Saggio di Bibliografia veneziana* (Venice: G. B. Merlo, 1847; facs. repr., Bologna: Forni Editore, 1967) mentions this publication as well.

[8] I-Paau, Codex 472: "2 novembris diem nobilitabit oratio in aede Cathedrali pro felici studiorum initio artistarum nomine habita a Iacobo Paduanino, quam sua praesentia reverendissimus episcopus et illustrissimus praeter urbisque praefectus cum magnifica artistarum universitae circumfusa frequenti nobilium studiosorum corona condecorarunt" (ff. 347–348). For modern transcriptions, see Silvio Bernardinello, *Le orazioni per l'annuale apertura degli studi nell'Università di Padova (dal 1405 al 1796)—Saggio bibliografico* (Padua: Società cooperativa tipografica, 1984), 378–379, and Lucia Rossetti, *Acta nationis germanicae artistarum (1616–1636)* (Padua: Editrice Antenore, 1967), 347.

[9] Luigi Morteani, *Storia di Montona* (Trieste: Tipo-Litografia Leghissa, 1963), 246.

[10] Giacomo de' Padovani, *Oratione all'illustrissimo Signor Girolamo Bembo nella partenza dal suo reggimento di Podestà a Montona. Di Giacomo Padovani Dottor di Filosofia, & Medicina,*

Although Padoani's presence in Istria in the late 1630s holds possibilities for the hypothesis that Antonia was born during his period of service there, baptismal records in Montona do not support the idea.[11] Padoani moved to Venice no later than the summer of 1641, when a patient, Cattarina Grigis, came to sign her will at the home of "Giac[om]o Padoani medico della contrà di S[an]ta Maria Mater D[omi]ni."[12] A census record for the neighborhood of Santa Maria Mater Domini at the end of that year lists the members of the household as Padoani, a woman, and a servant.[13] The "woman" in question may well have been his wife, Diana, but the census did not mention her by name.

Little is known about the family of Padoani's wife, Diana Paresco (1609–1676), but a few relationships can be deduced from surviving documents. Like her husband, she had ties to Vicenza and Padua as well as to Venice.[14] In his will of 1662, Giacomo referred to his father-in-law as the "late Camillo Paresco" ("già S[igno]r Camillo Paresco") (doc. 12).[15] A notarized act from 1655 concerns Diana's aunt Isabella Rosan, there named as the daughter of Giulio Rosan and the widow of Antonio Moreschi (his fourth wife).[16] If the biographical situation of Diana Paresco seems somewhat puzzling, even more so is that of her daughter, Antonia, about whom more questions than answers arise regarding the circumstances of her birth.

The census record of 1641 makes no mention of a daughter in the Padoani

---

Medico ordinario de detta Terra (Venice: Pietro Miloco, 1640). The Biblioteca del Museo Civico Correr owns this rare print.

[11] Hr-Ppa, Battesimi, 1586–1644 and 1645–1736; the Padoani family name does not appear in either register. Padoani would return to work in Istria at a later date; in 1663 he contacted Raimondo Fini, a lawyer in Capodistria, to help him retrieve money for services rendered in Buje, a town to the northwest of Montona across the Quieto River (I-Vas, Notarile, *Atti,* Camillo Lion, b. 8029, minute, 1663, 2 January).

[12] I-Vas, Notarile, *Testamenti,* Pietro Reggia, b. 831, n. 24 (1641, 27 August). Padoani also served as the treating physician when she died on 1 January 1642.

[13] I-Vas, Provedditori alla sanità, b. 571: "Giacomo Padovani D[otto]r fisico," "Nume[ro] Delle Anime di casa: 3; Nume[ro] Delli huomini da 18 sin 50: 1; Nume[ro] Delle donne: 1; Nume[ro] delle Massere: 1." "o" is given under the category "Nume[ro] Delle putte sino li 18." Girolamo Brinis, Padoani's notary, is listed just above his entry among the "Cittadini" (the other two categories are "Nobili" and "Artefici"). Thanks are due to Beth Glixon for showing me this census record.

[14] Her dates have been determined by her death notice, which gives her age at the time of decease: I-Pas, Ufficio di Sanità, b. 482. I thank Beth Glixon for this reference.

[15] I-Vas, Notarile, *Atti,* Pietro Bracchi e Girolamo Brinis, b. 871, protocollo (1649, 17 February), mentions Isabetta Giacomoni, the widow of "Giacomo Paresco di Vicenza," who signed an agreement in Venice in 1649, but it is unclear how this couple is related to Diana.

[16] I-Vas, Notarile, *Atti,* Pietro Bracchi e Girolamo Brinis, b. 842, protocollo 1655, ff. 51–52. Rosan drew up this document for Diana, who stood to inherit from her; the inheritance record can be found in I-Vas, Notarile, *Atti,* Camillo Lion, b. 8029, minute (1663, 22 June and 12 July).

household, nor do baptismal records.[17] Yet the descriptions of Antonia in 1654 suggest that she was born no later than about 1640. That the records of baptisms in Montona do not mention her birth in the likely years does not eliminate the possibility that Diana Paresco may have returned to her parents' home in order to deliver her daughter; Antonia herself would do so when she bore at least two of her children in Padua in the 1660s.[18] If it were possible to discover more information about Diana's family, perhaps Antonia's birth date could be ascertained; an estimation of 1640 must suffice.

Padoani's will of 1651 suggests that Antonia had a somewhat willful character. He wrote that she, his "only and beloved daughter," would one day inherit everything from him on the condition that she "should obey her mother . . . if [she] displeases . . . Signora Diana can deprive her of everything that [he is] leaving her."[19] Padoani's threat of disinheritance may reflect his daughter's obstinate behavior. Obedience to her mother would remain an important requirement for Padoani. In his subsequent will he returned to the theme when he accused Antonia of treating her disrespectfully, mentioning the significant role that Diana had played in her education (doc. 12).

In February 1653 Padoani signed an agreement to rent the house of Zan Francesco Balbi in Dorsoduro in the parish of San Pantalon *in salizada,* that is, in one of the streets leading away from the church.[20] This house would remain the Venetian residence of the Padoani family for the next twenty years: when Antonia married in 1659 she would live there with her husband, and her widowed mother still resided in the house in 1673.[21] The Padoani family maintained residences there as well as in Padua during the 1660s.

Soon after the move to San Pantalon, the Duke of Mantua, Carlo II Gonzaga, invited the doctor to serve at his court. The correspondence between them, preserved at the Archivio Gonzaga of Mantua, provides somewhat cryptic information about the doctor, his wife and daughter, and the musicians Francesco Corbetta (c. 1615–1681) and Francesco Cavalli (1602–1676). Al-

---

[17] According to the Archivio storico del Patriarcato di Venezia, the baptismal records for Santa Maria Mater Domini reside at the church of San Cassiano. Despite two visits to the church, I was unable to find the records there. Her name does not figure among the births listed in the relevant years of the baptismal records for San Cassiano.

[18] I-Vas, Avogaria di Comun, *Processi per Nobiltà,* b. 294/12, no. 23, for example, gives details of the circumstances under which her first son, Andrea, was born.

[19] I-Vas, Notarile, *Testamenti chiusi,* Girolamo Brinis, b. 642, nos. 31–35 (1651, 19 October), f. 1.

[20] The terms of the rental agreements are found in I-Vas, Notarile, *Atti,* Girolamo Brinis, protocollo, b. 840, ff. 48–50v, and minute, b. 871 (1653, 19 March); and Notarile, *Atti,* Giorgio Emo, b. 5508, ff. 195–195v.

[21] I-Vas, Notarile, *Atti,* Girolamo Brinis, b. 885, f. 518v (1658, 5 October) and Notarile, *Atti,* Camillo Lion, b. 8022, f. 174v (1660, 27 March). Discussion of the Padoanis' homes in Venice and Padua are found in I-Vas, Notarile, *Atti,* Giovanni Antonio Mora, b. 8636, ff. 108v–109v (1673, 14 May).

though the letters ostensibly concern employing Padoani, nearly every exchange also mentions his daughter.

A letter addressed to the duke in March 1654 finds Padoani in the midst of negotiating his employment at the Gonzaga court, a process that he described as having gone on for several months and that involved the "Residente" Antonio Bosso, a Mantuan envoy working for the duke in Venice (doc. 2).

> Your Most Serene Highness,
>
> It pleased Your Most Serene Highness in the past months to invite me into the service that I had already longed for myself; the extent of your kindness did not stop there: your envoy Bosso also explained to me the comforts that I would have received. And since, on one hand, I have not heard anything more about this and, on the other, it being time for me to resume my most important engagements in this city, I have decided to send in my place the Latin teacher ["maestro di grammatica"] of my only daughter, to beg your Highness humbly and devotedly to command me to do whatever pleases you more, if I move or if I stay. In one case I would enjoy great happiness, and in the other I would have the pleasure of serving you. My daughter continues to make good progress studying with Signor Cavalli; she is humbly devoted to the sublime merit of your Highness and, with me, bows down before you as I, together with her mother, in the depth of deference, salute the most Serene Archduchess.
>
> Your Lordship's humblest, most devoted, and most respectful servant,
> Giacomo Padovani, Physician [22]

Although Padoani's signature would seem to indicate that he was to come to work as a doctor in Mantua, he decided to send the "maestro di grammatica" in his stead. He provides here several details of Antonia's studies in music and letters, the two disciplines constituting the core curriculum in the education of the few girls fortunate enough to have tutors.[23] The unnamed "maestro di grammatica" held a title denoting his role as a teacher of Latin grammar

---

[22] I am grateful to Beth Glixon, who uncovered this letter in 1993, as well as Docs. 3–4; her discovery led me to look at the documents first on microfilm at Venice's Fondazione Giorgio Cini in 1994, and then further into the actual holdings of the Archivio di Stato of Mantua in 1996.

[23] Paul F. Grendler devoted a section of his study on the history of education to the question, "What Should Girls Learn?" and found that only "a significant minority of girls studied the Latin humanities, usually with all household tutors," in *Schooling in Renaissance Italy: Literacy and Learning, 1300–1600* (Baltimore: Johns Hopkins University Press, 1989), 93. Home studies with tutors or parents paralleled those of the convents, which generally offered instruction in music, reading, and writing. The Venetian writer Moderata Fonte (Modesta da Pozzo, 1555–1592), for example, "learned Latin, wrote vernacular poetry, did arithmetic, played lute and harpsichord, sang, [and] sewed" (94). Fonte's education suggests a model for the type that Padoani may have established for his daughter.

and language, reading, and composition.[24] Like the Padoani family, the eminent composer Francesco Cavalli lived in the parish of San Pantalon, within the magnificent Palazzo Balbi on the Grand Canal, but at the back, facing the Corte di Marconi.[25] A further degree of connectedness is suggested by the fact that, in 1652, during the final illness of Cavalli's cherished wife Maria, one of Padoani's acquaintances from Padua, Raimondo Zanforti (?–d. 1678), served as the attending physician.[26]

No sign of the matter of Padoani's appointment in Mantua follows the March 1654 letter until a flurry of documents appears in July of that year. This time, Padoani addressed his letter to Giulio Cesare Gonzaga (1618–1676), one of the Mantuan courtiers who had been assigned the task of negotiating the appointment.[27] Even four months later, little seems to have altered in the stalled employment process and, worse yet, an intrigue complicated matters on both sides. Padoani required a license, assurance of a salary, and arrangements for his daughter before he could leave Venice and go to serve the duke. Yet the impasse proved injurious to his reputation in Mantua; he alluded to gossip going around and of people speaking badly of him because some secret information had gotten into the wrong hands. His worry—that someone with "malicious curiosity" was prying into the affair—caused him to ask if the message that Giulio Cesare Gonzaga had received with an earlier letter of 7 July (one not found in the archive) was truly what he had written (doc. 3):

Most Illustrious and Most Esteemed Sir, and Most Honorable Patron,
I have before me the letter of Your Excellency [Giulio Cesare Gonzaga] and that of the Most Serene Highness [the duke], both together. I am deliberating about complying, because I owe it to His Highness and to Your

---

[24] See Grendler, Schooling, 4–5.

[25] The 1661 census for Dorsoduro-San Pantalon shows Cavalli living there; see I-Vas, X Savi alle decime, b. 424, no. 407. The rent on the entire property amounted to 600 ducats a year; no separate figure appears for Cavalli's quarters. On average the other homes in San Pantalon rented for 60 ducats a year.

[26] I-Vsp, Morti dal 1632 al 1652, f. 147: "La Sig[no]ra Maria moglie del Sig[no]r Franc[esc]o Cavalli Organista di S[an] Marco d'anni 40 in c[irc]a amalata da febre gia mesi uno, et mezzo. Il Medico [Raimondo] Z[an] Forte." Jane Glover, Cavalli (New York: St. Martin's Press, 1978), 36, n. 55, gives 16 September 1652 as the date of the opening of Maria Cavalli's testament, and the necrology cited here reveals her death the day before.

[27] Primarily a politician and member of the militia, Giulio Cesare Gonzaga served Ferdinand III in Vienna and Cosimo III in Florence. He did not belong to the branch of the family that ruled the duchy. See Pompeo Litta, Famiglie celebri italiane, "Gonzaga di Mantova," Part II, Index 49, fascicle 50. His interest in the arts might be divined from the fact that he is recorded as having been part of a four-person team ("squadra") that represented Jason at a spectacle— Festa del combattimento a cavallo dei mostri—staged for a state Carnival celebration in 1652; see Angiolo Tarachia, Feste celebrate in Mantova alla venuta de' Serenissimi Archiduchi Ferdinando Carlo e Sigismundo Francesco d'Austria et Arciduchessa Anna Medici, Il Carnevale dell'Anno 1652 (Mantua: Osanna, 1652), 44–52.

Excellency, but I wish to reveal once again the error of those who pretend that I am just trying to make excuses about not coming. I know that Your Excellency will work on getting the license, in accordance with all the things that were said, and with the promised letters that only have to do with the girl. Nevertheless, I beg you fervently that the first year be paid in advance with one hundred doblas, so that in the ensuing time I won't have to beg for money and—as I have said before—so that it won't be necessary to blush when asking for it. Because if I relinquish my daily earnings here, I know that I will not be able to earn very much in Mantua visiting the sick. This is my greatest concern, the only thing that makes me hesitate; this is what scares me, and why I must make these demands. If you arrange things in the way that I wish and send me the license, along with the money for the first year, I will set to work with arranging my departure, and at just 15 or 20 days' notice I will be able to get the boat to pick me up, along with my belongings and my family. I think that by the time these things are done, Mantua's bad air will be past and, God willing, I will have completed my work here. And that is all that I can tell Your Excellency from my side, confiding the rest to the magnanimity of His Highness, which he shows me with his letters, and to the protection of Your Excellency, who will be my protector. Meanwhile I beg you to look at the attached, written above, and let me know if it is the same as the letter that you sent to me with yours of the 7th of this month, because I have come to believe that malicious curiosity is at work. Likewise I beg you to let His Highness know most liberally of my readiness to serve him, so that if something is in the air—setting fires and making a mess—it will be known as fraudulent. And do believe me, Your Excellency: because it may seem that I might be making this up, I do not mean to speak flippantly when I recall Aesop's fable about the serpent nursed in the breast.[28]

I've said too much but it will never be too much.

Venice, 13 July 1654

Your Most Illustrious Excellency's most obliged and devoted servant,

Giacomo Padovani

In order to be sure that there had been no forgery or misrepresentation, as his reference to the fable suggests, he added a postscript indicating his worry: "I beg you to see that these letters were still sealed when they were received."

---

[28] Pietro Pancrazi related the following tale in *L'Esopo moderno* (Florence: E. Ariani, 1930): "*Il contadino e il serpe*. D'inverno, un contadino trovò un serpe tramortito dal freddo. Ne ebbe pietà, lo raccolse e se lo mise in seno. Rinvivito dal calore, quello ritornò serpe, e morse il contadino. Il quale, mentre già moriva: —Ben mi sta, disse; perché aver pietà d'un cattivo?" (82). An English edition practically contemporary with Padoani's letter, John Ogilby's *The Fables of Aesop* (1668; repr. edn. Los Angeles: William Andrews Clark Memorial Library, University of California, 1965), gives the moral of the tale as follows: "Ungrateful men are Marshal'd in three Ranks, / This not returns, the Second gives no Thanks. / Evil the last for Good repayes, and this / Of all Hell's Monsters the most Horrid is" (44).

His letter arrived quickly in Mantua; it took only two days for Giulio Cesare Gonzaga to receive and forward it to the duke with the following message (doc. 4):

Most Serene Prince,

See, Doctor Padovani is cured of his madness ["pazzia"], and seems to me to be very interested and concerned with satisfying Your Most Serene Highness and—leaving every other respect aside—it is now sure that there is someone who wanted to gossip, because my last letter was still open, the one in which I was writing about what Your Most Serene Highness had ordered me to do and I had sent it with the same letter to Your Highness, as I did because it was more convenient. You will see in the meanwhile what the doctor has written to me; when you send the letter back, tell me how I should answer it, so that with all punctuality I can obey you, as I do now and always will be careful with that which concerns you.

Your Most Serene Highness's humblest, most devoted, and most obliged servant,

Giulio Cesare Gonzaga

At 7 p.m. the enclosed arrived with the post from Verona.[29]

Gonzaga forwarded the doctor's letter to the duke with his own, in which he confirmed that Padoani's suspicions were not unfounded and revealed that the unnamed gossip had seen his letter before he sent it: his "last letter was still open." The lost letter of 7 July might have cleared up this mystery.

In March, Padoani had referred to Antonia as "la figliuola" (doc. 2) in training with two tutors. Now, as "la damigella" (doc. 3), he mentions her as a critical part of his employment prospects in Mantua. Subsequent references to her as "the girl who sings" (Docs. 5–6) at once clarify the nature of her music lessons with Cavalli, and also help to interpret his later description of her education: "the many efforts of my poor wife in raising my . . . daughter and in giving her tutors, and my own for (one would almost say) having fed her soul, in order to make her succeed, in 'virtù,' to the astonishment of the world" (doc. 12). The quality of "virtù" simultaneously referred to moral as well as artistic goodness, and in this case it appears to have been the latter quality that Padoani emphasized;[30] that she inspired wonder suggests that she possessed the qualities of a child prodigy. Cavalli seems to have had something of a subspecialty in teaching female pupils who, in addition to the nobles Fiorenza Grimani and Betta Mocenigo, most notably included the

---

[29] The "enclosed" letters were probably those of Padoani (13 July) and Bosso (14 July), brought by the "ordinary Saturday courier" running from Venice to Mantua via Verona (doc. 8).

[30] See Fredrika H. Jacobs, *Defining the Renaissance Virtuosa: Women Artists and the Language of Art History and Criticism* (Cambridge: Cambridge University Press, 1997), 9.

singer-composer Barbara Strozzi.[31] Antonia's prodigious vocal talent apparently caused the duke to seek her out, in keeping with the tradition of the northern Italian courts to employ such marvels as marks of distinction and prestige.

Meanwhile, the day before in Venice, Bosso also wrote to the duke (doc. 5):

1654, 14 July
My Most Serene Sir, Signore and Most Merciful Patron,
Before leaving for Germany, Signor Francesco Corbetta comes to the feet of Your Most Serene Highness in order to humbly greet you. From him Your Highness will certainly hear more about the father of the girl who sings, and likewise I trust that Your Highness by now will have been informed by me or otherwise about the matter of which I wrote in my last mailing. But in any case I reverently beg Your Most Serene Highness to excuse me for the tedium that I hand you, and I bow down deeply before you.
Your Most Serene Highness's humblest, most devoted, and reverent servant, the most faithful and most indebted
Antonio Bosso

This letter introduces yet another level of complexity to the situation. Although not mentioned by name, "the father of the girl who sings" and "Giacomo Padovani Medico" represent the same person. Bosso wrote that Francesco Corbetta came to him in order to convey his greetings to the duke, who would hear more directly about Padoani. Giulio Cesare had referred to Padoani's "pazzia" (madness); Bosso's next letter, written six days later, used a similar description to describe the doctor as one of the three *pazzi* (doc. 6). Perhaps it was Bosso's "malicious curiosity" that Padoani feared?

My Most Serene Sir my Signore, Signore and Most Merciful Patron,
Francesco Corbetta returns to Your Most Serene Highness's feet; from him you will hear directly regarding the girl who sings, of what interest I have not been able to understand because I have been completely tricked by him behind my back; neither Bartolo nor Baldo can come close to explaining their strategies.[32] But for now, all this means for Your Highness is that they are a cage of crazies ["una Gabia di Pazzi"] whose interests only

---

[31] In Strozzi's preface to op. 2, she thanks Cavalli as one of her teachers; see Ellen Rosand, ed., *Cantatas by Barbara Strozzi, 1619–c. 1664,* The Italian Cantata in the Seventeenth Century, vol. 5 (New York: Garland, 1986), 3. Grimani and Mocenigo appear in Glover, *Cavalli,* 32.

[32] Bosso probably referred to the fourteenth-century jurist, Bartolo da Sassoferrato, "Bartolo," whose student Baldo degli Ubaldi was known as "Baldo." The pair of jurists co-authored a number of works (see *Dizionario biografico degli italiani,* s.v. "Bartolo da Sassoferrato" by Francesco Calasso, 6: 640–669). The fact that Bosso used the phrase in passing suggests that, in learned circles of the early modern period, the pair represented the proverbial last word in legal matters.

have pernicious goals. What's more, I call to the attention of Your Highness that, in addition to the doctor falling into a frenzy (even though the
most mincing voice would say that he is possessed by the devil), the girl
who sings suffers from epilepsy brought on by the frenetic fears of her father, who has handed her over in marriage to Signor Corbetta and has
signed on with a private letter, clearly entirely charmed. All of this news
will be to show you with what esteem I hold Your Most Serene Highness,
to whom I deeply bow down.

Venice, 21 July 1654

Your Most Serene Highness's humblest, most devoted, and reverent
servant, the most faithful and most indebted,

Antonio Bosso

This comic scene further corroborates Antonia's description as Padoani's
daughter and as singer, but what of this matchmaking?

Francesco Corbetta, one of the foremost guitarists of the seventeenth century, had served the Mantuan court in the previous decade. Under the regency of Maria Gonzaga, mother of Carlo II, the court in 1644 had granted
him an *attestatione* (a "passport") that allowed him to travel abroad freely.[33] A
year before that, nicknamed "il Capriccioso" as a new member of the Academy of the Erranti of Brescia, Corbetta had dedicated a book of his guitar
music to Carlo II Gonzaga.[34] By 1652 he had profited from his passport; his

---

[33] I-MAa, Archivio Gonzaga, *Mandati* 52 (1644, 10 December). This document has not appeared in previous studies of music at the Gonzaga court, perhaps because Corbetta is not identified in it as a musician. The letter confirms the continuing patronage of Carlo II, to whom
Corbetta had dedicated his book of guitar music, *Varii capricii*, of 1643. Richard T. Pinnell's study
of the composer offers comprehensive biographical and musical information; see his *Francesco
Corbetta and the Baroque Guitar: With a Transcription of his Works* (Ann Arbor: UMI Research Press,
1980). Short biographies of the musician include Philip H. Highfill, Jr., Kalman A. Burnim, and
Edward A. Langhans, *A Biographical Dictionary of Actors, Actresses, Musicians, Dancers, Managers, and
Other Stage Personnel in London, 1660–1800* (Carbondale: Southern Illinois University Press, 1975),
3: 490; Marco di Pasquale, "Corbetta, Francesco," in *Dizionario enciclopedico universale della musica
e dei musicisti. Le biografie* (Torino: UTET, 1985), 314; Axel Fischer, "Hannover," in *Die Musik in
Geschichte und Gegenwart* (Kassel: Bärenreiter, 1996), Sachteil 4, col. 26; and the prefaces to facsimile editions of the music by Paolo Paolini (Florence: Studio per edizioni scelte, 1980).

[34] *Varii capricii per la ghittara spagnuola* (Milan, 1643; repr. Florence: Studio per edizioni scelte,
1980), intro. by Paolo Paolini. Corbetta published this book on 30 October 1643, half a year after
his acceptance as academician of the Erranti. I-BRas, Archivio antico municipale, *Accademi Erranti*, b. 142, mazzo 13, f. 18v gives the date of his acceptance as 31 May 1643. Corbetta's academic sobriquet, "il Capriccioso," clearly derives from his activity as a performer of "capricii."
On the Academy of the Erranti of Brescia, see Michele Maylender, *Storia delle accademie d'Italia*
(Bologna: Licinio Cappelli, 1926–1930), 2: 305–308; see too *Capitoli ed ordini per l'Accademia de
gli Erranti di Brescia* (Brescia: Giovanni Maria Rizzardi, 1635) in I-Vas, Riformatori allo Studio di
Padova, b. 539.

travels had brought him to Paris, as well as to Germany, where he enjoyed more lucrative work than he had found in Mantua (doc. 7):

My Most Serene Signore,
    Captain Luca, in the employ of Your Highness, has written in order to ask me to return to service. I offer humble thanks to Your Most Serene Highness, but, due to my previous scanty earnings it has been necessary for me to work with the Prince of Lüneburg, who has granted me many favors, as many in Paris as here. I beg Your Highness to excuse me, for I have tried many times with little success to work for Your Most Serene Highness. . . .
    Venice, 1652, 12 March
    Your Most Serene Highness's most devoted and obliged servant,
    Francesco Corbetta

Corbetta's continuing employment with the "Prince of Lüneburg" prompted Bosso to write two years later of his "leaving for Germany" (doc. 5). More about Corbetta's patronage in the north comes from the preface to a later publication in which he reminisced about the past.[35] There he identified the "prince" as "Giorgio Guglielmo, Duca di Bronsvich e' Luneburg" (1624–1705), the eldest of the three Dukes of Braunschweig-Lüneburg of the Calenberg line, along with Johann Friedrich (1625–1679) and Ernst August (1629–1698).[36] By the mid-1650s the dukes paid annual visits to Venice at Carnival time, staying in a *palazzo* on the Grand Canal adjacent to Palazzo Balbi.[37]

What was the connection between Padoani and Corbetta? The Gonzaga court sought out both men for their skills. Corbetta, the younger of the two, had enjoyed Mantuan patronage before finding greater fame and earnings abroad; Padoani, already at the height of his career by the time of the court's offer, had a lot more to lose with a family to provide for and a talented daughter's future to plan. Perhaps Corbetta had encouraged Antonia's vocal training and lessons with Cavalli during his sojourn in Venice in 1652. Might that explain the duke's interest in her singing?[38]

---

[35] *La Guitarre royalle* (Paris: Bonneüil, 1674). Corbetta here referred to a book of music that he had composed for Georg Wilhelm, Duke of Braunschweig-Lüneburg; the book has not yet turned up in any library catalogue and is presumed lost.

[36] Norbert Dubowy clarified the family relationships in "Ernst August, Giannettini, und die Serenata in Venedig (1685/86)," *Analecta musicologica* 30 (1998): 167–235.

[37] The 1661 census for Dorsoduro-San Pantalon gives the location of their house at the Cà Foscari bridge with no rental payment listed for a "casa del N.H. Alvise Foscari q. Franc[esc]o habitata dalli Sig[no]ri Prencipi di Bransvich"; see I-Vas, X Savi alle decime, b. 424, no. 419. See, too, Dubowy, "Ernst August," 169–170. The *palazzo* now belongs to the Università degli Studi di Venezia, Cà Foscari.

[38] Paola Besutti has shown that Carlo II Gonzaga sang baritone and often sent for vocal music; see her "Produzione e trasmissione di cantate romani nel mezzo del Seicento," in *La mu-*

No surviving document reveals what Corbetta had to tell the duke, but Bosso's letter of 21 July provided the information that the guitarist had not yet left Venice and that the situation with Antonia and her father had become still more complicated. One wonders about Padoani's associations with madness, given that both Bosso and Gonzaga used that adjective to describe him, and whether Bosso exaggerated in describing Antonia's reaction as epileptic or whether she really suffered from the disease. Bosso wrote a postscript that he included with his letter of 21 July (doc. 8):

> My Most Serene Sir my Signore, Signore and Most Merciful Patron,
>   After having written the enclosed letter—which was to have been given to Signor Francesco Corbetta, who did not wish to pick it up as he was about to miss the hour of his departure—I thought it better to keep it and to send it to your Highness by the shortest possible route to Verona, with the ordinary Saturday courier, so that Your Highness will be advised about the capricious matrimony of said Corbetta.[39]

After this date no mention is made of them; Padoani's appointment apparently never took place, nor did the marriage.[40]

What is to be made of these exchanges between Venice and Mantua? The letters, although they only elliptically allude to music, lead to the speculation that Antonia Padoani and Francesco Corbetta together performed music for voice and guitar. Carlo II Gonzaga's interests in music and his own musical abilities probably prompted his exchanges with Padoani, Corbetta, and, later, Barbara Strozzi. Padoani may have coveted the connections to the musical world offered by the duke and by Corbetta, but Antonia herself encountered a different fate.

Bembo's Wife

Sometime prior to the spring of 1658 Antonia Padoani met her prospective husband, the noble Venetian Lorenzo Bembo. He was born on 15 July 1637, fifteen years after the marriage of his parents, Andrea Bembo and Faustina

---

sica a Roma attraverso le fonti d'archivio, ed. Bianca Maria Antolini (Lucca: Libreria musicale italiana, 1994), 137–166. Beth Glixon uncovered letters in the Archivio Gonzaga revealing that Strozzi sent vocal music to the duke during his stay in Paris in 1655; see her "New Light," 322, 334, n. 88.

[39] The reference to Corbetta's "capricioso [sic] matrimonio" suggests a word play on the guitarist's sobriquet in the Academy of the Erranti, "il Capriccioso."

[40] Padoani's name does not figure among the practicing physicians of Mantua (I-MAa, Schede Davari, indice 92, no. 6, Medici, 1232–1706). Several of his Paduan colleagues—Alessandro Borromeo, Zanforti, and Frigimelica—come up in later correspondence as "medici" (such

Briani (fig. 1.1).[41] Although no other children of the union are known, he may have had siblings who perished in the second plague in Venice, at its peak in the early years of the 1630s; that he was not named after either of his grandfathers suggests that he was not a first-born son.[42] Lorenzo lost his mother sometime prior to the early 1650s, when his father married Laura Querini, who bore four sons.[43] Andrea Bembo held the position of *Camerlengo* ("treasurer") of Padua from 1654 until his death in the summer of 1658, leaving his widow in sole command—as *tutrice et governatrice*—of their three surviving boys.[44]

Where might Lorenzo and Antonia have met? In Padua, where his father was working? While no documentation for the 1650s has yet come to light regarding Giacomo Padoani's activity in that city, he maintained ties with his Paduan colleagues, and in the 1660s he and his wife, Diana, would be residents of the Paduan district of Borgo dei Vignali. What of the Venetian neighborhood of San Pantalon? Some of Lorenzo's relatives owned houses there, such as his aunt Orseta Corner Bembo, who had an act notarized at her home late in 1652.[45] To judge from his close relationship with her only son Zan Mattio Bembo and from her will, Lorenzo may have spent a good amount of time with her; perhaps she stepped in after his mother's death. His uncle, Piero Bembo, had a house in the Campo di Moschiello just over the bridge from the church of San Pantalon, one street away from the Balbi house that the Padoanis rented.

At this point, it is worth recalling Giacomo Padoani's oration for Girolamo Bembo in Montona in 1640. Although Girolamo shared the family name with Lorenzo, the relationship is extremely distant; Girolamo would marry Bianca Bembo in the 1660s, herself no close relative to either. Padoani's oration testifies to his long-standing admiration of the Bembo family. He mined the family history in this speech, naming several famous ancestors—Pietro Bembo, the illustrious writer and cardinal (1470–1547); the nun Illuminata Bembo

---

as in I-MAa, Archivio Gonzaga, *Carteggi d'Inviati* (Venezia), b. 1571 [1659, Abbate Tinti and Diversi] and b. 1574 [1664, 1665]).

[41] I-Vas, Avogaria di Comun, *Nascite,* reg. 59/IX, 30v. The couple was married on 22 September 1622; the wedding contract is registered in I-Vas, Notarile, *Atti,* Giulio Figolin, b. 5940, ff. 462–464.

[42] On the plague, see John Julius Norwich, *A History of Venice* (New York: Vintage Books, 1989), 540–541. Andrea's father was Zan Mattio; Faustina's, Zambattista.

[43] Zan Mattio (1653–1740), Antonio (1655–1716), and Nicolo (1658–1683) lived to maturity; Alvise died as an infant.

[44] Andrea was elected to the position on 31 March 1654; see I-Vnm, Ms. It. VII, 854 (8923), f. 127. "Tutrice et governatrice" follows Laura Querini Bembo's name in the notarial documents after Andrea died without leaving a will (*ab intestato*); for this information, see I-Vbc, Ms. P.D.C., b. 2706/8, the *Terminaz[ion]e di tutella* that Querini received on 30 December 1661.

[45] I-Vas, Notarile, *Atti,* Tadeo Fedrici, b. 6055, ff. 201v–202.

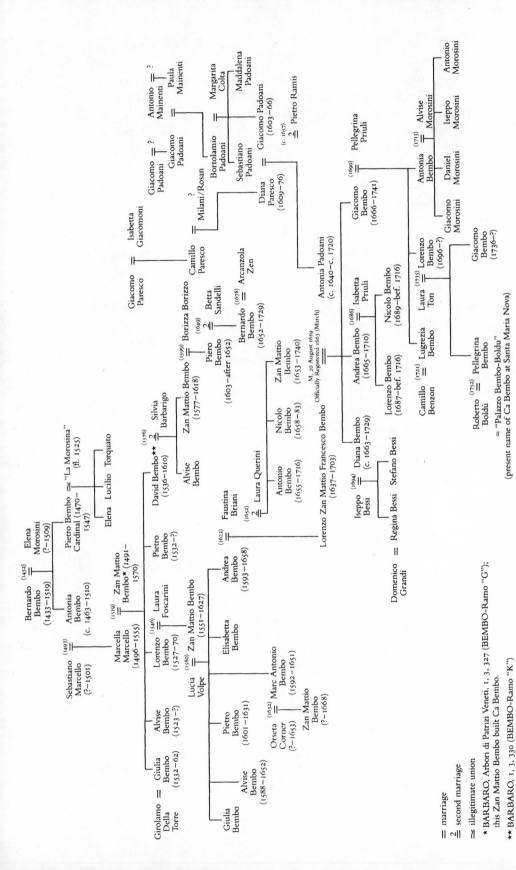

FIGURE 1.1 Bembo Family Genealogy and Palazzo Bembo-Boldù Lineage

(d. 1483); and the fourteenth-century bishop of Aquilea, Leone Bembo—and provided a brief genealogy of Girolamo's father and grandfather, important political figures. Padoani specifically mentioned the branch of the family from which Antonia's future husband descended.[46]

Although Lorenzo appeared to "marry down" in choosing Antonia, the child of two *cittadini* who were relative newcomers to Venice, the professional success of Padoani and the decline of the Bembo family fortunes effectively resulted in their economic parity. Clearly both families enjoyed a comfortable existence, although by no means a wealthy one. Lorenzo traced his ancestry to Cardinal Pietro Bembo through his sister Antonia Bembo Marcello, but more directly to Zan Mattio Bembo (1491–1570), the founder of Cà Bembo—the family house constructed at Santa Maria Nova (Cannaregio) in the late Trecento—now known as the Palazzo Bembo-Boldù.[47] By the mid-seventeenth century, the former days of glory were past and the Bembo family wealth, like that of much of the patriciate, dispersed.[48] Padoani's upward social mobility gave him a modicum of power, both professional and financial, in the Venetian class structure. By this time, it was not at all uncommon for nobles and *cittadini* to intermarry; several Bembo ancestors had begun the practice already in the previous century.[49]

Just months before his father's death, Lorenzo made plans to marry Antonia; he and Giacomo Padoani signed the wedding contract in Venice in May 1658 (doc. 9).[50] The contract stands as an important agreement insofar as it illuminates the financial status of both families; it would serve as the basis for the legal manipulations of the couple and their progeny well into the next century. The *dote* (dowry) that Giacomo offered Lorenzo for the hand of Antonia consisted of a total of 3,000 ducats in goods, money, and a two-year residence for the couple in the Padoani family home; the figure represents the

---

[46] Padovani, *Oratione,* 8–11. Padoani recounted the victories of Lorenzo's great-great-grandfather and great-grandfather, "Gio:Matteo & Lorenzo suo figlio, ambedui [*sic*] più volte Generali, & delle spoglie Ottomane vittoriosi & trionfanti" (8).

[47] For magnificent interior and exterior views, and greater detail about Cà Bembo, see Patricia Fortini Brown, *Private Lives in Renaisssance Venice: Art, Architecture, and the Family* (New Haven: Yale University Press, 2004): 188–197. See, too, Pompeo Molmenti, *La storia di Venezia nella vita privata,* 6th ed. (Bergamo: Istituto italiano d'artigrafia, 1925), 2: 376, n. 2; and the epilogue to Patricia Fortini Brown, *Venice and Antiquity* (New Haven: Yale University Press, 1996), 285–286.

[48] See J. C. Davis, *The Decline of the Venetian Nobility as a Ruling Class* (Baltimore: Johns Hopkins University Press, 1962).

[49] For more about the practice of intermarriage between *cittadini* and nobles, see Alexander F. Cowan, "Love, Honour and the Avogaria di Comun in Early Modern Venice," *Archivio Veneto,* 5th ser., 144 (1995): 5–19; see also his "New Families in the Venetian Patriciate, 1646–1718," *Ateneo Veneto,* n.s. 23 (1985): 55–75.

[50] I thank Marinella Laini for uncovering this critical document.

standard amount with which people of the time began married life.[51] It was fairly common practice for the bride's family to open its home to the groom, and the couple accepted the offer to reside at Salizada San Pantalon.

Lorenzo offered 3,000 ducats as *controdote* (counterdowry), a voluntary contribution offered "for the love" of Antonia in equal proportion to the obligatory *dote,* resulting in a total sum of 6,000 ducats (doc. 9):

> Giacomo Padovani, father-in-law . . . and . . . Nobleman Lorenzo Bembo, son of Nobleman Andrea, his son-in-law, have together presented to me, the notary, that which is written below, . . . which will serve as the wedding contract of the Illustrious Signora Antonia, daughter of the aforementioned Excellent Signor Giacomo, and wife of aforementioned Illustrious Signor Lorenzo . . . seen by me the notary and by Signor Christoforo Brombilla as witness. . . . And for the love that the said Nobleman Lorenzo holds for the aforementioned Illustrious Signora his wife, to the above he liberally adds to the dowry from his own goods as a counterdowry, or wedding gift . . . [in the amount of] 3,000 ducats.

Lorenzo's inheritance from his aunt Orseta constituted a substantial portion of this *controdote.* Orseta Corner Bembo had owned considerable property in the Vicentino: a house in the town of Nanto and land in the Bosco di Nanto, both lying directly to the south of Vicenza. Widowed in the early 1650s, Orseta willed these properties to Lorenzo and to her only son Zan Mattio.[52] The division of the Bosco di Nanto lands led to some disagreements between the cousins that would arise again in the next century during discussions of inheritance issues and disputes.

The preparations for the marriage of Lorenzo and Antonia continued well into 1659, when they were wed in August at the Palladian church of the Redentore on the island of Giudecca.[53] The attention paid by the wedding contract to Antonia's bridal attire evokes the splendor of the occasion (doc. 9):

---

[51] S.v. "dote" in Marco Ferro, *Dizionario del diritto comune e veneto,* 2nd ed. (Venice: Andrea Santini e figlio, 1845), 1: 640–649.

[52] Orseta Corner Bembo, widow of Marc'Antonio Bembo (Andrea's brother, both sons of Zan Mattio), had divided her property between herself and Zan Mattio (22 October 1652, see I-Vas, Notarile, *Atti,* Tadeo Fedrici, b. 6055). Then, in a codicil to her will, dated 30 November 1652, she left her "portione" to Lorenzo (I-Vas, Notarile, *Testamenti,* Tadeo Fedrici, b. 433, no. 421); she died the following February. Zan Mattio and Lorenzo worked on the divisions of the property at Nanto in the spring before Lorenzo's wedding (I-Vas, Notarile, *Atti,* Battista Ernest, b. 5487, ff. 6v–7v). The matter was still not resolved one year later, when Lorenzo named a procurator to try to set things straight between them (on 1 April 1660, I-Vas, Notarile, *Atti,* Battista Ernest, b. 5488, ff. 13–13v).

[53] I-Vas, Avogaria di Comun, *Matrimoni, Sposalici,* b. 100, f. 1.

For the dowry of said Signora the bride, her father this Most Excellent Signor Giacomo promises to give to this Most Illustrious spouse 3,000 ducats in cash . . . : 400 ducats in cash currency, of which . . . Signor Giacomo will spend most—that is, about 300 ducats—for the aforementioned bride's wedding clothes; the remainder will be given to the Most Illustrious spouse. Likewise all of the jewels that belong to the aforementioned bride will be estimated by those present . . . Signor Giacomo must pay two years' rental of the pearls that the bride will wear.

Lorenzo's career got off to a good start the following autumn, when he began service as "Avogador in Rialto," one of the lawyers appointed from the ranks of the Venetian nobles through the privilege of social standing rather than through formal legal study.[54] But the specter of financial difficulties raised by the contested Nanto lands foreshadowed a lifetime of monetary burden and preoccupation. The couple's troubles had already begun during the first summer of their engagement, when the documents take on an anxious tone not at all apparent in the optimism of the wedding contract.[55] The untimely death of Lorenzo's father and his stepmother's burden of raising three young sons—his half brothers—contributed to the family's financial troubles. Having inherited little from his father, it was fortunate that another aunt, Marina Briani, also provided for him in her will.[56] To judge from the attentions of his aunts, it seems all the more likely that Lorenzo lost his mother quite early on.

During his engagement and first year of marriage, Lorenzo bought land from his uncle, Piero Bembo, and sold jewelry.[57] Presumably he did all of this in an effort to provide the *controdote* that he had promised in the wedding contract, prompting a scramble for cash after his father's untimely death. The two-year stay in the house at San Pantalon normally would have lasted through August 1661, but little more than a half year elapsed before Padoani filed a complaint, chiding his son-in-law's behavior and giving him four months' notice (through August 1660). Vacillations between adjectives palpably attest to Padoani's anger (doc. 10):

[54] He was elected on 16 October 1659; see I-Vnm Ms. It., VII 845 (8924), f. 229. For a description of the office, see s.v. "Avvocati ordinarii" in Ferro, *Dizionario,* 1: 210–211. I would like to thank Jonathan Glixon for his help with reconstructing Lorenzo Bembo's career through the *fondo* of the "consegi" at the Biblioteca Nazionale Marciana, as well as with its interpretive material.

[55] These include I-Vas, Notarile, *Atti,* Lio Fabio Turighello, b. 5049; I-Vas, Consiglio de' Dieci, *Parti Criminali,* filza 91; and I-Vas, Notarile, *Atti,* Pietro Bracchi e Girolamo Brinis, b. 885.

[56] For mention of Briani, see I-Vas, Notarile, *Atti,* Lio Fabio Turighello, b. 5049, f. 216 (1659, 18 December).

[57] Idem.

The improper [*crossed out:* "unbearable"] ways in which you, Nobleman Lorenzo Bembo . . . continually [*crossed out:* "incorrigibly"] disturb my peace of mind and the tranquility of my house, necessitates me to resolve . . . that I cannot keep you any longer in my . . . house, and this regards the other protests made to you many times before, and that continue to be made. My reasons are only too well known to you so I do not need to write them on this paper . . . you have four months to find yourself another place to live. If you protest and do not leave . . . , I shall insist with violence and without question I shall summon the authority of the Excellent Chiefs of the Council of Ten in order to get back at you for your oppression and all of the time that I have suffered from it. . . .

Lorenzo denied any wrongdoing and wrote back (doc. 11):

This is an inappropriate form that you, Excellent Signor Doctor Giacomo Padoani, use with me, Lorenzo Bembo . . . and accuse me without cause. . . . You are moved to write to me in this letter what seems to me an order conceived far from the truth, invented with artificial advantage with the goal that I will leave in the most unfair way and that you won't give me what is mine. . . . This is what I intended to say in response to your writing, to which I protest that all parts of it are nil. . . . [58]

In November 1660 Lorenzo sought restitution for the unused rent that Padoani had offered as part of the *dote;* by the terms of the wedding contract, he had agreed to give money to the couple if they did not stay for the entire two-year period.[59] They did not move away from the neighborhood immediately; Lorenzo's notary came to see him "in confinio San Pantalon" in late December of that year.[60] Padoani's annoyance with the young couple evidently motivated his rental of a studio on the nearby Fondamenta dei Tolentini, the month before he filed this complaint.[61]

From his studio two years later, Padoani wrote a new will in which he mentioned the lack of respect shown him by both his daughter and Lorenzo (doc. 12). Apparently Antonia took her husband's side during the period of discord between the two men. In order to scold the couple for their misbehavior, Padoani added a clause in which he proposed to instill in them "the

---

[58] Probably not coincidentally, Lorenzo tried to resolve financial matters regarding the Nanto property with his cousin at precisely the same time (I-Vas, Notarile, *Atti,* Battista Ernest, b. 5488, ff. 113r–v).

[59] The negotiation itself posed no difficulty. Padoani asked his son-in-law to leave his home, thereby reneging on his original offer; he knew that he would have to pay to get back his "tranquility" (I-Vas, Notarile, *Atti,* Pietro Bracchi e Girolamo Brinis 842, ff. 194v–195).

[60] I-Vas, Notarile, *Atti,* Tadeo Fedrici, b. 6063, ff. 171v–172.

[61] I-Vas, Notarile, *Atti,* Camillo Lion, b. 8022, f. 134. As with his San Pantalon home, he rented from the nobility; the studio belonged to Scipion Boldù.

fear of God" by threatening to give as their inheritance just a pair of devotional paintings:

> I leave to Illustrious Signor Lorenzo Bembo, my son-in-law, for now and forever, my *Redentore*, a copy of one by Titian, kept in the *Fontego dei Tedeschi*. Likewise I leave to Antonia, my only daughter, a painting of Saint Anthony of Padua made in the house of Joseph Heinz, painter at San Polo, and this is all I can leave for now. . . . I cannot leave anything else, neither to one nor to the other, due to the little respect and lack of kindness that both have shown me and my wife as compensation for all of my poor wife's labors in raising my aforementioned daughter and in getting her taught, and I, for having guided her way and (one would almost say) nourished her soul, in order to make her succeed in 'virtù," to the astonishment of the world, and to accompany her as I did, having given her the dowry that neither paternal obligation nor the powers of my meagre fortune permitted me, beyond the large expenditures that I bore after having paid the dowry; for which I deserve to be excused by God, by the law, and by the world, and so by them. I add that I do all of this so that my poor wife will not have to suffer insults from them, but will be known and treated as a mother, as good conscience and the laws of God and of nature oblige them to do. I add still more, that I leave to them these devotional paintings so that it will happen that the fear of God will come before all else. In order, then, to take the greatest possible advantage of my legacy that they will receive, as contained here, they will treat my aforementioned wife and inheritor in the way that God, the laws of princes, and nature oblige them.

Despite his concerns about his daughter's lack of respect, Padoani took pride in the union of the Bembo and Padoani families; he treasured a set of *sottocoppe* (saucers) engraved with their respective coats of arms on which he had inscribed a special motto for their union: "Munus nunqua[m] eliminandum."[62] A clear echo of the Montona oration touchingly affirms that the honor of linking with Venetian nobility meant a great deal to him. Indeed, he wrote that if the couple improved their conduct, Antonia stood to receive his entire legacy (doc. 12):

> That Signora Antonia, wife of Signor Lorenzo Bembo and their children, will be the sole universal inheritor following the death of her aforementioned mother and of me. . . .

Antonia and Lorenzo officially registered their marriage on 8 March 1663;[63] four days earlier, Lorenzo had been elected to the zoning board of

[62] I-Vas, Notarile, *Testamenti*, Camillo Lion, b. 591, no. 87, f. 3: "A gift must never be disposed of."

[63] I-Vas, Avogaria di Comun, *Matrimoni, Sposalici*, b. 100, f. 1r. The entry here states that

Venice, the *Giudici del Piovego*.[64] The registration of the wedding presumably reflected the need to further assure the legitimacy of the noble Venetian status of their children; during their engagement period they had already filed one official document to that end.[65] Now Antonia was expecting their first child, Diana, whose birth date can be estimated as October 1663 from later records; upon Diana's later acceptance as an *educanda* at the convent of Santa Maria dell'Orazione (Malamocco) on 12 November 1683, her age was recorded as 20 with the figure 19 crossed out, thereby suggesting a recent birthday.[66]

In contrast to Diana's birth, the exact dates and times of those of her two brothers are readily available. According to Venetian custom, noble parents of sons born outside the city proper had to instigate a *Processo di Nobiltà* (a nobility trial) in order to assure their status and to be listed in the *Libri d'oro,* the "Golden Books" that recorded significant events in the lives of the patriciate. The *processi* give details about the circumstances of the births (date, time, place, witnesses, and baptism); these also offer important information about the Padoanis' milieu in Padua.

Antonia and Lorenzo's first son was born at the Padoanis' home at Borgo dei Vignali on Sunday 8 February 1665 at 11 p.m.[67] He was named Andrea Giacomo, his parents observing the custom of giving the paternal grandfather's name first, the maternal second. Two women witnessed the birth: Theresia Donghella, Diana Padoani's maid; and Lugrezia Capona, Antonia's servant. Antonia had asked that the *compadri* (male witnesses) at the baptism be Conte Girolamo Frigimelica Roberti and Raimondo Zanforti, described as "lettori publici" ("public lecturers"). The baptism took place at the church of San Zorzi on 17 February.

The doctors Frigimelica and Zanforti were highly respected in the Veneto; evidently Padoani made their acquaintance during his student years and stayed in touch with them. In 1633, Frigimelica had been appointed professor of medicine at the University of Padua,[68] where he may have served as one of Padoani's mentors. Zanforti, originally from Verona, practiced in both Padua and Venice.[69] Padoani did not hold the same status as Frigimelica and

---

the date of the wedding was first entered erroneously into the Avogaria di Comun. See also I-Vas, Libri d'Oro, *Matrimoni* V/92, f. 103v.

[64] I-Vnm, Ms. It. VII, 846 (8925), f. 199 (1663, 4 March).

[65] I-Vas, Consiglio de' Dieci, b. 108 (1658, 19 September).

[66] I-Vas, Corporazioni religiose, *Santa Maria dell'Orazione di Malamocco*, b. 7, Libro di Capitoli.

[67] I-Vas, Avogaria di Comun, *Processi per Nobiltà*, b. 294/12, no. 23.

[68] Charles Patin, *Lyceum Patavinum* (Padua: Frambotti, 1682), 12–13.

[69] See his biography in Nicolai Comneni Papadopoli, *Historia Gymnasi Patavinii* (Venice: Sebastian Coleti, 1726), 1: 317, with an explanation of the etymology of his name: Raymundus Joannes Fortis in Latin, Raimondo Zanforti in Italian.

Zanforti; a seventeenth-century update of Sansovino's study of Venice by Martinioni lists the two doctors as belonging to the Collegio del Veneto, and Padoani as one of the doctors *not* belonging to it.[70]

Frigimelica belonged to the Paduan Academy of the Ricovrati, a society founded around the turn of the seventeenth century to honor distinguished scientists and thinkers; he directed the Ricovrati from 1668 until his death in 1683.[71] It is intriguing to consider the possibility of Antonia's connection to this academy when, many years later, she would set to music poetry by Élis-abeth-Sophie Chéron (1648–1711), one of its numerous French women aca-demicians.[72] Frigimelica's younger namesake was active as a Venetian librett-ist in the late seventeenth century.[73] Given the highly literate circles in which Padoani moved—as deduced from the Mantuan correspondence as well as from his other writings—it is not surprising to encounter these two impor-tant public figures at the baptism of his grandson.

The inventories of several Bembo households only rarely reveal any kind of interest in the things that must have occupied Antonia, such as poetry or music. One of the relatives with whom Lorenzo had nearly continuous con-tact was his cousin (twice removed) Bernardo (1652–1729), son of Piero Bembo. In order to celebrate his 25th birthday, Bernardo traced the origins of the Bembo family.[74] Among his papers is the inventory of a singer, Bar-bara Riccioni Forestier, who left her harpsichord at his home for a period of

---

[70] "Iacopo Padoani" appears in the "Terzo Catalogo dei Medici, che sono in Venetia, Dot-torati in Filosofia, & Medicina, così quelli, che hanno ottenuto luogo nel Collegio quì della Città, come quelli, che sono fuori di detto Collegio, quali tutti hanno facoltà per Decreto del Senato di poter Medicare," among "Quelli, che non sono del Collegio" (2: 17). "Girolamo Frizi-melega" and "Raimondo Gianforte, Letter Primario in Padoua," appear in Giustiniano Martin-ioni, additions to Francesco Sansovino, *Venetia città nobilissima et singolare*, 2: 16. Girolamo Ales-sandro Cappellari Vivaro Vicentino, *Emporio universale delle famiglie*, refers to Martinioni's entry (Ms., I-VIbcb), 8: 254v.

[71] Diego Valeri, *L'Accademia dei Ricovrati* (Padua: La sede dell'Accademia, 1987), 20.

[72] The French connection to the academy came via Charles Patin (1633–1693), the expa-triate doctor who took over as leader of the Ricovrati following the death of Frigimelica and under whom women became academicians. See Attilio Maggiolo, "Elena Lucrezia Cornaro Pi-scopia e le altre donne aggregate all'Accademia patavina dei Ricovrati," *Padova e la sua provincia* 24 n.s., no. 11/12 (November–December 1978): 33–36; and F. Ravaisson, *Archives de la Bastille, Règne de Louis XIV* (Paris: A. Durand et Pedone-Lauriel, 1874), 227–230.

[73] Many of his operas were produced at San Giovanni Grisostomo; see Marinella Laini, *La raccolta zeniana di drammi per musica veneziani della Biblioteca Nazionale Marciana 1637–1700* (Lucca: Libreria Musicale Italiana, 1995), nos. 399, 405, 410–411, 413–414, and 421.

[74] I-Vnm, Ms. It. VII, 14 (7418): Cronica di tuttè le cose dell'inclitta Città di Ven.a: L'armè di tutti li Gentilhuomeni vènuti ad habitar in essa; et hora Nobili Venetiani, li quali sono state nella dignità del gran conseglio d'essa Città di Tempo in tempo; dalla Natività di Nostro Signor Jesu X.to del 421 adì 25 marzo, il giorno dell'Annuntiatione dalla quale è dichiarito l'origine di quèlla; e da che loco sono venuti; racolte al prèsente da Altre Assaisime. Pèr mè Bernardo Bembo fu de Pièro, L'anno 1677, nèl mio quinto lustro" (f. 1).

time; his aunt, Marcella Bembo Balbi, also numbered a keyboard instrument among her possessions.[75] This branch of the Bembo family, also resident in the parish of San Pantalon, may well have been an important source of companionship for Antonia, but no documents have surfaced to confirm the possibility.[76] Bernardo did not mention her in his *Cronica;* not surprising, given that all of the other members mentioned there were men or religious women. The household of her father-in-law shows no particular interest in music or letters, according to an inventory made shortly following his death and just prior to her wedding. The closest objects are some paintings, listed without attribution to an artist; the collection of firearms, by contrast, was remarkable.[77]

Antonia and Lorenzo's third and last child, Giacomo, was also born in the city of Padua, but not at Borgo dei Vignali. Giacomo Padoani would not live to see the baby; on 11 May 1666, the doctor died in Padua in the parish of San Zorzi.[78] The Podestà of Padua, Giovanni Cavalli, testified for the *Processo di Nobiltà;* he reported that the boy was born in a house in the district of Ponte Corvo at 5 p.m. on 10 November 1666.[79]

The War of Candia

Not even half a year after the birth of his third child, Lorenzo Bembo entered the service of the Venetian Republic in the final battles of the War of Candia (1631–1669). He joined the nobles who set sail with Captain Francesco Morosini for Candia, the Greek island now known as Crete, in order to try to put an end to the war against the Turks. By the second half of the 1660s, forces from all over western Europe would join together to protect this eastern region against the incursions of the "infidel."[80] In March 1667, Lo-

[75] Bernardo Bembo left much of his estate to the four *ospedali* for foundlings; his papers are preserved in I-Vas, Ospedali e luoghi pii diversi, bb. 236–239. The two harpsichord references are found in b. 236, *Processo B*, f. 40 (1715, 12 March, regarding Riccioni Forestier) and *Processo C*, f. 11 (c. 1661, regarding Bembo Balbi).

[76] I-Vas, Ospedali e luoghi pii diversi, b. 236, *Processo B*, f. 45 shows the location of this house in San Pantalon's "Campiel delle Mosche."

[77] I-Vas, Notarile, *Atti*, Battista Ernest, b. 5487, ff. 129v–131v (1659, 13 January). With little lighting in the streets of Venice at night, solitary walkers were in peril; many reports of assaults and murders in the city survive. Given these dangers Andrea Bembo might have collected suitably defensive arms.

[78] I-Pas, Ufficio di Sanità, *Registri dei morti*, reg. 479 (1663–1666), f. 118; I-Pav, S. Georgii, *Mortuorum (1614–1746)*, no. 56.

[79] I-Vas, Avogaria di Comun, *Processi per Nobiltà*, b. 294/12, no. 24. The two sons' births were entered into the *Libri d'Oro*; see I-Vas, Libri d'Oro, *Nascite*, X/60, 79 and XI/61, 44. The churches also list their births and baptisms. For Andrea, see I-Pav, S. Georgii, *Battesimi 1643 sino 1687*, reg. 4, n.f.; for Giacomo, see I-Pav, S. Laurentij, *Liber Baptizator*, reg. 7, f. 179.

[80] For an eyewitness account of the War of Candia by one of the Venetian nobles who for

renzo drew up a *procura* (power of attorney) from the Venetian neighborhood of San Moisè, which allowed Antonia to make transactions on his behalf during his absence at war, and allowed his cousin Zan Mattio to do the same for his three half brothers.[81] The address for the *procura* would suggest that the couple moved back to Venice soon after the birth of their third child, which an earlier document corroborates by providing an address for them at San Vidal early the year before.[82]

Lorenzo fought in a triumphant but bloody battle off the coast of Crete, present-day Iraklion, as told in an account by the eighteenth-century historian Cappellari Vivaro: "Lorenzo Bembo, son of Andrea, fought valorously in a victory against the Turks in 1668, but was severely injured."[83] A later author provided vivid details of the battle between the forces of the Turkish vizir and the Venetian leader Morosini (doc. 13):

> At the beginning of March the Vizir—who wished to conquer the Venetians living on Crete—quietly brought in a squadron to fight that of Lorenzo Corner, charging Pasha Halil and the well-known Durac to stand guard while he surprised the Venetian ships, capturing one of the ports and fortifying it, in order to burn and destroy the fleet of the Venetian Republic. But Francesco Morosini and his ships immediately left Crete and gathered twenty galleys together on the night of the seventh of March, so that the Turks—thinking that they were confronted with Corner's customary small squadron—were taken unawares and assaulted with great force and equal courage. The battle was hard and bitter; the most frightening thing was that it took place in the darkness of night. Two enemy galleys that assaulted the forces of the Republic were captured by the Venetians; Durac was trying to overtake the galley of Nicolò Polani when Morosini, by the light of his torch, brought in his troops. People thought this sudden display of light came from the fireworks; the Turks were so overwhelmed that Durac fell to the ground and his militia was outdone. The Venetians were victorious, taking with them five of the Turks' galleys and four hundred

---

several years served in the Greek islands, among other offices as *Provveditore delle tre isole* (Corfù, Zakynthos, and Cefalonia), see Andrea Valier, *Historia della guerra di Candia* (Venice: Paulo Baglioni, 1687). Paolo Preto has brought together both historical accounts and modern studies of the war in *Venezia e i Turchi* (Florence: G. C. Sansoni, 1975) and in "Venezia e la difesa dei Turchi nel Seicento," *Römische historische Mitteilungen* 26 (1984): 289–302.

[81] I-Vas, Notarile, *Atti,* Battista Ernest, b. 5493, ff. 22v–25, for Antonia's *procura;* for Zan Mattio's, see I-Vas, Notarile, *Atti,* Giovanni Antonio Mora, b. 8629, f. 23 (1667, 30 March).

[82] I-Vas, Giudici del Forestier, *Estraordinario,* b. 122, f. 64 (1666 [1665 m.v.], 27 February). I am grateful to Beth Glixon for sending this reference.

[83] Girolamo Alessandro Cappellari Vivaro, *Il campidoglio veneto,* I-Vas, Miscellanea Codici III, Codici Soranzo 31 (già Miscell. Add. 856): "Lorenzo Bembo figliuolo di Andrea, nella vittoria riportata sopra Turchi l'anno 1668, valorosamente combattendo, vi rimase gravemente ferito" (1: 394). On p. 697, Valier's *Historia* mentions Lorenzo Bembo in the 1668 battle.

prisoners, liberating more than one thousand Christian slaves; for all of this Morosini was highly praised and named a *cavaliere*.[84]

Lorenzo Bembo's glory reflected that of Morosini's navy; he must have been among those who invaded the ship that dazzled Durac and caused him to faint. Morosini served as the *Capitano generale da mar* in 1668; the battle described above took place at Santa Pelagia (Aghia Pelaghìa), just to the west of Iraklion.[85]

Although the general war accounts do not mention particular members of his forces, Morosini's weekly dispatches to the Republic provide more detail. One week after the victorious battle, he named three of the wounded as "the illustrious noblemen Zorzi of Cà Grego, Lorenzo Bembo, and Marco Balbi— the first one wounded by a musket in his arm, the second with his leg fractured, and the third one hit by two muskets in both of his hands."[86] A later dispatch provides still further information about the severity of Bembo's injury: "the illustrious nobleman Lorenzo Bembo survived; there was little hope for him [after the battle], for he was in critical condition and he almost lost his leg."[87]

A document that Antonia drafted during the following summer shows that Lorenzo did not go back to Venice with those who had petitioned to do so. She made use of her power of attorney to obtain some money from the rental of the Nanto property. The notary Battista Ernest emphasized that the household stood in particularly dire straits because it "had been left in the hands of a woman,"[88] but made no mention of the reason for her husband's prolonged absence. Clearly the monetary restitution for fighting against the Turks was not enough to support a wife and three children (by this time aged about one, three, and four).

Lorenzo returned to Venice late in the summer of 1669, shortly after Antonia's transaction with the notary; he came back defeated, for the Turks ultimately beat the Venetians.[89] Lorenzo's next position again took him away, this time to serve as "Rector and Procurator" at Cattaro, Orzi Novi—a town

[84] S. Romanin, *Storia documentata di Venezia* (Venice: Pietro Naratovich, 1858), 7: 453–454.

[85] *Venezia e la difesa del Levante, da Lepanto a Candia 1570–1670* (Venice: Arsenale Editrice, 1986), "cronologia" by Paolo Preto.

[86] I-Vas, Senato, *Provveditori da terra e da mar*, Armada, Capitano . . . Francesco Morosini, b. 1114, ff. 104–117v (dispatch no. 78 of 1668, 16 March). These dispatches survive in very fragile condition—their right halves nearly worn away—making it difficult to gain a coherent narrative from them.

[87] Ibid., f. 134v (dispatch no. 81 of 1668, 6 April).

[88] I-Vas, Notarile, *Atti*, Battista Ernest, b. 5494, ff. 129–130 (1668, 23 August). I am indebted to Beth Glixon for this find.

[89] Preto, *Venezia e la difesa del Levante*, "1669, 6 Sett." On that date, Francesco Morosini ceded Crete to the Turks; upon his return to Venice on 20 September 1669, he was named a Procurator of San Marco for his heroism during the war.

near Crema to the southwest of Brescia.[90] By the autumn of 1670, he could return to the armed forces as one of the guards of the slaves on the galley ships.

The financial hardships that Antonia suffered during Lorenzo's absences led to the devastation of their family life. In autumn 1672, she pressed charges against him in the Patriarchal Court to get a divorce for, among other things, having abandoned the family for five years and left her alone with little income to care for their three small children.[91] She leveled five accusations against her husband, who denied each one in the margins of the divorce suit (doc. 14):

> First that in word and deed, the nobleman Lorenzo Bembo has treated the noblewoman Antonia his wife badly many times, having fucked her [colloquial: "*fotendola*"] even more than once while she was pregnant.
> [*margin*]: To the first position of interrogation: "None of it is true."
> Second that this nobleman Lorenzo Bembo took the household belongings of said noblewoman—such as food, clothes, and jewels—in order to spend them for his own enjoyment.
> [*margin*]: To the second position of interrogation: "None of it is true."
> Third that he has had sex with the women of the household, each time insulting the said noblewoman Antonia.
> [*margin*]: To the third position of interrogation: "None of it is true."
> Fourth that the aforementioned nobleman has been away from his said wife for five years, and for most of that time has left her without money for food, with three children to support.
> [*margin*]: To the fourth position of interrogation: "None of it is true."
> Fifth that while he was in the army he continually had sex with other women, by whom he has also had children.
> [*margin*]: To the fifth position of interrogation: "None of it is true."

These accusations appear against the background of the dispute between Dr. Padoani and Lorenzo in 1660; Lorenzo's denials uncannily echo that exchange (doc. 11). At that point, though, Antonia had taken her husband's side; now it was her turn to make the accusations.

Antonia hired lawyer Marc'Antonio Ferro to come to her defense in the case.[92] The documents, spanning the period from 30 September through 12

---

[90] I-Vnm, Ms. VII, 847 (8926), f. 250 (1669, 23 June).

[91] I-Vasp, Curia Patriarcale, *Sezione antica:Actorum, mandatorum, et præceptorum*, b. 116. This document was uncovered by Jonathan Glixon.

[92] I-Vas, Notarile, *Atti*, Giorgio Emo, b. 5521, ff. 160v–161 (1672, 13 November), a document brought to my attention by Beth Glixon. Ferro is associated here with the Flemish businessman "Giusto Van Eick," who, perhaps not coincidentally, had resided in Cannaregio in the early 1660s and rented a storage area from the singer Barbara Strozzi. Beyond the Mantuan letters of the 1650s, this is the only document linking Antonia Bembo and Barbara Strozzi. I am grateful to Beth Glixon for bringing the possible importance of Van Eick to my attention; for the Strozzi-Van Eick rental negotiations, see her "New Light on Barbara Strozzi," 317.

December 1672, show that the couple was living separately: Antonia in the parish of Santa Fosca (Cannaregio), Lorenzo at San Barnaba (Dorsoduro). He took some precautions against her charges and five days before the first notarized document regarding the divorce, he rented out his portion of the Bembo house at Santa Maria Nova for a five-year period. Three days after, he transferred allegiances to his stepmother, Laura Querini, naming her as his executor.[93] He very likely sought refuge with Querini and his half brothers Zan Mattio, Antonio, and Nicolo at San Barnaba.

Clearly justice was not on Antonia's side. The divorce case was dropped following the list of accusations of December 1672; she was not able to get her money back for the possessions that Lorenzo had taken from her, nor did she receive an official apology. Perhaps he came through with some money for the family, quieting the legal proceedings. Antonia's remained "sua consorte" ("his wife") in subsequent notarized documents, confirming the continuation of their legally married state.

Matters came to a head about four years later when, following the death of Antonia's mother, Lorenzo and his half brothers engaged in an active correspondence. Throughout the tense summer of 1676, notarized letters went back and forth among them, full of angry accusations but with little substance about the nature of the argument. As he had done before to his father-in-law and wife, Lorenzo denied any wrongdoing, while the brothers wrote of scandal and of legal actions against him. The bickering among the brothers turned inward as well; Antonio and Nicolo argued in the closing letter of the series.[94]

The evidence thus far provides enough detail to sketch the personalities of both Antonia and Lorenzo. Lorenzo, the orphan who made an advantageous marriage, seems to have run almost constantly into financial difficulty and to have caused conflicts with those around him. The letters exchanged with Padoani and the comments appended to Antonia's accusations reveal his tendency to deny what others called misdeeds; many more such written testimonies follow in the numerous notarized exchanges—usually having to do with family property—with his cousins, Bernardo and Zan Mattio, as well as with his half brothers. For some time the force of his captivating personality helped him to get away with his offences. One imagines a terrifically charm-

---

[93] I-Vas, Notarile, *Atti*, Vincenzo Vincenti, b. 13887 (1672, 25 September and 2 October). Also in this month, an addition was made by the notary Pietro Bracchi to the original wedding contract of 7 June 1658 and to an addendum of 18 January 1661 pertaining to the balancing of dowry accounts between Lorenzo and his father-in-law. See I-Vas, Signori di Notte al Civil, *Pagamenti, e assicurazion di dotte,* b. 46, reg. 47, ff. 11–12, which gives the date of the addition as 3 October 1672. The papers of the notary, however, do not contain any corroboration of it (I-Vas, Notarile, *Atti*, Pietro Bracchi e Girolamo Brinis: *alfabeto* [b. 881, for 1665–1678] and *protocollo* [b. 912, for 1673, 11 August 1672–28 February]).

[94] I-Vas, Notarile, *Atti*, Vincenzo Vincenti, b. 13845 (1676): correspondence of 8, 12, 18, 30 June; 21 and 30 July; and 17 August.

ing man, to judge from his aunts' affections, from Antonia's initial love that caused her to side with him against her parents, as well as from his reputation as a ladies' man in Greece. The years spent away at war, which apparently caused a severe case of post-traumatic stress, soured relations with his wife; his ally against her father in 1662, now she turned against him. If his larceny went unpunished in 1672, clemency would not continue when he stole from the Republic of Venice in the following decade.

Escape

In a study of Venetian inscriptions, the nineteenth-century historiographer Emmanuele Cicogna noted that

> Under Abbess Giulia Marchiori [Melchiori] (1673–1676) Antonia Padoani, commoner, wife of the noble[man] Lorenzo Bembo, deposited at the convent jewels, pearls, and furniture, of which there is a list. There is nothing remarkable about it, except for a silver-lined crystal reliquary. The inventory was made on 30 March 1685. Antonia went to Paris (we do not know what motivated her to go), where she died between 1683 and 1685. She had a daughter, Diana Bembo, a nun at Santa Maria dell'Orazione on Malamocco.[95]

Cicogna found these papers in the archive of the convent of San Bernardo of Murano and presumed that Antonia's death prompted the inventory.[96] But Antonia did not die in the years he gave; 1683–1685 represents the period by which financial matters had deteriorated to the extent that most of her things had to be appraised and sold in order to pay the fees for her daughter's continuing stay at the convent. She left for Paris well before, and the foregoing has elucidated the reasons motivating her departure. The convent's capitular books reveal that Melchiori served as abbess from 14 February 1674 until her death on 20 November 1676.[97] Three additional pieces of evidence support the idea that Antonia escaped from Venice in the winter of 1676–1677: (1) the death of her mother, (2) a *procura* from Lorenzo, and (3) another encounter with Francesco Corbetta.

[95] Emmanuele Antonio Cicogna, *Delle inscrizioni veneziane* (Venice: Picotti, 1824–1853; facs. repr., Bologna: Forni Editore, 1983), vol. 6, pt. 1 (1853): "1685. Sotto l'abbadessa Giulia Marchiori (1673–1676) Antonia Padoanì popolare moglie del nobile *Lorenzo Bembo* depositò nel monistero gioie, perle, e mobili de' quali evvi elenco. Non veggo di curioso se non se un *Reliquiario di cristal di montagna fornito d'argento.* L'inventario fu fatto nel 30 marzo 1685. Antonia, non si sa per qual motivo, andata a Parigi, quivi morì tra il 1683 e il 1685. Essa aveva figliuola Diana Bembo monaca in S. Maria dell'Orazione a Malamocco" (354).

[96] I-Vas, Corporazioni religiose, *San Bernardo di Murano,* b. 18.

[97] I-Vas, Corporazioni religiose, *San Bernardo di Murano,* b. 7, Libero di chapitolo.

Described as "the wife of Pietro Ramis of Montagnana," Diana Padoani died in Padua on 29 April 1676.[98] Even if her mother's second marriage may have complicated matters, Antonia undoubtedly inherited most of the Padoani family estate. In one of two letters that she wrote from Paris in 1682, she declared that the goods that she had deposited in the convent—sometime prior to November 1676—"legally belonged to [her] and not to Lorenzo" (doc. 16). Moreover, a *procura* from Lorenzo dated January 1679 refers to further items that she left in the city "with a few people" before her departure (doc. 15).

Lorenzo sought money from the sale of Antonia's items, for he owed two years' worth of payments for his daughter's expenses at the convent of San Bernardo of Murano: February 1677–January 1679. The debt to the convent took most of the profit that he gained from the transaction. He paid L. [*lire*] 32 for the transportation of the goods, gave the convent L. 992, and ended up with L. 37.4 for himself.[99] Having deposited her valuables at San Bernardo di Murano toward the end of 1676, Antonia apparently delayed taking her daughter to live there until the eve of her departure for Paris.

In his *procura*, Lorenzo named Domenico Selles "procurator" of the belongings that Antonia had left in the city (doc. 15). Another set of documents reveals that the same "Domenico Selles, luthier at San Moisè" figures as the most crucial person of those holding her last-minute items. She had left her spinet in Selles's safekeeping.[100] This information simultaneously brings into the composer's biography the first mention of a musical instrument and furthers the hypothesis that the guitarist Francesco Corbetta aided her escape.[101]

Bembo described having "been abandoned by the person who took [her] away from Venice" (doc. 1). Although her words do not specify gender, surely a man escorted her to Paris, it being difficult for women of the time to move freely across borders. Corbetta—an international traveler who frequented both Venice and Paris, an acquaintance of hers from the 1650s, and a resident of both London and Paris during the 1670s[102]—received the following official travel document from the royal Whitehall Office on 13 December 1676:

[98] I-Pas, Ufficio di Sanità, b. 482. No last will and testament for Diana Paresco Padoani Ramis has surfaced at the Archivio di Stato of Venice.

[99] I-Vas, Notarile, *Atti*, Giovanni Antonio Mora, b. 8651 bis, f. 210 (1679, 3 March).

[100] I-Vas, Giudici del Forestier, *Estraordinario*, b. 206, f. 107v (1682, 17 March): "nelle mani di d[omin]o Dome[ne]g.o Seles Lauter a S[an] moise tutto quello & di ragion del N[obil] H[uomo] Lorenzo Bembo, et in particolar la spinetta di raggion di detto N[obil] H[uomo] sive il tutto della medema dattalli da vender dalla Rev[eren]da M[adre] Abbadessa di Murano."

[101] I-Vas, Esaminador, *Interdetti*, reg. 198, f. 94v (1679 [1678 m.v.], 27 February; reg. 206, f. 107v (1682, 17 March); and reg. 206, f. 131 (1682, 8 April). I am grateful to Beth and Jonathan Glixon for sending me transcriptions of the Selles documents from Venice early in 2005.

[102] James Tyler and Paul Sparks, *The Guitar and its Music: From the Renaissance to the Classical Era* (Oxford: Oxford University Press, 2002), 125.

Pass for Francesco Corbetti, one of the Italian musicians of the King's Bed-chamber, who is going to France and other foreign parts.[103]

Quite conceivably, Corbetta—having heard directly from Bembo of her plight—planned first to make arrangements in Paris for her to stay among the Italians living there, and next to travel on to Venice. Having been to Paris before his encounter with the Padoani family in 1654, he may well have spoken to Antonia then of the wonders of the French court, thereby lending credence to her claim that she had admired Louis XIV "since childhood." With abundant travels throughout southern and northern Europe, and several compositions suitable for voice and guitar, Corbetta's qualifications match Bembo's description of having been presented at the French court as "talent[ed] in singing" (doc. 1). This hypothesis explains the plausibility of Bembo's initial five-year stay with people from the Italian community in Paris and also elucidates the nature of her escape. Quite likely Corbetta's alibi consisted in going to his Venetian luthier,[104] where Antonia would meet him. It being Carnival season, masks may well have facilitated their departure.

---

[103] M. A. Everett Green, F. Bickley, and F. H. B. Daniell, eds., *Great Britain, Public Record Office, Calendar of State Papers, Domestic Series* (London: Longmans, Green, Reader, Dyer, and Roberts, 1860–1939; reprint, Nendeln, Liechtenstein: Kraus, 1968), 28: 451 cites the Home Office, *Warrant Book* 1: 331.

[104] See Tyler and Sparks, *The Guitar,* 113, plate 7.5, for a photograph of a five-course guitar made by Domenico Selles in Venice, c. 1670, preserved in the National Music Museum at the University of South Dakota. Selles's name also appears as "Sellas" and "Seles."

Chapter 2
OUR LADY OF GOOD NEWS

A ntonia Bembo's departure from Venice in the winter of 1676–1677 effectively sealed her fate and future life in France. Two decades later, she would write that, when she first came to Paris, she lived in the neighborhood of "Notre Dame de Bonne Nouvelle"—"Our Lady of Good News"—and that a royal pension subsequently provided her "a more suitable place" in a "holy refuge" (doc. 1). This chapter furthers the hypothesis that Corbetta not only helped her to escape but also introduced her to King Louis XIV and arranged for her first to live with fellow Italian expatriates in Paris. Five years later, she would move to her definitive home at the Petite Union Chrétienne, a semi-cloistered women's community associated with the church of Notre Dame de Bonne Nouvelle. The Comédie Italienne and the Petite Union Chrétienne belonged to the same neighborhood: the *paroisse* of Notre Dame de Bonne Nouvelle, circumscribed at the western edge of the city by the Porte Saint Denis and leading along rue Saint Denis to the rue du Petit Lion to the northeast, and by rue Poissonnière to the southeast (fig. 2.1).

The Jewels

The first document pertaining to Bembo in Paris comes from the source that Cicogna located in Venice: the papers of San Bernardo of Murano, among which are preserved two letters that she wrote in March and June 1682 to Abbess Isabella Campana, Melchiori's successor.[1] In a letter dated 21 Febru-

---

[1] Isabella Campana became abbess on 21 December 1679, a position that she held until the election of Degna Merita Vendramin on 30 April 1683; the two women alternated the leadership of the convent through 20 December 1697 (I-Vas, Corporazioni religiose, *San Bernardo di Murano*, b. 7).

Figure 2.1   Map of Paris in 1675 by Jouvin de Rochefort. *Source*: Harvard Map Collection.

ary—mentioned here but no longer extant—Campana had written to Bembo in Paris about the belongings that she had left at the convent, and about her daughter and husband, to which she replied (doc. 16):

Paris, 11 March 1682

Your Illustrious and Reverend Christian Ladyship,

I am obliged to your Reverend Ladyship for the expression of your courteous affection in your letter of the 21st of the last month, and I am particularly indebted to you for the advice that you gave me regarding my daughter's well-being. Since I did not receive from Lorenzo the jewels that Your Reverence keeps safe for me, I remain convinced that you must not be upset by his actions. I can always legally refuse him the jewels, so please keep them with you until such a time as I make a new arrangement. I intend for this to be at the end of three months; if I shall not be able to attend to these matters, I wish that your Reverend Ladyship will take care of them for me. The last of my wishes is that my daughter absolutely must not leave the convent; if she decides to leave, it will not have been with my consent. I add here—thanking you for your kind witness—that I pray heaven may grant you every wish, happily giving affectionate regards to Sister Maria Giordana and also to my daughter.

Your Illustrious and Reverend Ladyship's most devoted and humble servant,

Antonia Bembo

Figure 2.2   Signature of Antonia Bembo, 11 March 1682. *Source*: Documenti 1682, 11 e 12 marzo. Archivio di Stato di Venezia, Corporazioni religiose soppresse, San Bernardo di Murano, b. 18. Un'immagine in bianco e nero. Reproduction by the Sezione di fotoriproduzioni dell'Archivio di Stato di Venezia. Atto di Concessione n. 58/2005, prot. 7629 V. 12.

Evidently Campana had reported to Bembo that Lorenzo had discovered the location of the remainder of the belongings not gathered up in 1679. The initial sale had rendered just enough money to pay the convent through February of that year, but now, three years later, he needed to pay a new and still larger debt and was trying to lay his hands on his wife's goods at the convent.

Antonia's injunction reveals her fear that Lorenzo's inability to pay the convent would result in their daughter's release. Perhaps Diana herself, now a young woman of nineteen, wished to leave. The jewels to which Antonia referred came from her Padoani heritage.[2] True to her word, she replied to the abbess three months later (doc. 17):

Paris, 10 June [1682]
    Illustrious Lady,
    I have received the latest letter of your Reverend Ladyship in which you asked me for the copies that I have of the receipts for the objects that you are keeping for me. I answer you by saying that I left two copies in the safe-keeping of the deceased abbess. Notwithstanding, this must suffice for the

---

[2] On the complexities of dowries and inheritance, see Stanley Chojnacki, "Dowries and Kinsmen in Early Renaissance Venice," *Journal of Interdisciplinary History* 5 (1975): 571–600; and Thomas Kuehn, "Some Ambiguities of Female Inheritance Ideology in the Renaissance," *Continuity and Change* 2 (1987): 11–36.

moment and in the meanwhile, you absolutely must not allow my belongings to leave your safekeeping until I give you new instructions. I will do everything possible to rid your Reverend Ladyship of this embarrassment. In closing, I pray you to honor me with my regards to Sister Maria Giordana, and I remain

Your Illustrious and Reverend Ladyship's most devoted and humble servant,
Antonia Bembo

In the first letter (fig. 2.2), Antonia had conveyed her regards to her daughter, but this second letter (fig. 2.3) contains no salutation to her; apparently having accepted that Diana had left the convent against her wishes, now her concern shifted to the precarious state of her deposited belongings. The second missing letter from Abbess Campana must have asked for her inventory, to which she replied that "two copies" had been left with "the deceased abbess," Giulia Melchiori. A receipt dated 15 June 1682 shows that Lorenzo had just paid a fee of 40 ducats for a half year's room and board for Diana's continued stay at San Bernardo. The treasurer, Maria Elena Muti, reported that she had just returned, but asserted that the family still owed 200 ducats

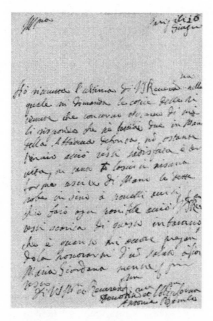

Figure 2.3   Signature of Antonia Bembo, 10 June [1682]. *Source*: Documenti 1682, 11 e 12 marzo. Archivio di Stato di Venezia, Corporazioni religiose soppresse, San Bernardo di Murano, b. 18. Un'immagine in bianco e nero. Reproduction by the Sezione di fotoriproduzioni dell'Archivio di Stato di Venezia. Atto di Concessione n. 58/2005, prot. 7629 V. 12.

for the unpaid interim, that is, three years at 80 ducats/year = 240 ducats for March 1679–March 1682 (doc. 18):

> Receipt from Sister Diana Bembo
>   Today 15 June 1682
>   I, Sister Maria Elena, Treasurer of the Convent of San Bernardo of Murano, have received from the Nobleman Lorenzo Bembo forty ducats for the next six months' board of the Illustrious Lady Diana his daughter, ending next December—forty ducats paid. I declare however with this receipt that I do not intend to deprive the convent of the two hundred ducats that are still owed to its credit for the past meals taken. She went home and now she is back ["and her aforementioned father" crossed out].

The receipt indicates Muti's suppressed words; she had wanted to say more about Lorenzo but evidently realized the impropriety of writing unrelated commentary on a financial statement.

Bembo sent regards in her two letters to *Suor* Maria Giordana Gozzi, a noblewoman who had entered the convent in 1663.[3] Gozzi kept track of her Parisian address, and of Diana's whereabouts during her absences from the convent, in a journal that the archive preserves among Bembo's papers. Perhaps Gozzi worked as an informant for Bembo, whose relations with her husband had been severed. In all likelihood, Bembo avoided writing to her brothers-in-law, who had to side with Lorenzo for the sake of family allegiance even if they fully empathized with her frustration. Gozzi became a literal and figurative "sister" (*suor*) for Bembo, who had no family members of her own after the death of her only adult blood relation, her mother, months before her departure. Even if her situation at the Petite Union Chrétienne did not require that she take the veil, she had become something of a *suor* herself by virtue of living among the religious.

Gozzi revealed several Venetian locations for Diana Bembo: "staying at Santi Apostoli past the bridge of the fruit merchant, Cà Belini at San Giovanni Nuovo, Cà Bembo at Santa Maria Nova, and Cà Formenti at San Marciliano."[4] Two of these places match the residences appearing in the supporting documentation: Cà Bembo and the home of Diana's uncle Antonio who lived near "Santi Apostoli just past the bridge of the fruit merchant."[5] A letter written to Lorenzo by his half brother Zan Mattio in autumn 1683 confirms

---

[3] See I-Vas, Corporazioni religiose, *San Bernardo di Murano,* b. 19, "Libro delle Investiture di Cecca et Altri Officij," f. 1. The convent's capitular book (b. 7) shows Gozzi's entry on 26 January 1663 [1662 m.v.], where she lived until her death on 28 October 1728, at age 82.

[4] I-Vas, Corporazioni religiose, *San Bernardo di Murano,* b. 19, Gozzi's booklet: "San Bernardo Murano:" "La Diana sta a San Apostolo pasa al Ponte di Barba frutariol, A San Zuane niovo cha belini, Santa Maria niova cha bembo" and "sta a San Marcilian cha formenti."

[5] I-Vbc, Ms. P.D.C., b. 2714/5, f. 164.

the supposition gleaned from the Parisian letters and Gozzi's journal: Diana had no fixed abode, but traveled back and forth between relatives' homes and the convent. Was it her wish to leave the convent, or her obligation every time the money ran out? Zan Mattio reprimanded Lorenzo for his inaction, despite repeated requests that he take Diana into his own home, select a convent for her, or repay him for the costs of her lodging (doc. 19):

2 October 1683

   I don't know how to understand the cause that makes you resist so much, Lorenzo Bembo, beloved brother to me, Zan Mattio, for I have asked you to return your daughter to the safety of a convent so many times without receiving an answer, only excuses, up to the point where you persuaded me that I should keep her in my own home and you would pay her expenses of 60 ducats until she returned to the convent. But many, many times, after much discussion about returning her to the convent, we had agreed that I would receive her and I did so, and told you. You led me to believe that this was what you wanted to do, and you said so, but you protested and then did not come to collect her within eight days' time. I declare that you are fully capable, being in the prime of life, to pay me 110 ducats for her expenses. For your own advantage and my great relief and also that of my house, I would like to be relieved of this debt, out of the sort of respect that you should know. I have said these things and warned you of them in the best way I know possible; I protest only that which is appropriate, and demand that you respond, otherwise I will be the last to protest.

The objections that Zan Mattio made for Lorenzo's poor behavior come as no surprise; they match the complaints of his wife, in-laws, and half brothers in the previous two decades. The total debt came to 110 ducats, suggesting that Diana had been with her uncle Zan Mattio for most of 1683, up to the time he drafted his letter to Lorenzo; it cost more to house her in the city than at the Muranese convent. That her uncle did not name a particular place suggests that he and Lorenzo sought a new situation for her, which they found at another Augustinian convent: Santa Maria dell'Orazione on Malamocco, the southern end of present-day Lido. On 30 August 1683 the capitular records note her entry there, with her confirmation as an *educanda* celebrated on 12 November 1683.[6] The archives of San Bernardo corroborate these events

---

[6] I-Vas, Corporazioni religiose, *Santa Maria dell'Orazione di Malamocco,* b. 7, "Libro di Capitoli." The confirmation gives her age as "20" with "19" crossed out, suggesting her date of birth as circa October 1663; I have not found a birthdate or birthplace for her elsewhere. On girls' education in convents, see Silvio Tramontin, "Ordini e congregazioni religiose," in *Storia della cultura veneta: Il Seicento,* ed. Girolamo Arnaldi and Manlio Pastore Stocchi (Vicenza: Neri Pozza, 1983): "Female monasteries and convents were also producers of culture. In fact during the seventeenth century the traditional custom of the patriciate (and not just of the patriciate but also of those who

and show that the Bembo family's debt indeed never rose above the formidable 200-ducat remainder recorded in 1682. Antonia wrote two letters to the abbess on 21 September and 21 November 1683—now lost—to arrange to repay the debt through the sale of her belongings, which also would yield enough to pay for the initial part of Diana's stay at Santa Maria dell'Orazione.[7]

It took some time to carry out Antonia's orders, but on the last four days of March 1685 several *Fanti*, representative members of the Council of Ten, executed the procedure at Lorenzo's request. After a locksmith had made a new key for them, a "small case and two chests" were opened before the *Fanti,* Abbess Vendramin, and a jeweler from the Rialto named Gasparo Romieri, revealing an array of treasures (doc. 20):

A pendant jewel (with various rubies, two *balas* rubies, and a pearl)	240 d.
A flower with diamonds	80 d.
The same with pearls	60 d.
A *goletta*[8] with pearls and emeralds	70 d.
A pair of earrings with emeralds	15 d.
A pair of same with six pairs of pendant pearls	20 d.
A watch with a filigreed gold case	40 d.
The same with an amber case	15 d.
Seven gilded black amber buttons	14 d.
A small heart [a prism] set in gold, a button, and two golden *capete*[9]	4 d.

---

had more than one daughter and limited financial resources) continued to entrust to the religious women the education of their *putte* or *fiole,* the latter name was that generally given to the girls sent to be educated" ["Anche i monasteri e conventi femminili furono produttori di cultura. Continuò infatti nel Seicento la tradizionale consuetudine del patriziato (e non solo del patriziato, ma pure di chi avesse più di una figlia e discrete risorse economiche) di affidare alle monache l'educazione delle loro putte o fiole, denominazione quest'ultima generalmente attribuita alle educande"] (48). Giacomo Padoani left part of his estate to the Augustinian order in Venice, perhaps of significance to Antonia when deciding where to entrust her jewels and daughter in the 1670s.

[7] I-Vas, Corporazioni religiose, *San Bernardo di Murano,* b. 18, Mazzo Q, Plica D, 28–31 March. In her journal, Gozzi recorded Antonia's address: "S[ore]lla la Bemba è in Parigi nella comunita delle Dame del unione christiana strada della Luna parochia della madona di buone novelle" (I-Vas, Corporazioni religiose, *San Bernardo di Murano,* b. 19, booklet "San Bernardo Murano" belonging to Gozzi), thereby confirming the residence that Antonia mentioned in the dedication to *Produzioni armoniche* (doc. 1).

[8] Giuseppe Boerio, *Dizionario del dialetto veneziano* (Venice: Giovanni Cecchini, 1856), s.v. "Golèta": "A collar made of lace and ribbons, ruffled in the shape of a lettuce. When women wore it with precious stones it was then called a wreath of jewels" ["Gorgiera; Collaretto di merletti e di fettucce increspate quasi a foggi di lattuga. Ne portano pure le Donne di pietre preziose e si dice Serto di gioie"].

[9] Ibid., s.v. "Capetà": "A jewel carved into the shape of a conch shell" ["Conchiglietta; Nicchietto. . . . piccoli Frastagli a foggia di Conchiglia"].

Five silver medals	1 d.
Four amber buttons covered in gold, a button with seed pearls, two garnet bunches of grapes	4 d.
A pair of golden bracelets with a braid	16 d.
A small silver chain	0.12
Fourteen pieces with emeralds	6 d.
Garnets; a claw set in silver	1 d.
A small box with corals, pearls, and *perosini*[10]	1 d.
An emerald heart, with an accompanying emerald medal with a figure	60 d.
A heart of *perosini* with a cross of mountain crystal and a golden medal	15 d.
Twelve silver buttons	3 d.
A spoon made of mother-of-pearl	0.12
A small heart with gold, a mushroom-shaped jasper, a wedding ring, a box with *perosini*, etc.	4 d.
A silver filigree cross	6 d.
A silver box with two lids	12 d.
Tortoiseshell binders with silver	4 d.
A mountain crystal reliquary with silver	2 d.
Three gold *perosini*	1 d.
A *pistoletta*[11] of gilded silver with a golden chain	5 d.
Various agates, carnelians, black amber, and other items in a box	2 d.
	702 d.

Antonia's original inventories having been misplaced during the succession of abbesses at San Bernardo, Romieri had been called in to make this official appraisal. Some shorter lists of jewels and linens among the papers preserved in the convent archive, however, may represent the "two copies" that she said she had left "in the safekeeping of the deceased abbess" (doc. 17). The group also inventoried her linens without an appraisal of their value, mistakenly declaring them as Lorenzo's (doc. 20):

Inventory of the linen of nobleman Lorenzo Bembo, found in storage at the convent of San Bernardo of Murano:

1. Sixty napkins	no. 60
2. Tablecloths	no. 4
3. Cotton tablecloths	no. 7
4. Pairs of sheets	no. 8

[10] Ibid., s.v. "Perosini": "Gold earrings with tiny pear-shaped pendants" ["Pendenti, sorta d'orecchini d'oro, che hanno per ciondoli delle parti fatte a foggia di minutissime pere"].

[11] Ibid., s.v. "Pistòla" and "Pistolese" represent the closest equivalents to this word in Boerio, who suggests for the interpretation of the second word a kind of knife usually worn by Pantalone in the *commedia*.

5. Aprons[12]	no. 4
6. A curtain of green *cendà*[13]	no. 1
7. Women's blouses	no. 2
8. Handkerchiefs	no. 12
9. Pairs of pillowcases	no. 8
10. Lace apron	no. 1
11. Pillows	no. 3
12. Turkish handkerchiefs with natural flowers	no. 8
13. Silk cradle covers	no. 2
14. Cradle cover of lace	no. 1
15. Black *telletti*[14]	no. 3
16. Kitchen cloths[15]	no. 10
17. A Turkish diaper cloth	no. 1
18. Two vessels for diapers	no. 2
19. A crystal pail	no. 1

Whereas the inventory of the jewelry notes its monetary value, that of the linens merely enumerates the quantity of its contents. The covers of silk and lace stored in the convent evidently belonged with one of the items that Lorenzo had sold six years before with Selles's assistance: a cradle.[16] The crystal reliquary that caught Cicogna's attention when he read this inventory stands alongside objects recalling Titian's Venetian beauties: the earrings, pendants, bracelets, gems, and buttons that had adorned Antonia and the women of her family.[17] One can imagine the excitement of hearing and seeing the lovely Antonia as she sang music as ravishing as the jewels she wore.

Having successfully sequestered her most valuable possessions, Bembo not only assured her independence from Lorenzo but also preserved the family wealth. Now she could pay the convent for Diana's accumulated fees, and

---

[12] Ibid., s.v. "Traversa": "Piece of cloth or other material, to tie in front and across the woman's waist; also called *Grembo* when the pinafore was folded and suitable to tuck in and carry something" ["Pezzo di pannolino o d'altra materia, che tengono dinanzi cinto le Donne, e che si chiama anche Grembo, quando il Grembiale sia piegato ed acconcio per mettervi dentro e portare che che sia"].

[13] Ibid., s.v. "Cendà o Cendal": "Fabric made of extremely light and notable silk that among eighteenth-century Venetian women became an almost national costume. By *Cendà* one meant the cloth; by *Cendaleto* the woman who covered herself with it" ["Drappo di seta leggerissimo e notissimo, di cui in quasi tutto il secolo ultimo scorso formavasi una specie d'abito, divenuto quasi nazionale delle Dame e Donne civili in Venezia; quindi per Cendà intendevasi anche il vestito, e per Cendaleto la Donna stessa quando n'era coperta"].

[14] Ibid., s.v. "Teletà": "finely-woven Venetian fabric" ["Teletta, Intendesi fra noi la Tela lavorata a opere minute"].

[15] Ibid., s.v. "Canevazza": "a kind of large and rough diaper" ["Canavaccio o Canovaccio; Sorta di pannolino grosso e ruvido"].

[16] I-Vas, Notarile, *Atti*, Giovanni Antonio Mora, b. 8651 bis: "una cuna di ferro" (f. 210).

[17] Cicogna, *Delle inscrizioni veneziane*, 6/1: 354.

then request that the remainder go toward her daughter's education at Santa Maria dell'Orazione. The closing statement of the group drawing up the inventories officially honored her request (doc. 21):

31 March 1685

Having heard the respectful petition of Nobleman Lorenzo Bembo, having seen the letter written by Noblewoman Antonia Bembo, his wife, of 21 November 1683, and having summoned and heard the Noblemen Anzolo Zusto and Vincenzo Vendramin, procurators of the venerable convent of San Bernardo of Murano, their Excellencies have determined that all books,[18] jewels, and other personal property existing in the inventory by order of their Excellencies, be it to possible advantage to sell by Anzolo Zusto, procurator of the aforementioned convent, and by one of the procurators of the convent of Santa Maria dell'Orazione of Malamocco, and that the same people owe the same procurators in the first place the abbess of the aforementioned convent of San Bernardo of Murano the sum of two hundred ducats, that will pay for the room and board accrued by the Noblewoman Diana Bembo, daughter of the aforementioned Lorenzo and Noblewoman Antonia Bembo for the time that she [Diana] stayed in said convent, and all the rest should be taken by the noblemen and deposited in the tribunal of the Heads [of the Council of Ten] because after it will be available for the time of taking the veil [for Diana], which should follow at the end of four months and absolutely must be given to the abbess of the aforementioned convent of Malamocco, for the account of the said daughter in said convent, and not otherwise, and to no one else.

The personal property and the linens, that will serve the needs of the said daughter when she becomes a nun, should be reserved [for her] by these procurators, and not sold. They must deposit both them and the inventory with the same abbess, who must keep them for the use of the same girl, when she takes the veil.

Vicenzo da Mula, Zaccaria Salamon, Giovanni Antonio Priuli,
Heads of the Council of Ten, [and] Maria Angelo di Negri,
Ducal Notary

Based on the new light shed on the packet of documents preserved in the archive, Cicogna's observations can now be qualified. He had inferred that Antonia's death had prompted the inventory and that Diana had become a nun at the convent of Santa Maria dell'Orazione. Instead, Antonia's absence from Venice made it necessary for the official treatment and dispensation of her belongings. It had certainly been the intention of the Council of Ten that Diana take the veil, but she lived in the convent for about ten years without

---

[18] Even though the document mentions "books," it gives no specific details of the contents of Antonia's library.

doing so and, at thirty-one, she would marry Iseppo Bessi, a Venetian *citta-dino*. One of the few extant descriptions of the Malamocco convent shows that it had received a subsidy from the Venetian Republic after having been found in decrepitude in the early part of the seventeenth century.[19]

Perhaps the tumult within the family circles caused Diana's sporadic residence in Venice in 1683. She was not the only one of the three children to suffer from her family's predicaments; that summer, troubles arose with her brother Andrea (doc. 22):

> On the evening of 27 June 1683, wandering through the city . . . [Andrea] met Antonio Gandiner who was going with all modesty enjoying the freedom of the city, when—without apparent motive—Andrea was seized by an impetuous fury to strike [Gandiner's] left breast and pierce it with a pointed weapon, from which [Gandiner] stood in mortal danger with copious bleeding. Having deliberately committed this dolorous act in the evil way described, he is sentenced by default.

The Council of Ten reprimanded Lorenzo for the behavior of his son, who was eighteen years old at the time of this incident, but it waited four years to draft this rather poetically phrased letter. By then, 17 December 1687, Andrea had been called into military service at Crema and his first son, Lorenzo, had just been born.[20] Andrea had married the noblewoman Isabetta Priuli in December 1686 at the Redentore in Venice, the church where his parents were wed.[21] Like Andrea himself, the child had been born at the maternal family home and not in Venice proper, so his parents had to file promptly in order to assure his status in the patriciate. The request to the *Avogaria di Comun* for the child's noble status probably prompted the sentence. Even if ordered to stand trial in January 1688, it seems unlikely that Andrea was incarcerated for his misdemeanor; his second son, Nicolo, was born in the autumn of the next year.[22] The Council of Ten awarded both sons their noble status.

The papers of Lorenzo's cousin Bernardo Bembo provide the richest source for information regarding the inheritance questions of Lorenzo and his kin, and for most of the data collected in the comprehensive genealogy of the Bembo family (fig. 1.1). Gozzi's journal corroborates Bernardo Bembo's records of the

---

[19] Andrea Da Mosto, *L'Archivio di Stato di Venezia: Indice generale, storico, descrittivo, ed analitico, 2: Archivi dell'amministrazione provinciale della Repubblica Veneta, archivi delle rappresentanze diplomatiche e consolari, archivi dei governi succeduti alla Repubblica Veneta, archivi degli istituti religiosi e archivi minori* (Rome: Biblioteca d'arte editrice, 1940): "nel 1614 era ridotto in così cattive condizioni che ebbe bisogno di un sussidio della Repubblica per essere restaurato" (172).

[20] I-Vas, Avogaria di Comun, *Processi per Nobiltà*, b. 294/12.

[21] Idem.

[22] For a useful study of the judicial system and its injustices in the period, see Gaetano Cozzi, *Giustizia 'contaminata'—Vicende giudiziarie di nobili ed ebrei nella Venezia del Seicento* (Venice: Fondazione Giorgio Cini, Marsilio Editori, 1996).

family properties, noting no fewer than four Venetian locations in which Diana spent her time away from the convent, the most important being the family house in Santa Maria Nova—Cà Bembo in Cannaregio—where Lorenzo lived in rooms entered through the side entrance off the Calle del Forno.[23] Because Bernardo had no children of his own, he left most of his estate to the home for the foundlings of the *Ospedale della Pietà*, whose archive preserves four large folders of precious documentation that he wrote or initiated.[24] Bernardo's record-keeping skills and sense of family responsibility stand in sharp contrast to Lorenzo's tendency to ignore matters of business and to take others' things. Bernardo did much historical work in order to determine who had legal rights to the properties that he and Lorenzo had inherited from the ancient estate of Zan Mattio Bembo.

Soon after Antonia sued for divorce, Lorenzo and his half brother Zan Mattio rented the part of Cà Bembo belonging to Bernardo.[25] This debt would only grow, and on 26 October 1683—just a few weeks after Zan Mattio had urged Lorenzo to take care of his daughter Diana's living arrangements (doc. 19)—Bernardo threatened to take the *inganator* (trickster) Lorenzo to court for evading his payments.[26] His repeated attempts to get Lorenzo to pay must have further prompted Antonia's letters in Fall 1683, possibly in reply to correspondence from Bernardo.[27] In addition to these bitter exchanges, the papers also describe the parts of Cà Bembo belonging to both cousins and the earnings that Lorenzo made on his rental property as he attempted to maintain a source of income.[28] Because of these rentals, it is unclear where Lorenzo himself lived after the mid-1670s.

Amphion

The period from Bembo's petition for divorce to her departure from Venice amounted to just over four years, 1672–1677, time enough to have made the necessary arrangements with Corbetta, by letter or in person when he returned to Venice on his tours. Once having brought Bembo to safety in Paris,

[23] I-Vas, Ospedali e luoghi pii diversi, b. 238, fascicle 1. See Brown, *Private Lives*, 195, for a view of the narrow Calle del Forno.

[24] I-Vas, Ospedali e luoghi pii diversi, bb. 236–239. "Foundling" refers to an infant abandoned by a living parent or parents.

[25] I-Vas, Ospedali e luoghi pii diversi, b. 238, Mazzo 7, ff. 26 (1675, 8 January), 29 (1675, 25 November), and 31.

[26] Ibid., f. II/3. Here Bernardo stated that Lorenzo had reneged on the debt settlement of 7 April 1681.

[27] Ibid., ff. II/2v–6 (1683, 13 October–1684, 27 March), III/1 (1684, 3 April). The debt given on f. III/1 amounted to a total of 965 ducats, of which a 444-ducat balance remained due.

[28] Ibid., fascicle 1.

however, he could not tarry there; by the end of the 1677 he was named the royal guitar master to Charles II's niece, Princess (later Queen) Anne (1664–1714).[29] In order to comprehend the *entrée* that Corbetta arranged for Bembo in Paris, it is necessary to provide further details of his French career.

The Mantuan correspondence (docs. 5–8) reveals new details of Corbetta's many Parisian connections and traces his activity in France back to the 1640s. He had already been in Paris at least four years before February 1656, when his name appeared there for the first time in print in the libretto for the ballet *La Galanterie du temps.*[30] A consideration of the events taking place in France in the 1650s pushes back the date of his first Parisian appearance to the previous decade; due to the upheaval of the Fronde, the Italians had been expelled from the city between 1648 and 1653.[31] Although his Mantuan passport of 1644 did not state where he was bound, he may have been called to Paris along with the many Italians hired by Cardinal Mazarin during the regency of Anne of Austria, including Brigida Fedeli (Aurelia Fedeli and Brigida Bianchi, pseuds.).[32] It was surely during the years prior to the Fronde that he taught guitar to the young Louis XIV.[33]

Corbetta's service to both the British and French courts took him back and forth across the channel in the 1660s and 1670s (fig. 2.4). A suite "sur la mort du Duc de Glocester" included in his publication of 1671, *La Guitarre royalle,* commemorates the English king's youngest brother, Henry, Duke of Gloucester (1639–1660), who died of smallpox.[34] In all likelihood, Corbetta arrived in England during the year of Henry's death upon the Restoration of King Charles II, to whom he served as courtier. Indeed, as Count Grammont

---

[29] GB-Lbl, Add. MS. 18958, "Establishment of the Duke of York . . . Christmas 1677": "Servants belonging to her Highness the Lady Ann . . . Guytarr Master Mr. Francisco Corbet, L. 100" (f. 8v).

[30] Henry Prunières, *L'Opéra italien en France avant Lulli* (Paris: Champion, 1913), 196. The name is found as "Corbetti" in the libretto (F-Pn, Rés. F. 679), with which no music survives. King Louis XIV himself appeared in *La Galanterie du temps,* a spectacle that included jokes made at the expense of Scaramouche, who sat in the audience unbeknownst to the actors. For the story, see Marie-Françoise Christout, *Le Ballet de cour de Louis XIV, 1643–1672* (Paris: Picard, 1967), 81. For the text of the play, see Victor Fournel, *Les Contemporains de Molière* (Paris: Firmin Didot, 1863–1875), 2: 437–447.

[31] Virginia Scott, *The Commedia dell'Arte in Paris, 1644–1697* (Charlottesville: University Press of Virginia, 1990), 19.

[32] Marcelle Benoit, *Versailles et les musiciens du roi* (Paris: Picard, 1971), 264.

[33] Pierre Bourdelot and Pierre Bonnet, *Histoire de la musique et de ses effets* (Paris: n.p., 1715), cited in Maria Rita Brondi, *Il liuto e la chitarra—Ricerche storiche sulla loro origine e sul loro sviluppo* (Turin: Fratelli Bocca Editori, 1926), 102, n. 1, and in Richard T. Pinnell, *Francesco Corbetta and the Baroque Guitar* (Ann Arbor: UMI Research Press, 1980), 1: 95. For a consideration of other possible candidates for the guitar teacher of Louis XIV, see Tyler and Sparks, *The Guitar,* 108.

[34] *La Guitarre royalle dediée au Roy de la Grande Bretagne composée par Francisque Corbett* (Paris: Bonneüil, 1671; reprint, Geneva: Éditions Minkoff, 1993).

FRANCESCO CORBETTA.

Figure 2.4   Engraving of Francesco Corbetta by S. van den Berghe, after S. Harding.
Source: The Harvard Theatre Collection, the Houghton Library.

(c. 1646–1707) recalled in his memoirs, the musician not only captivated his audience but also brought about a craze for his instrument:

> There was a certain Italian at court, famous for the guitar: he had a genius for music, and he was the only man who could make anything of the gui-tar: his style of play was so full of grace and tenderness, that he would have given harmony to the most discordant instruments. The truth is, nothing was so difficult as to play like this foreigner. The king's relish for his com-positions had brought the instrument so much into vogue, that every per-

son played upon it, well or ill; and you were as sure to see a guitar on a lady's toilet as rouge or patches. The Duke of York played upon it tolerably well, and the Earl of Arran like Francisco himself. This Francisco had composed a saraband, which either charmed or infatuated every person; for the whole *guitarery* at court were trying at it; and God knows what an universal strumming there was.[35]

La Guitarre royalle of 1671 contains several sarabandes, one of which may represent the one mentioned here. When Grammont was to return to Paris, King Charles II requested that he take along Corbetta's music lessons for guitar to give to his sister, "Madame" Henrietta, Duchess of Orleans (1644–1670).[36] Might the sarabande that Corbetta included as part of the *Tombeau* for Henrietta be very piece that so "infatuated" the English court?[37] That same sarabande received bilingual texts penned in French by "Mlle. Des Iardins," and in Italian by "Seig[neur] Cintio," the latter the stage name of Marc'Antonio Romagnesi. The only son of Brigida Fedeli, both played leading roles in the Parisian *commedia dell'arte*.[38]

The proximate worlds of Corbetta, Romagnesi, and Henrietta suggest at least an acquaintance among them. Furthermore, Corbetta's music for Henrietta is not unimportant when circling back to Bembo's dedication, for "Madame" figured prominently in the establishment of the church of Notre Dame de Bonne Nouvelle. Henrietta's portrait, along with her three children and Saint François de Sales, held a prominent position on the walls of the edifice, hanging next to a portrait of herself with the mother of Louis XIV, Anne of Austria. Both works have been attributed to the school of Philippe de Champaigne (1602–1674) and Pierre Mignard (1612–1695).[39] Henrietta's patronage for Corbetta and her love of music, as well as her piety, suggest lofty precedents for Bembo's work in producing music for both secular and sacred settings, as well as strengthen the hypothesis that Corbetta's network paved the way for Bembo's Parisian *entrée*.

In 1674 Corbetta published in France an eponymous *La Guitarre royalle,* now dedicated to Louis XIV.[40] With frequent voyages across the English

---

[35] Anthony Hamilton, *Memoirs of Count Grammont* (New York: Merrill and Baker, n.d.), 204.

[36] Richard Keith, "The Guitar Cult in the Courts of Louis XIV and Charles II," *Guitar Review* 26 (June 1962): 7, and "'La Guitare Royale'," 81. Pinnell identified these lessons, now lost, as being entered into the English catalogues of 1677; see *Francesco Corbetta*, 1: 183.

[37] *Le Tombeau sur la mort de Madame d'Orleans* is found on pp. 10–11, followed by *La Sarabande* on p. 11 with the same music texted ("La mesme en musiq[ue]") on pp. 93–95, there titled *Sarab[an]de Tombeau de Madame*.

[38] Scott, *Commedia dell'Arte in Paris*, 39.

[39] Maurice Dumolin and Geroges Outardel, *Les Églises de France: Paris et la Seine* (Paris: Le Touzey et Ané, 1936): "Notre Dame de Bonne Nouvelle," 214.

[40] Francesco Corbetta, *La Guitarre royalle dediée au Roy, composée par Francisque Corbet* (Paris: Bonneüil, 1674; reprint, Bologna: Forni Editore, 1983).

Channel, as well as service to both courts as guitar master, it was only fitting that he would produce a book of "royal guitar" music for each monarch. Moreover, he had been forced by the Test Act of March 1673 to reside in Paris until the summer of 1674,[41] when he returned as one of four guitarists performing in a masque at the Whitehall Palace, London, in 1675—Crowne's and Staggins's *Calisto*—after which he went back to Paris.[42]

Otherwise little is known of Corbetta's last years. In April 1681 the *Mercure galant* published an epitaph on the death of "Francisque" in Paris, touting his prowess as a musician as well as his popularity among many rulers:[43]

Cy gist l'Amphion de nos jours,	Here lies the Amphion of our time
Francisque, cet homme si rare	Francisque, such a rare man,
qui fit parler à sa Guitarre	who could make his guitar
le vray langage des Amours.	speak the true language of love.
Il gagna par son harmonie	With his harmonic skill
les cœurs des Princes et des Roys,	he won over the hearts of princes and kings,
et plusieurs ont cru qu'un Génie	and many believed that a genius
prenoit le soin de co[n]duire ses doigts.	took care to guide his fingers.
Passant, si tu n'as pas entendu ces merveilles,	If you have not heard these marvels,
apprens qu'il ne devoit jamais finir son Sort,	learn that he should never have met his destiny,
et qu'il auroit charmé la Mort;	and that he would have charmed Death herself,
mais, helas! Par malheur, elle n'a point d'oreilles.	but, alas! Unfortunately, she has no ears at all.

Bembo's allusion to having been abandoned by the person who brought her from Venice suggests a euphemism for Corbetta's death. "Habbi pieta di me," no. 16 from *Produzioni armoniche*, represents the likely piece that she and Corbetta performed in order to obtain the king's pension to stay at the Comédie Italienne; following the guitarist's death, Bembo obtained from the king "a more suitable place . . . in [a] holy refuge." Indeed, only one year elapsed between Corbetta's death and the king's *lettres patentes* in 1682 that es-

---

[41] See Tyler and Sparks, *The Guitar*, for an explanation of the Test Act, which "specified that . . . every office holder had to publicly take communion in the Church of England . . . [and] something approaching an exodus ensued" (125).

[42] Henry Cart De Lafontaine, *The King's Musick. A Transcript of Records Relating to Music and Musicians (1470–1700)* (London: Novello, 1909), ix, 281, cited in Pinnell, *Francesco Corbetta*, 1: 213, n. 2. On the masque, see Olive Baldwin and Thelma Wilson, "An English Calisto," *Musical Times* 112 (1971): 651–653.

[43] *Mercure galant*, April 1681, 127–139 at 132–133.

tablished her definitive home at the Petite Union Chrétienne. The hypothesis established here for Corbetta's assistance of Bembo provides a plausible scenario for both of their Parisian careers during the 1677–1681 period.

Comédie Italienne

Where did Bembo spend her first years in Paris among the Italian expatriates? Several intersections between the careers of Brigida Fedeli and her son Marc'Antonio Romagnesi with those of Corbetta and Bembo offer possible answers. The somewhat pejorative tone that Bembo used to compare her initial residence to the "more suitable place" at the "holy refuge" of the Petite Union Chrétienne suggests temporary quarters in the home of a host (doc. 1). Furthermore, the words "Parole d'Aurelia Fedeli" appear in the table of contents to *Produzioni armoniche* just above the entry listed for p. 160 (fig. 2.5), with a bracket in the left margin grouping together the three arias "In amor ci vuol ardir," "E ch'havete bell'Ingrato," and "Non creder a sguardi a 2." The stage name of the Italian actress and poet Brigida Fedeli, "Aurelia Fedeli," represents the only outright attribution to a poet found in all of Bembo's manuscripts of music. Fedeli's biography establishes by association a second hypothesis about the composer's cultural sphere in Paris. Fedeli not only lived in the neighborhood of Notre Dame de Bonne Nouvelle but in the 1660s and 1670s she and her son, Marc'Antonio Romagnesi, published poetry in the style of much of the unattributed amorous verse set to music in *Produzioni armoniche*.

Fedeli (c. 1613–1704) performed with the Italian *commedia dell'arte* in Paris for much of her career.[44] A native of Serviliano, she enjoyed much success throughout Italy playing the role of the *innamorata*, Aurelia, with the troupe of comedians.[45] The actors' renown attracted the attention of Anne of Austria and Cardinal Mazarin, who invited them to visit Paris on many occasions. Fedeli starred at the French court from the late 1630s intermittently until the 1660s, when the troupe made Paris its permanent home. Her three marriages and the resulting variety of her names have made for some confusion in the scholarship, not least of it the fact that she published her work under two different names—for her 1659 book with her married name, "Brigida Bianchi, the comedian known as *Aurelia*," and for her 1666 book with her *nom de plume*, Aurelia Fedeli.[46] Her French papers naturalize her legal name as "Brigide

---

[44] See Claire Fontijn, "Baroque Women: Brigida Bianchi, Comica detta Aurelia," *Goldberg Early Music Magazine* 9 (1999): 106–109, for a concise biography of the actress.

[45] See the lists of actors for 1644–1648 and 1653–1659 in Scott, *Commedia dell'Arte in Paris*, 50–51. For more about the location of Serviliano, see the discussion of her naturalization papers below.

[46] Brigida Bianchi, Comica detta Aurelia, *L'inganno fortunato, overo l'amata aborrita, comedia bellissima, transportata dallo spagnuolo, con alcune poesie musicali composte in diversi tempi* (Paris: Claudio

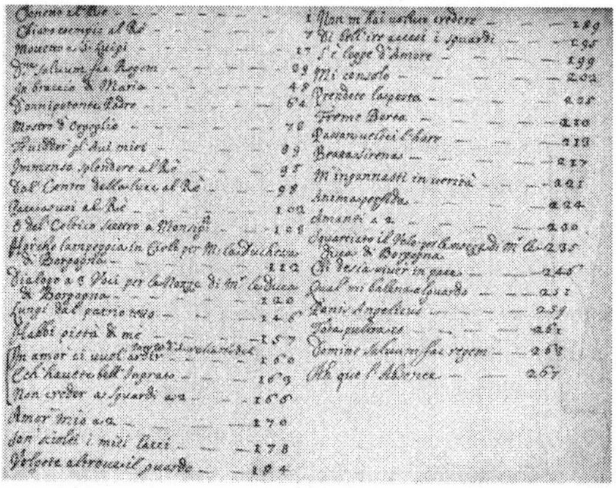

Figure 2.5   Table of contents, F-Pn, Rés. Vm¹117, p. 269. *Source*: Bibliothèque Nationale de France, Paris.

Fidelle," presumably reflecting her maiden name, Brigida Fedeli.[47] The identity of her first husband is not known, but her second was Augustin Romagnesi, the father of her only child, Marc'Antonio (c. 1633–1706).[48] Her third and last husband was Marc'Antonio Bianchi; both her second and third husbands played Orazio to her Aurelia as the comedy's famed pair of lovers on stage.[49] Her husband Bianchi died quite suddenly in Paris in 1660.[50] Thereafter she made the city her permanent home and never remarried.

In his first *La Guitarre royalle* of 1671, Corbetta had attributed to "Seig[neur]

Cramoisy, 1659); and Aurelia Fedeli, *I rifiuti di Pindo* (Paris: C. Chenault, 1666). Fedeli's signatures on notarized pension payments drafted during her final years, when she was close to ninety years old, reveal the continuing multiplicity of her names. As the widow of the actor Bianchi, she received one pension, which she signed as "Aurelia Brigida Bianqhi" (F-Pan MC, XCI, 538, 15 March 1700, doc. 2, f. 2). On another, signed the same day, she received a pension for her work as an actress, thus signing with her legal name "Brigida fedelij" (F-Pan, MC, XCI, 538, 15 March 1700, doc. 1, f. 2). On an earlier pension payment, she crossed out the initial letters "Aure-" and continued on with "Brigida fedelij" (F-Pan, MC, XCI, 504 bis, 5 February 1695, f. 2). For a reproduction of the three signatures, see my "Antonia Bembo," 147.

[47] F-Pan O¹★29, f. 520: "The record of naturalization papers accorded to Brigide Fidelle, native of Serviliano near Rome, given at Versailles on 25 November 1685" ["Relief d'adresse sur lettres de naturalité accordés a Brigide Fidelle native de Serviliano prés Rome a Versailles le xxv.ᵉ Novembre 1685"]. A town in Umbria named Servigliano lies not far from Ancona to the north and from Foligno and Spoleto to the east.

[48] Her second husband's full name appears in at least two archival documents, one preserved in F-Pan MC CXI, 563, f. 1: "veuve en Seconde noces d'Augustin Romagniecy," the other in F-Pap 5 AZ 1744 (1): "veuve en secondes noces d'Augustin Romagnesy" (f. 1r).

[49] F-Pan, MC, CXI, 563, f. 1 and F-Pap, 5 AZ 1744, f. 1r both give the name of her third and last husband as "Marc Antoine Blanchy," his name gallicized for the French legal documents.

[50] Maurice Sand, *Masques et bouffons (Comédie Italienne)* (Paris: M. Lévy, 1860), 180, stated that it was Romagnesi who died that year, but this may again be the fault of the confusion of

Cintio," the stage name of Fedeli's son Marc'Antonio Romagnesi, a poem to fit the sarabande for the *Tombeau* marking the death in 1670 of Henrietta, Duchess of Orleans. Born around 1633 in Verona, Romagnesi pursued a thorough liberal arts education at the Collegio Clementino in Rome.[51] His parents had a busy touring schedule; his fluency in French suggests frequent visits to France at an early age. According to his colleague in France, the actor Ange Lolli, Romagnesi wrote one play per week for the Italian troupe.[52] In 1673 he produced a substantial book of poetry that takes on the style of his mother's two publications in its dedications to poets, musicians, Italian rulers, and members of the French court. Most of the poems are in Italian, but a Frenchman wrote the penultimate one in Romagnesi's honor.[53] Like his mother, Romagnesi possessed musical talent that he vividly expressed in his poetry for musicians and in several of his poems designated "per musica." Many such poems are found in the three volumes that mother and son published in France.

Romagnesi dedicated a significant number of poems to people he knew in Italy, notably in Rome and Mantua. Apparently his father, Augustin Romagnesi, came from Mantua, for Marc'Antonio reclaimed his home in that city after his years of study in Rome. According to the Mantuan scholar Davari, the ducal family had been using the empty house for its own purposes when Romagnesi returned to settle in the city, and they "graciously gave it back to him."[54] He lived in Mantua with his wife, Elisabetta Giulia della Chiesa, until

---

names and of the order of husbands. At any rate, "Marc'Antoine Bianky" received a *"pension"* payment of 210 *livres* as an actor working in Paris on 28 June 1659; see F-Pan, MC, LXXIII, 441 (cited in Madeleine Jurgens, *Documents du Minutier Central concernant l'histoire littéraire [1650–1700]* [Paris: Presses Universitaires de France, 1960], 86).

[51] Romagnesi's naturalization papers, dating from the same period as those of Fedeli and many members of the Italian troupe who had been residents of Paris for at least twenty years, confirm his Veronese birth: "Marc'Antoine Romagnesy, natif de Veronne" (F-Pan Z^{1F}607, ff. 121r–v). Fedeli's naturalization process through various levels of the administration is found in this source (ff. 71v–72r) as well as in F-Pan O^{1*}29, f. 520. On Romagnesi's education at the Collegio Clementino, see Scott, *Commedia dell'Arte in Paris,* 180. In a poem close to the end of his magnum opus, *Poesie liriche di Marc-Antonio Romagnesi divise in quattro parti, consecate all'immortal nome di Luigi XIV* (Paris: Denys Langlois, 1673), 463, Romagnesi wrote of his return to the Collegio Clementino "after many years."

[52] Scott, *Commedia dell'Arte in Paris,* 182, cited this information from a periodical written by Robinet, *Lettres en vers et en prose,* 21 April 1668: "[he] furnishes [the troupe] a new [play] every week without any difficulty." Romagnesi gave Lolli's horoscope reading on pp. 124–125 of *Poesie liriche.*

[53] Romagnesi, *Poesie liriche,* "De Monsieur Gio. Rob. Avoc.," 508–516.

[54] I-MAa, Schede Davari, Ms., #14, ff. 1r–v. One of the last poems in Romagnesi's *Poesie liriche* refers to his "sequestered" family home in Mantua; the poem is dedicated to Duke Carlo II Gonzaga, in thanks for having returned the house to him: "Al Serenissimo Duca di Mantova: Per la liberazione d'una Casa dell'Autore, SUPPLICA: per cui Alt. Concesse generosamente la gratia" (471).

his mother called them to Paris in 1666 following the death of her patron Anne of Austria.[55]

Romagnesi's ties to the Mantuan court stretched back to the period of the 1650s, during the time of the negotiations of Antonia, her father, and Corbetta with Carlo II Gonzaga. The preface to a publication written by the grandfather after whom he was named reveals that the Mantuan–French connection went back still further, for he related that "we came back into the city to the ancient patrimony of this crown and our ruler protected us in Casale with the most memorable actions of the century, as well as in our city of Mantua."[56] Romagnesi's son Augusten maintained the family's connection to the Gonzaga; he signed his grandmother Fedeli's inventory in 1704 as "interpreter of languages to the Duke of Mantua."[57] The linguistic skills passed easily from one generation to the next, in a manner typical of artisan families who honed the talents of their trade over time.

The mutual political interests and entertainment needs of Mantua and Paris reveal common circles of actors and musicians. Many putative ties connect Marc'Antonio Romagnesi with Francesco Corbetta, who were associated with both courts during the same years. First, the two poems by "Seig[neur] Cintio" that Corbetta set to music in his 1671 book fit the *poesie per musica* genres in which Fedeli and Romagnesi specialized. Second, Corbetta composed an *Allemande Canossa,* in honor of the brothers Orazio and Luigi Canossa, major figures at the Mantuan court; Romagnesi would also dedicate a pair of poems to them in his *Poesie liriche.*[58] Third, Carlo II Gonzaga asked Scaramouche— the stage name of the famed actor Tiberio Fiorilli (1608–1694)—and several other Italian actors to come to Mantua in 1651, right around the time when he requested Corbetta's return to service; Romagnesi's poetry reveals a close relationship to the Mantuan duchy.[59] Fourth, in the 1656 production of *La Galanterie du temps* Corbetta joined the famed singer Anna Bergerotti, whom Ro-

---

[55] In her dedication to *I rifiuti di Pindo,* Fedeli asked Louis XIV for continuing support by reminding him of her career as the actress who had often entertained his parents.

[56] See Marc'Antonio Romagnesi, *Dichiaratione del Rè Christianissime, publicata nel parlamento, nel quale S.M. si ritrovò il giorno 18 di Gennaro 1634* (Venice: Giacomo Scalia, 1634); preserved in F-Pn, Rés. L³⁶b3791. Scott wrote that this Marc'Antonio played the parts of *Pantalone* and *Cintio* in the *commedia dell'arte* troupe in Mantua in 1620 (*Commedia dell'Arte in Paris,* 180), citing Vito Pandolfi, *La commedia dell'arte: storia e testi* (Florence: Sansoni Antiquariato, 1957–1961), 5: 400.

[57] F-Pan MC XCI, 563: "interprete des langues aydes de Chambre d'honneur de son Ex. Serenissime Monseigneur Le Due de Mantoue d[emeuran]t en lad[it]e rue S[ain]t Denis paroisse Saint Laurent" (f. 1). By this date, Ferdinando Carlo (1650–1708), son of Carlo II and Isabella Clara, served as the Duke of Mantua.

[58] *La Guitarre royalle,* 54, and Romagnesi, *Poesie liriche,* 155–156.

[59] Scott, *Commedia dell'Arte in Paris,* 35. Fiorilli wrote to the duke on 2 July 1651, according to Pandolfi, *La commedia,* 5: 398. Romagnesi's poems in honor of Carlo II and his son and successor, Ferdinando Carlo, appear throughout *Poesie liriche,* such as in the former's epitaph, 381–385.

magnesi would later address as "virtuosissima cantatrice."[60] Finally, Charles II invited the actors of the Comédie Italienne to perform in England from April through September 1673 and again during the next couple of years. Like Corbetta, Romagnesi focused on Henrietta, Duchess of Orleans, offering her an outright epitaph in his book of poetry in addition to the poetry included in Corbetta's *La Guitarre royalle*.[61] The Count of Grammont, who had brought Corbetta's lessons to Henrietta in France during the 1660s, also received a dedicatory poem in Romagnesi's work.[62] Given Corbetta's and Romagnesi's travels across the Channel in these years, their mutual service at the courts of Carlo II Gonzaga, Louis XIV, and Charles II, their acquaintance seems most probable, even if no tangible source confirms it. Clearly, they moved in the same circles.

In light of the hypothesis that Corbetta provided Bembo with connections in Paris, and the fact that Bembo set texts by Fedeli, substantial evidence presumes the two women's acquaintance. Corbetta, Romagnesi, and Fedeli shared a common bond in the two decades preceding Bembo's arrival as fellow Italians in the service of the French court. They played key roles in the musico-dramatic culture of France, where the best features of Italian entertainment culture married the sophistication of the French stage tradition in such works as Lully's *tragédies en musique* and Molière's comedies, which adopted many of the stock characters of the *commedia dell'arte*. Corbetta's technical skill allowed him to participate at every level of international musical culture. In the preface to *La Guitarre royalle* of 1671, he wrote that he had played in a multi-guitar *entrée* as part "of a ballet composed by the most famous Sir Gio[vanni] Battista Lulli" ("d'un balleto composto dal famosissimo S[ieu]r Gio[vanni] Battista Lulli"). This corroborates the libretto of the performance of *La Galanterie du temps,* where he had appeared along with four other named musicians: "Mademoiselle de la Barre, La Signora Anna Bergerotti, Corbetti, Les deux la Barre, frères, & les petits violons."[63]

Fedeli's starring role in the 1656 drama by Abbé Le Pure, *La Prétieuse,* produced by the Comédie Italienne, placed her at the forefront of the burgeoning French comedic genre.[64] Three years later, according to the following passage from the verse chronicle *La Muze historique*, Anne of Austria generously rewarded Fedeli's first publication:[65]

[60] Romagnesi, *Poesie liriche*, 90–94.

[61] Ibid., for "Enrichetta," 377–379.

[62] Ibid., "All'Illustrissimo et Eccellentissimo Signor Duca di Gramont, Marescial di Francia," 398.

[63] *La Guitarre royalle*, 4, and F-Pn, Rés. F. 679.

[64] See Colin Timms, "Brigida Bianchi's *Poesie Musicali* and Their Settings," in *I quaderni della civica scuola di musica,* numero speciale dedicato a "La cantata da camera nel barocco italiano," 19–20 (December 1990): 20, and Roger Lathuillère, *La Préciosité: Étude historique et linguistique* (Geneva: Droz, 1966), 1: 89, n. 253.

[65] Jean Loret, *La Muze historique,* 28 June 1659, ed. Ch.-L. Livet (Paris: Daffis, 1878), 3: 71.

Pour recompenser Aurélie,	To repay Aurelia
de la Pièce belle et jolie	for the beautiful and pretty piece
(sous le nom de Comédia)	(named "Comedia")
qu'à la Reine elle dédia,	that she dedicated to the queen,
cette Princesse libérale	that generous princess—
dont l'Ame est, tout à fait, royale,	whose soul is completely royal,
au jugement des mieux sensez,	to judge by those who know best—
luy fit prézent, ces jours passez,	gave her a present these past few days
d'un paire de pendans-d'oreilles,	of a pair of pendant earrings
de diamans beaux à merveilles,	made of marvelously beautiful diamonds,
ouvrage exquis, rare et brillant,	exquisite workmanship, rare and brilliant,
travaillé des mieux, et valant	made by the best, and worth
(ainsi que m'a dit certain Homme)	(so someone has told me)
de trois cens pistoles la somme.	three hundred *pistoles.*

The eighteenth-century comedian Riccoboni recounted an amusing story when he traced back to the late 1630s Fedeli's privileged pride of place to this "princess," Anne of Austria. The Queen Mother invited her and Scaramouche into the room of the dauphin Louis XIV. Disconsolate, he wailed when they arrived and would not stop crying. Fiorilli held and comforted the baby dauphin, who then laughed so uproariously that he wet his pants and Fiorilli. Louis's fondness for the Italian comedians began at an early age and he continued his mother's passion for the arts.[66]

Fedeli's beautiful singing voice complemented her thespian virtuosity.[67] After one of her performances in 1634, Giuliano Rossi measured the many talents of *Aurelia* ("oro/Aure-") through double-entendre with the precious metal:[68]

Comm'un Giove in tri de' do sommo choro,	Like a triple Jove in the supreme choir,
così in talenti, in gratia, in dote canto	such talents, grace, and the gift of song,
fra ri comici *Aurelia* và un tesoro.	among the comedians Aurelia is worth a fortune.
Ben l'è unna donna d'oro,	Good is she, a woman of gold,

---

[66] Cited in Scott, *Commedia dell'Arte in Paris,* who gave the source for Riccoboni's story in F-Po, Ms. Rés. 625, Thomas-Simon Gueullette, *Histoire du théâtre italien establi en France depuis l'année 1577 jusqu'en l'année 1750 et les années suivantes,* ff. 62r–v.

[67] According to Benedetto Croce, *Anedotti di varia letteratura,* 2nd ed. (Bari: Laterza, 1953), 193; Ada Zapperi, *Dizionario biografico degli Italiani,* s.v. "Bianchi," 71; and Pierre Louis Duchartre, *The Italian Comedy,* trans. Randolph T. Weaver (London: Harrap, 1929), 72.

[68] Luigi Rasi, *I comici italiani: Biografia, bibliografia, iconografia* (Florence: Bocca, 1897), 1: 419. Rasi's source for this poem was G. Scribe, "Aurelia comica," *Caffaro,* 28 March 1886.

s'infin ro nomme mostra à ra desteisa	in short, the name shows the same thing
ch'insomma à và tant'oro quant'a peisa.	so that, all in all, she is worth her weight in gold.

Both of Fedeli's publications attest to her strongly interdependent talents in drama, improvisation, music, and poetry.[69] Although her first book includes some poetry in addition to the play that so pleased Anne, her second contains only verse, some reprinted from the first publication. Many of these *poesie per musica* represent pieces that she could sing as she improvised on stage.[70] Although none of the musical improvisations written in her own hand survive, the large number of composers of the time who set her poetry attests not only to her widespread popularity throughout France and Italy but also to the international dissemination of her publications. Prompted by his interest in the many chamber duets of Agostino Steffani based on Fedeli's poetry, Colin Timms identified several other prominent composers who also set her poems to music: Domenico Rena, Carlo Pallavicino, Marco Marazzoli, Giuseppe Antonio Bernabei, Giovanni Buonaventura Viviani, Giovanni Carlo Rossi, Alessandro Melani, and Francesco Cavalli.[71] Fedeli's connection with Cavalli is particularly interesting in light of Bembo's studies with him and the latter's new setting of Buti's *L'Ercole amante* (1707), which Cavalli had set to music for the French court in the early 1660s.

The Italian comedians of Paris lived and worked at the Hôtel de Bourgogne and Théâtre de Bourgogne, a large complex located at the intersection between rue Pavée and rue Montorgueil. A map drawn by Jouvin de Rochefort in 1675 depicts the northwest quadrant of Paris just prior to Bembo's arrival in the city (fig. 2.6) and shows several locations close to or bordering the Hôtel de Bourgogne where Fedeli signed her name on legal documents. In 1683 the notary came to the rue Pavée, in 1686 to the rue du Petit Lion (see, too, the map of fig. 2.1), in 1689 to the rue de la Truanderie, and from 1695 to 1700 again to the rue du Petit Lion.[72] The rapid changes in the actors'

[69] Fedeli was known to have been proficient in several languages. In her first book she translated a Spanish play into Italian. In his *Notizie istoriche de' comici italiani che fiorirono intorno all'anno MDL fino a' giorni presenti*, Francesco Bartoli reported that she was decorated with "l'ornamento delle varie lingue" ("the ornament of several languages") (Padua: Conzatti a S. Lorenzo, 1782), 124, cited in Timms, "Brigida Bianchi's *Poesie Musicali*," 21.

[70] She said as much in the introduction to *L'inganno fortunato*: "Quanto alla Poesia, la Musica m'hà dato l'impulso di componerle" ("As for the poetry, music gave me the impulse to compose them").

[71] See the *Catalogue of Brigida Bianchi's Poesie musicali and their musical settings* in Timms, "Brigida Bianchi's *Poesie Musicali*," 32–37. The link with Cavalli suggests that Bembo may have known of Fedeli's work before her arrival in Paris in 1677; her settings of Fedeli's poetry are not found in any of the latter's publications, nor were they known to Timms.

[72] F-Pan, MC, XV, 292, f. 1; F-Pan, MC, CXIII, 129; F-Pan, MC, LXXVII, 35; and F-

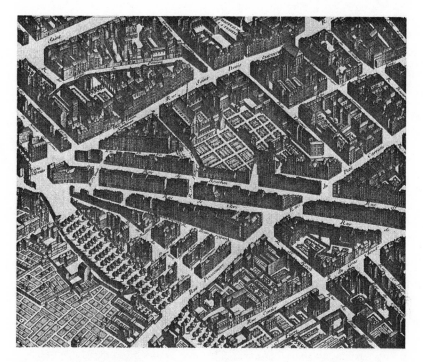

Figure 2.6   Map of Paris in 1742 by Turgot. *Source*: Harvard Map Collection.

households may not necessarily represent actual physical moves, but rather the places they came to sign legal documents.

Given this information it seems rather unlikely that Fedeli changed residences so frequently in her last years of life. From her *inventaire après décès,* the inventory of her household that was made when she died on 11 December 1704, we learn that she passed away in a house "near and adjoining" ("proche et atenant") the Hôtel Saint Chaumond.[73] The quantities of jewels given as gifts for her performances apparently adorned her throughout her life; reports state that she had remained an elegant and fashionable woman even into her nineties.[74] One of the most significant items in her household was a "harpsi-

Pan, MC, XCI, 504 bis, f. 2. The first two documents constitute notarized pension payments for the entire *commedia* troupe in Paris, located by Jurgens in *Documents,* 122 and 129.

[73] F-Pan MC, XCI, 563, ff. 1–10 at f. 2v.

[74] Rasi, *I comici italiani:* "Bianchi was a very beautiful woman; she always had the most cultivated taste in adorning herself . . . an Italian actor known as *Leandro* was said to have seen her in her bed, from which she no longer could get up, exceedingly adorned and still entirely in vogue with the latest fashions" ["La Bianchi fu bellissima donna; e serbò sempre un gusto de' più raffinati nell'adornarsi . . . attore della Commedia italiana sotto il nome di *Leandro,* gli dicesse di averla veduta nel suo letto, donde ormai non usciva più, eccessivamente ornata, e pur sempre conformantesi al sopravvenir delle mode"] (1: 422).

chord with one manual on a gilded wooden stand, covered with an Indian tapestry valued at 20 *livres*," thereby suggesting the possibility that she possessed musical skills on the keyboard as well as the voice.[75]

As Rochefort's map shows, the Hôtel Saint Chaumond and the Hôtel de Bourgogne lay quite close to each other as well as to the community in which Bembo eventually settled; close enough for her to describe the Italian community as "Notre Dame de Bonne Nouvelle" in her dedication to *Produzioni armoniche.* That Fedeli would retire in her final years to the Hôtel Saint Chaumond, adjoining the Union Chrétienne, makes still more plausible her acquaintance with Bembo, who by that time had been a resident of the community for some twenty years. Another comedian in the troupe, Françoise Biancolelli, entered the Union Chrétienne in the late 1690s. The daughter of the actors Domenico Biancolelli (Arlequin) and Orsola Cortesi (Eularia), Françoise played the new *innamorata* known as Isabelle when Fedeli retired in 1683. She entered the community in the last years of the century, following a tumultuous separation from a husband whose family had opposed his marriage to an actress.[76]

No document confirms the hypothesis that Corbetta and the actors of the Italian community in Paris provided shelter for Bembo, but the evidence points strongly to the supposition. That new actors hired by Romagnesi as a talent scout for the Comédie Italienne during a trip to Italy sometime prior to 1683 were housed on the rue du Petit Lion and the rue Montorgueil lends further credence to the likelihood that Corbetta had gone to Romagnesi for help in establishing temporary quarters for Bembo in 1676.[77] Might Romagnesi, like his mother, also have supplied some of the poetry for Bembo's vocal work? Given the number of people to whom he dedicated poetry, perhaps he added Bembo to his circle of acquaintances and some of the poetry that she set to music represents his subsequent writing after 1673.

Turgot's map affords by far the clearest view of Bembo's home at the Petite Union Chrétienne, on the rue de la Lune at its intersection with rue St. Étienne (fig. 2.6). The map also shows the larger institution of which the Petite Union Chrétienne was an offshoot, the "Filles de l'Union Chrétienne"

---

[75] F-Pan MC, XCI, 563, f. 4v. Witnesses for the inventory included her son, "Marc Antoine Romagnesi," and the first of his many children, who signed his name "Augusten" (f. 10).

[76] Biancolelli lived at the community until her death in 1747 and was buried at the church of Notre Dame de Bonne Nouvelle. See Scott, *Commedia dell'Arte in Paris,* 346.

[77] Scott, *Commedia dell'Arte in Paris,* 250, who cited Auguste Jal, *Dictionnaire critique de biographie et d'histoire* (Paris: Plon, 1867), s.v. "Romagnesi." Romagnesi asked for a passport and the allowance that had been given to his predecessor, Zanotti (*Octave*): "it is necessary that I go to Rome, Venice, Genoa, Ferrara, Bologna, Padua, and other places where the troupes are in order to find out about them and to meet the ambassadors of France who are at Rome and Venice. This is why I beg very humbly Mons. Colbert to give me some little sum of money to defray my expenses, for M. Octave has always had 200 ecus and he went only to Bologna and Venice."

in the Hôtel Saint Chaumond on rue Saint Denis. The undeveloped land on Rochefort's map was known as "la Villeneuve," to designate the new part of the city delimited by the Porte Saint Denis. Turgot's map testifies to continual urban expansion: by the mid-eighteenth century, the fields that Bembo had once overlooked to the west now contained houses incorporated into the city.

The Bridge of Sighs

Shortly before Antonia's departure, the *consegi*—the weekly record of election tallies of the *Maggior consiglio* and the *Senato* distributed in a report—elected Lorenzo to serve as a customs official at the Fontego dei Tedeschi.[78] In this building—Venice's present-day central post office—foreigners from German-speaking territories rented locked rooms and cabinets to store their valuables, somewhat like a modern safety deposit box in a bank. The *consegi* regularly elected Lorenzo to the Fontego for the following years up to 1689,[79] and he had a chance for a happier life with his daughter's financial problems and domestic arrangements sorted out by 1685. A curious tale of the storage of a mythical unicorn's horn by two citizens of Graz—Franz Christoph Amtman and Anna Hizzel—is found in the register where Lorenzo signed his name in April and May 1686 as *Visdomino,* one of the highest-ranking officials empowered to transact and sign official documents at the Fontego and to collect money for rooms rented there.[80] Several more entries concern the unicorn's horn until early in 1690, when it was reported as missing.[81] On 30 January, the register's entry—signed by Lorenzo and two other *Visdomini*—states that

---

[78] I-Vnm, It. VII, 849 (8928), f. 90 shows his election to the position on 30 September 1676. According to entries made in Bernardo's papers, he had already served in this capacity by 10 August and 25 November 1675 (I-Vas, Ospedali e luoghi pii diversi, b. 238, mazzo 7, ff. 28–29. I-Vas, Cinque savi alla mercanzia, b. 74 bis, nuova serie, *Capitolari dell'Offitio del Fontego dei Tedeschi, 1329–1797,* ff. 173v–175 describe the operations of the *Fontego*).

[79] I-Vnm, It. VII, 849 (8928), f. 181 (1678, 19 June), f. 253v (1679, 30 September); I-Vnm, It. VII 851 (8930), f. 199 (1688, 4 January), f. 328 (1689, 5 April).

[80] I-Vas, Cinque savi alla mercanzia, b. 74 bis, nuova serie, ff. 181–182v.

[81] Usually it was the horn of the narwal that passed for the mythical unicorn's horn. About twenty such horns were preserved throughout Europe at the beginning of the seventeenth century, of which one was in the treasury of San Marco. By the time of the Fontego case, skeptics were beginning to question the horn's curative powers and indeed the existence of the very creature itself; nevertheless, the rarity of the long, straight horn made it affordable only to the Church or to wealthy aristocrats. See Antoine Schnapper, *Le Géant, la licorne, la tulipe—collections françaises au XVIIe siècle* (Paris: Flammarion, 1988), 87–91, and 371 for a photo of one that was kept as part of the treasure of the Parisian church of Saint Denis. For a study of the fascination with the peculiarities of nature at the time, see, especially, Katharine Park and Lorraine Daston, *Wonders and the Order of Nature, 1150–1750* (New York: Zone Books, 1998), 74–75 about the unicorn's horn. Both works look back to the standard work on the subject by Odell Shepard, *The Lore of the Unicorn* (Boston: Houghton Mifflin, 1930).

the object had been taken for safekeeping in the monastery of the *Carmini;* two weeks later, Hizzel demanded an inspection of her storage space and came in person to do so, along with the *Visdomini* and other officials of the Fontego.[82] Finally the object was found.

Lorenzo signed no further entries as a customs official and lost everything in the wake of the case of the unicorn's horn. Following the Hizzel affair, the Council of Ten harshly condemned him and his accomplice for stealing, not just from the Fontego but from the Republic of Venice (doc. 23):

> 1690, 26 September in the Council of Ten.
>
> Lorenzo Bembo, son of the late Andrea and former *Visdomino* at the Fontego di [*sic*] Tedeschi, and Bortolo Bortoleti, the auditor in this office, are hereby charged with neglect of faith owed to the Republic and of accuracy that they should have demonstrated in their jobs. They made illegal profit from public patrimony and, in order to carry out his nefarious schemes with the illicit objects mentioned above, Bembo remained in his position for more years than was normal. He took large sums of money several times from particular clients who had left a rental account for a room inside the Fontego, keeping the receipts instead of putting them in the public cash box. He did not record his daily borrowings in the monthly account books of the office, thereby using public money as his own and wreaking havoc with the treasury itself. This all took place in collaboration with said Bortoleti, master of depraved faith, with whom he carried out this fraudulent act, writing false entries in the books and public papers that stated that this non-existent money had been entered into the public treasury.
>
> With the aforementioned damnable acts he [Bembo] has also taken advantage of the circumstances and formality of the office to take more sums of money, such as in the present case of the customs duty pertaining to the goods belonging to the citizens of Graz, which he unfaithfully converted into money for his own use, thereby displaying complete lack of respect for the government and a detestable spoiling of the cash accounts.

The decree continues with the condemnation of Bortoleti, who had been carrying out his fraudulent practices for far longer and in collusion with more people than Lorenzo had been. An equally damning sentence for both appears in conclusion, stating that "each one has respectively committed crimes—of falsity, fraud, plunder of the public money, spoiling of the cash department— [which were] carried out in detestable, odious, and dreadful ways."

The *Capi,* or Heads, of the Council of Ten, summoned Bembo and Bortoleti to appear in the Jail of the Presentadi within four months' time. Indeed, beginning in January 1691, records kept by the *Capi* show that Lorenzo was jailed in the prison cells adjoining the Ducal Palace, reached by crossing the

---

[82] I-Vas, Cinque savi alla mercanzia, b. 74 bis, nuova serie, ff. 181v (1690, 30 January and 10 February) and 182v (1690, 11 February).

Bridge of Sighs. Within the Presentadi he stayed in various cells known as the Callina, Franzona, Lovara, and Avogadra; he also served time in one of the cells of the Jail of the Condanati (Condemned), the Priggion Fornetto.[83] Not dark dungeons, these cells occupied the part of the jail that got some light, "alla luce," a privilege accorded Bembo's noble status.[84] The prison records show solitary confinement for months and sometimes more than a year at a time: July–September 1691, May 1692–November 1693, May 1694–January 1695, June 1698–January 1699, and August 1702.

In October 1694 Diana drew up her wedding contract in order to marry Iseppo Bessi, a Venetian commoner ("cittadino veneto").[85] Notwithstanding her father's solitary confinement in the Priggion Callina, he needed to give his official approval for the couple's marriage; his signature confirms his assent.[86] The documents for the engagement and wedding respect the family's integrity with no explicit mention of his incarceration, even if a discreet clause in the wedding contract includes an annual payment of 60 ducats to the Jail of the Presentadi for the rest of Diana's life.[87] Never having taken vows of celibacy at Santa Maria dell'Orazione, she had maintained her status as an *educanda*.[88] The wedding contract mentions several of the articles of clothing and jewels from the 1685 inventory saved for Diana's use.[89] She wrote that she had received all of her mother's belongings not sold the decade before, except for the watch with a filigreed gold case (valued on the inventory at 40 ducats), which was to be kept *in pegno* at San Bernardo for the family's remaining debt to the convent at the time of her November wedding.[90]

After October 1702, the prison records no longer mention Lorenzo; he suffered from sciatica in his foot for his final nine months and died of fever in the Jail of the Presentadi. On 20 August 1703 the attending physician at the

[83] I-Vas, Capi del Consiglio de' Dieci, *Note di prigioni*, b. 1 (secolo XVII) and b. 2 (secolo XVIII).

[84] Ibid., b. 1, November 1691.

[85] I-Vas, Signori di Notte al Civil, *Pagamenti, e assicurazion di dotte*, b. 53, reg. 72, ff. 43–47v.

[86] Ibid., ff. 43–44v; see also a copy of the wedding contract in I-Vas, Corporazioni religiose, *Santa Maria dell'Orazione di Malamocco*, b. 2, "Carte della q[uonda]m N[obil] D[onna] Diana Bembo che trata delle Valli Con l'agiustam[en]to e nuova fitanza fata al Sig[no]r Vicenzo Genoni primo Feb[ra]ro 1739 Vendute al N[obil] H[uomo] Alvise Nani nel 1753."

[87] I-Vas, Signori di Notte al Civil, *Pagamenti, e assicurazion di dotte*, b. 53, reg. 72, f. 44.

[88] I-Vas, Corporazioni religiose, *Santa Maria dell'Orazione di Malamocco*, b. 7. The convent's capitular book lists Diana Bembo's election by the convent to be received as one to educate ("ricever ad educatione") as late as age twenty-seven (1691, 29 March).

[89] I-Vas, Signori di Notte al Civil, *Pagamenti, e assicurazion di dotte*, b. 53, reg. 72, ff. 45–46v.

[90] I-Vas, Corporazioni religiose, *San Bernardo di Murano*, b. 18, Mazzo Q, Plica D ("Ricever della N.D. Diana Bemba," 4 November 1694). Diana's dowry description gives new lists of Antonia's jewels and linens not sold in the 28–31 March 1685 transaction. They were reappraised here at the occasion of the wedding, with some narrow fluctuations in value from the decade before.

Presentadi, Dr. Franco Paganoni, declared that Lorenzo had died in his cell the day before.[91] Perhaps the leg injury from the Candian battle of 1668 made his foot vulnerable to disease. He lived out his last 13 years in the prison, a punishment grim enough for what he had done.

Lorenzo's death set in motion a series of inheritance issues to resolve among his closest surviving family members: his children, his widow in Paris, and his cousin, Bernardo Bembo. Bernardo's careful bookkeeping managed to preserve the only extant document drafted in France that concerns Antonia Bembo and on which she signed her full legal name (fig. 2.7). A fuller examination of the papers concerning the inheritance reveals that this was the second such document written by the Parisian notaries, Mathieu Bailly and Mathieu-Antoine Gaillardie. The first document, deemed invalid when presented to the Venetian authorities in March 1704, had been written without the legal witness of a Venetian potentate. This matter was resolved one year after Lorenzo's death,[92] when the two notaries, along with the Venetian ambassador and his secretary, came together to Antonia's home on the rue de la Lune (doc. 24; emphasis mine):

> Before the undersigned notaries in Paris was present the Illustrious Antonia Padovani—widow of the deceased Illustrious Lorenzo Bembo, Noble Venetian, son of Andrea—living now in this city of Paris on rue de la Lune in the community of the Union Chrétienne in the parish of Notre Dame de Bonne Nouvelle.
>
> To which she adds to the *procura* already made in our study of 14 November 1703, *of which we have no record,* in favor of the Illustrious Andrea and Giacomo Bembo—her children, who are also Noble Venetians and children of the Illustrious Lorenzo Bembo—to whom she gives again the power, faculty, and authority to the law to arbitrate in the Venetian manner without the approval of any other person. . . . With all binding promises kept, this act was drawn up and passed in Paris in the home of said Woman Constituent who is declared above. The year seventeen hundred four, the nineteenth day of August, and undersigned
> Antonia Padoani Bembo
> Gaillardie, Bailly

This power of attorney provides much important information. First, it preserves the only known specimen of the composer's full legal name with a definitive spelling of her maiden name: Antonia Padoani Bembo. Along with the signatures on the two letters that she wrote to the convent in 1682—figures 2.2, 2.3, and 2.7—these bear comparison to the six music manuscripts

---

[91] I-Vasp, San Marco, *Registri dei morti,* V, f. 48r.

[92] It is curious that both the death of Lorenzo and the second *procura* took place on the 44th and 45th anniversaries, respectively, of his wedding to Antonia (20 August 1659).

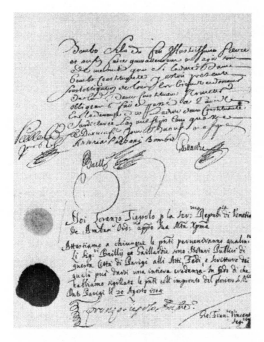

Figure 2.7   Signature of Antonia Padoani Bembo, 20 August 1704

examined in the ensuing chapters. Second, this *procura* represents the only
preserved French legal paper about Bembo—the notaries state explicitly that
they neither kept a copy in their *études* nor saved either one—and corroborates Gozzi's journal regarding her residence at the Petite Union Chrétienne
on rue de la Lune.[93] Third, Bailly's name appears on documents for both
the "grand Saint Chaumond" on rue Saint Denis (Union Chrétienne) and the
"petit Saint Chaumond" on rue de la Lune (Petite Union Chrétienne) for the
period 1699–1722. Both notaries signed individually on the aforementioned
retirement and pension statements of Brigida Fedeli in the 1680s, thereby
confirming that they served the residents of the larger community around
Notre Dame de Bonne Nouvelle.

The *procura* underscores the Venetian inheritance practice whereby only
male children could be beneficiaries of their mother's inheritance. Even though
only the brothers Andrea and Giacomo had those rights, Bembo had previously allocated funds specifically to her daughter. Papers preserved at the convents of San Bernardo and of Santa Maria dell'Orazione show that she au-
thorized a *donatione* to Diana in 1687 that gave her daughter rights to some of
the properties designated as her own in the 1658–1659 wedding contracts.[94]

---

[93] Their *études* contain no mention of Bembo: F-Pan, MC, LXXVII for Mathieu Bailly (fl.
1687–1723) and MC, XV, for Mathieu-Antoine Gaillardie (fl. 1694–1727).

[94] I-Vas, Corporazioni religiose, *Santa Maria dell'Orazione di Malamocco*, b. 2, "Carte della

In addition to the lack of a proper witness for the first *procura* of November 1703, the foreign language posed a problem upon the presentation of the second one in Venice in August 1704. To translate the document into Italian, the Venetians chose Apostolo Zeno (1688–1750), a learned man and librettist for numerous eighteenth-century Venetian operas.[95] Completed promptly, Zeno's translation furthered the procedure in Venice and allowed the conclusion of the transaction in the following month.[96] Bernardo Bembo's notary, Pietro Antonio Ciola, saved the original French document and its Italian translation.

Not irrelevant to Antonia Bembo's biography, the inheritance matters permit an estimation of how much longer she was to live, even if no mention of her precise date of decease can be found. Bernardo had placed an *interdetto* (a hold) on the inheritance proceedings in spring 1704.[97] On 18 March 1704, the first *procura* had been presented to the *Giudici del Proprio,* the Venetian governmental office in charge of distributing the payment, but the court judged it invalid four days later. Documents from then through 2 June reveal that outstanding debts had to be taken care of and the court stated that Antonia was responsible for paying Bernardo a certain sum of ducats.[98] Lorenzo's long-standing debts to Bernardo made for several complexities pertaining to the administration of the former's estate. He had sold or rented several parts of his property in the early years of his marriage to Antonia.[99] Four inherited properties were in question:

1. Lorenzo's portion of the house at Santa Maria Nova
2. A property near Padua, the Villa di Bovolenta in Contrà di Brea
3. Fishing wetlands in Cavarzere at Canal Doge, and, in Loreo, the Cà Negra; the Villa di Bosco
4. A property in a village near Vicenza, the Villa di Nanto

---

q.m N.D. Diana Bembo che trata delle Valli" (1687, 27 March) ("donatione fatta 1687. 27 Marzo dalla N.D. Antonia Bembo sua Madre") and *San Bernardo di Murano,* b. 18, Mazzo Q, Plica D (1687, 18 September).

[95] I-Vas, Notarile, *Atti,* Pietro Antonio Ciola, b. 4032, minute, ff. 4–5. For a complete listing of Apostolo Zeno's collection of *libretti,* see Laini, *La raccolta zeniana.*

[96] I-Vas, Notarile, *Atti,* Pietro Antonio Ciola, b. 3984–3985, protocollo (1704, 22–23 September).

[97] I-Vas, Signori di Notte al Civil, *Pagamenti, e assicurazion di dotte,* b. 46, reg. 47, ff. 9–12 (1704, 18 March) and 19–20 (1704, 22 March).

[98] Ibid., f. 19, marginalia (1704, 28 March and 7 April); I-Vas, Notarile, *Atti,* Pietro Antonio Ciola, b. 3984–3985 (1704, 2 June); and I-Vas, Corti di Palazzo, *Giudici del Proprio,* Interdetti, reg. 24 (1704, 7 April).

[99] Several sources in I-Vas refer to various transactions made from 1658 to 1661, many of these perhaps related to Lorenzo's father's untimely demise in August 1658 and to Antonia's father's insistence that the couple find another place to live in April 1660: Signori di Notte al Civil, *Pagamenti, e assicurazion di dotte,* b. 46, reg. 47, ff. 9–12 (1658, 23 May, 7 June, and 3 August; 1660 [m.v.],

Present-day maps of the Veneto show the towns in which these properties stood. The second and third holdings—Bovolenta, Cavarzere, Loreo, and Villa di Bosco—all refer to a large agricultural area to the south of Padua and immediately to the southwest of Piove di Sacco (fig. 2.8). The village of Bovolenta lies on the banks of the Bacchiglione River, an area to which the papers refer as "del Bachilion."[100] The villages of Cavarzere and Loreo lie to the southeast of Bovolenta, east of Rovigo above the Po River. Many noble Venetian families received as part of their income the harvests from the wetlands of the *terra ferma*.

Several parties held claims to the four properties. Antonia's earlier donation had given to Diana part of the wetlands ("le valli") at Cavarzere and at Nanto. The part of Cà Bembo that Lorenzo had rented out for many years stood in disrepair, and the renters complained about its decrepit state.[101] Antonia's legal document could not transfer the properties before the debts and repairs were taken care of. No further actions were required of her, however; the second *procura* achieved its goal of passing legal rights to her sons.

In 1710 Antonia and Lorenzo's son Andrea passed away, and his widow, Isabetta, in turn, claimed her dowry (*vadimonio*).[102] Inheritance issues seem to have been resolved peacefully between her and her sister Pellegrina, wife of his brother Giacomo, with whom Bernardo would continue to work out the inheritance matters even a decade following Antonia's *procura*. Diana's 1694 marriage contract dictated her responsibility for paying the prison of the Presentadi for the remainder of her days; it also gave her income from the rental of the properties at Cavarzere and Nanto from her mother's earlier donation.[103] Once Andrea died, these could be divided evenly between the two surviving siblings, Diana and Giacomo.

Known chiefly for its olive oil and valuable stones, the village of Nanto

---

18 January); Signori di Notte al Civil, *Pagamenti, e assicurazion di dotte*, b. 50, reg. 63, ff. 26v and 108v (1661, 22 August); Corti di Palazzo, *Giudici del Proprio*, Minutarum, reg. 51, ff. 11v–12r (1661, 14 March and 28 May); Notarile, *Atti*, Pietro Antonio Ciola, b. 3979, f. 290v (1659, 15 March), and bb. 3984–3985, ff. 1r–v (1660, 24 March) and ff. 2v (1659, 12 November; 10, 12 December).

[100] I-Vas, Signori di Notte al Civil, *Pagamenti, e assicurazion di dotte*, b. 50, reg. 63, f. 108 (1714, 5 April).

[101] I-Vas, Notarile, *Atti*, Pietro Antonio Bozini, b. 1021 (protocollo), ff. 201v–202v (1660, 30 December and 1661, 14 March and 28 May); I-Vas, Signori di Notte al Civil, *Pagamenti, e assicurazion di dotte*, b. 50, reg. 61, ff. 154v–155 (1713, 22 April); and I-Vas, Corti di Palazzo, *Giudici del Proprio*, Minutarum, reg. 51, ff. 11v–12r (1713, 22 April).

[102] For the inheritance, see I-Vas, Signori di Notte al Civil, *Pagamenti, e assicurazion di dotte*, b. 54, reg. 77, f. 15v (1713, 15 April) and I-Vas, Signori di Notte al Civil, *Lettere*, b. 220, reg. 27, f. 34v (1713, 19 April). Andrea died at Santa Maria Nova on 14 February (I-Vas, Avogaria di Comun, *Necrologi dei Nobili*, b. 159, no. 2).

[103] I-Vas, Signori di Notte al Civil, *Pagamenti, e assicurazion di dotte*, b. 53, reg. 72, f. 43–47v (1694, 12 October and 1719, 5 and 8 April); I-Vas, Corporazioni religiose, *Santa Maria dell'Orazione di Malamocco*, b. 7, "Libro di Capitoli" (1717, 15 April).

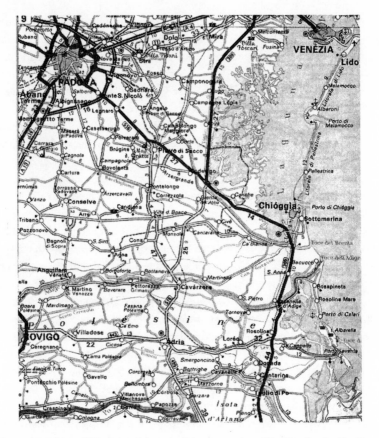

Figure 2.8   Map of Venice and the *terra ferma* properties of the Bembo family. *Source*:
© Cartografia del Touring Club Italiano—autorizazzione del 9 maggio 2001.

lies directly to the south of Vicenza in the *Monti Berici*. Orseta Corner Bembo
willed the lands at Nanto to her nephew Lorenzo in the early 1650s, prior to
the birth of his three half brothers. At least one of those brothers, Antonio
Bembo, inherited some of the Nanto land. In addition to his house in Venice
at Santi Apostoli, which had provided refuge for Diana on at least one occasion, he began purchasing more land in and around Nanto in 1680. Documents legalized by both Vicentine and Bergamask notaries provide details of
these holdings: in 1688 property at Campo San Piero; in 1691 a house and
land at Villa di Nanto; in 1693 land at Contrà della Piaza; in 1695 an "oste-
ria"; more property at Villa di Nanto near the Fontana secca in the following year and, in 1700 and 1702, respectively, more lands in Nanto's Contrà
della Crosara and del Ponte.[104] In the wake of Lorenzo's death, Antonio ac-

[104] I-Vbc, Ms. P.D.C., b. 2714/5, ff. 1 (1680, 10 October), 10 (1693, 11 May), 12 (1696, 13
October), 13 (1700, 23 September), 82 (1702, 6 November), 164 (1686, 4 January; 1688, 25 October; 1691, 25 October), and 165 (1695, 14 December).

quired from Andrea Bembo part of Orseta Corner's ancestral lands in Bosco di Nanto.[105] An inscription at the church of Saint Anthony of Padua in Nanto testifies to Antonio Bembo's distinguished position as a wealthy landowner and cherished citizen of the town.[106]

In 1713–1714 Giacomo Bembo approached the *Signori di Notte al Civil* to make the payments not resolved by Antonia's *procura* a decade before. This branch of the Venetian government dealt with the *vadimonio* and the *pagamenti di dotte,* dowry payments of a deceased mother to her children, at its annual meetings in March and April. These record some house repairs for Cà Bembo.[107] The convent archives of Santa Maria dell'Orazione also show dealings with the Bembo family during the same years, noting that Diana paid the prison for arrears; perhaps the payments requested by Giacomo from the *Signori di Notte al Civil* liberated some of the funds that she needed in order to make that payment, in addition to the money that she received annually from the family holdings around Padua and Vicenza.[108] In 1717 her daughter Regina went to live as an *educanda* at Santa Maria dell'Orazione, where she later became a nun.[109] Diana had to pay off her father's prison debt until her own death in 1729, the same year that Bernardo Bembo passed away.[110] Afterward Giacomo Bembo and his wife, Pellegrina, received the full inheritance from Lorenzo's branch of the family, and Cà Bembo at Santa Maria Nova passed to their children upon Giacomo's death in 1741.[111]

On 2 June 1724, Diana petitioned the *Signori di Notte al Civil* for the *pagamento di dotte* of "Antonia Padouani, who was her mother, and who died without a testament in Paris."[112] Many of the other payments in this source

---

[105] I-Vbc, Ms. P.D.C., b. 2714/5, f. 172 (1703, 26 November).

[106] See Gaetano Maccà, *Storia del territorio Vicentino* (Caldogno: Gio. Battista Menegatti, 1812–1816), 4: 298, 311. The inscription dates to 1712; Antonio lived until 1716 (I-Vbc, Ms. P.D.C., b. 2714/5, f. 1v deals with the divisions of his former property between his son, Angelo Maria, and Giacomo [Antonia and Lorenzo's son] on 8 March 1718).

[107] I-Vas, Signori di Notte al Civil, *Pagamenti, e assicurazion di dotte,* b. 50, reg. 61, ff. 154v–155 (1713, 22 March); I-Vas, Corti di Palazzo, *Giudici del Proprio,* Minutarum, reg. 51 (1713, 22 April); and I-Vas, Signori di Notte al Civil, *Pagamenti, e assicurazion di dotte,* b. 50, reg. 63, ff. 26v, 108r–v (1714, 28 March, 4–5 April).

[108] I-Vas, Corporazioni religiose, *Santa Maria dell'Orazione di Malamocco,* b. 2, "Carte della q[uonda]m N[obil] D[onna] Diana Bembo che trata delle Valli . . . Vendute al N[obil] H[uomo] Alvise Nani nel 1753" (1713, 26 March, 30 June, 23 September, and 29 December; 1714, 26 March and 6 July).

[109] I-Vas, Corporazioni religiose, *Santa Maria dell'Orazione di Malamocco,* b. 7 (1717, 15 April and 1719, 13 May).

[110] He drew up his testament on 14 June 1711, which was presented just after his death on 29 November 1729. See I-Vas, Giudici di Petizion, *Inventari,* b. 426/91, no. 50. Diana is the late, "quondam," Diana Bembo Bessi by 9 April 1729.

[111] I-Vas, Avogaria di Comun, *Necrologi dei Nobili,* b. 159, no. 2 (1741, 13 September).

[112] I-Vas, Corti di Palazzo, *Giudici del Proprio,* Successioni, reg. 52, f. 63r: "Ant[oni]a Padouani fù sua Madre morta ab intestato in Parigi."

do tell the date of decease of the woman in question, but none appears here. Given that she dedicated most of her music to Louis XIV, a date of c. 1720 can be presumed for her death.

La Petite Union Chrétienne

This biography concludes with a description of the Parisian environment in which Bembo lived and worked for close to 40 years (c. 1682–c. 1720). By the summer of the 1704, when the *procura* was notarized at her home on rue de la Lune, she had already completed her first music manuscript for the king and was well on her way to finishing her second for the birth of the son of Marie-Adélaïde, Duchess of Burgundy. Her compositional career had officially begun around 1682 at the Petite Union Chrétienne, also known as the "petit Saint Chaumond."

Originally founded by Saint Vincent de Paul and Marie Pollalion, the order known as "Les Filles de l'Union Chrétienne ou Filles de Saint-Chaumont" established itself at the Hôtel Saint Chaumond on rue Saint Denis in 1661 after its move from a village outside the city, Charonne.[113] This *hôtel,* a large house, had been built in 1631 by the Marquis de Saint-Chamond. In its new location on rue Saint Denis, the Union Chrétienne ingeniously adapted the marquis's appellation by naming as its patron saint the seventh-century martyr, Saint Chaumont, Bishop of Lyon, and fusing their orthographies. This establishment was more familiarly known as the "grand Saint Chaumond."

The community extended its charitable mission by opening a new sister house in 1682, called the Petite Union Chrétienne, or "petit Saint Chaumond." That house, purchased from François Berthelot and his wife Marie Regnault, lay just a few blocks from the Hôtel Saint Chaumond, quite close to the church of Notre Dame de Bonne Nouvelle.[114] Berthelot held royal connections, then serving as the "Secrétaire des Commendements" to the dauphine Marie-Anne-Christine-Victoire of Bavaria (1660–1690), wife of "Monseigneur" (Louis XIV's first-born son). The Berthelot house had been used briefly as a hospital for wounded soldiers, but Louis XIV had decided to construct a larger hospital elsewhere, the well-known Hôtel des Invalides.[115]

---

[113] Paul Biver and Marie-Louise Biver, *Abbayes, monastères, couvents de femmes à Paris des origines à la fin du XVIIIe siècle* (Vendôme: Presses Universitaires de France, 1975), 61–62. Both *Charonne* and *Bonne Nouvelle* are nowadays metro stops that correspond to the former locations of these convents. For archival descriptions of the community's days at Charonne, see, for example, F-Pan LL. 1668. F-Pan L. 1056 preserves a printed booklet of the history of the present-day institution that lists these founders; see *Institut de l'Union Chrétienne—Maison séminaire de Poitiers* (Poitiers: Chaperon, 1935).

[114] Biver, *Abbayes,* 65.

[115] Jacques Hillairet, *Dictionnaire historique des rues de Paris* (Paris: Éditions de minuit, 1964), 2: 79.

Berthelot sold the property to the community on 13 May 1682[116] and the king's *lettres patentes* of February 1685 made the transfer official.[117]

The royal family had played a crucial role in the establishment of the parish of Notre Dame de Bonne Nouvelle. The building of the church, "Our Lady of the Annunciation ['Good News']," began in April 1628, with the first stone laid by Anne of Austria (fig. 2.9).[118] The church had a small chapel dedicated to her patron saint Anne.[119] Two paintings of Anne of Austria (mother of Louis XIV) and Henrietta (his sister-in-law) graced its walls: one depicted them together and the other placed Henrietta and her three children with François de Sales in a symbolic confirmation of the English princess's devotion to Catholicism. Both of these women had played an important role in supporting the artistic work in France of Fedeli, Romagnesi, and Corbetta; it was no coincidence that the church of Notre Dame de Bonne Nouvelle lay close to the Comédie Italienne. Perhaps Berthelot's service to the dauphine Marie-Anne-Christine-Victoire provided further royal connections for the sister community through the 1680s. That Louis XIV sponsored the establishment of the Petite Union Chrétienne at Berthelot's house suggests a conscious continuation of his family's efforts to provide for the women of the greater community and to promote the unifying Catholic faith of his kingdom (for the "Nouvelles Catholiques"). Even if Bembo's dedication suggests that her "pension" had been one from which she personally benefited (doc. 1), more likely the king's *lettres patentes* offered general financial support to the community of which she was part.[120] Although playing a secondary role to that of the king, the powerful nexus of royal women devoted in several ways to the religious community—all of foreign origin—provides a likely group among whom Bembo found patronage.

Bembo's profile matches the cohort of secular "dames pensionnaires" who lived as lay sisters in "la communauté de l'Union chrétienne dite du petit St. Chaumont établi à Paris, rue de la Lune."[121] The Petite Union Chrétienne had a twofold mission: first, to educate girls who had newly converted to Catholicism and house them if they had done so against their parents' will and, second, to provide a respectable home for the *demoiselles* and *dames pensionnaires*.[122] A comprehensive study of women's religious communities carried out by Paul and Marie-Louise Biver shows that some of the funds used

[116] F-Pan, X^{1a}8679, f. 273.

[117] F-Pan, L. 1056, no. 33.

[118] Maurice Dumolin and Georges Outardel, *Les Églises de France: Paris et la Seine* (Paris: Le Touzey et Ané, 1936), 213. The rebuilt church of the nineteenth century preserved the stone by placing it at its center.

[119] Biver, *Abbayes*, 66.

[120] F-Pan O^1*630 and O^{1}656 contain the pensions for the period.

[121] F-Pan, L. 1056.

[122] Hillairet, *Dictionnaire historique*, 2: 400.

NOTRE-DAME-DE-BONNE-NOUVELLE.

1628.

ANNE D'AVTRICHE Par La GRACE DE DIEV ROYNE DE FRANCE ET DE NAVAREAMIS ET POSE'CESTE PREMIERE PIERRE DV CŒVR DE L'ESGLISE DE NOSTRE DAME DE BONNE NOVVELLES AV MOIS D'AVRIL DE L'ANNEE 162 8

Pierre. — Haut. o™,79; larg. o™,55.

Figure 2.9   First stone of the Church of Notre Dame de Bonne Nouvelle

to support the Petite Union Chrétienne came from the latter group.[123] The Archives Nationales preserve few documents about their constituency, and it appears that most of their papers were destroyed during the French Revolution.[124]

Mathieu Bailly served as one of the most frequently employed notaries to both the communities, the Petite Union Chrétienne and the Union Chrétienne, as his signatures appear on numerous documents.[125] It comes as no surprise, then, that Bembo would have called on his offices to notarize her power of attorney in 1704. The picture of life at the Petite Union Chrétienne

[123] Biver, *Abbayes,* 66.

[124] Personal communication in June 1995 with M. Richard, Mother Superior of the Union Chrétienne de Saint Chaumond, presently established in Poitiers. The few surviving lists of *dames pensionnaires* can be found in F-Pan H^5*4168–4169 and LL. 1667.

[125] The most important sources for the Petite Union Chrétienne at the Archives Nationales include F-Pan H^{5}4211 (Religieuses de St. Chaumont et de Ste. Aure, Rentes du XVIIIe s.) in which Bailly's name appears with some frequency in LL. 1667 (Filles de St. Chaumont, Registres capitulaires, 1685–1784) and LL. 1669 (Filles de St. Chaumont, Règles et constitutions).

gathered from archival evidence reveals a highly regulated environment existing alongside the religious order on which it depended. The division of the house on rue de la Lune provided apartments for the *dames pensionnaires,* who numbered no fewer than ten and no more than forty at any given time.[126]

To some extent, Antonia's daily schedule must have mirrored the canonical hours of the religious community:[127]

5 am	Arise for Orison
6 am	Prime and Tierce
7.30 am	Common Prayer
8 am	Holy Mass [8.30 am on Sundays and Feast Days]
	Breakfast
9 am	Silence, reading, *cantique spirituel*
10 am	Chapel and Chapelet[128] (3 days/week, one or the other)
	[on Sunday, reading in the garden or in one's room until 10.45 am]
11 am	Sext and None; the Miserere
11.30 am	Dinner in the Refectory in Silence, followed by the Angelus; recreation until 1 pm
1.30 pm	Vespers
3.30 pm	Compline
5.45 pm	Preparation for Orison
6–6.30 pm	Orison
6.30 pm	Supper, followed by recreation until 8 pm
8 pm	Matins, marking the end of recreation
8.15 pm	Evening Prayer
10 pm	Candles extinguished

The community surely made some use of a composer-singer of Bembo's caliber in the musical parts of their services. The sisters sang *cantiques spirituels* every day at 9 am, and each was instructed, if she had a good voice, to "consecrate it to the Lord" with "canticles and spiritual hymns."[129] Beginning in 1692, the community held an annual celebration of the feast of Saint Chaumont on September 28.[130] Presided over by the Father Superior—to whom the Mother Superior was allegiant—the feast represented one of the highlights of the community's liturgical year. As on other feast days, the sisters were to "sing the Te Deum" upon his entrance into the church.[131]

---

[126] F-Pan, LL. 1669, f. 87v.

[127] Ibid., ff. 55r–56r.

[128] "Chapelet" refers to an object like a rosary, occupying the fingers during the recitation of prayers.

[129] F-Pan, LL. 1669, ff. 38r, 50r.

[130] F-Pan, LL. 1667, p. 37.

[131] F-Pan, LL. 1669, f. 63v.

Perhaps some of the modifications made to the capitular records came about as a direct result of petitions for entrance into the community from women with needs much like those of Bembo. The regulation that the community's officials would "not admit women separated from their husbands" was crossed out in entirety in one of the capitular books. The next regulation stipulates that they would "not admit those who have been involved in scandal . . . or those who have had cumbersome legal problems"—to which was added, apparently in the same hand as the one that crossed out the previous rule—"until they have been resolved."[132] Both Bembo and Biancolelli lived at the Union Chrétienne separated from their husbands.

Although the relaxation of those rules must have followed the petitions of a requisite number of needy women, the life of the *pensionnaires* was still strictly regulated. The religious life was not to be disrupted by the lay sisters who, thanks to their charity, lived down the street. The capitular records state that the "pensionnaires' apartments will be separated from those of the rest of the community, and they will have no commerce with the sisters without the permission of the Mother Superior and the *Maitresse des Pensionnaires*."[133] Moreover, "the sister selected [as *Maitresse des Pensionnaires*] will often reflect on the terrifying truth advanced by Jesus Christ that it would be more advantageous to be thrown into the bottom of the sea than to give any occasion for scandal involving an innocent soul."[134] When the *pensionnaires* attended services with the religious, they were to be modestly dressed with no jewelry, and were to keep their distance from the main part of the sanctuary when the Priest officiated.[135]

The community was also explicit in its prohibitions against "working for men" and allowing men without an official position into the apartments of the "petit Saint Chaumond."[136] The "Regulations for Visits" recorded in 1690 dictate that only in the case of illness may a doctor enter the apartment of a *pensionnaire*.[137] That Bembo drafted her *procura* on rue de la Lune in the presence of at least four men—notaries Bailly and Gaillardie, and Ambassador Tiepolo with his Secretary Vincenti—presupposes that her home had a common room in which to receive male visitors. It also suggests a place where music—of a spiritual rather than a worldly nature—might have been made with the male voices for which many of her compositions call.

Although the sisters were never to "sing worldly songs," as the capitular records stiffly dictate, they did receive instruction on the harpsichord and the voice as part of a curriculum that also included drawing lessons.[138] Perhaps

---

[132] Ibid., unnumbered folio between ff. 3–4, regulations 4–5.

[133] Ibid., f. 31v.

[134] Ibid., f. 79v; Matthew 18:6.

[135] F-Pan, LL. 1667, pp. 27–28, regulations 8 and 12.

[136] F-Pan, LL. 1669, f. 86v.

[137] F-Pan, LL. 1667, p. 26, regulation 4.

[138] F-Pan, LL. 1669, f. 38r, and LL. 1667, p. 26.

Bembo worked in an unofficial capacity as one of the community's music teachers who could provide instruction in harmony, keyboard, voice, and composition. Although a different venue must be assigned her "worldly songs" (opera, aria, air, and sonnet), the Petite Union Chrétienne and the larger community around Notre Dame de Bonne Nouvelle offered optimal spaces for her to produce her sacred music, with the harpsichords and organs required for the basso continuo notated throughout. Indeed, much of her œuvre falls loosely under the categories named in the capitular records:

1. "Cantiques spirituels." Such works Bembo composed in three languages: in French, the seven penitential psalms found in F-Pn, Rés. Vm¹116; in Italian, the three *cantate spirituali*, nos. 5–7 in *Produzioni armoniche*, F-Pn, Rés. Vm¹117; and, in Latin, the psalm setting *Exaudiat te, Dominus*, F-Pn, Rés. Vm¹115.
2. Hymns. The *petits motets*, nos. 3–4 and 38–40 in *Produzioni armoniche*.
3. *Te Deum* settings. Each of these works occupies one manuscript: F-Pn, Rés. Vm¹112 and Rés. Vm¹114.

The worldly music intermingled with the sacred in *Produzioni armoniche* constitutes the subject of the next chapter. Thanks to the quasi-secular environment that the Petite Union Chrétienne provided, Bembo could continue to associate with the Comédie Italienne, setting amorous texts by Fedeli and Romagnesi; forge new ties with French artists in the city, such as Chéron, author of the psalm paraphrases, and perhaps La Guerre, whose *tragédie en musique* may have inspired *L'Ercole amante;* as well as with the court of Versailles, where her royal dedicatees—invariably compared with Greek gods—received her somewhat "other-worldly" songs.

Part II

The Music

Chapter 3
HARMONIC PRODUCTIONS

In *Produzioni armoniche,* Antonia Bembo compiled a wide variety of pieces that display her skill in composing music for her own voice, a high soprano, as well as for those that could accompany it. The manuscript's table of contents enumerates 41 pieces intended for both sacred and secular performance in a wide range of formal settings and keys (fig. 2.5, table 3.1). King Louis XIV accepted it as a gift for his library, for which it was bound in red leather and stamped with his coat of arms and initial "L" (fig. 3.1). Today it remains at the Bibliothèque Nationale, preserved as F-Pn Rés. Vm^{1}117. Bembo collected the pieces at the turn of the century, as deduced from the circumstances of two of its dedicatees: the music celebrating the wedding of the Duke and Duchess of Burgundy dates to December 1697, with that honoring Monsieur—the king's brother Philippe, Duke of Orleans—offered prior to his death in June 1701. *Produzioni armoniche* represents the first in the series of Bembo's six music manuscripts.

The title presents a group of diverse "harmonic" or "harmonious productions," in all likelihood composed over a lifetime in Venice and in Paris. Although her dedication states that these compositions were "made" in the "holy refuge," where she lived from the 1680s on, the style of several Italian arias and cantatas suggests the earlier creations of "the girl who sings." For instance, "Lamento della Vergine," no. 6, bears direct comparison with the narrative frame and structure of Barbara Strozzi's "Il Lamento" from op. 2 (reprinted in op. 3), and "Mi basta così," no. 22, with a similar aria from Strozzi's op. 7. Strozzi had both pieces published in Venice during the 1650s, the decade when both singers studied with Francesco Cavalli. Even if some fraction of the collection may pre-date Bembo's arrival in France, its majority attests to some twenty years of musical writing at the Petite Union Chrétienne. Nos. 8, 15, and 16 closely parallel her biography and offer a point of departure for an examination of the manuscript.

TABLE 3.1 Contents of *Produzioni armoniche* (F-Pn, Rés. Vm^{1}117)

No.	Title in Manuscript	Incipit	Key	Scoring	Genre
1.	Sonetto al Re	Gran Re, che tutto a tutti	D	S, b.c.	encomium
2.	Al Re	Chiaro esempio di gloria	D	S, V^1, V^2, b.c.	encomium
3.	Pour Saint Louis	Triumphet astris Lodovici	C	S, V, b.c.	petit motet
4.	—	Domine salvum fac regem	a	2S, b.c.	petit motet
5.	Per il Natale	In braccio di Maria	b	S, V^1, V^2, b.c.	sacred cantata
6.	Lamento della Vergine	D'onnipotente Padre	f	S, b.c.	sacred cantata
7.	Martirio di S[an]ta Regina	Mostro d'orgoglio insano	b	S, b.c.	sacred cantata
8.	—	Te vider gli avi miei	c	S, b.c.	cantata
9.	Al Re	Immenso splendore	F	S, b.c.	encomium
10.	Al Re	Dal centro della luce	a	S, b.c.	encomium
11.	Al Re	Pace a voi, pioggie beate	d	S, b.c.	encomium
12.	A Monseigneur	O del celtico scettro	C	S, b.c.	encomium
13.	A Mad[a]me la Duch[ess]a di Borgogna	Hor che lampeggia in cielo	G	S, b.c.	wedding cantata
14.	Per le nozze di Mad[am]a la Duch[ess]a di Borgogna	Qual ti rischiara il ciglio	g	2S, HC, V^1, V^2, b.c.	wedding dialogue
15.	Clizia amante del sole	Lungi dal patrio tetto	a	S, b.c.	cantata
16.	Aria adagio	Habbi pietà di me	f/f#	S, b.c.	d.c. aria
17.	Aria	In amor ci vuol ardir	a	S, b.c.	aria
18.	Aria	E ch'avete bell'ingrato	Bb	S, b.c.	refrain aria
19.	Aria a 2	Non creder a sguardi	a	S, T, b.c.	duet, sectional aria
20.	Affettuoso	Amor mio, facciam la pace	D	2S, b.c.	duet, d.c. aria
21.	Aria allegra	Son sciolti i miei laci	a	S, b.c.	binary aria
22.	Aria	Mi basta così	F	S, b.c.	refrain aria
23.	Aria	Volgete altrove il guardo	Bb	S, b.c.	sectional aria
24.	Aria allegra	Non m'hai voluto credere	b	S, b.c.	binary aria
—	Blank pages (193–194)	—	—	—	—
25.	Aria	Di bell'ire accesi i sguardi	Bb	S, b.c.	binary aria
26.	Aria affettuosa	S'è legge d'amore	c	S, b.c.	d.c. aria
27.	Aria allegra	Mi consolo, non son solo	E	S, b.c.	d.c. aria
28.	Aria	Prendete la porta	Bb	S, b.c.	refrain aria
29.	Aria	Freme Borea	A	S, b.c.	binary aria
30.	Aria	Passan veloci l'ore	a	S, b.c.	sectional aria
31.	Aria	Beata sirena, deh frena	e	S, b.c.	binary aria
32.	Aria	M'ingannasti in verità	e	S, b.c.	binary aria
33.	—	Anima perfida, ingrato cor	a	S, b.c.	refrain aria
34.	Aria a due	Amanti a costo di pianti	C	S, B, b.c.	refrain aria
35.	Per le Nozze di Madama la Duchessa di Borgogna Epitalamio	Squarciato il velo ai fati	A	S, b.c.	wedding epithalamium
36.	Aria Allegro	Chi desia viver in pace	d	S, b.c.	binary aria
37.	Per Monsieur	Qual mi balena al guardo	e	S, b.c.	encomium
38.	—	Panis angelicus	a	S, b.c.	petit motet
39.	—	Tota pulcra es, amica mea	e	S, b.c.	petit motet
40.	—	Domine salvum fac regem	C	S, b.c.	petit motet
41.	Air	Ha, que l'absence	a	S, b.c.	air

Figure 3.1   Coat of arms of King Louis XIV and initial "L" brass

Metamorphosis and Metaphor

Bembo described herself as a musician whose song convinced the Sun King to offer her support; she further noted that she had admired him since childhood ("infanzia"). The paired nos. 15–16 echo this story in music. As a clever metaphor for Bembo's own situation, "Clizia amante del sole" uses Ovid's tale of the nymph Clytie, in love with the sun, "Sol," who scorned her when he turned his attentions to another woman, whose father threw Clytie in a ditch to die. Her metamorphosis into a sunflower allowed her to possess the sun by turning her face to him along his diurnal path. A popular tale during the Sun King's reign, it encapsulates the mission of many who sought his protection. In the melancholic key of A minor, the solo cantata opens with the words of the narrator who introduces the drama at midpoint, describing the nymph "far from her home land, despised by the stars and scorned by fortune" who "fixed her eager glances on the beautiful sun" (CD tr. 1). After this short introduction, Clytie enters, telling of her abandonment: "you depart and leave me here entangled in an abyss of horrors." She beseeches the "Magnificent King of the Sunbeams" to accept the wishes of the "handmaiden" ("ancelle") who hopes to render him "eternal homage." Two passages in the anonymous poem closely resemble phrases in the poetry of Marc'Antonio Romagnesi:

Bembo, "ne geme il fonte e ne sospira il vento"

Romagnesi, "e geme il monte, e ne sospira il pianto"

Bembo, "e s'avvien ch'io m'avvampi"

Romagnesi, "e se m'accende in amoroso ardore"

In addition, Romagnesi's own work contains numerous references to Clytie.[1] Perhaps he penned the poem for Bembo with her circumstances in mind: Corbetta's euphemistic departure referring to his death in 1681 and Louis XIV the "Magnificent King."

At the center of the work, an aria-recitative pair prepares the way for Clytie's metamorphosis and employs *chiaroscuro* effects for figurative light in the major mode and shadow in the minor. In the G-major aria, the nymph sings confidently to her "sweet object of desire"; the recitative contrasts distance from the sun in the minor mode ("languisco," mm. 79–80) and proximity to it in the major ("m'avvivo," mm. 80–81) (ex. 3.1). The sun's rays offer life and their absence signals imminent death, a thought illustrated by thick shadows that hide the sun and thereby halt nature and the nymph in their tracks (mm. 81–84). Clytie discovers her own inner light as she turns into a flower in the company of nature: a fountain, the wind, and a meadow. The contrasting triple meters precipitate this metamorphosis as the return of the light (in D major, 3/4) yields to the flower's laughter and celebration (in 3/8). The brightest possible keys vividly produce the opening of the yellow petals borne of the powerful golden rays of the sun. The parallel minor returns as the ephemeral sunflower promises eternal servitude.

The concluding recitative leaves no doubt as to the identity of the sun, depicted now as the "King of Brilliance" ("Re di Luce"), the metaphorical Sun King who sustains the Venetian *girasole*, Antonia. She could not have found a more fitting poem with which to amplify the story told in the dedication. Clytie/Antonia, "far from her homeland" and abandoned by Corbetta after the "abyss of horrors" she had left behind in Venice, sought sustenance from Sol/Louis whose light/pension meant the difference between destitution and the continuation of her life. Although the words "desire" ("desio") and "lover" ("amante") might imply the physical nature of the nymph's feelings for Sol, her telling identity as a "handmaiden" ("ancelle") who offers an "eternal obsequy" ("ossequio eterno") signals the more pressing need for the king's patronage.

The tale metamorphoses actual people (Louis, Antonia) into Ovid's classical roles (Sol, Clytie the Sunflower) who finally transform themselves into another pair, God and Nature's handmaiden. The thinly veiled allusion to God's "handmaiden," *ancilla Domini*, recasts the King of Brilliance as a savior for the powerless nymph, whose "faith" is "reborn" after having inherited the "immortal glory" of his "celestial rays." The many other artisans working for the king's glory—here depicted as the company of nature in whose midst the sunflower appears—had done the same. Metrical means join forces with madrigalism to conclude the work, wherein a rebirth of climbing eighth notes ascend the scale in 6/8 time before slowly descending to death, resting

---

[1] *Poesie liriche*, 51, 102, 253, and 324; the two quoted lines come from 139 and 271.

Example 3.1   F-Pn, Rés. Vm¹117, no. 15, mm. 79–84

Away from you, I languish, close by, I am enlivened;
If you are hidden I do not live; if I see you I rejoice.

peacefully in the assurance of faith. Such madrigalism, the embodiment of the meaning of a word or phrase in music, serves as a prominent tool throughout the composer's oeuvre.

Through these multiple metaphorical metamorphoses, Bembo—apparently with Romagnesi's help—attracted the king's attention in order to obtain his aid. Yet even with his support, the cantata underscores the precarious state of her existence; it does not triumph in the major mode, nor does the rebirth remain in the lofty position toward which it had climbed. Rather, it concludes down in the same A-minor ditch where it had begun. The final recitative provides the message that faith alone provides hope. Not long after Bembo's arrival in France the story was featured in the popular periodical *Mercure galant* as "Clytie énigme" (fig. 3.2). A common pedagogical tool of the time consisted in deciphering such enigmas, or emblems. The cantata holds not only a metaphor for religious faith—the flicker of light within each hopeful believer who has witnessed the greatest sustaining life force imaginable—but also a brilliant solution to the riddle of the composer's hope for Christian redemption and for a place among the king's artisans of glory.[2]

The da capo aria "Habbi pietà di me," no. 16, offers a likely candidate for the music Bembo described in her dedication as having convinced the king that she "had some talent in singing." Conceivably, she sang it to the accompaniment of Corbetta's guitar. The *Aria adagio,* divided in contrasting halves with a da capo marking, reinforces Clytie's plea in more direct terms, devoid

[2] Orest Ranum coined the phrase in *Artisans of Glory: Writers and Historical Thought in Seventeenth-Century France* (Chapel Hill: University of North Carolina Press, 1980).

Figure 3.2   "Clytie énigme," *Mercure galant*, September 1679. *Source*: Cliché Bibliothèque nationale de France, Paris.

of classical allusion. The mournful first syllable cries out, catching the listener's attention with a falling fourth and scalar descent completing the piteous opening (ex. 3.2, CD tr. 2).

A section

Habbi pietà di me,	Have pity on me,
non mi lasciar morir.	do not let me die.
Non merta la mia fé,	My faith does not deserve it,
non vole il mio soffrir.	my suffering does not wish for it.

B section

Rio tenor d'ingrata sorte	The evil way of an ungrateful fate
mi condanna a mille pene,	condemns me to a thousand pains;
il mio mal vien dal mio bene,	my suffering comes from my beloved,
la mia vita mi da morte	my life gives me death
senza sperar mercé	without hoping for a reward
al mio lungo servir.	for my long servitude.

Through quick-paced recitative, the B section takes on a rebellious tone to rage against the unjust ravages of destiny. The dual tonality in F minor and

Example 3.2   F-Pn, Rés. Vm¹117, no. 16, p. 157, mm. 1–3

Have pity on me, do not let me die.

F-sharp minor, side by side in the key signature, appears nowhere else in the compilation. Perhaps these signal the divergences in pitch between Venice and Paris that would have affected the composer immediately upon arrival in France. F-sharp minor at a French low pitch standard would bring the aria into the range of a singer used to performing at Venetian high pitch, where F minor would have sufficed.[3] The dual tonality seems to commemorate that moment in her compilation and lends further credence to the idea that "Habbi pietà di me" represents the very music with which Bembo and Corbetta may have courted the king's support for the soon-to-be-abandoned Venetian noblewoman.

Continuing with the idea that Bembo's selection of texts may shed light on her biography, no. 8, "Te vider gli avi miei," progresses from the previous pair. After having established her role as one of the king's artisans of glory, she worked within the confines of willing servitude. Again through classical allegory, now with the tale of Icarus, the piece explores the idea of pride coming before a fall; he did not see the limits of his mortality and flew too close to the sun, thereby melting his wax wings and sending him tumbling down to his death in the sea below. The poetry and music have to do with heights and abysses, as well as with mortal fate and pride. The voice of Romagnesi returns in this text's multiple references to Icarus, Dedalus, the mountains of Olympus and Ossa, and concern with pride—all of which appear frequently in his poems.[4] At the outset, the narrator states in a brief introduction that "[her] ancestors saw you, proud monument, lifting yourself up to emulate Olympus and Ossa," where the two characters signify both composer ("my ancestors") and dedicatee ("proud monument"). The dangers

[3] See Jean Saint-Arroman, L'Interprétation de la musique française 1661–1789. I. Dictionnaire d'interprétation (Initiation) (Paris: Honoré Champion, 1983), 133. This dictionary provides definitions for terms with a list of musical examples and sources for each. A variety of diapasons existed in the chapel, the convents, for chamber ensembles, and for opera during the period in question just in Paris and Versailles alone, but the standard French pitch for present purposes is A (G) = 392 Hz.

[4] Romagnesi, Poesie liriche: references to Icarus (96, 298, 313), Dedalus (96, 80, 130, 298, 319), and Olympus and Ossa (27, 393).

of pride affect all mortals, Louis XIV included; while the sun, "proud mon-ument," can be "uprooted and shaken by cruel Saturn," the audacious narra-tor must beware of a fatal sunburn. It is worth noting here Romagnesi's pre-occupation with astrological forces; amongst his poems, he included charted readings for several acquaintances.

Best defined as a cantata in nine distinct sections flowing seamlessly from one to the next, no. 8 exhibits some complexity of form. The cantata should be performed straight through at first, but an indication on the system begin-ning the fourth section, "Alla sfera del sol volti la carta" ("turn back here after 'Alla sfera del sol,'" the ninth section), matches an indication at the end of the piece to return to repeat that section through the eighth, where the cantata concludes at the flourish, the characteristic double bar of *Produzioni armoniche* (ex. 3.3). Only four of the sections employ illustrating rubrics; Bembo indi-cated the majority through meter change or dividing double bar.

After the brief introduction establishes tonic as C minor, the rubrics *Aria,* *R[ecitativ]o,* and *Aria,* define the movement of the second (ex. 3.4), third, and fourth sections. The first *Aria* begins with a four-measure phrase in the con-tinuo that the voice repeats, revealing the words that shaped its being: "su-perbo mortale, che pensi, che tenti?" (mm. 14–18, 18–22). Identical to the opening mm. 14–18, the third repetition of the phrase, mm. 22–26, sets up an antiphonal ostinato between the two parts. The falling tetrachord $c–G$, mm. 19–22, seems to promise not just a fitting harmony for the voice but also

Example 3.3   F-Pn, Rés. Vm^{1}117, no. 8, p. 92, mm. 107–122

. . . the ladder to heaven. To the spheres of the sun, without thinking, [Icarus was] spurred on to fearless flight.

Example 3.4   F-Pn, Rés. Vm¹117, no. 8, mm. 14–22

Proud mortal, what do you think? What do you dare?

a lament for the doomed mortal's fate. However, in m. 26 this foreshortened ostinato gives way to an imitative motivic kernel elaborated in the eighth section with a vivid madrigalism on "scala" (ex. 3.3, systems 1–3). In the fifth section, strong imperatives seem aimed at the mortal who, like Icarus, climbs too high: "Stop the flight! Come down! Fall! Repent!" This idea returns in the next set of encomiastic pieces to encapsulate fear of overstepping modesty, a vexing problem for a refugee singer needing discretion. The sixth section, marked *Adagio,* delivers the sobering message that "in the hands of death, human fate cannot rise again," another way of describing the Fall from grace. A notable French touch with a *petite reprise,* marked *Piano,* instructs the singer to repeat the second half of the phrase gently and quietly. The moral of the story appears in the eighth section, delivered in repetition as the final section of the cantata: "humility has always been the ladder to heaven" (ex. 3.3). Sequential melismatic triads on "scala" first descend (systems 1–2), then climb (systems 2–3), cleverly conjuring through music a tangible image of Jacob's ladder—the more dependable way to climb to heaven than on Icarus's melting wings. A similar caveat appeared at the close of Clytie's tale, where she concluded, "should I burn myself on your celestial rays . . . from my death, my faith will be reborn." Christian faith thereby trumps and incontrovertibly supersedes mythological and astrological belief.

Encomia for the Triumvirate

The foregoing interpretation of "Te vider gli avi miei" as biography presupposed the extent to which its writer projected a persona and raison d'être dependent on the king for identity. Lacking a title, the piece mediates between that group of biographical pieces and the genre of the encomiastic cantata.

Unified by an overarching tonality and presented in sections divided by related key, by meter, or by formal labels such as aria or recitativo, such encomia function as cantatas, in praise of the king, his brother, his son, and granddaughter-in-law. Cantata no. 8, then, overlaps with a group of encomia—effusive laudatory statements—dedicated to the "triumvirate": music for the king and his son (nos. 1–3, 9–12), with that for his brother (no. 37) placed close to the end of the manuscript.

By the time of the compilation of *Produzioni armoniche,* King Louis XIV had a long and distinguished career behind him. He had proven himself expert at unifying France through his military campaigns, his politics, and a rigorous agenda of religious integration. With generous patronage of the arts and music, he assured the diffusion of the knowledge of his bold exploits. The many buildings, sculptures, paintings, and musical works that survive in and around Paris reflect this support as the outward symbols of his power. The image of a strong monarch was celebrated daily during his reign, as the French people thrived on his heroic depiction.[5] Of all the allegories, that of the sun held the most potential for his encomia. In 1653 he had appeared in costume as the sun in a ballet produced by Isaac de Benserade (1612–1691). While countless rulers of yore had invoked solar images to invest their positions with importance, the king's early symbolic association increased as his reign flourished and far surpassed that of earlier Gallic monarchs. During the next decades, Versailles celebrated his solar image in the construction of gardens, fountains, grottoes, and pools. Such writers as La Fontaine and Molière equated his image with the mythological sun god, Apollo, a figure associated with positive properties.[6] The texts of Bembo's songs specifically addressed to the king contribute to an understanding of his literary and musical depiction as Sun King and elaborate on well-established Apollonian imagery. But herein lies implicitly the ambivalent relationship that the composer held toward her gift of song and her status as a foreign woman who stood, unlike her French colleague La Guerre, outside the royal patronage system.

Produzioni armoniche opens with a "Sonetto al Re," a cantata in classic sonnet form that continues the royal praise begun in the dedication. The rhyming *endecasillabi* (eleven-syllable lines), divide into two *quartine* of eight lines and two *terzine* of six:

---

[5] Along with Ranum, numerous writers have treated this subject, including Jean-Marie Apostolidès, *Le Roi-Machine: Spectacle et politique au temps de Louis XIV* (Paris: Éditions de minuit, 1981); Peter Burke, *The Fabrication of Louis XIV* (New Haven: Yale University Press, 1992); Louis Marin, *Portrait of the King,* Martha M. Houle, trans. (Minneapolis: University of Minnesota Press, 1988 [1981]); Jean-Pierre Néraudau, *L'Olympe du Roi-Soleil—Mythologie et idéologie royale au Grand Siècle* (Paris: Société d'Édition "Les Belles Lettres," 1986); and Nicole Ferrier-Caverivière, *L'Image de Louis XIV dans la littérature française de 1660 à 1715* (Paris: Presses Universitaires de France, 1981).

[6] Ferrier-Caverivière, *L'Image de Louis XIV,* 73–80.

Gran Re, che tutto a tutti, eccelso
  in terra,
	Great King, who is everything
	  to everyone,

tutto puoi, tutto reggi e a tutti
  imperi,
	supreme on earth, all-powerful,
	  sovereign, and imperial,

e pure a meditar gli alti misteri	even while pondering the highest mysteries
il tutto annullar cerchi sotterra.	you seek to subdue all subterranean stirrings.

Tu che vide l'Europa in pace e
  in guerra
	You, whom Europe saw in peace and
	  in war,

dar glorioso effetto a tuoi pensieri,	give glorious effect to your thoughts,

tu che miri al tuo pie schiavi
  gl'imperi
	you behold at your feet the enslaved
	  empires

con quel poter ch'ogni potenza
  atterra.
	with that strength that fells any other
	  power.

La discordia impulsasti entro il
  profondo,
	You pushed discord down to the
	  depths,

e in ferma fede e sacrosanto zelo,	and with firm faith and holy zeal,

da te scacciasti il Calvinismo
  immondo.
	you banished corrupt Calvinism from
	  your sight.

Non ha più raggi a circondarti Delo,	Delos has not enough rays to encircle you;

non ha più glorie a tributtarti il
  mondo,
	the world has not enough glory to
	  bestow on you;

non ha più stelle a coronarti il cielo.	heaven has not enough stars to crown you.

The depiction of the king ruling heaven and earth contrasts with "sotterra" and continues with the glorification of his political and religious actions. A decidedly Catholic chastisement of Calvinism lends support to the cause of France's unification. At the conclusion, Louis is made to surpass monarchy through an allusion to Apollo, said to have been born on the Greek island of Delos.

No. 2, "Chiaro esempio di gloria," continues the sonnet's D-major tonality, adding to the ensemble two instrumental parts—labeled here and throughout as V1 and V2 (ex. 3.5, CD tr. 3). The texts reveal an author concerned with the uses of both sound and silence, referring to the voice as a glorious "bright trumpet" ("questa lingua è chiara tromba," ex. 3.5, mm. 22–25, and "tromba sia la gloria stessa," in no. 10), to "lips" loosening "to song" ("sciolgo i labri al canto," no. 2), and to the resonance of the chest ("dal mio petto ogn'hor rimbomba," no. 2). Ideally two trumpets in D would accompany the voice in no. 2. The strophic middle portion of the piece appears in example 3.5 with its

Example 3.5   F-Pn, Rés. Vm^{1}117, no. 2, mm. 18–25

1. This voice is a bright trumpet of
   your glorious, generous spirits...
2. If you resemble the blond god,
   I too wish to participate in
   echoing your memory...

motto, an imitative theme with a triadic profile that moves between the treble
parts (m. 18) to the voice (m. 20). Bembo used such obbligato treble instruments sparingly in *Produzioni armoniche* (nos. 2–3, 5, and 14), as if in preparation for extensive usage of the practice in her later work. She would also quote
the concluding phrase of no. 2 in her dedication to the *Tè Deum-Exaudiat te,
Dominus* manuscript (doc. 26): "chi dà quanto può, dà quanto deve" ("[she]

who gives as much as [she] can, gives what [she] owes"). The phrase underscores her ever-present sense of indebtedness to the king's patronage, as well as of an identity forged through glorifying him in vocal music.

As the allegorical sun, Louis stood at the center of the solar system, with all the other planets, or figurative countries, revolving around him. This cosmological image begins no. 3, "Pour Saint Louis," a motet in Latin in which the voice and the instrumental *dessus* perform antiphonally in order to sound the triumph of the stars ruled by Louis, the central solar power: "Triumphet astris Lodovici gloria." The motet's triadic motto closely resembles that shown in example 3.5, but transposed to C major in even rhythms. In contrast to the mythological representations offered by the Italian pieces, "Pour Saint Louis" evokes the king's ancestor, Louis IX "the Pious" (1214–1270), to promote an image that combines religious, political, and historical themes, thereby elevating the monarch to the role of religious as well as terrestrial hero. Commensurate with his constantly evolving mystique, the king's set of encomia evokes a legendary world combining Greek mythology with Christian lives of saints in order to pay him tribute in ways that he and his society would have found highly acceptable. In her work on imagery, Nicole Ferrier-Caverivière noted the widespread use of the depiction of Saint Louis whereby contemporary authors often moved seamlessly between Apollonian and Christian evocations in a "transposition of Christian dogma."[7]

As if to echo the opening sonnet, "Pour Saint Louis" contains a verse condemning Calvinism, surely a reference to the revocation of the Edict of Nantes in 1685. The poem casts the Calvinists as barbarians ("barbarorum"), heretics who had divided France, now depicted as a metaphorical "monster" killed by Louis's forces ("heresis monstrum jacet"), where the monster represents any force running counter to Catholicism. The poem's bellicose tone invokes the king's image as a military leader whose triumph and glory come from the spoils of war. In this violent depiction Saint Louis appears alongside Louis XIII, thereby conflating the present king with his immediate and past ancestors: the first stanza calls up the "memory of Louis" ("Lodovici memoria") and the second suggests the vestiges of the past "holy prince" ("sancti principis"). The last stanza, the most explicit, states that Louis follows willingly "the example of the father" ("Exemplum Patris alter en Lodovix"). The militant nature of this poem extends to Christ, the avenger ("Ultricis Christi"), as if to recall the participation of Saint Louis in the Crusades.

Bembo deliberately ordered *Produzioni armoniche* with grouped selections to celebrate royal members of court and to mirror her own identity. No. 3 showed that the king was an important religious figure in addition to a political hero. She expanded the tribute by offering another motet, a prayer for the kingdom in French style, no. 4. Analyzed together in that context, the

---

[7] Ferrier-Caverivière, *L'Image de Louis XIV,* "une transposition du dogme chrétien" (80).

two motets constitute a religious offering that complements the encomiastic sonnet-cantata pair of nos. 1–2. Both texts celebrate his attributes: no. 3 with a lengthy story of the vanquishing of Calvinism and no. 4 with the final tercet from Psalm 20 (set again in no. 40). While no. 1 denounces "corrupt Calvinism" ("il Calvinismo immondo")—the problem that Louis XIV had to address—no. 3 highlights the triumphant nature of the two kings' common mission. Nos. 3 and 4 seem to represent the "hymns of glory to . . . [the king's] name" promised by the poem of cantata no. 2, "Al Re." Motet no. 3, one of only four pieces in the compilation scored for an ensemble with obbligato instrumentation, foreshadows the expansion procedures taken up later in the concerted works. The larger ensembles called for in nos. 2–4 appropriately celebrate a great king, amplifying the sound offered by the initial sonnet. The sacred cantatas, nos. 5–7, continue the motets' religious theme and function as an interlude set for the royal encomia.

Cast in binary form, "Domine salvum fac regem," no. 4, calls for an ensemble of two sopranos with continuo (ex. 3.6). The first section explores close imitation between the two voices, which establish the motet's key of A minor, while the second engages the continuo as a third imitative voice. At the outset of the second section, mm. 23–24, the basso continuo (b.c.) imitates the first soprano at the distance of one quarter note on "et exaudi nos in die," and, starting in m. 27, the three parts proceed around the circle of fifths (D–G–C) and cadence together in F major at m. 30. A moment of silence—the curious rest on the third beat of m. 24—represents a recurrent feature of Bembo's music. Indeed, silence itself appears as an important recourse for the singer delivering these poems. This motet also contains a clue to the range of the instrument intended to play the continuo part; the bass avoids a descent down to BB on the second beat of m. 37, when it would have been more logical to go down to that note and then to have jumped up the octave on beat three, rather than displacing the C–B into an awkward seventh at mm. 37–38. The continuo instrument of choice for a sacred work would have been the organ, whose keyboard ended at C. The evidence is further borne out by the lowest note of the compilation, AA on p. 157 of "Clizia amante del sole." Quite conceivably, the organ played the sacred work, the harpsichord or a plucked instrument the secular.

The poetry of no. 9 describes the sun's rays:

. . . ma quale in mezzo a l'etra	. . . which other majestic monarch
maestoso monarca	spreads rays of glory
raggi di gloria spande?	from the middle of the sky?
O, che prodigio, questi è Luigi	O, what a marvel, this is Louis
il Grande.	the Great.
Ei dunque in grado accetti	So therefore with respect, accept
gl'ossequiosi affetti	the humble affections
de miei devoti carmi	of my devoted songs

Example 3.6   F-Pn, Rés. Vm¹117, no. 4, mm. 23–30

And hear us in the day that we shall call upon you

In faithful song and utter admiration, the end of the recitative section names the monarch: "Luigi il grande." It furthers the sonnet's concept of encircling Delos and echoes a poem by La Fontaine that compares the monarch to both Phoebus Apollo and the sun:[8]

L'un et l'autre soleil, unique en son espèce, étale aux regardants sa pompe et sa richesse.

The one and the other sun, unique to its kind, spreads pomp and wealth before the spectators.

[8] Cited by Ferrier-Caverivière, *L'Image de Louis XIV,* 79; the complete poem is found in *Œuvres complètes* (Paris: Bibliothèque de la Pléiade, 1958), 2: 185.

Phébus brille à l'envi du monarque français;	Phoebus shines with envy of the French monarch;
on ne sait bien souvent à qui donner sa voix.	often one knows not to whom to give one's voice.
Tous deux sont pleins d'éclat et rayonnants de gloire.	Both are full of charm and radiate glory.

The cantatas examined here present the beneficent qualities of the Sun King—the qualities of Apollo, the perceived goodness of unified Catholic faith, the welcome warmth of an Aegean island—as well as the danger of getting too close to the sun. Just as the sun is all-powerful, so can it be dangerous to the sungazer: like no. 8, cantata no. 10 warns of Icarus's derring-do. It opens with the narrator's admiration of the rays of light flooding the *Piranei,* perhaps alluding to the Peace of the Pyrenees, achieved by the strategic marriage between Maria Teresa of Spain and Louis XIV in 1660. In recalling that moment, one of the king's early "trophies," Bembo drew attention to her claim to fame: her family's close acquaintance with Cavalli prior to his invitation to compose an opera in France in celebration of that royal wedding.

Dal centro della luce, orbi rottanti,	From the center of the light, rotating orbs,
sovra Luigi eterni rai versate	pour your eternal rays on Louis
et incurvando i Piranei giganti,	and curving around the gigantic Pyrenees,
ai trofei della Francia archi inalzate.	raise up arches to the trophies of France.

Melismatic silhouettes sinuously trace the curves of the French triumphal arches, which inspire images of the mountain range dividing France and Spain (ex. 3.7). The setting of "archi" features a brief rising sequence in mm. 11–12, followed by the G-major scaling of the mountaintop reached in m. 13. The bright keys of C, D, and G here broadcast the celebratory juncture.

The next section commands all things to call out Louis's praises—the breezes, waves, and branches should make a joyful noise in his honor ("sia loquace ogn'aura, ogn'onda"). Yet, at the conclusion of the piece, the narrator recoils in horror, now negating the exaltation of a moment before and chastising the injunction to celebrate him in sound:

Ma scendi incauto cor, su l'alta mole	But descend, imprudent heart; if you put down your Icarian flight
se poni icareo il vol, rovine attendi.	on the high boulder, ruin will await you.
Taci, deh taci, e qual Egittio apprendi	Be quiet, yes be quiet and, like an Egyptian, learn
a idolatrar co' tuoi silenzii il sole.	to adore the sun with your silences.

Example 3.7   F-Pn, Rés. Vm¹117, no. 10, mm. 10–14

raise up arches to the trophies of France.

The allusion to Icarus's high flying and the connection to singing as a dangerous act both highlight the risk of approaching the Sun King too closely. Ironically, the very musical skill that had provided Bembo with the occasion to appear before him may have required great courage to use. The texts suggest that humility and silence would be more appropriate forms of devotion. Egyptian priests were reputed to celebrate the power of the sun by keeping quiet until it rose, when they would intone a hymn of thanksgiving.[9] The "humble affections of devoted songs" in no. 9 above take the sunrise ritual in reverse order, for the silence of the heart and soul soon quiet the songs:

Qui tacque l'alma e le sue glorie honora,
s'adoran co 'l silenzio i numi ancora.

Here the soul fell silent and honored his glories,
deities are also adored with silence.

The narrator concludes by promoting the merits of quietly adoring Louis XIV, the temporal deity, and recalls one of its musical embodiments: the "silent" interjection in m. 24 of no. 4 (ex. 3.6).

No. 12, a cantata for the king's son, Louis, the Grand Dauphin (1661–1711), titled "A Monseigneur," directly follows the second set of encomia for the king. Its bilingual titles—Italian in the table of contents, French in the score—distinguish it from that set as well as from the other encomia, which all bear Italian titles. The cantata contains four unlabeled sections and contrasts the unassuming role of the admiring narrator with the exploits of

[9] On the importance of Egypt in Louis XIV's France, see Erik Iversen, *The Myth of Egypt and its Hieroglyphs in European Tradition* (Copenhagen: Gec Gad, 1961; reprint, Princeton: Princeton University Press, 1993), 124–126.

Monseigneur, "inheritor of the Gallic scepter," brave in battle and "not less" than his father. A similar phrase is found in Romagnesi's poetry, where his "maggior d'Ulisse, e non minor d'Achille" can be compared with Bembo's line here, "maggior di tutti e non minor del Padre."[10] The textual relationship between narrator and object of praise, however, exhibits little of the intensity found in the king's encomia. Musically, too, little time is given to dwelling on any particular bit of text or to modulatory detours. The highpoint comes in the third section, an aria describing the terrestrial and martial powers of the man who exceeds Caesar in war; repeated sixteenth-note figures make the most of the rhymed words "guerra" and "atterra." The final section proclaims that there are "three Louis on earth" ("tre Luigi in terra"): Louis XIV, Monseigneur, and his own son, Louis, Duke of Burgundy, revealing another new "triumvirate."

"Per Monsieur," no. 37, demonstrates lavish care for dramatic text setting in an encomiastic cantata for the king's brother Philippe, Duke of Orleans (1640–1701). With a more subjective tone omitting the customary statements of humility, it suggests a closer relationship between narrator and dedicatee. The first of the piece's three sections proceeds in arioso style in E minor, opening the work with close interplay between singer and continuo (ex. 3.8). Through a lengthy melisma shared in imitative dialogue on the verb "balena" ("flashes"), both parts illustrate the strong ray of light emanating from Monsieur. Bembo found an appropriate madrigalism to portray that ray with an ascending E-minor scale on "raggio" over a sustained continuo (mm. 4–5). The second section sings Philippe's praises with an aria in the relative major, G: "the heart yearns for him, every soul sighs to him." The third section, in recitative, returns to the home key as it proclaims the dual glories of the duke and the king in their home city: "to Paris's astonishment . . . the king lives in Philippe, he in Louis" ("con stupor di Parigi . . . il re vive in Filippe, egli in Luigi"). The cantata's tripartite harmonic trajectory, *mi–sol–mi* (e–G–e), underpins their mutually glorious solar depiction, as suggested by the Italian *solfeggio* phrase, "mi sol(e) mi(o)" ("my sun, mine").

The poetic texts reveal the composer herself; their persona clearly reflects her own circumstances, displaying unquestionable knowledge of the craft of vocality, of setting Italian poems written in France, and of exploring the nature of servitude to the king. The obsequious pledges found in the poetry go beyond the expressions of humility given by most contemporary composers who produced music at court, perhaps because Bembo's lack of affiliation meant that she did not have official permission to be a musician. As a result, her talent in song carried with it the fear of overstepping the boundaries proscribing her actions. Her status as a foreign woman outside the professional scene restricted her access to musical performance and, hence, to composition

[10] Romagnesi, *Poesie liriche*, 395.

Example 3.8   F-Pn, Rés. Vm¹117, no. 37, mm. 1–6

Qual mi ba- le -   -   -   -   -   -   -

-na   al guar - do   rag   -   -   -   gio d'e-ter-no fuo- co?

What ray of eternal fire flashes before my eyes?

and publication, a problem explored quite effectively by these pieces. As a woman seeking an appropriate mode of conduct in France, she had some formidable obstacles to overcome. Romagnesi may well have understood her precarious status in France and have had a hand in writing these poems for her.

Sacred Cantatas

Placed between the two groups of encomia in the manuscript, the three *cantate spirituali* (sacred cantatas nos. 5–7)[11] further elucidate the composer's interests and confirm her own religious fervor as well as adherence to the king's program of Catholic unity. The first two give voice to the Blessed Virgin Mary with a celebratory Christmas cantata ("Per il Natale," no. 5) and a mournful "Lament of the Virgin" ("Lamento della Vergine," no. 6). The third recounts the tale of a fourth-century Burgundian woman with "The Martyrdom of Saint Reine" ("Martirio di Santa Regina," no. 7). In her summary of *Produzioni armoniche*, Rokseth singled out "Per il Natale" and "Martirio di Santa Regina," noting their exceptional beauty and fine construction.[12] A recording of the lament, the first piece of Bembo's to become commercially

[11] For a useful overview, see Gloria Rose, "The Italian Cantata of the Baroque Period," in *Gattungen der Musik in Einzeldarstellungen, Gedenkschrift Leo Schrade*, ed. Wulf Arlt, Ernst Lichtenhahn, Hans Oesch, and Max Haas (Bern: Francke Verlag, 1973), 655–677, especially 655, 669. See, too, the facsimile of Giacomo Antonio Perti's *Cantate morali, e spirituali* (Bologna: Giacomo Monti, 1688; reprint, Bologna: Arnaldo Forni, 1990).

[12] Rokseth, "Antonia Bembo," 150–151.

available, confirms its place among these favorites (CD tr. 4). Indeed, the three *cantate spirituali* have much in common. Nos. 5 and 7, both set in B minor, contain scenes with an assumed *turba* (simulations of the crowd from the oratorio tradition), the former adding two obbligato instruments for a pastoral effect. Nos. 6 and 7 call for two characters beyond the narrator's role. The degree of complexity increases with each: in no. 5, seven sections feature three composite scenes (narrator–Mary–narrator); in no. 6, twelve sections contain five (narrator–Mary–narrator–Christ–narrator); and in no. 7, thirteen sections yield nine such scenes (tables 3.2 and 3.3).

The sacred cantatas make use of the narrative technique later used in "Clizia amante del sole," where the soloist takes on multiple roles to portray a narrator as well as one or two dramatic characters. In turn, it appears that Bembo may have modeled them on several pieces by Strozzi that employ a narrative/first-person voice/narrative format, in which the narrator provides a framework for the subjective story told in the first-person voice by the character or characters concerned. Such formats appear with some frequency in Marian devotional music of Seicento Italy, focusing on exactly the highpoints of the Christian calendar year found in nos. 5–6 here: a lullaby for Christmastime and a lament for Holy Week.[13] The first-person female voice approached an ideal characterization of the Virgin Mary, and Bembo apparently drew on this tradition for her own Marian settings as well as for her dramatization of Clytie's metamorphosis and Reine's martyrdom.

Mary's character displays a wide range of emotion in "Per il Natale," a quasi lullaby whose dramatic action takes place shortly after the birth of Jesus.[14] Scored in B minor for two obbligato upper parts with voice and continuo, it shares instrumentation with no. 2, "Al Re," there for a pair of trumpets; the pastoral setting here suggests rather a pair of transverse flutes or violins. The instruments perform everywhere except in the recitative portions, set apart by double bar or change in meter rather than by rubric. The narrator takes up the thematic material provided by the opening instrumental prelude and presents Mary, in whose loving arms the divine child "breathe[s] breezes of peace [un]to the world." A short bass descent to the relative major, D, marks the beginning of her narrative whose imitative thematic material recalls that of nos. 2–3. A recitative divided in half by a double bar comes next. In the first section Mary basks in the glory of her accomplishment, noting the

---

[13] Contrary to what one might expect, it appears that few contemporary women composers used the first-person female voice in song. For a discussion of Bembo's two Marian settings in the context of the Seicento tradition, see Claire Fontijn, "The Virgin's Voice: Representations of Mary in Seventeenth-Century Italian Song," in *Maternal Measures—Figuring Caregiving in the Early Modern Period,* ed. Naomi J. Miller and Naomi Yavneh (Aldershot, U.K.: Ashgate, 2000), 135–162.

[14] For a critical performing edition of the cantata, see Claire Fontijn, ed., *Per il Natale* (Fayetteville, AR: Clar-Nan Editions, 1999).

onlookers' admiration of the holy birth. In the second section a sudden shift to the relative minor marks her realization that her thoughts are "vainglorious" as she shrinks back to find that she has been so presumptuous as to assume that she would be glorified along with her son (mm. 47–57).[15] She asks him for pardon—"Figlio perdona"—and then finds a rationale for her imaginings; she reassures herself with the thought that "if a god without original sin / sprang from the womb of his mother / then I am without sin." The obbligato instruments return for the following aria in which several appearances of a descending sequence of suspensions suggest Mary's devotion to the "supreme mysteries" that she honors and adores (mm. 63–78). In the final arioso the narrator returns, framing the scene of mother and son with objective commentary. The entire ensemble concludes the cantata with imitative effects symbolizing the "eternal echoes" of the Christmas miracle as "the onlookers cry out, 'Gloria!'."

The "Lamento della Vergine" addresses the crucifixion from the perspective of the Virgin Mary (CD tr. 4). Its setting in F minor, appropriately chosen to lend its effect to the scene of acute distress, recalls the alternate key signature for "Habbi pietà di me"; it appears nowhere else in *Produzioni armoniche*. The cantata contains twelve sections, with the actual lament appearing in the sixth section as its literal centerpiece (table 3.2).

Bembo apparently modeled the entire piece after Strozzi's "Il Lamento," op. 2 (1651), which dramatizes the beheading of Henri de Cinq Mars in 1642. The reprint of "Il Lamento" in her op. 3 (1654) suggests its popularity. The actual lament features a basso ostinato pattern repeated thirteen times, as if to underscore the misfortune of the French squire but also to mark its importance as the work's centerpiece. Davide Daolmi and Emanuele Senici have posited that with "Il Lamento" she crafted a male lament that would have appealed to Giulio Strozzi's academy, employing a replacement for the more customary female lament because of the putative homosexual relations between the French king Louis XIII and the squire Henri.[16] She transposed the ostinato for another male lament in the pastoral serenata of op. 8 (1664).

In Venice, the composer would have known all three of Strozzi's publications, and they may well have served as a template for her "Lament of the Virgin," which draws on the tradition of the female lament rather than on the twist that might have been taken for the purposes of the Academy of the Incogniti. In Bembo's centerpiece, the lament found in the sixth section, straightforward rhyme and even meter in two quatrains of *senari* (six-syllable lines) dictated an aria setting appropriate for meditation on the moment of the crucifixion. An even 3/4 meter offers the steadiness of a walking bass in

---

[15] Mm. 47–57 and 63–78 of "Per il Natale" appear in Fontijn, "The Virgin's Voice," 142–144.

[16] Davide Daolmi and Emanuele Senici, " 'L'omosessualità è un modo di cantare'—Il contributo *queer* all'indagine sull'opera in musica," *Il saggiatore musicale* 7/1 (2002): 137–178.

TABLE 3.2 Analysis of *Produzioni armoniche,* no. 6, "Lamento della Vergine"

Character	Rubric	Key	Action
1. Narrator	[Recitativo]	f	Description of Christ on the cross
2. Narrator	[Aria]	f	The world responds to Mary's weeping
3. Narrator	Recitativo	d (vi)	Introduces Mary
4. Mary	Aria vivace	d	Mary's outrage and anger
5. Mary	Re[citativ]o	F	Mary's wish for eternal life in Christ
6. Mary	Aria-Seconda	f	Centerpiece: the Virgin's lament
7. Mary	Recitativo	bb/d	Death vs. eternal life in God
8. Mary	[repeat of section 4]	d	Mary's outrage and anger
9. Mary	Aria	d	Mary's anger with the monster
10. Narrator	Re[citativ]o	bb (iv)/f	Introduces Christ's last utterances
11. Christ	Affettuoso assai	f	Christ's last words
12. Narrator	[Recitativo]	f	Narrator concludes with Christ's death

eighth or quarter notes, while the voice gently sings a mournful minor triadic figure at the first and second (*Seconda*) verses (ex. 3.9).

Staccato dal ramo	Torn away from the branch
di pianta fatale,	of a fatal tree;
il fallo d'Adamo	Adam's fall
diè frutto mortale.	bore deadly fruit.
Seconda	
Con pena infinita	With infinite pain
cangiò trista sorte,	sad fate transformed
quell'arbor di vita	that tree of life
in arbor di morte.	into a tree of death.

A four-measure bass ritornello (mm. 83–87, 106–110, 129–133) frames the voice and acts as an interlude between the two verses (mm. 87–105, 110–128). In mm. 99–100 the cadence touches briefly upon A-flat, the relative major, after which *Rep[lic]a p[ia]no* presents a slightly varied, softer repetition of the singer's phrase in mm. 95–100 softly transposed to the tonic key in mm. 100–105. A striking resemblance obtains between the singer's phrase in mm. 87–90 and mm. 18–21 of no. 8 (ex. 3.4): both set in triple-time minor keys, the identical phrases begin and end on the same note with which they started, diverging only in the ways that they approach the cadence. Indeed, the tetrachord in the b.c. of no. 8 posited a foreshortened lament (mm. 19–22); the true lament here receives lengthier development. The three identical ritornello statements appear with four ostinato interjections: the continuo repeats the emblem of lament, the tetrachord descending from f to c (mm. 88–91) twice more after that shown in example 3.9. As if to further highlight its importance as musical centerpiece for the "Lament of the Virgin," Bembo in-

Example 3.9   F-Pn, Rés. Vm¹117, no. 6, mm. 83–106

Torn away from the branch of a fatal tree, Adam's fall bore deadly fruit.

cluded a diminution of the music of the ritornello in the fourth and eighth sections, which becomes the fierce accompaniment to Mary's outrage in the *Aria vivace,* "Che fai, che tenti?"[17] As in no. 5, Mary's forceful rebellion against the "tiranna, pessima" ("tyrannical . . . shadow") dramatizes her invincibility as Christ's mother; the phrase also recalls motet no. 3, which names as a "monster" a similar opposing force. Nos. 5 and 6 both cast the Virgin Mary in a feminist manner as a powerful, active force, an image that stands in sharp contrast with the more customary one of the meek, submissive Pietà.

Christ's words in the eleventh section reinforce the tonic key as he cries out to God the Father: "why do you abandon me, alas?" ("perche mi lasci, ohimè?"). The paraliturgical context for this cantata offered the opportunity

[17] For a transcription of the *Aria vivace* see Fontijn, "The Virgin's Voice," 145.

to dwell on the sentiments of Mary as no biblical text does. The slurred paired notes of Christ's beseeching render a powerful sighing effect that drives home the very real fear of mother and son: knowing that his crucifixion meant his death, did they also know of his resurrection? While the deaths in the secular cantatas and arias seen thus far assured the possibility of some kind of salvation, the passion scene of the Savior's mortal ending offers no such hope; the composer froze the frame on the scene of death alone.

The assurance of Christ's salvation lends strong hope and faith to the third *cantata spirituale*, "Martirio di Santa Regina," as Reine battles against her oppressor, the tyrant Olybrius (table 3.3). Reine's father, Clement, a non-Christian of the Burgundian town of Alise, had given her to another woman to raise after her mother died in childbirth.[18] By the time that she reached maturity, she had become a Christian and chose to live as a shepherdess. Her father scorned her choice until Olybrius, a local governor, asked for her hand in marriage. Because she refused his proposal, she was thrown into a dungeon and tortured. The night before her beheading, she had a vision of the cross and of her deliverance; to the astonishment of the spectators just before her public execution, they beheld a shining dove above her, leading many to convert to Christianity.

The straightforward terms *Aria* appear in sections 2 and 8, and *Recitativo* in sections 3, 10, and 13, but imaginative adjectives modify the labels of sections 4–7: *Aria spiritosa, Aria violente, R[ecitativ]o con forza,* and *R[ecitativ]o affett[uos]o.* The expressive rubrics devised for those movements show the degree of further sophistication with which Bembo infused the genre, revealing her flair for dramatic text setting as a composer living in France; such rubrics reappear extensively in the *tragedia, L'Ercole amante.* As in the "Lament of the Virgin," the protagonist speaks in the penultimate section. In the *Aria Adagio e affettuoso,* Reine beseeches Christ in smooth, slurred phrases—"dear spouse," "caro sposo"—to save her in her dying moments, as had Christ himself when he pleaded for God to come to his aid and to comfort his mother. Reine's steadfast confidence in Christ contrasts markedly with the precarious Passion scene of the crucifixion. Her faith and courage stem from the assurance that she will be saved from cruelty by succumbing to her martyrdom.

Bembo's sacred cantatas cast the spiritual quest from a female perspective as Mary and Reine take center stage in each dramatic situation; Olybrius and Christ assume bit roles next to these formidable women. Mary's triumph as the progenitor of Christ, her anger and outrage at his loss, and Reine's defiance offer a wide range of emotion to the powerful female protagonists. With

---

[18] Saint Reine's story is told in Donald Attwater and Herbert Thurston, S.J., eds. *Butler's Lives of the Saints* (New York: P. J. Kenedy & Sons, 1956), 3: 500–501, and in the *Petit Larousse illustré* (Paris: Larousse, 1976), 1572. Claude Boillon notes a resurgence of interest in Reine during the late seventeenth century; see *Bibliotheca Sanctorum,* s.v. "Regina" (Rome: Città Nuova Editrice, 1968), 11: 71–72.

TABLE 3.3 Analysis of *Produzioni armoniche*, no. 7, "Martirio di Santa Regina"

Character	Rubric	Key	Action
1. Narrator	—	B	Purity vs. impurity
2. Narrator	Aria	B	Reine taken prisoner
3. Narrator	Recitativo	A	Introduces Reine
4. Reine	Aria spiritosa	A	Sings of courage and faith
5. Reine	Aria violente	A	Challenges Olybrius
6. Reine	R[ecitativ]o con forza	A–D	Faith in eternal life
7. Narrator	R[ecitativ]o affett[uos]o	f#	Reine's torture/introduction
8. Reine	Aria	f#	Reine impervious to suffering
9. Reine	—	D	The instruments of torture
10. Olybrius/ Narrator	Rec[i]t[ativ]o	a–A	Olybrius's torture; moral offered
11. Narrator	Affettuoso	A–e	Introduces Reine's last words
12. Reine	Aria Adagio e affettuoso	E	Reine's address to Christ
13. Narrator	R[ecitativ]o	E–b	Reine received into heaven

the exception of the *Stabat Mater,* crucifixion stories rarely focus on the pain suffered by Mary; the poem's paraliturgical concern reflects a point of view troped into the biblical settings that more typically focus on the male figures of the Trinity.

While nos. 5 and 6 could conceivably date from Bembo's Venetian years, no. 7's dwelling on a minor French saint represents a selection made by one situated in France with a mission to further French Catholicism. Her casting of the French saint's tale in Italian and in first-person vocal narrative style make it a most unusual work within a set of pieces already quite different from the music produced in Paris at the time. Moreover, no. 7 furthered one of the goals of the Petite Union Chrétienne: to protect girls who had adopted the Catholic faith against the will of their families. In 1697 such sacred cantatas meshed nicely with the growing corpus of *cantiques spirituels* in France, which reflected Louis XIV's growing piety under the influence of Madame de Maintenon. The Italian cantata was soon to bear fruit in France; by the early eighteenth century, composers such as La Guerre would devote entire published books to cantatas on religious themes. Although Bembo's influence on this trend cannot be assumed, these works appear to pre-date French efforts taken with the genre of the sacred cantata.

Lovers' Song

Arias on amorous texts constitute the majority of works in *Produzioni armoniche,* with just under half titled as *Aria* (nos. 17–18, 22–23, 25, 28–32) or some modification thereof (nos. 16, 19–21, 24, 26–27, 34, 36, 41). With few exceptions, the anonymous *poesie per musica* concern unrequited or problematic love, a theme common to the period and also shared by the three poems attributed to Aurelia Fedeli. Composers of seventeenth-century vocal chamber works tended to follow the exigencies of the texts in which the poet determined the type of music that would result from a given form; Monteverdi's *seconda prattica* ideal—the domination of words over music—reigned supreme. Closed forms required an aria, while prose phrases resulted in arioso- or recitative-style musical settings.[19] The analyses presented here follow Bembo's designations and define short sectional works as arias, like "Habbi pietà di me," and longer pieces with more sections as cantatas, like "Clizia amante del sole." Unlike Strozzi, Bembo did not use the word cantata, but with "aria" she intended a short single- or multi-sectioned work on an amorous subject, without distinction as to the formal procedure used within. Strozzi's op. 7 offers a likely model for considering Bembo's works as large (*cantate*) or small (*ariette*). A pattern emerges from examining the pieces with aria titles in the collection: interdependent sections linked together appear in the sectional aria (nos. 19, 23, 30); in the binary aria (nos. 21, 24–25, 29, 31–32, 36) the B section balances the A section; and in the da capo aria (nos. 16, 20, 26–27), the B section returns both textually and musically to the beginning. Repetition weaves a constant message through both refrain (nos. 18, 22, 28, 33–34, 41) and sectional arias.

In her study of *Produzioni armoniche,* Marinella Laini found several distinctions between pieces and identified two types of cantatas: "cantate spirituali" and cantatas either of a "lirico-amoroso" (lyrico-amorous) or of an "encomiastico" (encomium) variety.[20] She grouped the arias into two large categories: (1) monostrophic ariettas within a cantata and (2) self-standing arias with an articulated formal structure. She also distinguished among the three types within the second group: da capo arias, binary arias (the most numerous), and arias in rondo form. These analytical guidelines serve as a point of departure for the present interpretations, which posit more groupings based on the recent archival and biographical corroboration of the manuscript. Ellen Rosand identified "such terms as arioso, mezz'aria, and arietta . . . to distinguish between lyrical passages that are integrated within recitative, short arias that are musically undeveloped, and light 'singsong' arias

---

[19] See Carolyn Gianturco, "The Italian Seventeenth-Century Cantata: A Textual Approach," in *The Well-Enchanting Skill: Music, Poetry, and Drama in the Culture of the Renaissance,* ed. John Caldwell, Edward Olleson, and Susan Wollenberg (Oxford: Clarendon Press, 1990), 48. Gianturco cited a similar argument by Gary Tomlinson in his "Music and the Claims of Text," *Critical Inquiry* 8 (1981–1982): 565–589.

[20] Laini, "Le 'Produzioni Armoniche,'" 89–98. Guides for genre classification also include Eleanor Caluori, *The Cantatas of Luigi Rossi* (Ann Arbor: UMI Research Press, 1981), and Robert Rau Holzer, "Music and Poetry in Seventeenth-Century Rome: Settings of the Canzonetta and Cantata Texts of Francesco Balducci, Domenico Benigni, Francesco Melosio, and Antonio Abati" (Ph.D. diss., University of Pennsylvania, 1990).

that are based on strongly metrical texts."[21] These terms serve to describe vocal passages midway between the metrical regularity of the aria and the speaking quality of the recitative.

Typical of the sectional aria, in no. 30, "Passan veloci l'ore," the word *Aria* functions simultaneously in the manuscript as a marker for the first section and as a title (CD tr. 5). Three more sections follow: *Aria affettuoso* (B), *Recitativo* (C), and an undesignated concluding portion borrowed as a fragment from the opening material (A¹), yielding the composite formula: ABCA¹. The first couplet of the initial four-line stanza returns foreshortened at the end (A¹), dovetailing with a rhyme identical to the recitative (C).

Aria (A)
Passan veloci l'ore (a)   The hours go by quickly
e pur quella non v'è (b)   and yet that hour does not arrive
che mi discopra, oimè, (b)   which will unveil for me, alas,
del bel idolo mio l'almo splendore. (a)   the pure splendor of my beautiful idol.

Aria affettuoso (B)
Dura pena è l'aspettar   Harshly painful is the waiting
quel diletto che non giunge.   for pleasure that does not materialize.
Mel figuro in vaneggiar   I imagine it in my dreaming
da vicino allor ch'è longe.   as near although it is far.

Recitativo (C)
O sciocca vanità di chi ha trafitto il   O foolish vanity of one whose heart
    core (a)   is wounded
e catenato il piè: (b)   and whose foot is chained:

(A¹)
passan veloci l'ore (a)   the hours go by quickly
e pur quella non v'è. (b)   and yet that hour does not arrive.

The aria encapsulates a brief, self-contained dramatic moment. A woman in love counts the hours until her beloved is to arrive, but he never does. An abrupt, quirky rhythmic figure brings the continuo and voice in on a syncopation, a clever metaphor for the initial message regarding time. A trill enhances the elegant ornamental flourish of the phrase as the hours fly by in a thirty-second-note madrigalism (ex. 3.10). A particularly noteworthy effect here accompanies the line "Dura pena è l'aspettar" ("Harshly painful is the waiting") in the *Aria affettuoso* (B section). The descending arpeggiated basso ostinato pattern undergirds the sentiment of the lover, held in musical stasis;

---

[21] Ellen Rosand, *Opera in Seventeenth-Century Venice: The Creation of a Genre* (Berkeley: University of California Press, 1991), 279–280.

Example 3.10   F-Pn, Rés. Vm^{1}117, no. 30, mm. 1–2

Pas - san ve -lo - - ci l'o - re,   e pur

The hours go by quickly, and yet that hour [does not arrive]

the slow motion here contrasts with the quick passage of time in the previous section. On the recording, an improvised, interpolated violin line strengthens the longing affect, followed by a repetition for voice and violin together. In the brief recitative that follows, the lover acknowledges her own folly. The sectional aria's conclusion in the home key offers a partial return of the initial phrase to reinforce the message, both textually and tonally. The encapsulation of the main ideas—time passes too quickly without bringing satisfaction—becomes the moral of the story as the clever phrase is cut short to leave the listener to imagine what may follow. In general, the other amorous arias share the statement of a moral that can be offered either in a poignant return to initial material or in a new final twist of text and music.

No. 23, "Volgete altrove il guardo," like "Passan veloci l'ore," features a return to the initial message and music of the A section, but compressed, concluding with a restatement of the initial couplet. Developing variations for the A section typify many of the aria settings: new keys, ornaments, new turns of phrase, and transpositions of melodic order in the vocal or basso continuo phrases. This aria's formal scheme thus emerges as A^{1}A^{2}A^1 / B^{1}B^{2}B^3 B^{2}B^3 / A^1:

A^1	Volgete altrove il guardo (7)	Look somewhere else,
	occhi di basilisco (7)	basilisk eyes;
A^2	mirar più non ardisco (7)	I don't dare to look any longer
	quel lampo onde tutt'ardo. (7)	at that light for which I burn with passion.
B^1	Per tragica sorte (6)	By tragic fate,
	mi scese nel seno (6)	your poison
	il vostro veleno (6)	entered my breast
	a darmi la morte. (6)	to kill me.
B^2	E dall' arco d'un ciglio esce quel dardo (11)	And from the arch of an eyebrow an arrow comes out
B^3	per cui, trafitto il cor, manco e languisco. (11)	by which, with pierced heart, I faint and languish.
A^1	Volgete altrove il guardo (7)	Look somewhere else,
	occhi di basilisco. (7)	basilisk eyes.

Inverted in the manuscript, 6/8 meter marks the time for the A sections, while the B sections move fluidly from common time to triple meter, written correctly as 3/8 and 3/4. Unlike "Passan veloci l'ore," no double bars delineate the sections; instead, poetic scansion determines the musical setting: eighth notes for *senari* and *settenari* (seven-syllable lines) and quarters for the longer *endecasillabi*. The theme of the aria explores treacherous love by comparison to the fatal glance and breath of the basilisk, a legendary reptile.[22] In Venetian dialect, a basilisk (rendered as *basalisco*) connotes negatively as it signifies a bestial, unkind, and therefore monstrous man.

The designation of refrain aria describes pieces that use a refrain in whole or in part: nos. 22 and 28 employ refrains at the beginning, middle, and end of the piece, while nos. 33–34 abandon the final refrain in order to conclude with a new idea suggesting a solution to the problem posed by the refrain subject. The refrain aria clearly appealed to the composer, who also employed it in no. 18, one of her settings of Fedeli's poetry, and in the French *Air* (no. 41).

The arias no. 22, "Mi basta così," and no. 28, "Prendete la porta," both feature a sturdy refrain (A) that frames the inner sections (B and C) with some tonal modifications (A^1 or A^2), yielding ABA^1CA^2 as the formal scheme for both. "Mi basta così" harks back to Venetian practices of the 1650s (ex. A.1)[23] and offers several striking points of similarity with Strozzi's "Basta così" from op. 7.[24] In the A section refrains, the b.c. features an accompanimental basso ostinato figure with scalar sixteenth notes in 12/8 meter (inverted as 8/12 in the manuscript), while the voice interjects several times with the phrase, "Mi basta così" ("I've had enough"). Tellingly, each of the four statements of that phrase in the refrain coincides with the cadential point of the b.c., tonic-dominant-tonic-dominant (mm. 1–2, 3, 4, 5–6). The B and C sections use motto technique to provide an imitative equal texture between the two parts and to elucidate the meaning of the refrain through *senari* set to music in triple meter (3/8). In the B section the couplet "Deluso, schernito (6)/Ho troppo patito (6)" ("Disillusioned, mocked, I have suffered too much") reveals the problem as scorned love. Recalling the metaphoric basilisk of no. 23, wild animal similes intensify this aria: "I was like a mole, blind to my well-being, I was like a lynx, stalking my destruction" ("fui talpa al mio bene, fui lince al mio mal"). As if once again to thwart the lover's expectation, a de-

---

[22] For more about the basilisk, see Park and Daston, *Wonders*, 45 and 173. For the next sentence, see Boerio, *Dizionario*, s.v. "basalisco."

[23] Appendix 2, example 1; hereafter ex. A.1.

[24] *Diporti di Euterpe overo cantate e ariette a voce sola di Barbara Strozzi Opera Settima* (Venice: Francesco Magni, 1659; reprint, Archivum Musicum: La Cantata barocca 3. Florence: Studio per edizioni scelte, 1980), 129–137. See the facsimile of this particular *arietta* in Ellen Rosand, ed., *Cantatas by Barbara Strozzi, 1619–c. 1664*, The Italian Cantata in the Seventeenth Century 5 (New York: Garland, 1986), 189–193.

ceptive cadence in m. 46 underscores "mal," which only finds resolution in
m. 50 on "dì."

A comparison of the two arias "Basta così" and "Mi basta così" points
strongly to the possibility that Bembo composed hers, too, in Venice. The
two arias share poetic themes, characteristic *tronco* scansion, tonalities, similar
titles, and identical musical form. The table of contents to Strozzi's op. 7 as-
cribes all poems to various authors, many of them members of the academy
for which she sang. Attributed to "Signor Pellicani," Strozzi's poem concerns
avoiding dangerous love, summed up in a telling phrase from the C section:
"Amor so che cos'è: è bello, è buono, ma pur non fa per me" ("I know what
love is: it is beautiful, it is good, but not for me"). Although F major sounds
as the tonic key of Bembo's aria, its secondary tonal area explores the main
key of Strozzi's aria, G minor (mm. 42–50). Like Strozzi's, Bembo's refrains
are set in measures of four beats with B and C sections in triple time. The interjecting nature of Bembo's title phrase "mi basta così" resembles Strozzi's
short phrases from the refrain, "basta così, v'ho inteso," or the settings of
"è bello, è buono." This piece therefore points to a composition date prior to
Bembo's French years and suggests another musical tribute, along with no. 6,
to the role model of her youth.

The refrain for no. 28, "Prendete la porta," uses motto imitation between
continuo and voice instead of independent roles. While similar poetic scansion in both arias dictated 12/8 meter (both inverted in the manuscript), here
a *senario tronco* line joins two *senari piani* to halt phrases in the pattern 6–6–5,
such as in the opening B-flat major music: "Prendete la porta / volate pen-
sieri / su l'ali d'amor" ("Go out the door, / fly, thoughts, / on wings of love").
Such short line lengths characterize much *poesie per musica,* and Venetian
opera arias of the period also frequently employed this verse type.[25] The stock
pastoral character found in this aria, "Filli" (Phyllis) appears frequently in
Seicento poetry, such as in Francesco de Lemene's 1699 "Fillide sempre bella,"
as well as in Romagnesi's work.[26] In the C section, longer phrases introduce
the man who hopes that disdainful Phyllis will finally be moved to pity when
the lily and the rose announce the news of his death: "Spunta il giglio con la
rosa / per moverla a pietate / aure del mio morir Filli d'estate." The suicidal
lover's last-ditch attempt to attract the object of his affection recalls the nature imagery evoked in Clytie's tale. One of Romagnesi's poems contains a
phrase astonishingly close—also with the rose and the lily—to that of Bembo's aria: "già spunta la rosa, e 'l giglio."[27] Soon after Bembo's arrival in France,

[25] See Harris Saunders, "The Repertoire of a Venetian Opera House (1675–1714): The
Teatro Grimani di San Giovanni Grisostomo" (Ph.D. diss., Harvard University, 1985), 192.

[26] The poem appears in an anthology edited by Lucio Felici, *Poesia italiana del Seicento*
(Milan: Aldo Garzanti, 1978), 283–285; Romagnesi's references to "Filli" are found in *Poesie liriche,*
79, 273, 345, and 464.

[27] Romagnesi, *Poesie liriche,* 56.

Paolo Lorenzani—a fellow Italian expatriate—employed "Filli" as one of the protagonists in his opera *Nicandro e Fileno* (1681), set to a libretto by Philippe-Julien Mancini, duc de Nevers.[28]

The theme of deceitful love takes center stage in no. 33, "Anima perfida," applicable to any wronged lover as the genders remain ambiguous. As if to avenge the lover's annoyance and to be better heard, the singer spits out the repeated two-word phrase in frantic transpositions (CD tr. 6). In vain: the attentions of the beloved have turned elsewhere. The refrain repeats numerous times the first line of the text in a lilting, melancholic A-minor melody linked to the B and C sections through rhymed returns, such as "ar-dor" with *tronco* scansion in the B section, returning to "cor" in the A.

(A)	Anima perfida,	Treacherous soul,
	ingrato cor . . .	ungrateful heart; . . .

(B)	. . . nutrendo in petto	holding greater passion
	per altro oggetto	for someone else
	più vivo ardor.	in your heart.

"Anima perfida" recalls the way in which "Passan veloci l'ore" connected back to its beginning; the overall analysis yields the formula ABA^1CA^2D. Peace obtains only in the sequence of 7–6 resolutions in the B section, identifying jealousy as the source of the lover's wrath. The D section employs a metaphor in its final tercet, where the jilted lover becomes a "fiery ball" who bounces off cold "marble." Set in 6/8 meter, this section offers the moral to the story with a new rhyme scheme that inspired a highly virtuosic style replete with fierce melismatic madrigalism for emphasis on the word "rintuzzata":

(D)	Tal se palla infocata incontra	If, similarly, a fiery ball meets a
	un marmo	marble object,
	quando il marmo colpisce	when it hits the marble,
	vien rintuzzata e 'l feritor	it bounces back, and injures the
	ferisce.	injurer.

Rather than concluding with the more customary refrain, the singer rages in quickly moving sixteenth notes. A *petite reprise* driving home the vengeful message of the last line reveals one of the French mannerisms adopted by the composer.

The Petrarchan binaries conjured up by the images—fire/ice, hot/cold, moving/still—succinctly illustrate the differences in emotion between lover and beloved. The moral shows the desire for revenge against the treacherous

---

[28] Paolo Lorenzani, *Nicandro e Fileno,* ed. Albert La France (Versailles: Éditions du Centre de Musique Baroque, Société Française de Musicologie, 1999).

lover, in self-defense. Although unlabeled in the compilation, the piece shares its formal refrain procedure with the following *Aria a due;* neither piece specifies gender, but the two voices of the duet, no. 34, sing as woman (soprano) and man (bass). Set in C major, the duet consoles the sad lover for whom "beauty cannot be bought by weeping" ("Amanti a costo di pianti, non si compra la beltà"). The bass part contains figured b.c. indications and sports a two-octave range that equals the virtuosity of the soprano part found in most of the arias. The form foreshortens the formula of the preceding number: ABAC, where the C section contrasts with the playful nature of the preceding material and reveals the moral of the tale: "If I'm not mistaken, / golden keys open doors of iron" ("Ma s'io non erro, / apron le chiavi d'or porte di ferro"). Felicitous thirds close the piece in a great melisma that opens up the very vista offered by the word "porte." A noteworthy similarity to a phrase in Romagnesi's poetry suggests either the popularity of the phrase, or once again the mark of his work: "chi sa, se chiave d'or non apra un giorno le ferree porte."[29]

"Habbi pietà di me," no. 16 treated above, marks the first of the four da capo arias of *Produzioni armoniche.* These binary pieces exhibit the following characteristics: the phrase "da capo" is written into the score, as in nos. 16 and 27, or the poem's textual incipit written at the end of the second section indicates a return to the beginning, as in nos. 20 and 26. No. 20, "Amor mio," stands out as one of the gems of the collection, with its theme of amorous contentment atypical of the aria group. The duet delights in the joys of mutual love,[30] as two sopranos chortle in consonances of thirds and sixths, their vocality symbolizing their reciprocal love. A sensual touch of dissonant chromaticism appears in the B section as the voices curl up together in a "knot of love" ("nodo d'amor").

In thematic content nos. 26 ("S'è legge d'amore") and 27 ("Mi consolo") appear as a pair of da capo arias in the compilation. The first, an *Aria affettuosa* in C minor, mournfully wallows in the "law of love" that dictates suffering. Like "Habbi pietà di me," the A section presents the problem and the B section protests against it. The opening musical treatment illustrates emotional stasis through the repetition of the title phrase "If it is the law of love to make me suffer, take my heart and let me die" (ex. 3.11). A basso ostinato pattern (mm. 2–5) structures the A section with eight repetitions, the first three providing the original pattern that the last three modify, while the middle two repetitions move into a new tonality. The ostinato undergirds the

---

[29] Romagnesi, *Poesie liriche,* 245.

[30] For a complete analysis and a performing edition with continuo realization of the duet, see Claire Fontijn, "Antonia Bembo," in *Women Composers: Music Through the Ages,* ed. Martha Furman Schleifer and Sylvia Glickman (New York: G. K. Hall, 1996), 2: 201–216, which also includes nos. 39 and 41. The three works can also be obtained individually (Bryn Mawr, PA: Hildegard, 1998).

Example 3.11   F-Pn, Rés. Vm¹117, no. 26, mm. 1–5

S'è leg - ge d'a - mo - re__ di far - mi sof - frir,

If it is the law of love to make me suffer,

textual repetitions, mired in obsessive sadness. An aching major seventh chord indicated by the figured bass harmony holds the voice and b.c. together on a mutual half note on the verb *fare* (m. 4), resolved by the subsequent cadence. That dissonance recurs for each of the ostinato's eight statements, as if to intensify the lover's anguish. The depicted character only finds temporary solace in the raging of the B section, where he asks for death as comfort. A "tyrannical beauty" ("tiranna beltà") holds his life in the balance, but he cannot be saved: the da capo returns to the inevitability of suffering.

No. 27, the following *Aria allegra,* offers a poem of consolation, seemingly a rejoinder to the desperate sadness of the preceding da capo aria (CD tr. 7). The theme resembles the soprano–bass duet in refrain aria no. 34 as it offers comfort to the broken-hearted lover, who learns that "a thousand crowds of people in love . . . deafen the [earth's] Pole / with their sighing."[31] Clearly misery deserves such company. Motto procedure develops motivic fragments in both A and B sections. At the outset the soprano answers the continuo with a reversal of the scalar direction that continues with a lachrymal madrigalism in the home key of E major: "Mi consolo . . . non solo a lacrimar" ("I am comforted, I am not alone in my weeping"). Once again the B section provides a strong emotional outlet for the A, now in *parlando* style: "mille turbe innamorate / fra l'incendio e le catene, / disperando aver mai bene" ("a thousand crowds of people in love, / caught between passion and bondage, / despair that they will never find satisfaction").

Where the da capo arias all reinforce their A section through obligatory repetition and ornamentation, the binary arias provide a locus for the composer's written-out embellishment, with the important message found in the final section. *Produzioni armoniche* contains seven arias in which two halves balance and contrast with each other in some way: nos. 21, 24–25, 29, 31–32, and 36. The most explicit binary arias, nos. 25 and 31, use the label *Seconda* to designate the embellished second half, with a verse equal in length to the

---

[31] Here, too, a similar phrase is found in Romagnesi's *Poesie liriche:* "d'urli horendi assordar la Terra e 'l Polo" (393).

first. The practice also occurs in a section within a larger work, such as the "Lament of the Virgin" above. Nos. 21, 24, and 32 display similarly paired halves, but only the first of these exhibits identical verse length and poetic scansion (a tacit *Seconda* designation). Nos. 29 and 36 repeat the first half with new material (A and A^1) before the second half of the poem. Formal considerations were determined by the poet and appear to have no bearing on the adjectives used to describe the mood of the aria, its subject matter, or the gender narrating the piece. Like the preceding arias, these poems explore from many points of view the dangers (and delights) of love and may suggest yet another Romagnesi–Bembo collaboration.

The arias labeled *Aria-Seconda* both feature a male narrator who expresses his love for a beautiful woman: in no. 25, Phyllis, the pastoral character encountered in the refrain aria no. 28 and, in no. 31, a Siren. In both cases, the love goes unrequited. The first stanza presents the problem (love's treachery) for which the second offers a solution (relief brought by death), and the two resulting parts complement each other with similar music. In the case of no. 31, "Beata sirena," the music for the two halves is largely identical and the piece operates as a strophic aria based on quasi-parallel poetic scansion; the penultimate line of the *Seconda* section offers a *tronco* halt on the word "dir":

Beata sirena,	Beautiful siren,
deh frena	o stop
gli accenti canori,	your singing;
e se fai preda de cori	and if you make prey of hearts
il mio lascia in libertà	leave mine in freedom;
uccider chi t'adora è crudeltà.	it is cruel to kill the one who adores you.

Seconda	
Se parli, se canti, m'incanti,	If you talk, if you sing, you enchant
quest'alma in petto	this soul in my breast,
è sì grand'il mio diletto	and my delight is so great
che la lingua nol può dir[e]	that the tongue cannot express it;
e pur canti l'essequie al mio morir.[32]	even so, sing obsequies at my death.

The second half thereby necessitated writing out, unlike the strophic superimposition of numbered stanzas found in cantata no. 2 (ex. 3.5), there somewhat to the detriment of the musical line. The aria's poetic themes of voice versus silence recall the conflict explored in the biographical set of encomia.

The fourteen-line verse set to music in the *Aria* "Di bell'ire accesi i sguardi" (no. 25) suggests the form of sonnet no. 1, which scanned in *ende-*

---

[32] Romagnesi's phrase "fanno essequie al mio gioire . . . la sentenza al mio morire" sounds very similar to the final line of this poem (*Poesie liriche*, 207).

Example 3.12   F-Pn, Rés. Vm¹117, no. 25, mm. 1 and 28

With beautiful anger lighting her looks...
If, due to contempt, [her face glares with lively] passion,

casillabi. Here, the scansion is irregular between the *Aria* and *Seconda* halves, which are divided into a quatrain and a tercet. Again, the word *Aria* functions simultaneously as title and as designation for the first half of the binary structure. The term *Seconda*—as used in cantata no. 6 and binary arias nos. 25 and 31—signals a variety of embellishments for the second of the two paired verses. In the second half of her binary arias, Bembo often developed a procedure used in the first. No. 25 provides a good example: where the soprano had introduced the rising fifth in the first part in common time, now the bass begins on the falling fifth, inverting it and placing it in a new meter (inverted as 8/6 in the manuscript) (ex. 3.12).

Both halves of the short aria "M'ingannasti in verità," no. 32, use a motto phrase initiated by the b.c. and repeated by the voice (CD tr. 8). The A section repeats that motto obsessively, delighting in the rhymes between "dispietato" and "ingrato." With its high tessitura, paired sixteenth notes, and quick tempo, the B section requires virtuosic singing.

Bembo's arias in particular display her magnificent vocal talent. The ornamented refrains found in such arias as "Anima perfida" and "Mi basta così" offer tonal transpositions and new turns of phrase for the opening material, but the binary aria "Chi desia viver in pace" goes beyond such ornamentation to offer variations as worthy as examples of the art of vocal embellishment as those found in contemporary theoretical treatises (ex. 3.13). Performance practice of the da capo aria essentially dictates that ornamentation must be added at the return of the A section, tacitly requiring improvisatory skill and virtuosity of the singer. The decorated A¹ section of no. 36 participates in efforts to prepare the way for such eighteenth-century conventions in chamber music and in opera. Akin to the Seicento strophic variation form in which the bass repeats the original material while the voice offers variation, the *Aria Allegro* "Chi desia viver in pace" decorates and transforms the bass in order to match the variation of the soprano and alter the harmonic progressions, with the formula AA¹B.[33]

[33] Rose, "Italian Cantata": "strophic variations, i.e. each strophe is set to the same or a slightly modified bass, over which the melody varies" (656).

Example 3.13   F-Pn, Rés. Vm¹117, no. 36, mm. 1–5, 38–40

Whoever wishes to live in peace should follow the path of love

Bembo tended to favor the introduction of the motive in the bass, and then to have the soprano imitate it, either in part or in entirety. In the first part of "Chi desia viver in pace," a motive appears first in the b.c. of the A section in 3/4 (m. 1), while the variation in the A¹ section begins with both the b.c. and soprano in simultaneous entrances in contrasting common time (m. 38). The embellishment of the A¹ section is effected through melodic intensification, with filled-in intervals and added ornaments, as well as through a metric shift allowing longer phrases. The ingenious manipulation of the original material results in a transformation from the motto procedure of the A section to the elaboration of both parts in contrapuntal style in the A¹, where a turn figure adorns and elongates the a¹ of the opening phrase and a correspondingly varied bass line proceeds simultaneously with the soprano. The A¹ section expands the tonality of D minor with a passage in the relative major that will cadence in the tonic at m. 48. The words "ove brilla" are set syllabically in the A section (mm. 15–16), while the A¹ section transforms them into a melismatic escapade (mm. 48–49) in both parts, wherein the b.c. borrows the f–c¹–f¹ pattern from mm. 15–16 and accelerates it by diminution. Alone, the b.c. winds down these vigorous passages, using the same motives as when it was simply an accompaniment, and cadences with a falling octave in m. 60 that brings the first half of the poem to a dramatic and virtuosic close. The B section restores the relative calm of constant love following the uncertainty of stormy passions as described in the A section, thereafter returning to 3/2 with a textual repetition.

The secular arias analyzed here demonstrate a great variety in symmetry and motivic procedure. Gianturco's poetic basis for analysis shows clearly that verse dictated its musical setting but that there existed much room for variety within those parameters. The number of coincidental phrases between Romagnesi's and Bembo's work points to the supposition that he authored the verse used here and possessed the type of sensitivity to musical forms required for the singer, or that she imitated his poetry. If he one day proves to have been the author of Bembo's anonymous poetry, *Produzioni armoniche* would hold the distinction as a unique site for the collaboration of mother—Aurelia Fedeli—and son.

The three poems ascribed to Aurelia Fedeli by the table of contents at the end of *Produzioni armoniche,* nos. 17–19, provide the only outright designation of authorship of verse in Bembo's entire œuvre (fig. 2.5). As in her son's work, Fedeli's two published books feature quantities of such *poesie per musica.*[34] The poetry and the music of nos. 17–19 may represent a collaborative effort between Fedeli and Bembo, for this manuscript appears to contain their only musical settings and unique source of transmission. Perhaps following her collaboration with the actress's son Romagnesi, Bembo asked Fedeli for poetry to set to music, knowing that it was her specialty. The poetry reflects the continuing creative output of the actress, who had retired from the stage in the 1680s. Indeed, a great deal of evidence posits Bembo's close tie to the Romagnesi-Fedeli family in Paris.

In keeping with much of Fedeli's published poetry, the three arias treat amorous problems. The first two are scored for soprano and b.c., and the third for a soprano and tenor with the figured bass doubling the tenor.[35] The duet offers three performance options: a vocal duet with the b.c. line doubled, a cappella, or an aria for soprano with instrumental accompaniment. The transcription in example A.3 omits the b.c. figures in the tenor part—the second option.

No. 17, "In amor ci vuol ardir," bears the following message: "One must be daring in love; banish fear from your heart forever if you desire it." Edited as part of a singer's anthology, the aria resembles an étude as it presents a virtual *moto perpetuo* of triplet sixteenths throughout. The challenge to the singer, in fact, matches the very message of the piece: dare! The piece is anomalous within the group of arias, as it delivers the poem's four lines in a straightforward, through-composed manner.

A jilted woman narrates no. 18 with a repetitive question: "What's wrong, o God, what's wrong?" ("E ch'avete, o Dio, ch'avete?") (ex. A.2). She attempts to provoke her stoic lover through repeated refrains, but all in vain. Even if

---

[34] Brigida Bianchi, Comica detta Aurelia, *L'inganno fortunato,* and Aurelia Fedeli, *I rifiuti di Pindo.*

[35] No. 17 appears in the anthology *Italian Arias of the Baroque and Classical Eras,* ed. John Glenn Paton (Van Nuys, CA: Alfred, 1994), 55–59. Nos. 18 and 19 are published for the first time in exx. A.2 and 3.

the setting yields a playful affect, the protagonist's anger recalls the strong emotional responses of other hurt women in Bembo's output, secular and sacred alike, such as the Virgin Mary, Reine, and the lover of the "basilisk." The framing structure of the refrain (mm. 7–9, 18–20, 28–32) resembles "Mi basta così" and "Prendete la porta," and its charming variations poke fun at a woman's alleged propensity to nag for attention—in every way a woman's song.

No. 19, the duet for soprano and tenor (ex. A.3), has a notable syllabic text setting, which it shares with the other duets discussed above (nos. 4, 20, 34). The tenor imitates the soprano, sometimes rhyming on words uttered simultaneously, such as in mm. 25–26: "spietati" ("deceitful") and "ingrati" ("thankless"). The theme offers a fitting conclusion to the set, for here Fedeli expounded on the unpredictable nature of love, underscored by the music's several metric shifts. In the first poem, Fedeli suggested that one be bold to find love, in the second she showed what happens once under its spell, and in this one—in rational retrospect—she warned to be careful. Placed together, the group forms a miniature cycle, a kind of before, during, and after vignette of an amorous encounter. The very close nature of the anonymous poetry and Fedeli's verse strengthens the supposition of Romagnesi's pen at work. At any rate, the *poesie per musica* produced in France bear many of the marks of their native culture and provide an abundance of exquisite musical settings.

French-style Works

Whereas the Italian works testify to the composer's skill in setting her own language to music, two layers of pieces in *Produzioni armoniche* show the influence of the French soundscape. The Latin *petits motets* nos. 3–4 and 38–40 fit French paraliturgical practice and no. 41, the *Air* "Ha, que l'absence," joins the tradition of popular urban song in Paris at the turn of the eighteenth century. The manuscript's final piece and its sole one in French, the *Air* follows the musical and textual lines of the *airs sérieux et à boire*. Starting in 1679, the printer Christophe Ballard published annual collections known as *Recueils* as a continuation of the *air de cour* tradition, which dated back to the previous century. Women composers began making contributions to the genre in 1694, when the *Recueils* increased to a monthly production rate.[36] Although never published by Ballard, Bembo's "Ha, que l'absence" belongs to the genre of *airs sérieux*.[37] It contains two quatrains, stanzas A and B, in rhyming couplets:

---

[36] See James R. Anthony, *French Baroque Music, from Beaujoyeulx to Rameau,* rev. and expanded ed. (Portland, OR: Amadeus Press, 1997), 418. See also Fontijn, "Antonia Bembo," chapter 3.

[37] See Claire Fontijn, ed., *Ha, que l'absence* (Bryn Mawr, PA: Hildegard, 1998).

(A)

Ha, que l'absence est un cruel martire, (a)	Ah, absence is a cruel martyrdom,
lorsqu'on aime tendrement (b)	when one loves tenderly
un objet tout charmant (b)	a charming object
et qu'on ne l'ose dire. (a)	and one does not dare say so.

(B)

L'on se plaint, l'on soupire, (a)	One complains, one sighs,
l'on chéri le tourment; (b)	one cherishes the torment;
et l'amour nous inspire (a)	and love inspires us
de répéter souvent: (b)	often to repeat:
Ha, que l'absence est un cruel martire. (a)	Ah, absence is a cruel martyrdom.

The appearance of the "a" rhyme at the end of stanza B marks a return to the beginning, where the text literally "inspires . . . to *repeat*" it and thereby acts as a refrain.

While form applies to any language, vocal style depends on a particular tongue. Bembo accordingly imbued her *Air* with French mannerism throughout: ornamentation (*tremblement mou* in mm. 6–7, *tremblement appuyé* in m. 11), rubric ("doucement" marked above the last three-measure phrase for a true *petite reprise*), highly contrapuntal texture, and largely conjunct melodic writing.[38] An air published in one of Ballard's *Recueils* by one of the Parisian women composers, a certain "Mademoiselle H.," offers a basis for confirming the French nature of Bembo's *Air* (ex. A.4). Both address the subject of the pain of distant love with an initial outcry ("Ah!" or "Ha!") that echoes the Italian arias in *Produzioni armoniche:* unrequited love. Unlike the neutral narrator of Bembo's poem, a lover too shy to declare passion to the beloved, that of Mademoiselle H. presents the plaint of a male lover who pines away for unkind Iris, thoroughly unresponsive to his passions:

Ah! n'est-ce pas assez de maux que j'ai soufferts? (a)	Ah! Have I not suffered enough?
Malgré la rigueur de mes fers, (a)	Despite the rigor of my chains,
Iris, absent de vous, (b)	away from you, Iris,
ma flame fût constante. (c)	my flame has been constant.
Vostre retour! helas! pour moy n'est pas plus doux; (b)	Your return! alas! it is no better for me,
cruelle, je ne vis que dans la triste attente (c)	cruel one, I live only in sad expectation
de mourir plus près de vous. (b)	to die closer to you.

---

[38] Saint-Arroman, *L'Interprétation de la musique française,* 400–401.

Even if the poems employ different rhyme schemes and scansion, both present their initial gambits within a classic alexandrine (twelve-syllable line). Both pit masculine endings against feminine endings—"fers" / "constante" in Mademoiselle H. and "tourment" / "inspire" in Bembo—with their musical settings closely hewn to the French accent. The two airs both function within A minor, touching on the dominant at midpoint. The smooth, conjunct motion of Mademoiselle H.'s air (mm. 3–5, 7–10, 13–15, last three bars) recalls that of Bembo's (mm. 1, 3–7, 8–10, 12–13, last three bars, with *petite reprise*). Mademoiselle H.'s despondent falling sevenths in the final measures on "mourir" work madrigalistically in the same vein as Bembo's falling tritone on "cruel" at the identical penultimate juncture. The pieces share many such characteristics, and their comparison shows the extent to which the composer adapted to the local popular culture.[39]

A mixture of French and Italian styles—"the united tastes," as François Couperin (1668–1733) would call them in *Les Goûts-réünis* of 1724—became characteristic for Bembo's settings of French and Latin texts alike. Example A.5, an instrumental duet from a work of Couperin's from the following year, pits the French style of Jean-Baptiste Lully (1632–1687) in the upper line against the Italian style of Arcangelo Corelli (1653–1713) in the accompanying line for the first air, and vice versa for the second. Conjunct motion typifies the French style here and ornamentation often serves to connect main notes through stepwise motion (such as in the first two systems of Lully's *Air léger*, where a series of falling triadic *tierce coulées* follow the initial *port de voix* in mm. 4–6). Corelli's *Second Air*, by contrast, is distinctive in its quirky, harmonically daring intervallic leaps in the initial measures, and the arpeggiated quality of the second half mirrors that of Corelli's accompaniment to Lully's *Air léger*. Significantly, the melancholic minor mode of the French air contrasts with the vivacious major mode of the Italian.

Bembo's *Air* offers a standard against which the Gallic nature of the collection's five *petits motets* might be measured. A second setting of "Domine salvum fac regem," no. 40, appears as the last of the group of three *petits motets* for soprano and continuo included at the end of the compilation. The analysis of the first such setting, no. 4 for two sopranos and continuo, adjoined the opening group of encomia for the king (ex. 3.6). Conceived in the exuberant key of C major, no. 40 offers a quasi-da capo form that restates part of the initial material (ABA'). The quick, sprightly triple movement of the A section in tonic (ex. 3.14) contrasts with the slower duple meter of the B section, which moves into D minor (mm. 39–42); the A' section closes the

---

[39] For more about poetic voice in airs at the turn of the century, see Catherine E. Gordon-Seifert, "Strong Men—Weak Women: Gender Representation and the Influence of Lully's 'Operatic Style' on French *Airs Sérieux* (1650–1700)," in *Musical Voices of Early Modern Women—Many-Headed Melodies*, ed. Thomasin La May (Aldershot, U.K.: Ashgate, 2005), 144, 154.

Example 3.14 F-Pn, Rés. Vm¹117, no. 40, mm. 1–9, 39–42

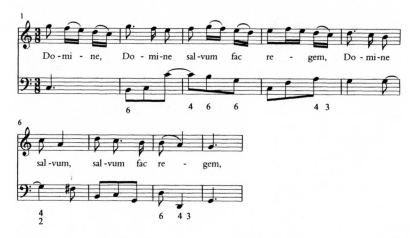

O Lord, save the king:

and hear us in the day that we shall call upon you.

motet with a return to the tonic key. Both settings of "Domine salvum fac regem" feature the French characteristics of pervasive counterpoint and, except for the triadic profile of the imitative material in no. 4, largely conjunct motion.

A useful comparison can be made with a setting of the same text from a *petit motet* scored for three sopranos and b.c. by Lully, the naturalized composer considered the epitome of French style at the time of Bembo's arrival in Paris.[40] Contrasts differentiate the first and second halves of the poem:

[40] *Mottets de feu Mr. de Lully* (Béziers: Société de Musicologie de Languedoc, n.d.), a facsimile of F-Pn, Rés. F. 668.

Example 3.15   Lully, *Domine salvum fac regem*, LWV 77/iv, mm. 32–37

...save the king: and hear us in the day...

"Domine salvum" in triple meter, "et exaudi nos" in duple (ex. 3.15). No. 40 takes the same strategy, while no. 4 employs thematic rather than metric contrast. In keeping with the French cadential practice of setting a feminine rhyme to music, the first syllable of Lully's "regem" (mm. 34–35) consistently receives emphasis with a longer note than the second syllable, apparently serving as a model for Bembo's motet no. 40 (mm. 8–9). While both of Bembo's "Domine salvum fac regem" motets suggest some knowledge of Lully's *petit motets,* no. 40 especially signals her conscious assumption of French style. A study of settings of the phrase "salvum fac regem" by Jean-Paul Montagnier confirms this typical French accentuation of the Latin phrase in motets by the composers Du Mont, Bernier, Nivers, and Lalande, also following the work of Lully. Montagnier drew upon Patricia Ranum's method of Latin *à la française* to note distinctions drawn at the time between French settings: those of traditional psalmody and those of the grammarians.[41]

Given that Bembo expressed her fervent wishes for the preservation of Louis XIV's kingdom throughout *Produzioni armoniche,* it comes as no surprise to find at its conclusion a second setting of this common prayer. This text comes from the final verse of Psalm 20, *Exaudiat te, Dominus,* which she later set in its entirety. Bembo quoted the final couplet of the vocal line for no. 2, "chi dà quanto può, dà quanto deve." The conscious strand of connections within and without *Produzioni armoniche* serve as a key to understanding the composer's oeuvre and her sense of obligation to the French royal family.

The elevation motet "Panis Angelicus," no. 38, also uses contrasting musical ideas for the two halves of the poem: in the first half, the soprano sings of transubstantiation ("the bread of angels becomes the bread of humankind;

[41] Jean-Paul Montagnier, "Modèles chorégraphiques dans les grands et petits motets français," in *Le Mouvement en musique à l'époque baroque,* ed. Hervé Lacombe (Metz: Éditions Serpenoise, 1996), 149–151. See, too, Patricia M. Ranum, *Méthode de la prononciation latine dite 'vulgaire' ou 'à la française'* (Arles: Actes Sud, 1991).

heavenly bread gives divine purpose to its form"), while in the second the b.c. assumes a walking bass over which the voice extols the miraculous nature of the Eucharist—with literally "elevating" lines—that fortifies the humble during Communion: "O miracle! The poor humble servant partakes of Our Lord." Cast in A minor, two mellifluous chromatic phrases adorn "pauper servus et humilis" and outline the span of an octave climbing up two consecutive tetrachords. A madrigalism depicts the servant's lowly status as the line drops a sixth on the word "humble," and an expressive French trill, a *tremblement mou,* extends the *b¹* in m. 32.[42] Such elongated cadential notes for the singer recur frequently in Bembo's corpus of works, signaling obligatory ornamentation.

The through-composed *petit motet* no. 39, "Tota pulcra es," bears an ambiguous notation in its final bar. In editing the piece, I provided a *petite reprise* to the final three measures with a dal segno marking, but it would also be possible to return to the beginning for a complete repeat.[43] The motet presents a five-line verse derived from the Song of Solomon (4: 7, 8, and 11). The rough nature of the Latin suggests that Bembo may have adapted the verse fragments herself; the somewhat ungrammatical phrases of no. 3 might also be explained in this way. Conjunct motion once again suggests the piece's conception in French style, with a walking bass characterizing the continuo part. The walking bass not only recalls the second section of the preceding motet but also the manner in which Couperin devised Lully's accompaniment of Corelli in the *Second Air* (ex. A.5).[44]

Bembo's models for the French style included her contemporaries: La Guerre, contributors to the Ballard *Recueils,* Lully, Charpentier, and Lalande. The two model French pieces cited here both post-date her work, yet they provide a standard against which to gauge the style and her contribution to its coalescence with Italian practice.

The Wedding of the Duke and Duchess of Burgundy

In three pieces of *Produzioni armoniche* Bembo lavished her attention upon the arrival in France of the Savoyard princess Marie-Adélaïde (1685–1712) for her wedding to Louis, Duke of Burgundy (1681–1712). Two of the pieces, a can-

---

[42] See Saint-Arroman, *L'Interprétation de la musique française,* 421, whose example of the *tremblement mou* comes from François Couperin's *Leçons de Ténèbres;* it was not usually indicated in the music (the interpreter must select where to place it), but occurs on the mediant in the minor key in pieces of plaintive affect.

[43] Claire Fontijn, ed., *Tota pulcra es* (Bryn Mawr, PA: Hildegard, 1998).

[44] The motet is associated with the elevation of the host; see Lionel H. Sawkins, "Chronol-

tata (no. 13) and a dialogue (*Dialogo,* no. 14), continue the spirit of the royal encomia for Louis XIV (nos. 8–11) and Monseigneur (no. 12). No. 14 shows the composer at her most expansive, with a trio of singers matched to an instrumental trio. The Italian-speaking princess who loved music and dance surely appreciated Bembo's efforts, for she would be the dedicatee and recipient of the entire next manuscript, Rés. Vm[1]112–113. The king adored Marie-Adélaïde and would have been no less delighted with the profusion of music for the girl who held bright promise for the future of the French kingdom. Nos. 13 and 14 figure as a pair; the first, scored in G major, announces the kingdom's triumph brought by the young bride, and the second, in G minor, celebrates her nuptials with the mythological characters Virtue, Music, and Apollo. The order of the three pieces follows the events of the glorious occasion: first the bridal presentation, then the celebration of the wedding, and, appropriately far-removed in the manuscript, a cantata in A major for the private setting of the bridal chamber, the "epithalamium" (no. 35).

I have argued elsewhere that Bembo sought patronage from Marie-Adélaïde by emphasizing their common background as Franco-Italians.[45] In support of this idea, it is worth noting that the titles given to the three pieces on the score of the music itself specify a dedication to the Duchess of Burgundy alone, whereas the table of contents gives only no. 13 to the duchess, but nos. 14 and 35 to both Duke and Duchess of Burgundy (compare fig. 2.5 with table 3.1). Both manuscript and table of contents signal the wedding "per le nozze" for nos. 14 and 35, leaving no. 13 as an encomium for the Duchess of Burgundy alone. These observations suggest that Bembo's titles appear in the body of the manuscript, and someone else wrote up the table of contents for the manuscript after the wedding and before the binding of the work for the king's library. Bembo was not alone in her efforts to capitalize on the duchess's proclivities for "les goûts réunis"; Romagnesi's *Poesie liriche* belonged among her library books, suggesting not only her support of the Italian comedian but another link to the poetry of *Produzioni armoniche.*

The elaborate imagery offered by no. 13 depicts Marie-Adélaïde as the "new heroine" ("nova eroina") who brought peace to France and Savoy; in exchange for the princess's hand in marriage, Savoy regained territory that had been lost to France for most of the previous century. In recitative style,

ogy and Evolution of the *grand motet* at the Court of Louis XIV: Evidence from the *Livres du Roi* and the Works of Perrin, the *sous-maîtres* and Lully," in *Jean-Baptiste Lully and the Music of the French Baroque: Essays in Honor of James R. Anthony,* ed. John Hajdu Heyer (Cambridge: Cambridge University Press, 1989), 56–57.

[45] See "In Honour of the Duchess of Burgundy," 45–89. For a recent biography, read Charles Elliott, *Princesse of Versailles—The Life of Marie Adelaide of Savoy* (New York: Ticknor and Fields, 1992), but the most comprehensive study remains that of Gabriel-Paul-Othenin de Cléron, comte d'Haussonville, *La Duchesse de Bourgogne et l'alliance savoyarde sous Louis XIV* (Paris: Calmann-Lévy, 1898–1908).

the cantata opens with "the star of eternal peace . . . sparkling in the sky," as Bellona, the goddess of war, puts down her weaponry. Madrigalism ornaments the poetry as melismas rage on the "furor" of war and "thundering canon[balls]" cascade down an octave. The joy of the union erases all previous trouble as great victory triumphs for all: "dunque, perfetta *gioia* / non interrotta mai da fantasmi di *noia.*" The same idea and felicitous rhyme recur in the first appearance of *Musica* in the wedding dialogue, where she embodies the very essence of music in "hymns of joy" and recalls the prologue to Monteverdi's *L'Orfeo.* This presentation cantata concludes on a scintillating "astral" g^2 for the word "victory," which brings the cantata full circle from the incipit announcing the bright star promising future peace: "hor che lampeggia in cielo astro d'eterna pace."[46]

The "Dialogo," no. 14, extends the dramatis personae to three characters for the only vocal trio of the compilation: Virtue and Music are notated on soprano clefs (C1), with the character of Apollo on tenor clef (C4).[47] The range of Apollo's part suggests either an *haute-contre* male or an alto female; low French pitch brings the part lower still. In performing the work, tenors have found the part to lie too high, such that they must transpose it or exchange certain lines with one of the accompanying instruments. If performed at the Petite Union Chrétienne, the part would have gone to a female singer. The C4 clef also appears as the lower line in Fedeli's duet, no. 19, suggesting a similar performer. The accompanying two *dessus* instruments recall those found in nos. 2 and 5; they match the top voices, and the b.c. matches that of Apollo. Most of Bembo's later works employ the same core instrumental trio.

The allegory of the "Dialogo," steeped in seventeenth-century masque tradition, introduces the wedding's attributes with the figurative king (Apollo), Marie-Adélaïde (Virtue), and composer (Music). The trio's prelude establishes G minor and introduces Apollo, who asks Virtue what she hears. She tells of the star's arrival—the image presented in the preparatory cantata—descending to give peace to the world.[48] Apollo's ensuing aria exhorts all to enjoy the long-awaited day. In a grand arrival, Music descends on steps of harmony; the musical "steps" ("gradi") that she takes descend chromatically in both the vocal and continuo parts as Virtue prompts all to banish fear and worry. The two arias sung by Apollo and Music, along with the opening prelude, represent the most spectacular moments of the "Dialogo." After Apollo "crowns peace on earth," Virtue sings of the "ever happy, fortunate day," later repeated as a duet and then as the only tutti number in the second to last

[46] This musical example, along with two others from no. 13, appear in Fontijn, "In Honour of the Duchess," 53–54.

[47] Ibid., 59–60, provides facsimiles of *Prodizioni armoniche* pp. 132 and 135–136 to show the scoring of the two trios for voices and instruments.

[48] Ibid., 57–58, contains this musical example, as well as one comparing the arrival of *Musica* to that of the eponymous singer in the prologue to Monteverdi's *L'Orfeo.*

section. The final number, a solo for Virtue, features frequent appearances of the instrumental trio, the first section of which is in a siciliano rhythm, while the middle section climbs up chromatically and stratospherically to b-flat^2 to symbolize the figurative "planetary poles," recalling a similar concept from the aria no. 27. The dialogue concludes with the solo soprano, rather than with a grand tutti finale, bringing the duchess's triumph into the foreground.

No. 35, the epithalamium "Squarciato il velo ai fati" ("Unveiled the fates"), begins with an arioso for the first five lines of the poem, which refer again to Bellona as in no. 13; now she is vanquished and "tired" ("stanca"). Marie-Adélaïde's symbol returns from the initial cantata: the olive branch of peace figuratively offered to the French prior to the wedding now transformed into a crown of olive branches.[49] Bembo's musical vision of the crowning ("cinto il crin," mm. 10–13) produced a lengthy melisma, an encircling figure on those words in the soprano line and to some extent in the bass. The melisma on "crin" resembles that found at the conclusion to the sonnet with which the compilation opens (no. 1), where the depiction of the crowning of the king also uses decorative notes to encircle the main ones. "Eternal April" ("eterno Aprile"), celebrated in the interior of the cantata, symbolizes not just the young princess but the potential renewal of the French monarchy through her marriage to the Duke of Burgundy. Madrigalism renders unmistakable the meanings of the words "eterno"—set with a lengthy melisma that would challenge even a singer of great endurance—and "Aprile," a classic reference to youth and fecundity. The final recitative underscores this future by its reference to the new triumvirate in "the threefold Louis" ("triplicato Luigi"): the Duke of Burgundy; his father, Monseigneur; and his grandfather, Louis XIV (the same group as the "tre Luigi in terra" of no. 37 above).

The epithalamium initiates the final group at the end of the collection, encompassing nos. 35–41. Considered together, these pieces point to a new path for the monarchy. The love poetry of nos. 36 and 41, an Italian aria and a French air, respectively, suggest association with the bilingual duchess's wedding, acting as a frame for the politically neutral Latin motets, nos. 38–40. By all appearances, the beauty of her nuptial music seems to have earned the composer the patronage of the Duchess of Burgundy—the subject of the next chapter, "Ties That Bind."

The poetry of *Produzioni armoniche* opens up a rich world of allusion and allegory that corroborates the biography of the composer who selected the works and made them her own through their musical setting. The French kingdom not only offered her refuge for her physical existence at Notre Dame de Bonne Nouvelle but salvation for her soul as she found living royal "gods" to worship who in turn organized their devotion around the Catho-

---

[49] Ibid., 53 and 62.

lic faith that so powerfully sustained them all. Terrestrial, astrological, and cosmological images make this amply clear throughout the composite narrative of this first collection of music.

Many of the poems celebrate the glorious bounty of nature: Clytie blossoms as a sunflower, a lover beckons the lily and the rose to move cold Phyllis's heart, lovers sing of the fire and ice of their passions, and spring burgeons forth in myrtle, olives, and roses at the regal wedding. The order of nature, however, thoroughly depended on a cosmos ruled by God and the Sun King, cast as Apollo, the god of Delos and, later, as David in the psalms and as Hercules in *L'Ercole amante*. The "stars" of the French court—rulers depicted as sun, astral bodies, rotating orbs—in turn pledged allegiance to the greater planetary forces and God above all. When Clytie had hard luck, it came from the "nausea of scorning stars and of fortune," an illness that only "the illustrious king of the sunbeams" could cure. When the hierarchy was threatened in some way, monstrosities of nature appeared: the basilisk came to make prey of the vulnerable lover, the lynx to pounce upon ill fate and, in the sacred sphere, monsters—Christ's crucifiers, Olybrius, and the Calvinists—upset the unity of faith in Catholicism. The sophistication of the poetry not only testifies to the fine education that Antonia Padoani received from her father and the illustrious tutors whom he hired to teach her but also to the richness of Venice's window to the Orient, as many of the verses long for Greece and, still further east, for Egypt, where in rituals people "admire[d] the sun with their silence" (no. 10) and mythic reptiles dangerously roamed free. Yet the poetry conjures a carefully delimited world. By selecting the cautionary tale of Icarus, Bembo confronted her humble position and with her stratospheric song journeyed along the geographical borders of Europe and up and down the poles of the globe. Her musical world thereby not only reflects the glories of the French kingdom but also its analogous cosmos.

Produzioni armoniche contains the seeds of Bembo's subsequent endeavors. Its arias, cantatas, dialogues, sacred cantatas, motets, and instrumental settings all come to fruition in the later works (fig. 3.3). She organized it in three distinct parts:

1. The establishment of her identity as an artisan of glory, nos. 1–16;
2. The demonstration of her Italian heritage in the arias and cantatas, nos. 17–34;
3. "Les goûts réunis," the new path for the monarchy and for her, nos. 35–41.

Bembo's heritage stands at the core of her compilation: the majority of her pieces feature chamber music in her native tongue in apparent emulation of the most published Venetian composer of the day, Barbara Strozzi. Her Italian-language tributes to the French royal family allowed her to work at the full

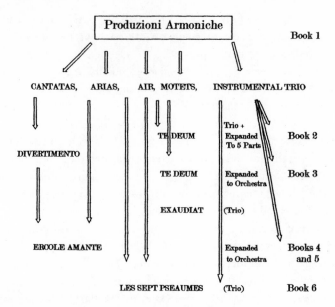

Figure 3.3   *Produzioni armoniche* as palette for Bembo's subsequent work

force of her powers. The pieces written in the style of her adoptive country, however, show mastery already at hand. The versatility of musical media— form, sacred and secular work, varied ensembles, Franco-Italian mixed style— makes this collection worthy of the rich poetic and mythic world that inspired it.

Chapter 4

TIES THAT BIND

B embo's music for the wedding of the Duke and Duchess of Burgundy in 1697 beautifully proclaimed her devotion to the royal family in *Produzioni armoniche* with festive pieces describing the duchess's pleasing manner (no. 13), bringing metaphorical characters into dialogue for the wedding (no. 14), and celebrating the bridal chamber (no. 35). The wedding dialogue, in particular, paved the way for Bembo's future endeavors in dramatic multi-section vocal work. Presumably having gained the approbation of the duchess, she anticipated the advent of her first child by selecting two new texts: the *Te Deum* in Latin, followed by a secular Italian poem of equivalent length. The dedication for the resulting musical settings brought together in the manuscript F-Pn, Rés. Vm^{1}112–113 discloses the composer's intention to follow French practice with a customary hymn of celebration (doc. 25):

> *Te Deum* to give thanks to God for the glorious delivery of your Royal Highness, who has brought into the world a prince so pleasing to all the universe and particularly to your Majesty. With the addition of a small *Divertimento* for the birth of the same prince.

With appropriate modesty, Bembo understated the size of her "addition." The *Divertimento* (Rés. Vm^{1}113) actually represents her first full-length dramatic work. A more effusive dedicatory statement follows, reaffirming the duchess's patronage:

> I beg your Royal Highness to graciously accept a *Te Deum*, which is intended to thank God for having given France a prince so dear to your Majesty and to all the court as the glorious Duke of Brittany. In addition to it, I present a *Divertimento* for the birth of this hero who fills all the world

with hope. All of this [is intended] as an unquestionable token of the humble zeal with which I present my profound respect, and with which I entrust myself to the lofty patronage of your Royal Highness and of all the royal family.

Reinforcing the idea of servitude to God and to the royal family so ener-getically and repeatedly emphasized by the encomia of *Produzioni armoniche,* the concluding soprano aria of the *Divertimento* expounds on the notion of eternal servitude to "Adelaide, Semi-Goddess." Here Bembo found new pos-sibilities for expression in the native language that she shared with the 18-year-old duchess, who delivered the Duke of Brittany to the French king-dom on 24 June 1704.

Marie-Adélaïde of Savoy, Semi-Goddess

As the nuptial music in *Produzioni armoniche* revealed, the joining of Marie-Adélaïde to Louis, Duke of Burgundy, marked the end of the War of the Pied-mont, a bitter battle raging between France and Savoy from 1690 through 1696 as the result of a long-standing dispute. By the terms of the Treaty of Cherasco of 1631, the Savoyards had been obliged to cede Pinerolo, lying at the heart of the Principality of Piedmont, to the French.[1] With Pinerolo the French held a corridor to the southeast located dangerously close to the Pied-montese capital of Turin, and during the following six decades the House of Savoy maneuvered to regain the region. By waging a military campaign against Louis XIV, Marie-Adélaïde's father Victor Amadeus II (1666–1732) hoped to restore the region to the Savoyards.[2] "Martial Bellona," the person-ification of war in cantata no. 13, put down her weaponry in July 1696 by Louis XIV's ratification of a treaty proclaiming that France would accept the hand of Marie-Adélaïde in exchange for Pinerolo.[3] In keeping with the

---

[1] Haussonville, *La Duchesse de Bourgogne:* "The Cherasco Treaty was a mistake. Pinerolo under French domination became what Calais under English rule was for the French two cen-turies before, a torn-out piece of flesh. . . . Until the end of the century, all of Savoy's politics would revolve around this unique goal: the restoration of the Pinerolo" ["le traité de Cherasco était une faute. Pignerol aux mains des Français devint ce qu'avait été deux siècles auparavant, pour la France, Calais aux mains des Anglais, le lambeau de chair arraché. . . . Jusqu'à la fin du siècle, nous allons voir toute la politique de la Savoie tourner autour de cet unique object: la resti-tution de Pignerol"] (1: 8–9).

[2] Ibid., 1: 17. Victor Amadeus II harbored strong anti-French sentiments that fired his de-sire to win the War of the Piedmont. See also Geoffrey Symcox, *Victor Amadeus II: Absolutism in the Savoyard State 1675–1730* (Berkeley: University of California Press, 1983), 106.

[3] Symcox, *Victor Amadeus II,* 116–117.

iconography of contemporary portraiture, the cantata vividly conjures the olive branch and laurels associated with Marie-Adélaïde's victory as peace-maker.[4]

The Duke and Duchess of Burgundy, third cousins, shared their descent from the same set of great-great-grandparents: Henri IV (1553–1610) and Marie de Médicis (1574–1642). The duchess's more immediate French female ancestors all had married into the House of Savoy. With no exceptions, these women knew how the patronage of music could bolster the political strength of their reigns. For instance, Christine (1606–1663)—daughter of Henri IV, sister of Louis XIII, who married Victor Amadeus I (1587–1637) in 1619—was an avid *mélomane* who promoted the formation of the first orchestra at the Savoy court.[5] Her daughter, Adélaïde (1636–1676), married Ferdinand Maria, Elector of Bavaria (1636–1679); under the couple's generous patronage, art and music thrived at the Munich court.[6] In the 1680s Christine's grand-son, Duke Victor Amadeus II, married Anne-Marie of Orleans (1666–1728, daughter of Monsieur, the dedicatee of *Produzioni armoniche,* no. 37). Fond of vocal music, Marie-Adélaïde's mother, Anne-Marie, supported the work of the singer Giuseppe Matteo Vacca; she may have been his student and the dedicatee of his musical treatise in French.[7] The considerable degree of Italo-French musical culture at the Savoy court attracted Marc-Roger Normand (1663–1734), a cousin of François Couperin. Nicknamed "il Coprino," Normand served as court musician in Turin during the late seventeenth century.[8]

By the time of her marriage, Marie-Adélaïde understood the ways in which displays of musical culture strengthened the eminence of a duchy or king-dom. After the announcement of her betrothal in Turin, a musical celebra-

---

[4] A portrait preserved in the Piedmontese Castello di Racconigi depicts the duchess with these attributes; see Fontijn, "In Honour of the Duchess," 50.

[5] On Christine of France, see Marie-Thérèse Bouquet-Boyer, "Turin et les musiciens de la Cour 1619–1775: Vie quotidienne et production artistique" (Doctoral diss., Université de Paris IV, Sorbonne, 1987), 59; Émile Magne, *Les Fêtes en Europe aux XVIIe siècle* (n.p., 1930), 311; and Monique Rollin, "La Musique de ballet dans les tablatures de luth: Souvenir et source d'inspi-ration," *Cahiers de l'Institut de recherches et d'histoire musicale des états de Savoie* 1 (1992): 53.

[6] See Elisabeth Jeannette Luin, "Das künstlerische Erbe der Kurfürstin Adelaide in ihren Kindern, Enkeln und Urenkeln," in *Festgabe für seine Königliche Hoheit Kronprinz Rupprecht von Bayern* (Munich: Verlag Bayerische Heimatforschung, 1953), 152–179. Luin signaled the activi-ties of the composers Johann Jakob Kerll, Agostino Steffani, and Ercole Bernabei at the Munich court. Adélaïde's daughter was Marie-Anne-Christine-Victoire of Bavaria, Dauphine of France from 1680 to 1690 and the mother of Louis, Duke of Burgundy.

[7] I-Tn, Ris. Mus. I/26, *Metodo elementare di musica composta da D. Giuseppe Matteo Vacca in francese* [MS]. Reference in Bouquet-Boyer, "Turin et les musiciens," 59, n. 1.

[8] Bouquet-Boyer, "Turin et les musiciens," 14, n. 3; 166–168. Pay records show that Marc-Roger Normand earned 200 *livres* when he played at Carnival in 1688 as an "aiutante di cam-era." He served as the harpsichord teacher to the princesses of Carignan in Turin. For more about his teaching in Savoy, see Augusta Lange, "Disegni e documenti di Guarino Guarini," *Guarino Guarini e l'internazionalità del Barocco* (Turin: Académie des Sciences de Turin, 1970), 1: 191, n. 2.

tion there brought together the characters of the Three Graces, Hercules, Cupid, Apollo, Mercury, and the Zephyrs, one of which "peek[ed] through the fog covering the future . . . and saw a son issuing from the union, who would be 'like Mars in war, but . . . with a face like Cupid'."[9] Upon the arrival of Marie-Adélaïde, André Cardinal Destouches (1672–1749) offered a heroic pastorale, in whose dedicatory poem he wrote: "In immortal verse, I may / lead Adélaïde to the foot of our altars, / there to sing of Hymen triumphant over War, / of the century, and of the assurance of happiness on earth."[10] In both of these celebrations, the duchess's political significance as a peace offering and as a potential bearer of a child superseded any personal attributes. By contrast, Bembo's Italian pieces for the duchess—the three in *Produzioni armoniche* and the present *Divertimento*—conform to the kingdom's greater political mission while capturing her specific attributes and, most importantly, acknowledging her agency. Bembo chose texts that vividly portray and reflect the allure of the girl who quickly became the center of attention at the French court.

Haussonville noted the intensity of Marie-Adélaïde's participation in court occasions during her teenage years, the period between her wedding and the birth of her first child (1697–1704). With her youthful energy, she brought to the royal family an atmosphere of excitement that had been lacking for some time. She exulted in dance, music, and masquerade at court, where at one point she appeared in costume as the goddess Flora followed by an entourage of nymphs. During the carnival seasons of 1699 and 1700, composers André Campra (1660–1744) and Pascal Collasse (1649–1709) produced operas that she enjoyed, the former on a specific commission to honor her with *Le Carnaval de Venise*. A summertime festivity of 1702 offered "excerpts from old operas" performed by François Couperin and his daughter Louise (c. 1675–1728), members of the musical dynasty the duchess had known in Turin.[11] Couperin's reflection on music at the turn of the century inspired his idea of uniting the tastes of France and Italy, as did his contact with Normand; Bembo's work in "les goûts réunis" may have advanced this notion, especially given the cultural nexus brought together by the Torinese duchess.

---

[9] Haussonville quoted the anonymous libretto, *Le Esperidi figurate sulle rive del Po per le nozze di Madama Adélaïde,* which is preserved in I-Tr: "les trois Grâces, Hercule, l'Amour, Apollon, Mercure, et les Zéphyrs . . . l'un de ces fabuleux personnages, perçant les brouillards de l'avenir, y voyait déjà apparaître un fils qui naîtrait de l'union projetée . . . : 'Tu seras Mars dans le combat; mais ton visage ressemblera à celui de l'Amour'" (1: 203–204).

[10] *Issé, pastorale héroïque* (Paris: Christophe Ballard, 1708), Épistre: "Que ne puis-je déjà dans des Vers immortels, / conduire ADELAIDE aux pieds de nos Autels, / y chanter ton Hymen triumphant de la Guerre, / l'Epoque, & le soutien du Bonheur de la Terre" (iv).

[11] Haussonville, *La Duchesse de Bourgogne,* 2: 116. This four-volume study examines each year of the duchess's life in microscopic detail. For the descriptions of the entertainment, see 1: 493–494 and 2: 12, 83, and 116.

Marie-Adélaïde's upbringing at court along with her education at the school run by Madame de Maintenon at Saint-Cyr helped to prepare her for her role as future ruler. She and her husband kept separate quarters for the first years of their marriage because they had been brought together at such a young age; however, by May 1701, the duchess's *dame d'honneur* Mademoiselle de Ludes declared her ready to bear children.[12] A touching poem from a contemporary *chansonnier* shows the duchess's valid anxieties regarding her obligation to produce a successor to the throne: "On that subject, the duchess, / ignoring all rumors, / reported the facts to the doctor / in a trembling and timid voice, / saying softly to him a thousand times: / 'am I or am I not?' "[13]

The long-awaited birth of the Duke of Brittany in the summer of 1704 prompted festivities throughout the kingdom and the hiring of the best musicians of the realm to mark the event. In the employ of the duchess, the marquis de Dangeau made arrangements for musical celebrations involving "les vingt-quatre violons du Roi" and choirs from the Opéra under the direction of André Danican Philidor (c. 1652–1730), as well as brass and percussion fanfares. The duchess herself was unable to take part in those festivities, but by August she could enjoy a performance in her salon by violins and oboes sounding in alternation with trumpet fanfares in the park outside.[14]

Most tragically, the young prince died of violent convulsions nine months later, on 13 April 1705.[15] Such a grievous blow left a terrible mark on the royal family; when Marie-Adélaïde gave birth to her second son in January 1707, Louis XIV ordered that there be no festivities.[16] Bembo would have obeyed the king's injunction, so there is little doubt that her celebratory *Te Deum* and *Divertimento* date to the 1704–1705 period.[17]

Louis XIV had provided Marie-Adélaïde with the Ménagerie, a small pavilion in the park of Versailles at some distance from the Grand Trianon. The pavilion had a library and a number of rooms, but no sleeping quarters; it was intended for dining, entertainment, and reading, rather than continual

[12] Haussonville devoted a section to "Maternité" in volume 2; the marriage was consummated in 1699 (2: 70).

[13] Henri Carré, *La Duchesse de Bourgogne: Une Princesse de Savoie à la cour de Louis XIV, 1685–1712* (Paris: Librairie Hachette, 1934): "La duchesse, sur ce sujet / ignorant tout ce qu'on décide, / au médecin conta le fait, / d'une voix tremblante et timide / lui disant mille fois tout bas: / le suis-je ou ne le suis-je pas?" (101).

[14] Ibid., 113. She left her bed in July and her first venture out of doors was not until August.

[15] Ibid., 115.

[16] Haussonville, *La Duchesse de Bourgogne,* cited the unpublished papers of Madame d'Aumâle, who wrote that "Le Roi, de plus en plus sensible aux calamités de son peuple, fit donner ordre à monsieur d'Argenson, alors lieutenant de police à Paris, d'empêcher qu'on y fît aucune dépense extraordinaire" (3: 118). It was only the third son, the Duke of Anjou, who would survive long enough to fulfill the Savoyard prophecy—he would become Louis XV.

[17] Rokseth provided this dating of the manuscript in "Antonia Bembo," 152.

Figure 4.1   Coat of arms of Marie-Adélaïde of Savoy, Duchess of Burgundy

habitation. The books in the duchess's library, dispersed in the late eighteenth century, all bear her coat of arms: three lilies of France with the cross of Savoy. The heraldists Olivier, Hermal, and Roton singled out five variations of the device representing the duchess's coat of arms on the books that they could identify in private collections and auctions. These books served as exemplars revealing five different brasses that had been used to inscribe their leather covers; the coat of arms on Bembo's book matches the fourth such brass, found on the *Almanach royal* of 1710, where two adult courtiers in profile flank the lilies and the cross (fig. 4.1). In their assessment of the library, the heraldists observed that "apart from several books of music . . . it . . . contained no more than serious books of theology and history."[18] Their description holds the distinct possibility that Bembo's book belonged alongside those that they identified.

F-Pn, Rés. Vm^{1}112–113 reflects both cultures of the young princess and matches the unifying symbolism of her coat of arms. In addition to the heraldists' exemplars, the Rare Book Room of the Bibliothèque Nationale owns a copy of Marc'Antonio Romagnesi's *Poesie liriche* (1673) whose cover bears the duchess's coat of arms.[19] As the foremost Italian poet in Paris, Ro-

---

[18] Eugène Olivier, Georges Hermal, and Robert de Roton, *Manuel de l'amateur de reliures armoriées françaises* (Paris: Charles Bosse, 1934), v. 26, *planche* 2511.

[19] The F-Pn book bears shelf number Rés.Yd.1232. I have worked from a microfilm of F-Pm, shelf number 43892.

magnesi belonged to the circle of Italians who could converse with the duchess in her native tongue. Like much of the poetry of *Produzioni armoniche,* that of the *Divertimento* suggests Romagnesi's influence if not his very pen. Given the high regard with which Romagnesi and his mother, Fedeli, were held at the center of court life in the decades prior to the duchess's arrival, it is most plausible that he would have acted as a kind of informal court poet to Marie-Adélaïde in the last years of his life.

A *Te Deum* for the Duke of Brittany

Marking many important occasions during the reign of Louis XIV, the *Te Deum* hymn accompanied military victories, recoveries from illness, and royal weddings and births. The *Menus Plaisirs* provide testimony to the frequency of the hymn's performance, often with indications of the date and location, but generally lacking the name of the composer who set it to music.[20] The largest possible ensemble performed the hymn for grand state ceremonies, for which the composers Lully, Marc-Antoine Charpentier (1643–1704), and Michel-Richard de Lalande (1657–1726) furthered the genre of the *grand motet* in music for one or more choirs with soloists and orchestra. Bembo would follow the *grand motet* tradition with her second *Te Deum* for the king himself, but here she chose the more intimate, smaller-scale *petit motet* for her hymn celebrating the triumph of Marie-Adélaïde's motherhood. Jean Duron considered both motets in his definition of the *Te Deum* genre, the first formal integration of Bembo's work into the musicological canon.[21]

The *Te Deum* for the birth of the Duke of Brittany—scored for two female sopranos and bass with an instrumental ensemble of two treble instruments and basso continuo—bears comparison with several works in *Produzioni armoniche.* With its six-part ensemble, the wedding dialogue (no. 14) offers the closest model for the vocal trio in the *Te Deum,* which substitutes the former's *haute-contre* with a bass. Two cantatas (nos. 2 and 5) also call for the instrumental trio but employ the solo soprano voice. These pieces exhibit Bembo's skill with the instrumental trio as a counterpart to the voice—such as the antiphony of no. 2 (ex. 3.5) and the exquisite B-minor prelude to no.

---

[20] F-Pan, O¹★2835: "Te Deum pour la Naissance du Monseigneur le Duc de Bretagne . . . État de la Depense fait en l'Extraordinaire des menus plaisirs et affaires de la Chambre du Roy pour le Te Deum Chanté en l'eglise notre Dame le 27 juin 1704 a cause de la naissance de Monseigneur le Duc de Bretagne" (ff. 87–87v).

[21] Jean Duron, "Te Deum," in *Dictionnaire de la musique en France au XVIIe et XVIIIe siècles,* ed. Marcelle Benoit (Paris: Fayard, 1992), 662–663. See the comprehensive article regarding the *Te Deum* genre by Jean-Paul C. Montagnier, "Le *Te Deum* en France à l'époque baroque—Un emblème royal," *Revue de Musicologie* 84 (1998): 218, n. 61.

14—and served as models on which to build the *Ritournelle* portions of the *Te Deum*. The amorous duets with continuo for soprano and tenor (no. 19; ex. A.3), two sopranos (no. 20), and soprano and bass (no. 34) offered earlier occasions for composition in duet texture. But the two groups of *petits motets* provided the most important points of departure, as these—nos. 3–4 and 38–40—employ the Latin language and exhibit features of the French style. Whereas Lully's music served as her model in those earlier works, in crafting her motet now at the turn of the eighteenth century she turned to the latest settings by Charpentier and Lalande.

Truly befitting bilingual composer and patron, Bembo provided both French and Italian rubrics in the score of the motet (table 4.1). Sections 2, 5, 11, and 13 bear the Italian tempo rubrics *Adagio* and *Allegro*, whereas the French *Ritournelle* indicates passages of considerable length for the instrumental trio: interjections offering repartee to the voices, or music for the instruments alone in sections 1, 6, 8–9, 11, and 13. Brief instrumental interlude passages usually omit the rubric. Unlike *Produzioni armoniche*, which left the two upper parts of the trio unspecified on G2 clefs (nos. 2 and 14), the *Te Deum* designates "violons" scored in the French manner with G1 clefs (ex. 4.1).

Dynamic markings, too, appear in French with the terms "fort" generally used for initial thematic statements, "doux" for their echoes. In the final section, for instance, the indication for "1.ᵉʳᵉ fois fort 2.ᵉ fois doux" specifies a

Example 4.1   F-Pn, Rés. Vm¹112, p. 1, mm. 1–7

We praise you, o God.

TABLE 4.1 Analysis of the *Te Deum* (F-Pn, Rés. Vm^{1}112)

Section	Text/Rubric	Key	Scoring	Measures
1.	Te Deum laudamus, te Dominum confitemur.	e	S, S, B, V^1, V^2, b.c.	1–59
	Ritournelle	e	V^1, V^2, b.c.	59–65
2.	*Adagio* Te æternum Patrem omnis terra veneratur, tibi omnes Angeli, tibi cæli et universæ potestates tibi Cherubim et Seraphim incessabili voce proclamant:	C	S, S, B, b.c.	66–82
	sanctus Dominus Deus Sabaoth!	b	S, S, B, V^1, V^2, b.c.	83–100
3.	Pleni sunt cæli et terra majestatis gloriæ tuæ, te gloriosus apostolarum chorus, te prophetarum laudabilis numerus, te martyrum candidatus laudat exercitus.	f#–E	S, S, B, V^1, V^2, b.c.	101–128
4.	Te per orbem terrarum sancta confitetur Ecclesia: Patrem immensæ majestatis, venerandum tuum verum	E–A a–e	S, S, B, V^1, V^2, b.c.	129–135 136–142
	et unicum Filium, sanctum quoque Paraclitum Spiritum.			
5.	*Allegro* Tu Rex gloriæ Christe, tu Patris sempiternus es Filius.	e–G	S, S, B, V^1, V^2, b.c.	143–151
6.	Tu ad liberandum suscepturus hominem, non horruisti Virginis uterum, tu devicto mortis aculeo, aperuisti credentibus regna cælorum.	G–E	S, S, b.c.	152–170
	Tu ad dexteram Dei sedes in gloria Patris, judex crederis esse venturus.	e–G	S, S, B, b.c.	171–185
	Ritournelle	G	V^1, V^2, b.c.	185–195
7.	Te ergo quæsumus famulis tuis subveni quos pretioso sanguine redemisti,	e–d	S, S, B, b.c.	196–203
	æterna fac cum sanctis tuis in gloria numerari.	Bb–F		204–216
8.	Salvum fac populum tuum Domine, et benedic hæreditati tuæ, et rege eos, et extolle illos usque in æternum.	F–d	S, S, B, V^1, V^2, b.c.	217–244
	Ritournelle	d	V^1, V^2, b.c.	245–252
9.	Per singulos dies benedicimus te, et laudamus nomen tuum in sæculum et in sæculum sæculi.	d–A	S, S, B, V^1, V^2, b.c.	253–288
	Ritournelle	d–A	V^1, V^2, b.c.	288–292
	Et laudamus nomen tuum in sæculum et in sæculum sæculi.	d	S, S, B, V, b.c.	292–301
	Ritournelle	d	V^1, V^2, b.c.	301–310
10.	Dignare Domine die isto, sine peccato nos custodire.	a	S, S, B, b.c.	311–324
11.	*Adagio*			
	Ritournelle	a	V^1, V^2, b.c.	325–328
	Miserere nostri Domine.	a	S, S, B, V^1, V^2, b.c.	328–359
	Ritournelle	a	V^1, V^2, b.c.	359–377
12.	Fiat misericordia tua Domine super nos, quemadmodum speravimus in te.	a	S, B, b.c.	378–387
13.	*Ritournelle*	e	V^1, V^2, b.c.	388–417
	Allegro: In te Domine speravi, non confundar in æternum.		S, S, B, V^1, V^2, b.c.	417–474

Example 4.2   F-Pn, Rés. Vm¹112, p. 64, mm. 387–394

. . . as we trust in you.

loud–soft performance for a series of repeated phrases by the instrumental trio, abbreviated as "fort" and "doux" for the remaining echoes (ex. 4.2).

As an extension of its bilingual rubrics, the motet contains music in both the French and Italian styles facilitated by their shared Latin language. Characteristic French qualities associated with the *petits motets* of *Produzioni armoniche* reappear in the *Te Deum:* smooth, mellifluous lines moving in conjunct, eighth-note motion often suggest an interpretation in *notes inégales*—a French practice whereby notated equal values are performed unequally in a lilting, swinging fashion—while lengthened notes at cadential points characterize the *récit* sections for solo voice. By contrast, the antiphonal effects for thematic imitation suggest Italian influences and models. Cavalli's *Messa concertata* from the *Musiche sacre* collection (1656) offers a familiar example as well as some points of similarity with Bembo's motet and may even explain some of her apparent idiosyncrasies—that is, those not associated with her French contemporaries.[22] Yet Italian influences in French music were already present by the time of Bembo's arrival. Even if vaunted as the quintessential French classical composer, Lully himself had Florentine origins; Charpentier's studies with Carissimi in Rome gave him easy access to matters of Italian style. The latter's *Te Deum* (H. 146), possibly composed for the French military vic-

[22] Francesco Cavalli, *Messa concertata,* ed. Raymond Leppard (London: Faber Music, 1966).

tory at Steinkerque in 1692, offers a good source of comparison for Bembo's motet,[23] despite their obvious contrasts of occasion: brass fanfares were *de rigueur* for his *grand motet* setting, while violins were more suitable for her *petit motet*.

A consideration of the construction of Bembo's motet, section by section, illustrates how the stylistic, bilingual, and harmonic elements function together (table 4.1).[24] The opening and closing tutti choruses, the longest sections of the motet, frame the work and ground it in E minor. Unlike Charpentier, who provided an instrumental prelude followed by a bass solo for the opening text, Bembo began in full six-part tutti texture (table 4.2), the voices all proclaiming, "Te Deum laudamus, te Dominum confitemur" ("We praise you, o God, we acknowledge you to be the Lord"). Two statements of the four-measure A phrase (mm. 1–9) begin the section with the instruments in imitative succession: basso continuo (b.c.), first violin (V1), and second violin (V2). After the first cadence in m. 5, the voices take up the phrase in equivalent registral order: bass (B), first soprano (S1), and second soprano (S2). All six parts reinforce the texture and come to a full cadence at m. 9. The rhythm of the words "Te Dé-um" determined the shape of a phrase in which the downbeat falls on the first syllable of the second word, rendering a musical setting in triple meter. Two four-measure units constitute the A phrases, which work together to establish a periodic, symmetrical structure with contrasts in texture between instruments and voices.

The B phrases reverse the order and double the length of the A phrases, such that the voices introduce material then echoed by the instruments (mm. 9–25). The word rhythm again defines the accents: "Dó–mi–num" dictated a dotted rhythm following the upbeat "te." The B phrases lend a celebratory tone to the section as they cadence in the relative major at mm. 17 and 25. The AB phrases combine the two rhythmic motives in two identical repetitions of full tutti texture (mm. 25–42, 42–59). Midway through each AB phrase (mm. 36 and 53), a major seventh chord on C propels motion toward a cadence in the dominant, followed by the ensemble's return to the home key (mm. 36–42, 53–59). The instrumental *Ritournelle* echoes this six-measure tail as a soft *petite reprise*, concluding the section in an understated manner. The instruments thereby frame the section and play one interlude as a central portion (mm. 17–25), a small-scale mirroring of the motet's larger harmonic structure (sections 1, 4–7, 13). With its even phrase lengths, balanced alternation between tutti and instrumental textures, and symmetrical harmonic scheme, section 1 begins the motet in an appropriately festive mood.

---

[23] Jean-Paul Montagnier, ed., *Charpentier, Te Deum, H. 146* (London: Ernst Eulenburg, 1996), Préface, IX.

[24] For all references to measure numbers, see the edition of Conrad Misch, *Te Deum laudamus* (Kassel: Furore Verlag, 2003).

TABLE 4.2 Analysis of the Opening Chorus, *Te Deum* (F-Pn, Rés. Vm¹112)

Measures	Phrases	Texture	Key
1–5	A (4)	Inst.	e–e (i)
5–9	A (4)	Tutti	e–e (i)
9–17	B (8)	Tutti	G (III)
17–25	B (8)	Inst.	G (III)
25–36–42	AB (10–6)	Tutti	B–e (V–i)
42–53–59	AB (10–6)	Tutti	B–e (V–i)
59–65	B (6)	*Ritournelle*	e–e

Section 2, *Adagio,* expands the C-major shadings heard briefly in the opening music (mm. 11, 35, and 52). At this same juncture, Charpentier brought in the four-voice chorus for the first time; Bembo, by contrast to her tutti opening, instead launched into imitative or independent solos and duets, the reduced textures rendering the text highly intelligible. A passage in quick declamatory style precedes the quotation in the fifth line of text (mm. 66–82):

Te æternum Patrem omnis terra veneratur,	All the earth worships you, Father everlasting,
tibi omnes Angeli,	to you all angels
tibi cæli et universæ potestates	to you the heavens and powers
tibi Cherubim et Seraphim incessabili voce proclamant:	to you Cherubim and Seraphim continually call out:
Sanctus Dominus Deus Sabaoth!	"Holy Lord, God of Hosts!"

The first soprano's line climbs to the very "heavens" in mm. 72–73, recalling similar madrigalistic moments in *Produzioni armoniche.* A bass solo (mm. 79–82) bridges the dramatic expectation built up through the "tibi" incipits of lines 2–4 with a succession of stretto entries on "Sanctus Deus Sabaoth!" (mm. 83–100). Effectively all six echoing parts illustrate the heavens, which "continually call out" to their creator. The singers declaim the complete text in homophony in mm. 88–97; as in section 1, the instrumental trio echoes their final material as a *petite reprise* (mm. 97–100).

Section 3 merges seamlessly with the previous music by means of a b.c. tag, which descends in conjunct motion from b to f-sharp. The major keys of this section match the laudatory nature of the text:

Pleni sunt cæli et terra	Heaven and earth are full
majestatis gloriæ tuæ,	of your majesty, of your glory;
te gloriosus apostolarum chorus,	the glorious company of the apostles,
te prophetarum laudabilis numerus,	the goodly fellowship of the prophets,
te martyrum candidatus laudat exercitus.	the noble army of martyrs, praise you!

The instrumental trio plays a brief prelude in triple meter with music derived from the word rhythms of the first line of the text (mm. 101–103), confirmed by the vocal entries in the order S1, S2-B. The bass and b.c. continue the phrase at m. 109 in unison on the second line of text, leading into a tutti section in duple meter. During this transition to ¢, the quarter note should remain constant; the 2/2 time signature of Misch's edition at m. 111 makes this clear. Via the descent of the b.c. through a 7-#6 chord on F-sharp, the tutti texture at m. 113 cadences in E major, the key of the next section. A lengthy melisma for the vocal ensemble in mm. 124–126 emphasizes "laudat," the verb found in line 5, and a full cadence in E-major homophony for all parts brings sections 1–3 to a satisfactory close.

A new procedure characterizes section 4, within which duple meter sustains two seven-measure halves (lines 1–2 and 2–3) wherein the voices sing in quasi-conversational style (mm. 129–135 and mm. 136–142). Lines 1–2 in the first half feature major-mode shadings (E-A), reversed to feature minor modes (a-e) in the second half:

1	Te per orbem terrarum sancta confitetur Ecclesia	The holy Church throughout all the world
2	Patrem immensæ majestatis, venerandum tuum verum	acknowledges you, the Father of immense majesty,
3	et unicum Filium, sanctum quoque Paraclitum Spiritum.	your venerable, true and only Son, the Holy Spirit and Comforter.

The first and second sopranos' beseeching upward leaps of a minor sixth (mm. 136–138) counterbalance the bass's falling sixth en route for an octave descent, a–A. The French-style mm. 140–142 imply the need for several ornamental flourishes, such as trills on the f-sharp^1 and d-sharp^2 and a port-de-voix on the climactic g^2 in the first soprano part. Her high tessitura soars above the ensemble, accompanied by the first violin, and then subsides through chromatic neighbor notes into the E-minor cadence.

Section 5 introduces the *Allegro* rubric for a section glorifying the "true and only Son," now mentioned by name: "Tu Rex gloriæ Christe, tu Patris sempiternus es Filius" ("You are the King of glory, o Christ, you are the everlasting Son of the Father"). The text engendered some of the earliest polyphonies and Bembo seems to have acknowledged that venerable tradition here, at the heart of the motet in the home key (sections 5–6). The dense accompaniment played by the instrumental ensemble weaves together the spaces between the imitative vocal entries: S1, S2, and SB (mm. 143–148). At the conclusion of the section, mm. 148–149, the first soprano again sails above the tutti texture with a prolonged g^2 on "sempiternus," illustrating the word's meaning through its duration. The exaggerated length of the cadential material on "Filius" recalls the elevation motet "Panis Angelicus" from *Produzioni armoniche;* the third beat of m. 150 needs careful placement by the second violin and continuo as the other parts all depend on them to resolve the somewhat precarious syncopation and elongation of those penultimate measures. A full cadence at mm. 150–151 confirms the relative major tonal area for the next section.

The emerging prominence of the first soprano in sections 4–5 prepares for the alternating soprano solos that sing, at the opening of section 6, of the divinely appointed body of the Virgin Mary:

Tu ad liberandum suscepturus hominem,	When it came time for you to deliver man,
non horruisti Virginis uterum.	you did not abhor the Virgin's womb.
Tu devicto mortis aculeo,	When you overcame the sharpness of death,
aperuisti credentibus regna cælorum.	you opened the kingdom of heaven to all believers.
Tu ad dexteram Dei sedes in gloria Patris,	You sit at the right hand of God, in the glory of the Father,
judex crederis esse venturus.	we believe that you will come to be our judge.

Bembo's interpretation of the passage stands in sharp contrast to Charpentier's, whose hymn for military might instead assigned the passage to a male trio. Such attention to the female body underscores the composer's orientation as a woman writing music for women to sing. While the first soprano sings the second line of text (mm. 154–156), the b.c. descends chromatically from d to A. The second soprano literally seconds the first by transposing her line up a whole step in a brief sequence, now undergirded by the descent e–B (mm. 158–159). Chromaticism becomes the medium of exchange between them as the first soprano interrupts the second's d-sharp^2 with a rejoinder on d-natural^2 (mm. 159–160). With a turn toward a *durus* (the hexachord's original designation for a sharp) note spelling on the word "*aculeo*" (f-sharp and f-sharp^1 octaves), Bembo cleverly alluded to the "sharpness" of death and bridged the transition into triple meter (mm. 161–162) on the word "aperuisti." The "opening of the kingdom of heaven" brings comfort from death's sting, as the first soprano moves into the quick and joyful character of a new triple meter section.

The two sopranos sing a passage together in thirds and sixths—reminiscent of the duet "Amor mio" from *Produzioni armoniche*—that completes the fourth line of the text (mm. 162–169). The prevailing quarter-eighth accompaniment in 3/8 remains constant while the measures double in length (6/8) in a new imitative section at m. 171; reduced scoring further facilitates the metric transition. The last two lines of text provide the material for the final part of section 6, which moves deftly from the home key into G major. Motivic embellishment confirms the joyfulness of the text, initiated by the soprano's flourish on the word "gloria" (m. 173), which is then taken up in solo, duet, and trio configurations and echoed by the instrumental trio in a concluding *Ritournelle* (mm. 190–195).

A tag leads from the relative major of section 6 back to the E minor of section 7, where the first soprano and b.c. initiate a modulatory passage concerned with the Eucharist (mm. 196–198). Above the linear descent e–D, the soprano descends chromatically, f-sharp^1–f-natural^1, touching the major and the minor modes of D. In mm. 200–201 simultaneous linear tritones in the soprano (b-flat^1 and e^1) and in the doubled bass and b.c. (g and c-sharp) lend proper solemnity to a meditation on Christ's "precious blood" ("pretioso sanguine"):

Te ergo quæsumus famulis tuis subveni	We therefore pray to you to help your servants
quos pretioso sanguine redemisti,	whom you have redeemed with precious blood;
æterna fac cum sanctis tuis in gloria numerari.	number them among your saints in eternal glory.

The soprano imitates the bass's previous tritone at the octave, g^1 and c-sharp^1, as if to emphasize the central idea of the Eucharist, after which the vocal trio sings in D-minor homophony (mm. 200–203). With its new key and time signatures, an entirely different mood accompanies the setting of line 3. In the first half of the line, set in 3/8, the three voices imitate each other in stretto fashion, S1–B–S2 (mm. 204–207), after which the two sopranos, now in 6/8, introduce a lengthy melisma on "gloria" that becomes the predominant concluding motive in all the voices (mm. 209–216). This part of the section builds upward in the first soprano part, first ascending the octave via a thirty-second-note flourish to f^2 (m. 211), underscored by triple octave Fs, then reaching the highpoint of a^2 (m. 213). The section concludes with a full cadence in F major at mm. 215–216, in which a momentary 3/4 meter effects a *ritardando*. Sections 4–7 belong together, just as do the next series of *récits* characterizing sections 8–10.

A variety of vocal and instrumental textures embody the idea of the diversity of the "people" ("populum") described in section 8, which continues in the key of F:

Salvum fac populum tuum Domine,	Save your people, o Lord,
et benedic hæreditati tuæ,	and bless your heritage,
et rege eos, et extolle illos usque in æternum.	and govern them, and lift them up for ever.

In a section beseeching God to come to the aid of the people, each performer has the opportunity to make an individual musical plea, and even the b.c. gets a brief solo (mm. 244–245). The first soprano sings a French-style *récit* on the first two lines, complete with an extended cadential point stretching through mm. 221–222. In the ensuing duet with the bass (mm. 222–226), the third line gives rise to a new motive: "et" provides an upbeat to two pairs of sixteenth notes on "re-ge." The b.c. moves into the relative minor for the remainder of the section through stepwise motion down to D for the second soprano's *récit*, which begins in m. 227 as a variation on the first soprano's music. This ravishing minor-mode *récit* recalls some of the impressive variations of thematic material in *Produzioni armoniche* (such as those illustrated in ex. 3.13). A melisma on "Domine" features written-out ornaments that progress from a^1 to c^2, replete with possibilities for improvised flourishes and *ports-de-voix,* below which a succession of sixth chords match the linear minor-sixth descent to a^1 on the word "hæreditati" (m. 230). The second soprano's *récit* concludes on a prolonged trill whose resolution overlaps with the following bass *récit,* in which the setting of a melisma on "Domine" expands out to an octave (mm. 233–234). The section concludes with antiphonal music for the entire ensemble (mm. 234–252) complete with a substantial *Ritournelle* that tapers the repeated phrases and strongly articulates a prolonged full cadence in D minor (mm. 251–252). Octaves emphasizing the continuo's dominant-tonic chords confirm the finality of the section, driving home the notion of eternity and providing the tonal context for the next.

Another series of *récits* follows in section 9:

Per singulos dies benedicimus te,	Day by day we magnify you,
et laudamus nomen tuum in sæculum	and we praise your name for ever
et in sæculum sæculi.	and ever.

Misch's edition assigns the first entry to the second soprano and the second entry to the first; Bembo's manuscript, however, indicates no such distinction. In all likelihood, she intended that only one voice sing the entire *récit* (mm. 253–283), in keeping with the normative practice, such as that demonstrated by Charpentier's setting for a solo soprano in section 7 ("Te ergo quæsumus") of H. 146. Another noteworthy point of comparison obtains between Bembo's scoring and cadential setting in mm. 281–283 and a passage from Lalande's motet *Super flumina Babilonis* (ex. 4.3), where both soprano and *dessus* also perform the upper parts with a strong second-beat ornament over V-I harmony resolving into a chord in octaves.

The violin part writing in Bembo's motet begins smoothly at m. 253, but disjunct leaps starting in m. 255 render the sound of jagged filler rather than a self-sufficient line. This problem also affects mm. 298–301 and suggests some contrapuntal difficulty. The vocal and the b.c. lines sound smooth and conse-

Example 4.3   Lalande, *Super flumina Babilonis,* S. 13, "Adhaereat lingua mea," mm. 61–63

quent, but the violin part almost seems like an afterthought. Similarly disjunct obbligato treble lines are found in motet no. 3 from *Produzioni armoniche,* as well as throughout *Les sept Pseaumes, de David* (F-Pn, Rés. Vm¹116).

Double bars in the manuscript at m. 310 mark the conclusion of section 9; section 10, mm. 311–324, flows from it and continues in the key of A minor. The simplest possible texture conveys a fervent wish for purity with "Dignare Domine die isto, sine peccato nos custodire" ("Deign to keep us this day without sin, o Lord"). The dialogue treatment of *récits* recalls that of Charpentier's H. 146, where a simple transposition of the theme occurs in section 4 ("Te per orbem"); by contrast, Bembo slightly varied each thematic statement. The first soprano sings mm. 311–315, moving to E minor, the second its inversion in mm. 316–320, moving toward C major, while the bass's final statement (mm. 321–324) closes in A minor.

Framed by introductory and closing *Ritournelles* that mimic or echo the text—"Miserere nostri Domine" ("Have mercy on us, o Lord")—section 11 presents both a new rubric, *Adagio,* and a new meter, 3/2. The three words constituting this plea receive multiple rhythmic settings. The introductory *Ritournelle* presages the opening vocal text; stretto entries typify the solemnity of the wish presented by the first and most important word of the phrase. The violins' interjection at m. 340 introduces a lively dotted figure, which the voices in mm. 341–342 confirm. The lengthy final *Ritournelle* develops without mimicking an absent text, giving independence to the instruments for the first time in the motet.

Section 12 declaims two statements of its text. Bembo's manuscript bears the indication "2e" ("seconde") on the system with which the duet for soprano and bass begins at m. 384; Misch logically interpreted it to mean the retroactive assignment of the solo to the second soprano in mm. 379–383.

Fiat misericordia tua Domine super nos,   Let your mercy be upon us, Lord,
quemadmodum speravimus in te.   as we trust in you.

The second soprano concludes the solo by dwelling on "speravimus" at the prolonged cadence of mm. 382–383.

The grand finale—set in triple-meter E minor—proclaims the last line of text: "In te Domine speravi, non confundar in æternum" ("We trust in you, God, we will not be troubled in eternity"). Like Charpentier, Bembo set the last section for a tutti performance; however, she presented the voices homophonically, where Charpentier instead capitalized on imitative textures. Bembo's *Ritournelle* presents a prelude with all of the thematic material first (mm. 388–417) before the voices enter in an exact repetition. Repeat signs indicate the first time through as "fort" ("loud") and the second time through as "doux" ("soft"), with the explicit intent for an echo performance (ex. 4.2). The *Allegro* appears at the vocal passages following the *Ritournelle* at m. 417, the instruments marked "doux" to echo the voices.

Bembo's witty setting of "non confundar" illustrates the very confusion that the motet's prayer asks not to encounter. At the initial statement, the instruments repeat one measure only (mm. 390–391), but in the vocal version of mm. 423–429, the repeat is not present as they sing the entire phrase "non confundar in æternum." The diversion from the prelude's scheme is obvious because up until now the voices literally replicated the *fort-doux* pattern. In mm. 438–442 the idea of the brief statement of "non confundar" mimics the prelude in yet another permutation. Bembo saved the motet's climax for the end. On the downbeat of m. 463, the final statement of the text, the first soprano reaches up to the motet's highest pitch b^2. The instruments echo the voices, but no soft marking is present; they should retain their loud volume for a grand conclusion.

As if to emphasize further the motet's French character and destination, the word "Fin" appears on the last page of the score (p. 75). With this touch—along with the *récits,* cadential figuration, implied ornamentation, rubrics, and genre—Bembo clearly intended to lend the piece a strong French accent, even if its antiphonal nature points to Venetian choral practice. The compositions of contemporaries in Venice and Paris served as clear models for Bembo's first full-length foray into sacred music, which stands squarely within the tradition of sacred music celebrating the triumphs of Louis XIV's reign.

The bicultural aspects of the motet would not have been lost on its dedicatee, nor would those of the second piece—"l'aggionto d'un picciolo divertimento"—with its allegory told in the language that the women shared. While retaining the three-part instrumental ensemble employed in both the wedding dialogue (no. 14) and in the *Te Deum* with which it is paired, the *Divertimento* augments the number of singers from three to five: two sopranos (C1 clefs), *haute-contre* (C3 clef), tenor (C4 clef), and bass (F4 clef).

Cupid's Beautiful Mother

The *Divertimento* presents its allegorical characters in a sequence of entries following the opening tutti chorus: Glory and Fame (sopranos) in sections 2 and 3, two Cupids (also sopranos) in section 4, and the Chorus of Graces (two sopranos with *haute-contre*) in section 5 (table 4.3). Only two additional singers—*haute-contre* and tenor—would have been needed to supplement those already present for the motet in order to constitute the five-part chorus of the tutti sections. Their presentation recalls that of the wedding dialogue, where Apollo (*haute-contre*) and Virtue and Music (sopranos) appear in short succession. Yet, as if influenced by the framing structure of the *Te Deum*, the *Divertimento* effectively expands the function of the chorus: here all five singers join together in the first and last sections as well as in sections 4 and 9, where the three singers of the wedding dialogue had engaged in only one tutti chorus placed at the middle of the composition. The opening choral music partially recurs in section 4 and once again in its entirety to conclude the work.

The binding together of the *Te Deum* and the *Divertimento*, along with the connection made between them in the dedication, strongly suggests that one follow the other in performance. A flexible orchestration of the instrumental trio, and especially the b.c., along with the supplementation of the two new singers, would not have precluded this possibility. The "violons" specified in the motet could play both works (ex. 4.1). In keeping with standard liturgical function, the *Te Deum* must have had an organ for its b.c. whereas, from the outset—with its invocation of the "cetra"—the *Divertimento* implies an obligatory plucked instrument, like a theorbo:

1	Risuoni per l'etra	Let the sweet sound
	di musica cetra	of the musical lyre
	soave clamor	resound through the air
	s'intreccin le palme,	let the palms be interwoven,
5	s'innalzin trofei,	let the trophies be raised,
	e con voce festiva	and with festive voice
	intuonin Francia e Spagna:	let France and Spain proclaim:
	"viva il bambino Duce di Bretagna,	"long live the child, Duke of Brittany,
	delle due monarchie chiaro splendor."	the bright splendor of both kingdoms!"

The inventory of Marie-Adélaïde's royal household includes just one musician who held the official title of "harpsichord player," "joüeur de clavessin" Jean-Baptiste Buterne (c. 1650–1727).[25] In addition, he held an appointment as one of the four organists employed by the Chapelle Royale in Versailles. In service to the duchess as musician and music teacher, the versatile keyboardist represents the likely player of the organ for the motet and the harpsichord for the *Divertimento*.[26] The violin and theorbo players are less easily

[25] F-Pan, O¹3715, f. 6r.

[26] The only surviving music by Buterne is a small booklet of harmony lessons preserved at

TABLE 4.3 Analysis of the *Divertimento* (F-Pn, Rés. Vm¹ 113)

Section	Textual Incipits	Key	Scoring	Measures
1. [Tutti]	Rittornello	A	V¹, V², b.c.	1–7
	Risuoni per l'etra di musica cetra soave clamor!		S¹, S², HC, T, B, V¹, V², b.c.	7–29
	Ritt[ornell]o	E	V¹, V², b.c.	29–36
	Risuoni per l'etra di musica cetra soave clamor!		S², b.c.	36–43
	Ritt[ornell]o		V¹, V², b.c.	43–50
	S'intreccin le palme . . .	E–f#	S¹, S², HC, T, B, V¹, V², b.c.	51–81
	Risuoni per l'etra di musica cetra soave clamor!	A	S¹, S², HC, T, B, V¹, V², b.c.	81–97
	Ritt[ornell]o		V¹, V², b.c.	97–116
2. La Gloria [recit.]	Gloriosa Adelaide, d'ogni cor e d'ogn'alma . . .	D	S, b.c.	117–129
3. La Fama, Aria	Arcieri, guerrieri, che fieri raggirate i brandi alteri . . .	b	S, V¹, V²	130–178
	Ritorn[ell]o		V¹, V²	179–185
4. Due Amorini, Aria	Alma dea di Pafo e Gnido, bella madre di Cupido . . .	f#	S, S, V¹, V², b.c.	186–200
[Tutti]	Ritorn[ell]o		V¹, V², b.c.	200–204
	Risuoni per l'etra di musica cetra soave clamor!	A	S¹, S², HC, T, B, V¹, V², b.c.	81–116
5. Coro di Gratie	Splendete, ardete (pupille) . . .	D–A	S¹, HC, b.c.	205–209
	Ritorn[ell]o		V¹, V², b.c.	210–214
	Splendete, ardete (pupille) . . .	A–D	S¹, S², b.c.	214–218
	Ritorn[ell]o		V¹, V², b.c.	218–222
	Splendete, ardete (pupille) . . .	A–b	S¹, S², V¹, V², b.c.	222–232
	Ritorn[ell]o	b	V¹, V², b.c.	232–235
	Splendete, ardete (pupille) . . .	b–D–A	S¹, S², HC, V¹, V², b.c.	235–267
	Splendete da Capo			235–267
6. Aria [la Prima Gratia]	Su cantate, su danzate, mentre stagion sì dolce . . .	a	S¹, V¹, V², b.c.	268–296
Gigue			V¹, V², b.c.	297–303

		Key	Instrumentation	Measures
7. Aria	*Rit[ornel]lo*	A	V¹, V², b.c.	303–305
	Da noi fuggite pianti e sospiri . . .		S¹, V¹, V², b.c.	305–327
	Rit[ornel]lo		V¹, V², b.c.	327–336
Menuet			V¹, V², b.c.	337–360
8. [recit.: A Grace?]	Dal Oriente al Occidente risuoni il grido . . .	a	S¹, b.c.	361–379
	Si riprende Su Cantate la Prima Grattia		S¹, V¹, V², b.c.	268–296
9. [Tutti]	Su dunque ai suoni, ai balli, ai canti, ai musici . . .	d	S¹, S², HC, T, B, V¹, V², b.c.	380–416
	Ritorn[el]lo		V¹, V², b.c.	417–421
10. Aria	*Rit[ornel]lo*	D	V¹, V², b.c.	422–429
	Sventure, fuggite, coi strali fatali mortali . . .	D	S, V¹, V², b.c.	429–463
11. Aria	*Rit[ornel]lo*	a	V¹, V², b.c.	464–466
	Trionfi sempre in questo loco, il riso e 'l gioco . . .	a	S, V¹, V², b.c.	466–506
12. Gigue		e	V¹, V², b.c.	507–537
Aria [Two Graces]	Soggetti di noi, vassalli di noi, da l'occaso ai lidi eoi . . .	G	S, HC, b.c.	538–543
	[Rittornello]	G	V¹, V², b.c.	543–545
	Delizie più care . . .	b	S, HC, b.c.	545–552
	[Rittornello]	e	V¹, V², b.c.	552–555
	Delizie più care . . .	e	S, HC, b.c.	555–565
	Rit[ornel]lo		V¹, V², b.c.	565–568
13. Aria	Ti rinnego o libertà . . .	C	S, V¹, V², b.c.	569–594
14. [repeat mvt. 6]	*Si riprende l'aria Su Cantate*	a	S¹, V¹, V², b.c.	268–296
15. [repeat mvt. 1]	*dopo si riprende il coro Risuoni per l'etra primo*	A	S¹, S², HC, T, B, V¹, V², b.c.	1–116

identifiable, however, the Marquis de Sources mentioned in his journal that the king came by the Ménagerie in 1710 during an impromptu concert performed for the duchess. There viola da gambist Antoine Forqueray (1672–1742), flutist René Pignon Descosteaux (c. 1645–1728), and theorbist Robert de Visée (c. 1660–c. 1732) joined Buterne.[27] If such musicians—the very best of their kind—played at her pavilion without prior official arrangement, other such occasions must have arisen. De Visée, then, may have been the "cetra" player whom Bembo had in mind, especially given that he was Corbetta's former guitar student. Louise Couperin, who joined her father at one known performance for the duchess in 1702, may also be considered as a candidate for the lead soprano parts of both works. These conjectures offer a sense of the high level of musical talents that would have been available for Bembo's conception of her works, even if it cannot be proven that any of them actually performed her music for the duchess.

The bright key of A major frames the *Divertimento* and also grounds the music of sections 4, 5, and 7. The ritornello, whether named *Ritournelle* in the motet or *Rittornello* here, serves to introduce or reinforce motivic ideas derived from the rhythms of the words and to offer a counterbalancing texture to the solo ensembles or tutti choral sections (ex. 4.4). The first *Rittornello* opens with an instrumental prelude derived from the word-rhythms of the first line of text, proclaimed by the voices corresponding to the instruments in range: two sopranos and bass ($S^1–S^2B$), followed by an echo in the three lower voices (T–HC–B).

The musical setting of "Risuoni"—a quarter-note upbeat to a dotted quarter and eighth note—presents a major-mode variation and augmentation of the theme from the A-minor duet for soprano and tenor from *Produzioni armoniche* (ex. A.3). A variety of motivic shapes appears in this first tutti chorus, schematized in table 4.4, with particular attention paid to the setting of the opening couplet (a, b, b^1, b^3, f). Madrigalism furthers the setting of lines 4–9, where brief interjections from two duets—S–S and HC–T—figuratively weave "the palms" (line 4) after which the tutti chorus can raise "the trophies" up to its highest registers (line 5) (ex. 4.5).

A dotted upbeat into m. 57 appropriately signals the intended "festive voice" (motive c, line 6). The poem celebrates the Duke of Brittany's descent

---

F-Pbsg, Ms. 3173: "Petites reigles pour l'accompagnement que Monsieur Buterne m'a donné par confiance et dont il fait grant cas et qu'il se réserve." One wonders from the personal tone adopted here if these are not the duchess's very keyboard lessons.

[27] Haussonville, *La Duchesse de Bourgogne*, 4: 52. Sources also described a theorbist dressed as a tiger during a masquerade in 1700 for Marie-Adélaïde, where she disguised herself as a sultane. The theorbist's name was not revealed there; see the citation in Marcelle Benoit, *Les Musiciens du roi de France (1661–1733)* (Paris: Presses Universitaires de France, 1982), 115.

Example 4.4   F-Pn, Rés. Vm¹113, p. 1, mm. 1–9

Let the sweet sound . . .

from French Louis XIV and Spanish Maria Teresa, yielding triple-meter downbeats on the phrase "intuonin Francia e Spagna" as if to conjure a joyous sound from both of these countries. Four imitative duet statements of motive d with basso continuo accompaniment—S^1–S^2 (mm. 60–62), S^2–HC (mm. 62–64), S^1-T (mm. 64–66), and an echo from the instrumental ensemble (mm. 66–68)—repeat this important proclamation of the boy's origins (ex. 4.6).

"Viva il Bambino" expresses a wish for the baby's health, the duple nature of the phrase rendered in common time (m. 68). A fanfare in E major deliv-

TABLE 4.4 Motives in the Opening Tutti Chorus of the *Divertimento*

Measures	Key	Line	Motive
1–22	A–E–B	1–3	a
22–35	E	1–3	b
35–50	E	1–3	b^1
50–56	E	4–5	b^2
56–60	D	6	c
60–68	E (D)	7	d
68–80	E–A–f#	8–9	e
81–91	A	1–3	b^3
92–97	A	1–3	f
97–116	A	(1–3)	b^3 + f

Example 4.5　F-Pn, Rés. Vm¹113, mm. 50–58

let the palms be interwoven, let the trophies be raised,
and with festive voice...

ers all of lines 8 and 9 (motive e) in a joyful antiphonal outpouring from all
the musicians.

A look at the manuscript reveals that the tutti concludes in F-sharp minor
(ex. 4.7), after which a tag in the b.c. moves back into the tonic key (mm. 81–
83) and restores the original triple meter with music related to the motives associated with the opening text (b³). The *segno* at m. 82 marks the spot to which
section 4 will return for a repetition of this music (mm. 82–116; motives b³

Example 4.6   F-Pn, Rés. Vm¹113, mm. 64–68

...let France and Spain proclaim: "long live the child..."

and f), which begins with quarter-note upbeats in the S^1–S^2–T parts launching into imitation on virtuosic eighth-note melismas. At m. 92, the two sopranos emphasize the word "soave" by adorning it with a trill on the first of a group of thirty-second notes; the other parts imitate this final embellishment (motive f). This substantial first section acts as a frame for the entire *Divertimento* and reveals the composer's skill with large-scale choral writing.

The personification of the duchess, "La Gloria," sings the first solo (section 2):

Gloriosa Adelaide, d'ogni cor e
    d'ogn'alma alta speranza,
cui s'inchinan divote anime e cori,
    ai cui sommi splendori
danno applauso immortali le
    monarchie.
Ecco gionto quel dì che al glorioso
    tuo parto sovrano
darà sommessi omaggi il Trace insano.

Glorious Adelaide, high hope of
    every heart and spirit,
before whom devoted souls and hearts
    bow down
and whose great splendors monarchs
    applaud.
The day has come on which the mad
    Turk
will give humble tribute to your
    glorious royal delivery.

Example 4.7   F-Pn, Rés. Vm¹113, p. 15, mm. 78–83

Let the sweet sound . . .

The poetry and its musical setting recall the encomia of *Produzioni armoniche,* which praise members of the royal family in simple soprano-b.c. arias and employ transparent madrigalism to mirror textual meaning. For "Adelaide, high hope of every heart," the opening soprano phrase rises from a¹ to the octave above, matched by the downward turn of phrase depicting her devoted bystanders ("cui s'inchinan divote anime") (ex. 4.8).

In this opening passage, the soprano delivers the text in recitative style above a series of harmonies moving from pedal Ds underscoring the key of the solo (mm. 117–119) through the circle of fifths via A (m. 120) and E (m. 122). The recitative introduces the aria for "La Fama." In addition to their recitative-aria distinction, the two soprano solos contrast by key and texture. Now in the relative minor, two violins accompany the allegory of Fame, without the b.c. (ex. 4.9):

Arcieri guerrieri	Archers of war,
che fieri raggirate	who arrogantly outsmart
i brandi alteri	proud swords,
e con pugna mentita	and in a sham battle
fulminate, saettate.	strike with a shower of arrows.
E al pargoletto eroe, d'eterno vanto erede,	And to the child hero, heir to eternal glory,
palma non sia che non gli baci il piede.	let there not be a single palm that does not kiss his foot.

Example 4.8   F-Pn, Rés. Vm¹113, mm. 117–122

Glorious Adelaide, high hope of every heart and spirit,
before whom devoted souls and hearts bow down

Throughout the aria, the second violin plays a *petite basse* role, allowing the first violin to introduce the motto of the soprano's lyric line (mm. 130–132), to play a duet with the second violin (mm. 133–134), and to accompany the voice (mm. 135–138).

In the aria's first full sentence, internal rhymes mimic repetitive martial

Example 4.9   F-Pn, Rés. Vm¹113, mm. 130–138

Archers of war, who arrogantly outsmart proud swords,

acts (ex. 4.9); the second sentence conveys the idea that the "child hero" embodies the union of France and Savoy. Wildly battling thirty-second-note flourishes in manic 3/8 time (mm. 130-149) give way to peaceful devotional admiration of the baby (mm. 150-178), with triple and duple meters sharing a restful quarter-note pulse. Repeated twice with new accompanimental material each time, the setting of "palma non sia" marks the climax of the aria with palms of victory waving high in the singer's range, music on which the following ritornello for violin duet elaborates.

Section 4 reunites the instrumental trio and brings together the sopranos in a duet for "Due Amorini" ("Two Cupids"). The poem presages the deadly arrows portrayed in section 10, but here they are amorous ones that mirror the iconography of the duchess. She appears in an exquisite oil portrait by Jean-Baptiste Santerre (1651–1717) in a bejeweled dress with an attendant winged Cupid (fig. 4.2). Moreover, the poet (Bembo? Romagnesi?) paraphrased Horace's classical ode beginning "O Venus, regina Cnidi Paphique, sperne dilectam Cypron" and interpolated a second line that compares the maternity of Marie-Adélaïde with that of Venus:

Alma Dea di Pafo e Gnido,	Sacred Goddess of Paphos and Cnidos,
bella madre di Cupido,	beautiful mother of Cupid,
lascia ormai Cipro e Cithera,	leave now Cyprus and Cythera;
qui si porti tutto il resto di tua schiera	let the remainder of your legions come here,
e i faretrati	and let the quivered
Amori alati,	winged Cupids,
che d'alm'e cor fan prede,	who make prey of soul and heart,
al famoso bambin baccino il piede.	kiss the famous child's foot.

The musical setting equals the resplendence of the poetry and art (ex. 4.10).

In the b.c., a *moto perpetuo* of running sixteenths simmers below the Cupids' duets (mm. 186–187, 189–190) and the violins' antiphonal imitation (mm. 187–188). A short ritornello following the section reinforces its key of F-sharp minor (m. 204), after which the score signals a return to the relative major of "Risuoni," the opening tutti chorus at m. 82. Sections 1 through 4 thereby come full circle and provide closure before the next dramatic scene.

Section 5 concludes the presentation of the characters of the *Divertimento* with the Chorus of Graces, a lengthy trio for two sopranos and *haute-contre* with full instrumental complement.[28] Internal rhymes characterize the poetry of the first and second couplets, in similar fashion to that of section 3:

---

[28] Scores survive from several Parisian convents—most notably Port Royal—that show women's names next to *haute-contre* parts, yet music in this range could go either way. See Catherine Cessac, *Marc-Antoine Charpentier* (Paris: Fayard, 1988), 480.

Figure 4.2   Jean-Baptiste Santerre, *Portrait de Marie-Adélaïde de Savoie* (1709). *Source*: Santerre, Jean Baptiste (1651–1717). Portrait of Marie-Adélaïde of Savoy / Duchess of Burgundy (1685–1712). 1709. Oil on canvas, 275 × 184 cm. Inv.: MV 2117. Photo: G. Blot / C. Jean. Copyright Réunion des Musées Nationaux / Art Resource, NY. Chateaux de Versailles et de Trianon, Versailles, France.

Splendete, ardete (pupille), o d'Adelaide	Shine, burn (pupils), o Adelaide's
belle pupille/ch'in voi sfaville/ chiaro splendor.	beautiful pupils/in you sparkles/ bright splendor.
Ridete o labri ch'i bei cinabri	Laugh, o lips, so that their beautiful cinnabar red
scaccin la noia e portin gioia ad ogni cor.	might banish boredom and bring joy to every heart.

The Chorus of Graces divides into two large parts, as shown in table 4.5, with most musical attention paid to the first line of verse, much like the opening tutti chorus.

Example 4.10   F–Pn, Rés. Vm¹113, mm. 186–190

Sacred Goddess of Paphos and Cnidos, beautiful mother of Cupid,

The music for the second line appears in brief portions labeled 2a, 2b, and 2c, which correspond to the breaks in the transcribed verse lines above. Part A sets the first couplet (mm. 205–235), Part B both couplets, repeated (mm. 235–267). At m. 267 the manuscript provides music for the first soprano on "Splendete," a segno marker, a *custos* guide—an indication at the end of the staff to show the initial pitch starting on the subsequent system—to the pitches f-sharp[2] and d for the first soprano and b.c., and the words "da capo." However, the *custos* guides indicate a return to the second setting of "Splendete" at m. 235 rather than a true da capo to m. 205; no segno appears at either juncture. Another oddity of the manuscript also merits scrutiny: on p. 36, mm. 206–207, the alto sings "pupille" while the soprano sings "ardete" (ex. 4.11). The simultaneously sounding words reinforce the text, echoed by the instruments.

Example 4.11   F-Pn, Rés. Vm¹113, p. 36, mm. 205–208

Shine, burn, o Adelaide's (pupils)

Santerre's portrait, although painted five years after the *Divertimento,* offers a fine visual analog to the poetic description of the duchess's large, limpid brown eyes and luscious, cinnabar red lips. A marked *Ritt[ornell]o* gracefully tapers off Part A and leads into the variation on the opening material for Part B at m. 235 (ex. 4.12), where all three parts concur with their text underlay and "ardete" is heard in the mezzo range. In the next tutti section, a sequence of

TABLE 4.5 Analysis of the Chorus of Graces from the *Divertimento* (F-Pn, Rés. Vm¹113)

7 (Measures)	Key	Line	Score
Part A			
205–9/210–14	D–A/D–A	1–2a	S¹HC bc/Rit
214–22/222–26	A–D/A–D	1–2a/1–2a–2b	SSbc–"Rit"/SSbc
226–28	e–F#	2b	SSbc–"Rit"
228–35	D–b	2b–c	Tutti/Rit
Part B[a]			
235–45	D	1	Tutti
245–50/250–7	D	2	Tutti/"Rit"
257–64/264–7	D–b–A	3–4	Tutti/"Rit"

[a]After part B reaches m. 267, it repeats beginning at m. 235.

Example 4.12   F-Pn, Rés. Vm¹113, p. 44, mm. 235–238

Shine, burn

three transpositions moves the phrase "belle pupille ch'in voi sfaville" up by
step—g–a–b in the continuo—and the ritornello literally echoes it (ex. 4.13).

Following the Chorus of Graces, the First Grace sings a solo aria with the
instrumental trio, which provides a brief introduction to her text in section 6:

Su cantate, su danzate,	Come, sing, come, dance
mentre stagion sì dolce, sì gradita	for such a sweet, pleasant season
a le gioie, ai piacer l'anime invita.	invites all souls to joy and pleasure.

Even if the name of the First Grace does not appear on the score at this place,
the indication for the repetition of this music following section 8 suggests that
she is the singer both times: "The First Grace repeats *Su Cantate*" (see table
4.3). Her extended trill on e^2 seems to "invite" people to the dance as the repeating notes in the accompanying instruments proclaim their readiness (ex.
4.14). The Gigue resumes the duple meter from "Su Cantate" and retains the
aria's key of A minor.

The aria's text, "mentre stagion sì dolce," suggests the composition and
performance of the *Divertimento* in summertime, the season of the boy's birth.
If Bembo's intention had been for Marie-Adélaïde to dance the Gigues and
Menuet of the *Divertimento*, the piece could have been performed no earlier

Example 4.13   F-Pn, Rés. Vm¹113, mm. 246–249

beautiful pupils, in you sparkles [bright splendor]

than August 1704. The duchess's strongest passion was for the dance, which she studied with Guillaume Raynal (?–1706), one of the founding members of the Académie royale de danse.[29] August 1704 represented a noteworthy period for the composer as well as for the duchess—it was then that Ambassador Tiepolo visited her so that she could sign the French legal document settling her Venetian estate.

The aria that follows the dance revisits a theme presented in "Triumphet astris Lodovici," no. 3 from *Produzioni armoniche,* and retains its antiphonal quality between the first violin and soprano in the bright tonic key. The theme's return from the earlier piece implies that the Duke and Duchess of Burgundy, along with their son, the Duke of Brittany, represent the fulfillment of Louis XIV: his triumphant stars. The text now imparts the idea that the birth has brought so much joy to the kingdom that it should dismiss all previous worries:

Da noi fuggite, pianti e sospiri,	Flee from us, cries and sighs,
dolglie e martiri,	aches and martyrdoms,
tormenti e guai;	torments and misfortunes;
fuggite, sì, per non tornar mai.	flee, o yes, flee, never to return!

The antiphonal treatment for the first half of line 1 echoes the message that all cares are to "flee from us." The second statement of the soprano presents the entire text. The music for the third verse line beginning at the upbeat to

---

[29] F-Pan O¹★3715, f. 5v. Household *Abrégé* of the Duchess of Burgundy; Raynal's name appears just above Buterne's.

Example 4.14   F-Pn, Rés. Vm¹113, mm. 290–298

...invites all souls.

m. 319 is repeated by the ritornello as a perfect lead-in for another dance, this time a Menuet whose two light upbeats elegantly define its meter (ex. A.6). In binary form, the Menuet features two four-measure phrases in the repeated A section (mm. 337–340, 341–344), with four three-measure phrases in the B section (mm. 345–348, 348–351, 351–354, 355–358). The score indicates a first and second ending in m. 344, a full repetition of the B section and a "2.e reprise" of the last phrase as a *petite reprise,* complete with a segno marking the internal repeat (mm. 355–358). The A section, largely composed of quarter-note rhythmic motives, contrasts with the B section, with its sprightly, snapped dotted-eighth and sixteenth notes on several downbeats (mm. 348, 351) followed by a cadential augmentation of the figure to close the dance (dotted-quarter and eighth notes, mm. 352, 354). Bembo's copyist misread the foreshortened rhythms of mm. 348 and 351 as each consisting of two measures in length; visible erasures and additions in the score, probably the composer's, correct those mistakes. A recitative following the Menuet recounts the august heritage of the baby boy:

Dal Oriente al Occidente, risuoni il grido per ogni lido:	From East to West, let the cry resound on every shore:
di Luigi il gran monarca,	of Louis the great monarch,
del glorioso Delfino,	of the glorious Dauphin,
del famoso bambino, dell'eroe di Borgogna,	of the famous child, of the heroes of Burgundy,
invitto padre di Dora e Senna, la feconda madre,	undefeated father of Dora and Seine, the fertile mother,
del gran Berri, del Duce d'Orleans,	of the great Berry, of the Duke of Orleans,
che seco rai di gloria spande:	from whom spread rays of glory:
"viva sempre Luigi, il forte, il grande."	"long live Louis, the strong, the great!"

Several of the people mentioned here received tributes in *Produzioni armoniche,* most notably "Louis, the strong, the great" and his son, "the glorious Dauphin" Monseigneur (*Produzioni armoniche,* no. 12). The king's brother Monsieur, Philippe, Duke of Orleans (*Produzioni armoniche,* no. 37) had just died, so the title of "Duce d'Orleans" now referred to his son Philippe II, Duke of Chartres and Orleans (1674–1723). The "heroes of Burgundy," the baby's parents, brought together two great rivers: the Dora, which flows through Turin in Savoy, and the Seine. The boy's uncle, brother of the Duke of Burgundy, was Charles, Duke of Berry (1686–1714).

The genealogy presented in this recitative honors the boy's family through its ranking in order of seniority: great-grandfather Louis XIV, grandfather Louis, the newborn Louis Duke of Brittany, his parents, his uncle Charles, and his great-uncle Philippe. Were it not for the fact that among his ancestors were foreign women from Bavaria (his grandmother Marie-Anne-Christine-Victoire) and from England (his great-great-aunt Henrietta), the baby's parents' degree of relatedness as third cousins would have been detrimental to their children. Marie-Adélaïde's mother, Anne-Marie of Orleans, and her husband's father, Monseigneur, were also cousins—the children of Monsieur and Louis XIV, respectively. The fact that the baby would not live long cannot be ascribed to inbreeding, however, since the third child of the Duke and Duchess of Burgundy, a son born in 1710, would live on as Louis XV until 1774, with his great-uncle Philippe acting as Regent after Louis XIV's death. The devastating deaths of the Duke and Duchess of Burgundy and their second son in 1712 left only this last-born child in their wake; a funeral orison for the young couple shows the customary weeping Cupid on the left panel, a sad counterpart to the *Amorini* adoring the living "Semi-Goddess" (fig. 4.3).

Figure 4.3   *Oraison funèbre. Source*: Paris: Bibliothèque Mazarine.

Nancy Mitford has argued that the boy would not have survived, had not the Duchess of Ventadour—his wet-nurse and governess—kept him safe and far away from the doctors' reach.[30]

A soprano delivers the genealogy of section 8 in A minor, the parallel mode to the Menuet (ex. 4.15). In keeping with the compositional procedures developed in *Produzioni armoniche,* the section opens with a tangible image: the rising of the sun in the East, "Oriente," as the voice leaps up to e^2, with a subsequent descent to e^1 for its setting in the West, "Occidente." An octave run restates the word "risuoni"—invested with meaning from section 1, now referring not to the lyre but to the announcement of the baby's heritage that should be made known "on every shore" (mm. 362–363). At the mention of Louis XIV's name, the continuo moves down by step by means of a 7-#6 cadence to G as the soprano dwells on a trilled e^2 before resolving upward to g^2 (mm. 365–366). After a strong cadence in A minor at m. 379, the First Grace repeats "Su Cantate" from section 6 (mm. 268–296). Logically, she should sing all of the intervening sections as well as this recitative in order to facilitate the execution of the interspersed arias and dances. A choral number, section 9, continues the celebration:

Su dunque ai suoni, ai balli, ai canti,	Arise then to sounds, to dances, to songs,
ai musici concenti;	to music's harmony;

---

[30] Nancy Mitford, *The Sun King* (New York: Harper and Row, 1966), 231–232.

Example 4.15   F-Pn, Rés. Vm¹113, mm. 361–366

Dal O - ri-en - te al Oc — ci - den - te, ri - suo — — ni il

7 6

gri - do per o - gni li - do: di Lu - i - gi il gran mo-nar - ca,

7   #6

From East to West, let the cry resound on every shore:
of Louis the great monarch,

  e qui risponda   and let here respond
  l'aria, la terra, il ciel, il mare   the air, the earth, the sky, the sea,
   e l'onda.   and the wave.

"Su" restates the First Grace's injunction from the previous music, as if the birth announcement has caused the natural world to join the celebratory voices and dances of humankind (ex. 4.16).

The section proclaims the text twice through in D minor, divided into two parts, A (mm. 380–399) and B (mm. 400–416) with a concluding ritornello (mm. 417–21). In Part A, the instruments introduce the motto (m. 380) that the tutti chorus takes up, featuring a brief interjection from the three lower voices (mm. 382–383). A segue into "ai musici concenti" begins with a brief trio for the two sopranos and bass that leads back into the tutti. "E qui risponda" prompts a madrigalistic series of imitations of the phrase from tutti chorus to ritornello, S-HC, and T-B, after which the listing of elements begins: air, earth, sky, sea, and wave (ex. 4.17).

Part B sets the verse anew; this time, the motto roles are reversed as the tutti chorus begins and the instruments reply. Much of Part B features antiphony between the choral writing for the voices and for the instruments. Between mm. 412 and 414, the bass voice drops out and returns for the penultimate bars to conclude the section with a full D-minor cadence. This chorus elicits a full sound matching the grandeur of the text through madrigalism, motivic development, imitative and antiphonal techniques, and harmonic skill. Section 9 represents the last number containing new music for the entire ensemble, as the next full tutti—that following section 15—will repeat the opening chorus to conclude the *Divertimento*.

The instruments move into the parallel major for section 10, a brief aria

Example 4.16   F-Pn, Rés. Vm¹113, mm. 380–383

Arise then to sounds, to dances, to songs,

for soprano and the instrumental trio. The text's internal triple rhymes recall the poetry of section 3:

Sventure, fuggite,   Flee misfortunes;
  coi strali fatali mortali in van mi   with your fatal deadly arrows, you
    seguite.   follow me in vain.

Example 4.17 F–Pn, Rés. Vm¹113, mm. 414–416

...the sea, and the wave.

Each of the soprano's three entrances imitates the instrumental group as an enactment of the "deadly arrows" following her (ex. 4.18).

The first two statements include the entire couplet, while the final statement stops after the initial imperative—the wish to obliterate misfortune—and concludes on two further repetitions of the verb, "fuggite." The instrumental parts' "piano" marks their final echo as the section "flees," successfully fulfilling the wish.

Section 11 creates a minor mode version of the theme composed to depict "fleeing" in section 7. Interestingly, it began as the antiphonal call for "Triumphet Astris" from *Produzioni armoniche* and now "triumphet" appears in Italian, "trionfi" (ex. 4.19). The setting here can also be compared with the duchess's pre-nuptial cantata no. 13, which concludes with melismas on "triumphant . . . victory":

Trionfi sempre	Let laughter and fun
in questo loco	always triumph
il riso e 'l gioco	in this place;
né cangi tempre	nor should the constant heart

Example 4.18   F-Pn, Rés. Vm¹113, mm. 422–437

Flee misfortunes; with your fatal deadly arrows, you follow me in vain.

Example 4.19   F-Pn, Rés. Vm¹113, mm. 464–469

Let [laughter and fun] always triumph in this place...

per girar d'ore   change character
costante il core.   with the passage of time.

The verse features five-syllable lines (*quinari*), rhyming abbacc. Such regularity is atypical of the *Divertimento*, much of it written in free verse, but rather more in keeping with the poetic structures found in the arias of *Produzioni armoniche*. The soprano sings the complete text twice through, accompanied by the instrumental trio. Defining madrigalisms on "riso" and "girar" evoke the sense of both words through their quick thirty-second-note motion, motives that pervade all parts in imitation at the second statement of the verse in mm. 489, 493, 497, and 500 (ex. 4.20). The sustained a^2 on "costante" recalls the madrigalism on the word "eterno" in the duchess's epithalamium. Bembo's acute sensitivity to verse and poetic meaning through madrigalism and registral placement followed the tradition established by her fellow Venetian composers Monteverdi, Cavalli, and Strozzi.

Section 12 begins with a second Gigue followed by an aria for soprano and *haute-contre:* the First and Third Graces. The double bar at the end of the dance would argue for its consideration as a section on its own, but it shares the 6/8 meter and E-minor tonality with the ensuing duet aria and functions rather as its prelude. Moreover, sections 6 and 7 suggested the same type of pairing, also with a double bar between them, although in each of those instances the dance followed the aria. Whereas the first Gigue was set in a duple meter (¢) based on duple subdivisions (ex. 4.14), this one uses compound meter (6/8) with triple subdivisions (ex. 4.21).

The elegant crafting of the Gigue's tonal construction ranks it with the best French chamber works of the day, such as those found in suites by Hotteterre and Dornel. Set in E minor with binary structure, the Gigue moves into related tonal areas in both halves:

||: e(i) – D(V of III) – G(III) :||: G(III) – D(V of III) – b(vi of D; v of e) – e(i) – G(III) – b(v) – e(i) :||

The b.c. receives pride of place, as it plays a solo as well as an accompanimental role in the antiphonal performance of the thematic material. It echoes the themes throughout and participates in the tutti portions closing each half. Eighth-note motives characterize the outset of the first half, with the introduction of snapped dotted motives (mm. 518–520) that will characterize the second half. The initial thematic material in E minor, which turned toward the dominant of G in the first half, returns midway through the second, there moving toward that relative major and thereafter toward the dominant to complete the Gigue. As had the Menuet of section 7, this Gigue indicates a full repeat as well as a *petite reprise* for the last measures, mm. 535–537, with *custos* guides as well as a segno in each of the three parts.

What might have been the desired instrumentation for the three dances of

Example 4.20   F-Pn, Rés. Vm¹113, mm. 488–506

...laughter and fun will not allow the constant heart to change character with the passage of time.

Example 4.21   F-Pn, Rés. Vm¹113, mm. 514–522

the *Divertimento?* Flutes doubling the strings would be appropriate for their range and pastoral mood, as well as for their associated arias. Bembo would call for such instrumentation in her second *Te Deum,* a *grand motet,* so it is possible to infer backward here that flutes could play the soft echoes to the strings' louder passages. She specified violins in the first *Te Deum,* but flutes may have supplemented the theorbo and harpsichord as additions to the *Divertimento.* Thanks to Sourches's journal we know that one of France's best flutists, Descosteaux, at one point performed at the duchess's pavilion. Performers of his calibre might have played the pieces examined here, given the duchess's fondness for dance and music.

The aria for the Two Graces in section 12 makes use of the instrumental trio from the second Gigue, but the two *dessus* parts only provide antiphonal echoes to the voices— they never play simultaneously. The first section of the aria distinctly recalls the final chorus of the *Te Deum,* "In te Domine speravi." Bembo chose an E-minor setting for both in 6/8 time, employing virtually identical music for their sixteen-syllable phrases: "dall'Occaso ai lidi Eoi, mai non furo né saranno" and "In te Domine speravi, non confundar in æternum":

Soggetti/Vassalli di noi,	Subjects/Vassals of ourselves
dall'Occaso ai lidi Eoi,	from the West to Eastern shores
mai non furo né saranno.	never existed nor shall exist.
Delizie più care,	Among these shining stars
più dolci contenti	the coming ages will not see
fra gl'astri lucenti,	dearer delights
i secoli futuri non vedranno.	or sweeter comforts.

The striking resemblance suggests that a paired performance of these bound-together works would allow the recognition of this thematic return, and of the similitude between the "vassals" ("vassalli") allegiant to the royal kingdom and "the servants" ("famulis tuis") who hope in God. The proximity of the French royal family to Christian or Greek divinity represents a conception of the cosmos thoroughly consistent with the arias of *Produzioni armoniche*. That both phrases share so much common material furthers the notion that the composer moved effortlessly between secular and sacred worlds as she participated in life at court as well as within her semi-cloistered community.

In the final aria of the *Divertimento*, the narrator expresses a wish "in chains . . . to languish and serve . . . Adelaide, Semi-Goddess":

Ti rinnego, o libertà,	I renounce you, o freedom,
tra catene io vuò languir	in chains I wish to languish
e servir sin'a l'ultimo sospir	and serve—until my final breath—
Adelaide, Semi Dea,	Adelaide, Semi-Goddess,
casta Dea de la beltà.	chaste Goddess of beauty.

The opening gambit indeed somewhat slavishly adheres to the motto introduced by the voice, echoed by the first violin, and restated a third time by the voice (mm. 568–571)—an apt madrigalism on which to portray such a wish for servitude. The "chains" echoing between the vocal melisma and violins (ex. 4.22) resemble the circulating, crowning figures of the sonnet opening *Produzioni armoniche*. Bembo thereby created a musical connection between her first manuscript for the *Pater familias* and the close of the second for the newest family member—an unequivocal musical expression of her goal to glorify the royal family.

One wonders whether Bembo herself, well into her sixties at this stage, would have sung this final aria, for she would have been by far and away its best narrator. Given the rather rudimentary nature of the poem set to music here, true *poesia per musica*, it would not be unreasonable to consider the possibility that she wrote the verse herself. However, if Romagnesi one day proves to have been the poet of the texts, then he managed in both cases to provide her with an appropriate manner to express her profound indebtedness to the French kingdom.

Example 4.22   F-Pn, Rés. Vm¹113, mm. 569–575

I renounce you, o freedom, in chains I wish to languish

The birth of the Duke of Brittany in 1704 inspired musical compositions abroad as well as in France. In Venice, the French Ambassador Joseph-Antoine Hennequin de Charmont Fontaine commissioned music for the occasion from one of the foremost composers, Benedetto Vinaccesi: the serenata, *Sfoghi di giubilo.* While the music has not survived, the poem has.[31] By contrast to Bembo's *Divertimento,* this text shows no sign of dances as part of the festivities. Although written for the same occasion, its emphasis differs from Bembo's. At the outset, Marie-Adélaïde is portrayed as the "pure goddess of Delos," but she is absent from the rest of the poem:

[31] It is preserved in F-Pamae, Correspondance politique, Venise, 139, ff. 221–226. The music does not accompany the poem and has not yet been located. As the ambassador explained on ff. 208v–209, he took the liberty of sending the poem but would bring the music only when he returned to France: "I will carry along with me all musical compositions that are beautiful and of particularly good taste, that are worthy of serving one day as an entertainment for your

Empi di rai più chiari	Fill the open path of heaven
le aperte vie del cielo,	with the brightest rays,
candida Dea di Delo,	pure Goddess of Delos,
ed ingombra di luce, e monti, e valli;	and fill the mountains and valleys with light
or che ha per fasce in cuna	now that Fortune's mane
il crin de la Fortuna,	has turned into swaddling clothes in the cradle,
E vaghisce Il BAMBIN Giove de' Galli.	and she can admire the CHILD, who is Jove of the French.

In the dedication, the poem, and dances, Bembo emphasized elements favored by the Duchess of Burgundy, just as she had for the set of three wedding pieces in *Produzioni armoniche*. The gathered evidence all points strongly to the duchess's patronage for the Venetian composer in her midst. These compositions suggest a specifically feminine interpretation of the occasions of wedding and birth that contrast markedly with those of her male contemporaries. If Vinaccesi and Destouches—whose dedication to *Issé* honored the occasion of the duchess's wedding—were the only representatives from the period, the duchess might appear to have been a marginal, minor figure in the wedding and the birth. Bembo's work forcefully dispels this notion by emphasizing her central importance to both occasions. The female perspective supplied here provides a new impression of the duchess as a peacemaker, an active role more powerful than that of political pawn promoted elsewhere. This music dramatizes the private, domestic world of the duchess and adds an important dimension to her public, strategic role. Bembo's hypothetical membership in Marie-Adélaïde's Italian circle may help to explain how she could take a more intimate approach to writing music for her than could the composers bound by commission and state obligation.

Scribal Considerations

Bembo's dedicatory words mention the duchess's "patronage." Might the inference suggest that the wedding pieces of *Produzioni armoniche* met with such approbation that the young princess asked her for more music and, with it, offered her some monetary support? Because Bembo's name does not appear

---

Majesty" ["Je porte avec moy toutes les compositions de musique qui sont belles et d'un goust particulier et digne de pouvoir servir un jour de divertissement a sa Majesté"]. In *Pallade Veneta*, Eleanor Selfridge-Field identified the four singers in the serenata, who represent Glory, Virtue, Public Confidence, and French Genius ["Gloria, Virtù, la Fede Publica," and "il Genio della Francia"] as Cattarina Inverardi, Madalena Zustiniani, Tomaso Fabris, and Stefano Romano (Venice: Fondazione Levi, 1985), 254. On *Sfoghi di giubilo*, see Michael Talbot, *Benedetto Vinaccesi:*

on any of the lists of the duchess's household, nor in the extraordinary expenses associated with it, the financial aspect remains ambiguous. Moreover, the *Abrégé* listing all those in service to the duchess recorded no payments to music scribes.

In her dedication, the composer noted that she presented the *Te Deum* and *Divertimento* as a pair, which the duchess had bound together in the red leather characteristic of the royal libraries along with her official imprimatur: the device uniting France and Savoy (figs. 4.1 and 4.3). The resulting manuscript, Bembo's second opus, is distinguished from *Produzioni armoniche* not just in its precise dating and dedicatee, but also in the hand of its copyist. If the duchess did indeed offer the composer financial assistance, it may have been for the copying of this manuscript.

In order to compare the scribal hands of F-Pn Rés. Vm^{1}117 and Rés. Vm^{1}112–113, this study makes use of the handwriting samples already provided: the two letters of 1682 and the *procura* signed in summer 1704 (figs. 2.2, 2.3, and 2.7) as well as the facsimile examples of the *Produzioni armoniche* manuscript (ex. 3.2 and 3.3), the *Te Deum* (ex. 4.1 and 4.2), and the *Divertimento* (ex. 4.7, 4.11, and 4.12).

No discrepancy exists between the hand that copied the *Te Deum* and *Divertimento*—these manuscripts represent Group 1, the three documents with Bembo's handwriting Group 2, and *Produzioni armoniche* Group 3. More differences than similarities exist across the groups. The capital letters "A" and "S" in Group 1 (ex. 4.11–4.12) resemble those found in Group 2 (figs. 2.2–2.3), but little else suggests that Bembo was the hand behind the music manuscript. Group 3 uses a cursive *a* (ex. 3.3). The capital "R" of "Reverendissima" in Group 2 (fig. 2.2) has nothing in common with that found for "Ritournelle" or "Rißsuoni" in Group 1 (ex. 4.2 and 4.7). Although the deltoid, lower-case "d" followed by "e" is found both in the correspondence of Group 2, such as "dimanda" and "defonta" (fig. 2.3) and in Group 1, "Splendete, ardete" (ex. 4.11–4.12), it is practically the only common calligraphy; the handwriting makes an extravagant backward curved loop absent in Group 1. "H" bears no resemblance between her letters, such as "Hò" (fig. 2.3) and the music of Group 3, "Habbi" (ex. 3.2).

The two scores, Groups 1 and 3, offer points of comparison among musical symbols. The soprano and bass clef demonstrate considerable differences: Group 3's large soprano clef has a protruding lower stemmed breve (ex. 3.2), while Group 1's is small and the breves line up (ex. 4.1). Group 3's

---

A Musician in Brescia and Venice in the Age of Corelli (Oxford: Clarendon Press, 1994), 89–90, 218, and 330. Talbot's research into the serenata genre has led to me consider Bembo's *Divertimento* as a lengthy cantata rather than as a serenata; see his "Vivaldi and a French Ambassador," *Informazioni e studi vivaldiani* 2 (1981): 31–41 and "The Serenata in Eighteenth-Century Venice," *Research Chronicle of the Royal Musical Association* 18 (1982): 1–50.

bass clef is neat, curling up like a snail on the F line of the staff (ex. 3.2), while Group 1's hangs down (ex. 4.1). The upright "#" in Group 3 (ex. 3.2) becomes a left-oriented symbol in Group 1 (ex. 4.7). Braces unite systems in Group 1 (ex. 4.2), whereas Group 1 leaves the systems unconnected (ex. 3.3).

Rokseth's pioneering article posited that all of Bembo's scores are autographs, but she did not have the Venetian correspondence to hand. With these documents available to view, it can be determined that Bembo sent her music out to be copied. Perhaps the patronage for which she thanked both Louis XIV and Marie-Adélaïde helped her to present her works to them in bindable fair copy. Even though the scribal hands are clear and the manuscripts preserved in excellent condition, no scholar has yet been able to ascribe them to a known copyist. Thanks to Bernardo Bembo's archive, the composer's signature on the August 1704 *procura* (fig. 2.7) dispels the notion that she copied her own manuscript of the *Te Deum* and *Divertimento* during the same summer season, if not the very same month.

Only in the last three manuscripts (one for the penitential psalms and two for the opera) would a third scribe be called upon; that hand provides yet another set of idiosyncrasies. With its offering of two more sacred motets, once again for Louis XIV, Bembo's third manuscript (F-Pn, Rés. Vm^{1}114–115), next examined in "The United Tastes," shares the scribal hand of her first *Te Deum* and her *Divertimento*.

Chapter 5

THE UNITED TASTES

The third manuscript, F-Pn, Rés. Vm^{1}114–115, revisits previous texts. Here the *Te Deum,* set for instrumental and vocal trios in F-Pn, Rés. Vm^{1}112, expands into a *grand motet* for chorus, soloists, and orchestra and, like its predecessor, takes first position in the pair of larger works. Here Psalm 20, whose final couplet had appeared twice in *Produzioni armoniche* (nos. 4 and 40), receives a complete setting as the *Exaudiat te, Dominus;* the psalm's orchestration mirrors that of the first *Te Deum,* with an instrumental trio matched in range to its vocal trio. Epitomizing early eighteenth-century chamber music, such trios contain music for two treble-range instruments balanced by a fundamental bass.

The manuscript's dedication reveals its chronology as the composer's "terzo laboro," offered to the entire royal family but especially to the king (doc. 26):

Te Deum to pray God for the preservation of a monarch as great as Louis XIV and [of] all his royal family. Accompanied by an Exaudiat. Composition of Antonia Bembo, Noble Venetian

Sire,

Louis the great, the strong, the wise, the invincible, supreme Jove of the earth, monarch of monarchs: I make so bold as to dedicate the third product of my weak efforts to your sacred Majesty. A Te Deum to render thanks to the divine Majesty (and also to pray for the preservation of a prince so dear to your Majesty, and to all the court, as the Duke of Brittany) with the addition of an Exaudiat. Sire, [she] who gives as much as [she] can, gives what [she] owes, and strong passions are better expressed by devoted silence than by fluent eloquence. Nevertheless I venture to sign my name below with the most meek and profound respect.

Your most Christian Majesty's faithful, submissive, and most respectful servant,

Antonia Bembo, Noble Venetian

Casting aside earlier Apollonian metaphor, Bembo now likened the king to Jupiter, "Jove," the god who fought the giants on earth and governed the heavens.[1] She emphasized her repeated gift-giving by quoting from her earlier work: "chi dà quanto può, dà quanto deve" (*Produzioni armoniche,* no. 2).[2] The final couplet of an earlier encomiastic cantata for the king, this quotation follows the statement that she has added "an Exaudiat" and implicitly refers to her two earlier settings of the psalm's final couplet. Similarly, the notion of "devoted silence" echoes an earlier concern that imprudent loquaciousness must learn silent adoration (*Produzioni armoniche,* no. 10). By contrast with the singerly art that won Bembo her royal pension in the early 1680s, it was composition that more closely aligned with the quasi-silent enterprise sought in this dedication. The question of authorship of the anonymous poetry raises itself one last time here, but still cannot be laid to rest. By quoting from the earlier cantata, did the composer bring the notion into play again to underline her own authorship and to reinforce its autobiographical significance? Notably, all of the texts set after 1704 come from the Bible and from readily identifiable contemporary authors. Moreover, Romagnesi—the putative author of the anonymous Italian poetry from her first and second manuscript—had died in 1706, before the production of this one.

Bembo may have offered her second *Te Deum* to celebrate the French military victory marked by the capture of the Catalan city of Tortosa in July 1708.[3] The dedication presents a wish for the continuation of the king's health as well as for that of the "Duca di Bretagna": the second Duke of Brittany, born on 8 January 1707.[4] Peter Burke's characterization of the "sunset" years encapsulates the court's general sentiment of defeat in the final decade of the reign of Louis XIV, when few practitioners of music or of poetry could match the former talents of Lully or Molière. Bembo's optimistic prayers responded to that sentiment by bolstering earlier images of Louis XIV's strength, wisdom, and invincibility. Her metaphorical "Giove" echoes the reference to the first Duke of Brittany in the dedication to Vinaccesi's *Sfoghi di giubilo.* The volume containing Bembo's paired works bears the king's coat of arms, marked with a brass stamp dating to the turn of the eighteenth century. Golden laurels outline the book's edges, with four decorative "L"s at each of the four corners of their inner square. Louis's initial "L"s and the cir-

---

[1] Néraudau, *L'Olympe du Roi-Soleil,* 63–64.

[2] A number of scholars have taken Marcel Mauss's *The Gift* (New York: Norton, 1967) and applied its ideas regarding patronage to the French court. See in particular Sharon Kettering, "Gift-Giving and Patronage in Early Modern France," *French History* 2 (1988): 131–151, and Natalie Zemon Davis, "Beyond the Market: Books as Gifts in Sixteenth-Century France," *Transactions of the Royal Historical Society* 33 (1983): 69–88, as well as Davis's book on the subject: *The Gift in Sixteenth-Century France* (Madison: University of Wisconsin Press, 2000).

[3] Burke, *The Fabrication of Louis XIV,* 112, with reference to the [*Recueil des*] *Gazettes* of 1708.

[4] Carré, *La Duchesse de Bourgogne,* 150.

cular crest holding three fleurs-de-lys contrast with the heraldry found on the cover of *Produzioni armoniche* (fig. 3.1).

Although no record survives to tell about the performance of either of the motets of F-Pn, Rés. Vm¹114–115—if it ever existed—their analysis reveals that they were composed with the foremost musical models in mind, especially those of Lalande. The only manuscript to employ Latin throughout, the liturgical language shared by both French- and Italian-speaking cultures provided the apt medium for Bembo to unify their styles in the motet.

"Les goûts réunis"

The *Te Deum* for Marie-Adélaïde mixed French and Italian rubrics in its closing movement, whereas the present *grand motet* and Psalm 20 employ French rubrics everywhere except at their conclusions, where both use the heading "Ritt[ornell]o" (tables 5.1 and 5.6). The *grand motet* begins with the quintessentially French "Symphonie" (ex. 5.1), whereas Psalm 20 employs the Latin term "Symphonia." These three motets evidently represent the Venetian composer's efforts to unite the two tastes she knew so well, brought together by word (Latin text, and rubrics in Italian, French, or their conflation) and music. Two prominent examples juxtaposing French and Italian styles frame the period of her activity in France: Lully's "Dialogue de la musique italienne et de la musique française" from the *Ballet de la Raillerie* (*Ballet of Mockery*, 1659), which deals with vocal music (ex. A.7), and instrumental music by François Couperin from 1725 (ex. A.5).

In Lully's "Dialogue," set in the key of G minor, the b.c. supports two alternating treble voices representing Italian Music and French Music (ex. A.7):

Italian Music (mm. 5–9): Kind French Music, how did my song offend you?
French Music (mm. 9–14): In so much as your songs often seem dull to me.
Italian Music (mm. 14–24): You are not capable of making anything but suffering and sad lamentations.
French Music (mm. 24–37): Do you believe that anyone prefers your long, boring humming?
Italian Music (mm. 37–41): Why should your taste make the rules for another's?
French Music (mm. 41–49): I'm not commanding your [taste], but I want to sing with mine.
Italian Music (mm. 49–63): I can sing more loudly than you because I love more than you do; he who feels a deathly pain cries out as loudly as he can, "have pity!"
French Music (mm. 63–82): The way that I sing expresses better my languishing; when this pain touches the heart, the voice is less bright.[5]

---

[5] Prunières, *L'Opéra italien*, Appendix, 16–19, which he transcribed from F-Pn, Vm⁶1.

Through mockery ("raillerie") and competition in the first three exchanges, the two musics come to define their own characteristics in the final one. Italian Music initiates the dialogue with a provocative question in imitation of the smooth octave descent of the solo bass line. French Music answers with two measures of even rhythms moving in conjunct intervals (mm. 9–11) and then mocks Italian Music's character-defining dotted rhythms propelling leaping fourths (mm. 11–12). Both characters find the other's music "dull" or "boring" ("languissants" mm. 13–14 / "languenti" mm. 16–21 / "ennuyeux" mm. 31–32, 36–37), which suggests a mutual lack of comprehension; Italian Music also finds the song of the French too "sad" ("mesti" mm. 22–23). Italian Music makes its accusation via a notable melisma (mm. 17–21) that French Music perceives as an excessive "humming" ("fredons"). French Music thereby identifies its counterpart's characteristics not just as melismatic but also sequential (mm. 27–30, 33–34). Italian Music continues with another provocative question, beginning with its own dotted, interval-leaping persona (fourth, m. 37, and minor sixth, m. 39), but, at the mention of "your taste," moving back into the smooth, flowing descent of its opening gambit (compare mm. 1–4, 8, and 39–41), further reinforcing the way that French Music flows stepwise in conjunct motion. Avowing a simple preference for its own taste, French Music dismisses the competition between them through its demonstration of a two-measure phrase drawn from the style of the air sérieux (A, mm. 43–45) with brief pseudo-double variations upon it (A^1, mm. 45–47, and A^2, mm. 47–49). A reveals a brief modal shift from G minor to G major (m. 44) that contrasts with the chromaticism characterizing Italian Music in mm. 55–60, A^1 subtly provides rhythmic decoration (m. 46), and A^2 takes up the syncopation of A^1 followed by even rhythms and conjunct motion with a cadence in the home key (mm. 47–49).

The fourth exchange leads to the revelation of each music's essence. Italian Music claims its own as: including more disjunct intervals set in dotted rhythms (mm. 49–53, 61–62), louder and therefore better (mm. 49–51), more passionate (mm. 51–55), and better at sustained chromaticism (mm. 55–60). French Music returns now to the concept of "langueur," turning what it regarded initially in pejorative terms as "boring" into a positive compliment whereby languor refers to its introverted, quiet response to existential "pain" ("mal" m. 73), by contrast with Italian Music's extroverted response to it (mm. 55–63). French Music hereby acknowledges *its* expressive mode—which Italian Music finds too "sad"—by stating its unabashed preference for its own music. In such a context, one can well imagine the hostility that Cavalli encountered from Lully two years later, when commissioned to compose an Italian opera for the French court. Bembo inherited Lully's definitions of national difference by virtue of having witnessed his last decade of activity in France.

Whereas Lully's dialogue emphasized the goal to differentiate between the two musics in order to define nascent French classical style, Couperin's efforts were to unite them in two instrumental works of 1724–1725.[6] It was Couperin's manner of incorporating into one's native musical style the attractive qualities of the other that Bembo anticipated in the decades preceding his two publications on the subject. In the *Préface* to *Les Goûts-réünis,* Couperin explained his acceptance of both tastes; however, in content the publication remained largely French in manner with a few nods to the Italians. The ninth *Concert* bears the title "Ritratto dell'amore," the tenth *Concert* includes a movement named "la Tromba," and "L'Apothéose de Corelli," which crowns the publication, contains a "Sonade" that uses "notes égales" to portray the quintessential Italian composer. The two airs reproduced in example A.5, discussed above in connection with *Produzioni armoniche,* come from Couperin's *Concert instrumental* of the following year: in the first air, Lully plays the tune and Corelli accompanies, and vice versa in the second air. In effect, Couperin's symbolic duo—Corelli and Lully—revisits Lully's "Dialogue," now providing actual composers rather than anonymous national representatives, instrumental rather than vocal music, and a conciliatory rather than a confrontational mode of presentation. French Music (Lully) is notated in French violin clefs with a squiggle for trills, with melodies in conjunct motion (or *tierces coulées* rendering the same effect), and largely conjunct bass lines. Italian Music (Corelli) is notated in G2 clefs with the + symbol for trills, more leaps within the melodic lines, and frequent Alberti bass figuration. Couperin's apt comparison between the consummate artists of the recent past justifies the unification that he proposed in order to bring about "perfection in music"[7]— notably on the eve of the eruption of the debates over the Paris production of Pergolesi's *La serva padrona,* which would lead to the Guerre des Bouffons. "La Paix de Parnasse," the musical equivalent of a political treaty, follows the Corelli-Lully exchange of airs.[8] In order to placate the French Muses, Couperin proposed terms that gallicize standard Italian ones, such as "cantade" and "sonade." Indeed, he further asserted that the first "Sonades Italiénes" appeared in Paris more than "thirty years ago,"[9] that is, prior to 1694.

Couperin's historical reference merits a small detour, as it provides testimony to the first known sonatas in France. In addition to the Corelli publications, these included works purchased for the Italian circle around Abbé Mathieu at Saint-André des Arts in Paris.[10] Couperin also undoubtedly re-

[6] François Couperin, *Les Goûts-réünis ou Nouveaux Concerts à l'usage de toutes les sortes d'instrumens [sic] de Musique augmentés d'une grande Sonade en Trio. Intitulée Le Parnasse ou l'Apothéose de Corelli* (Paris: Boivin, 1724; reprint, New York: Performers' Facsimiles, n.d. [2001?]), and *Concert instrumental sous le Titre d'Apotheose [sic] Composé à la mémoire immortelle de l'incomparable Monsieur de Lully* (Paris: Boivin, 1725; reprint, New York: Performers' Facsimiles, n.d. [2001?]).

[7] Couperin, *Concert instrumental,* 12.

[8] Ibid., 16.

[9] Couperin, *Les Goûts-réünis,* Préface.

[10] Michel le Moël, "Un Foyer d'italianisme à la fin du XVIIe siècle: Nicolas Mathieu, curé de Saint-André-des-Arts," *"Recherches" sur la musique française classique* 3 (1963): 43–48.

ferred to La Guerre's instrumental music, including the "tocade" of her first book of harpsichord music from 1687, and imitated the Italianate nature of her unpublished *sonates en trio* that apparently date from the early part of the 1690s.

Borrowed here for an earlier time and altogether different repertory, the phrase "les goûts réunis" applies to Bembo's settings of Latin texts. Her *grand motet* bears numerous signs of having adopted the French style: (1) the timbre of the *haute-contre* voice; (2) the instruments of its ensembles, including the named transverse flute and the bassoon for the soft echoes, and the implied *hautes-contre de violon* for the inner parts; (3) the disposition of the work for soloists, five-part chorus, and orchestra; and (4) in the *récits,* the languorous quality ascribed to French Music in Lully's "Dialogue," mm. 67–70, and also found in his *petits motets* (ex. 3.15). Although consciously fewer in number, some Italian elements remain recognizable: prominent, high-register thirds at cadences already noted in the first *Te Deum;* split scoring; and the ritornello found in the concluding section.

With Bembo's music and models of influence in mind, Psalm 20 can be considered as another forum for exploring "les goûts réunis." By 1708, she had lived in Paris for more than thirty years. Chapter 3 posited a quest for redemption via the selected texts and dedicatory message; here, through religious music in Latin, she found a balanced synthesis of the reigning tastes of her time. Their neutral language prefigures Couperin's idea of reconciliation, even if the singers interpreting them sang the motets with a French accent.

The Model of the *grand motet*

During the lengthy reign of the Sun King, the *grand motet* typified musical productions offered in the Chapelle Royale. Like the *tragédie en musique,* it offered a new musical genre unique to the French.[11] Henry Du Mont (c. 1610–1684) worked almost exclusively in the sacred sphere and established the formal scheme of the *grand motet* genre—based on earlier models by Guillaume Bouzignac (c. 1587–after 1642) and Nicolas Formé (1567–1638)—that served as the foundation for its later development.[12]

Dating back to the reign of Louis XIII and the regency of Anne of Austria in the first half of the seventeenth century, the *grand motet* genre juxtaposes two groups of singers, the *grand chœur* (large chorus) and the *petit chœur* (usually vocal soloists), accompanied by a group of instrumentalists, the *chœur de symphonie.* In the first half of Louis's reign, shawms ("cromornes") and serpents joined the strings and organ in the orchestra. Advances in French instrument development and construction led to the replacement of these older instruments with the newer transverse flutes in the upper *dessus* parts, and of

[11] Laurence Decobert, "La Naissance du grand motet," in *Henry Du Mont à Versailles* (Arles: Actes Sud, 1992), 21.

[12] Ibid., 22.

the serpent with the bassoon in the b.c. After Du Mont's death, it would be Lalande who would elevate the genre to still higher status, so that the *grand motet* would be performed at court as well as in the city's Concert Spirituel throughout the eighteenth century until the Revolution.

Even though the performance venue for the *petits motets* of *Produzioni armoniche* remains unknown, they fit the repertory that the king's *sous-maîtres* (music-masters) devised for daily worship in the *Messe basse* (low Mass) and the Divine Office. These were celebrated at the many châteaux and churches at which the "nomadic" court assumed residence prior to its definitive installation at Versailles in the 1680s.[13] One *sous-maître* was appointed per semester of the year; musicologist Laurence Decobert noted that their small and large motets mostly predate their appointment to royal service. Bembo's two groups of *petits motets* in *Produzioni armoniche*—nos. 3–4 ("Pour Saint Louis" and the first of the "Domine salvum fac regem" settings, for two sopranos) and nos. 38–40 ("Panis angelicus," "Tota pulcra es," and the "Domine salvum fac regem" setting for solo soprano)—belong to the same tradition as those produced by the *sous-maîtres*, among whom were Pierre Robert (1618–1699), Thomas Gobert (c. 1600–1672), and Gabriel Expilly (c. 1630–c. 1690), in addition to Du Mont and Lully.[14] Bembo may have attended some of the occasions celebrating the morning *Messe basse* or the offices; in any case, her models of French music came from the composers in royal service and her *petits motets* match the liturgy of her religious community within the Union Chrétienne.

Lalande's 77 *grands motets* and the paraliturgical poetry found in the *Cantica pro Capella Regis* of Pierre Perrin evidently served as models for Bembo's second *Te Deum*.[15] Here she tightened the structure, compressing into 11 sections what had previously extended into 13 (compare tables 4.1 and 5.1). Both settings reveal cognizance of the Phrygian mode of the original plainchant

[13] Ibid., 25. The court moved between the urban châteaux of the Louvre and the Tuileries as well as among the country residences at Versailles, Chambord, St. Germain-en-Laye, and Fontainebleau. The king often attended Mass at the Parisian church of St.-Germain-l'Auxerrois, close to the Louvre.

[14] For a detailed study of their work and influence on the development of the *grand motet*, see Lionel H. Sawkins, "Chronology and Evolution of the *grand motet* at the Court of Louis XIV: Evidence from the *Livres du Roi* and the Works of Perrin, the *sous-maîtres* and Lully," in *Jean-Baptiste Lully and the Music of the French Baroque: Essays in Honor of James R. Anthony*, ed. John Hajdu Heyer (Cambridge: Cambridge University Press, 1989), 41–79. See, too, Jérôme de La Gorce and Herbert Schneider, eds. *Quellenstudien zu Jean-Baptiste Lully—Hommage à Lionel Sawkins*. Musikwissenschaftliche Publikationen 13 (Hildesheim: Georg Olms, 1999), and Jérôme de La Gorce and Herbert Schneider, eds., *Jean-Baptiste Lully—Actes du colloque Saint-Germain-en-Laye/Kongreßbericht Heidelberg 1987*. Neue Heidelberger Studien zur Musikwissenschaft, vol. 18 (Laaber: Laaber-Verlag, 1990).

[15] See the transcription of the dedication and preface to this work, originally published by Robert Ballard in Paris in 1665, in Louis E. Auld, *The Lyric Art of Pierre Perrin, Founder of French Opera*, Part 2, *Lyric Theory and Practice* (Henryville, PA: Institute of Mediæval Music, 1986), Appendix, 165–170. See, too, Montagnier, "Le *Te Deum*," 203.

TABLE 5.1 Analysis of the *Te Deum* (F-Pn, Rés. Vm¹114)

Section	Text/Rubric	Key	Scoring	Measures
1.	*Symphonie*	A	Ch. de symphonie, Fl., Bsn.	1–33
	Te Deum laudamus, / te Dominum confitemur.		Ch. de voix	33–78
2.	Te æternum Patrem omnis terra veneratur / tibi omnes Angeli, tibi cœli et universæ potestates.	D	S¹, V¹, b.c.	79–87
	Ritournelle		V¹, V², b.c.	87–90
	Tibi Cherubim et Seraphim incessabili voce proclamant:	D–b	S¹, S², B, V¹, V², b.c.	91–107
	sanctus Dominus Deus Sabaoth!	e	Ch. de symphonie, Ch. de voix	108–123
3.	*[Ritournelle]*	e–B	Fl¹, Fl², HCV¹, HCV², b.c.	124–129
	Pleni sunt cœli et terra majestatis gloriæ tuæ.	e–B	S¹, Fl¹, b.c.	130–135
	Te gloriosus apostolarum chorus, / te prophetarum laudabilis numerus, / te martyrum candidatus laudat exercitus.	b–D	S¹, S², B, Fl¹, b.c.	136–143
	Ritournelle	D	Fl¹, Fl², Fl³, b.c.	143–146
	Te per orbem terrarum sancta confitetur Ecclesia:	D–[G]	S¹, V¹, b.c.	146–149
	Patrem immensæ majestatis, / venerandum tuum verum et unicum Filium, / sanctum quoque Paraclitum Spiritum.	E–A	S¹, S², B, V¹, b.c.	149–156
4.	Tu Rex gloriæ Christe, tu Patris sempiternus es Filius.	A–E	S¹, S², B, V¹, b.c.	157–169
	Ritournelle	E	Ch. de symphonie	169–177
	Tu Patris sempiternus es Filius.	E–A	S¹, S², B, Ch. de symphonie	177–187
	Ritournelle		Ch. de symphonie	187–194
5.	Tu ad liberandum suscepturus hominem, / non horruisti Virginis uterum, tu devicto mortis aculeo, / aperuisti credentibus regna cælorum.	A–D	HC, HC, B, b.c.	195–204 bis
	Tu ad dexteram Dei sedes in gloria Patris,	D–E	S¹, B, V¹, V², b.c.	195–212
	judex crederis esse venturus.	E–A	Ch. de symphonie, Ch. de voix	212–220
	Ritournelle	A	Ch. de symphonie	220–232

6.	Te ergo quaesumus famulis tuis subveni / quos pretioso sanguine redemisti, / æterna fac cum sanctis tuis in gloria numerari.	a–e	S^1, V^1, b.c.	233–238
	Ritournelle	C–G	S^1, S^2, B, V^1, b.c.	239–246
		G	Ch. de symphonie	246–249
7.	Salvum fac populum tuum Domine,	G–A	S^1, V^1, b.c.	250–254
	et benedic hæreditati tuæ,		S^2, V^2, b.c.	254–258
	et rege eos, et extolle illos usque in æternum.	A–e	HC, B, b.c.	259–263
	[repeat of text]	e–b	S^1, S^2, B, V^1, b.c.	264–269
	Ritournelle	b	Ch. de symphonie	269–281
8.	*Ritournelle*	b–F#	V^1, V^2, HCV^1, HCV^2/b.c.	282–85 bis
	Per singulos dies benedicimus te, etc.	b–b	S, V^1, b.c.	285–332 bis
	Ritournelle	b–F#	Ch. de symphonie	282–286
	Per singulos dies benedicimus te, / et laudamus nomen tuum / in sæculum et in sæculum sæculi.	b–A	B, V^1, V^2, b.c.	286–298
	Ritournelle	A	Ch. de voix	298–302
		A–E	Ch. de symphonie	302–306
	[repeat of text]	E–A	S^1, S^2, B, V^1, V^2, b.c.	306–320
	Ritournelle	A	Ch. de symphonie	320–327
9.	Dignare Domine die isto, sine peccato nos custodire.	e–D	S^1, S^2, V^1, V^2, b.c.	328–336
	Miserere nostri Domine.	d	S^1, S^2, B, V^1, b.c.	337–346
	Fort lent[ement] et tendrem[en]t		Ch. de symphonie	346–356
10.	Fiat misericordia tua Domine / super nos,	a–e	S^1, V^1, b.c.	357–363
		e–B	S^2, V^2, b.c.	363–367
	quemadmodum speravimus in te.	B–E	HC, B, b.c.	367–370
11.	*Ritt[ornell]o*	A	Ch. de symphonie	371–383
	In te Domine speravi, non confundar in æternum.		Ch. de symphonie, Ch. de voix	383–412

Example 5.1   F-Pn, Rés. Vm¹114, p. 1, mm. 1–9

ascribed to St. Ambrose of Milan[16] in their use of E minor: the first as tonic throughout, the second as the key for the threefold repetition of the Sanctus.

Bembo's *grand motet* represents a remarkable first foray into full choral and orchestral scoring. In sections 5 and 8, she provided alternative settings for the same text, labeled in table 5.1 as "bis" measures. In the tutti sections, a five-part full chorus ("chœur de voix")—the same disposition of two sopranos, *haute-contre,* tenor, and bass as found in the *Divertimento*—is matched with a five-part string orchestra containing two violins, two *hautes-contre de violon,* and b.c. ("chœur de symphonie"). The score calls for flutes, bassoon, and solo violin at special junctures. Throughout, the instrumental *Ritournelle* offers a flexibility of scoring that features the entire "chœur de symphonie" (such as in section 1), the instrumental trio (section 2), or the four upper string parts alone (section 8).

This analysis refers to the first performance edition, prepared by Wolfgang Fürlinger, in tandem with the manuscript.[17] The words "symphonie, fort,

[16] Sawkins, "Chronology and Evolution," 29–30.

[17] Antonia Bembo, *Te Deum laudamus,* ed. Wolfgang Fürlinger with epilogue by Claire Fontijn. *Musik des 17. Jahrhunderts,* Band 17 (Altötting: Musikverlag Coppenrath, 1999). This edition is not an *Urtext.* It gives only "2 Flöten oder 2 Oboen und Fagott ad lib" without specifying the instruments, and the rubrics bear no relation to the manuscript. The two b.c. parts are combined in a homogenization that loses sight of some notes (see table 5.1). Ex. 5.1–5.4 and 5.7, facsimiles from the manuscript, and appendix 2, ex. A.8–9, supply some of those abridged elements.

Example 5.2 F-Pn, Rés. Vm¹114, pp. 6–7, mm. 33–39

We praise you, o God

doux," and "flutes," respectively (ex. 5.1), reveal the name of the full orchestral group, show dynamics employed in the same manner as in the first *Te Deum,* and associate the flutes with the soft, "doux," echoes. The grand opening for the "chœur de symphonie" in mm. 1–33 prefigures the melodic rendition of the text that the "chœur de voix" presents in mm. 33–78 (ex. 5.2), whose entrance prompted the shift into split scoring that Rokseth identified as an Italianate feature.[18] The voices appear (C1, C1, C3, C4, and F4) on the *verso* folio, supported by the "Basse Cont.," a figured b.c., which would be played by the organ, theorbo, or other instruments capable of realizing the designated harmonies.

The "chœur de symphonie" (G1, G1, C3, C3, and F4) appears on the *recto* folio, undergirded by an unfigured bass part to be doubled by the viola da gamba and bassoon in the *fort* sections and by bassoon alone in the *doux.* These sustaining instruments usually double the b.c. part but sometimes diverge from it by filling out the upper harmonies, notably at cadential points (mm. 35–36). The composer indicated that the bassoon should play with the flute at the soft, *doux* dynamic (upbeat to m. 49), followed by the "fort" marking the violin parts (m. 50) (ex. 5.3).[19]

The *Symphonie* begins with antiphonal, celebratory repartee, alternating loud passages for all instruments with soft passages in which reduced performing forces echo the tutti. Through contrasting dynamic levels and varied orchestration, Bembo achieved an apt aural hierarchy. Table 5.2 eluci-

[18] Rokseth, "Antonia Bembo," 156, n. 9. When split scoring is in effect, the figured b.c. part that appears below the unfigured F4 part in the instrumental *symphonie* migrates to the left-hand "chœur de voix" brace in the sections for all forces (*Tous*) (see ex. 5.1 and 5.3).

[19] The edition indicates "ad libitum" for flutes, oboes, bassoon, and contrabassoon, but the manuscript contains no indications for oboes or contrabassoon.

Example 5.3   F-Pn, Rés. Vm¹114, p. 11, mm. 46–50

dates the symmetrical structure of the first section, where the instrumental music from mm. 1–33 appears on the upper row and the tutti music from mm. 33–62 on the lower row. It also illustrates the nature of the *petite reprise,* in parentheses above the upper row (following mm. 29–33), which overlays the analogous closing material of mm. 62–78.

Whereas the first *Te Deum* had integrated voices and instruments from the outset, the separation of the larger vocal and instrumental forces here permits an entire symphonic iteration of the vocal music prior to the entry of the "chœur de voix." Motive A consists of a two-measure phrase with a strong upbeat to the first full measure corresponding to "Te Deum laudamus," in which a dotted-quarter note accentuates the second syllable (corresponding to "De-um"). The first echo repeats motive A in mm. 2–4/35–37. Motives A and B appear consecutively in mm. 4–11/37–44; the dotted-eighth–sixteenth-note downbeat rhythm of motive B responds to the second line of the text: "te Dominum confitemur." The following phrases, mm. 11–21 (23)/44–54 (56), develop motive A exclusively as they expose several reduced textures in sequential imitation. Table 5.2 separates mm. 21–23 (violin entries) and mm. 54–56 (soprano entries corresponding in range to the violins) in order to show that the choral material of mm. 62–64 will be derived from them. Mm. 11–23 feature the following order of entries: 1. Fl¹-Fl²-HCV¹-HCV² ([*doux*]), 2. HCV¹-HCV²-Vdg/Bn-b.c. ([*doux*]), 3. Fl²-HCV¹-HCV²-b.c. (*doux*), 4. Tutti (*fort*), 5. V²-HCV¹-HCV²-b.c. ([*fort*]), and 6. V¹-V²-b.c. ([*fort*]). When the vocal ensemble restates this material at mm. 44–56, it mimics the

TABLE 5.2 Analysis of the "Symphonie," *Te Deum* (F-Pn, Rés. Vm¹114)

Measures	1–2	2–4	4–11	11–21	21–23	23–29	29–33	(21–23)	(23–29)	(29–33)
	Symph. [fort]	Fl. doux	Symph. fort	Fl.-Symph. doux-fort	V¹,V², b.c.	Symph. fort	Fl. doux			
Motive A	A	A	A–B	A	A	B	B	A	B	B

Measures	33–35	35–37	37–44	44–54	54–56	56–62	62–64	64–70	70–74	74–78
	Tous Fl.	Fl.	Tous	Tous Chorus w/bassoon doux-fort	S¹, S², b.c.	Tous fort	Fl., b.c. doux	Symph.	Chorus	Symph. doux

instrumental texture. The *Symphonie* concludes with a decisive proclamation of motive B, characterized by two descending fifths in the *dessus* parts followed by sinuous conjunct lines replete with characteristically French cadential ornamentation (mm. 70–78). Its majestic character sets the tone for the showcase of instrumental, solo, and choral numbers that follows.

The nomenclature employed here to designate the middle parts of both the vocal and instrumental textures necessitates an explanation of French classical performance practice, which favored the *haute-contre* (alto or high tenor) voice for the C3 clef scoring and usually used the alto-range string instruments associated with *les vingt-quatre violons du Roi* ("The King's 24 Violins"). Instead of modern violas, a historically informed performance today might employ such instruments as the *haute-contre de violon* and the *taille de violon*.[20] The orchestral scoring corresponds to the five- and six-part string orchestra in use at the Chapelle Royale in Versailles in the first decade of the eighteenth century.

More problematic is the interpretation of the alto vocal part. In the *Divertimento,* the C3 clef figured as the lowest part of the trio for the Three Graces, implicitly a woman's role. However, in that discussion it was assumed that there would only have been one singer to a part. This *grand motet,* by contrast, adheres to a tradition renowned for performance by large numbers of singers in the *grand chœur;* Decobert cited testimonies of over one hundred choral singers at early performances of works in the genre.[21] Such a massive performance of Bembo's *grand chœur* would certainly have attracted the attention of contemporary chroniclers; in the absence of such mention, it is safer to assume a more modest choir size that, in this case, would surely have emulated the Chapelle Royale, possibly employing male *hautes-contre* alongside female ones and in general at least a few voices per part.

Whereas Bembo's *petits motets* could have been performed at the Petite Union Chrétienne, her *grand motet* exceeds the descriptions of any music found in its liturgy. Moreover, it is doubtful that her community could have afforded musicians of the calibre required to interpret her *grand motet*. Given that by 1708 the *grand motet* moved easily between sacred and secular performance spaces, it could conceivably have been performed in the large octagonal salon found on the main floor of the Duchess of Burgundy's pavilion.[22] The finest musicians came to the Ménagerie for chamber music, and perhaps performed the first *Te Deum* paired with the *Divertimento;* by adding a few

[20] René Ouvrard defined *haute-contre* range as scored on the C3 or C4 clef; see Jean Duron, "haute-contre," in Marcelle Benoit, ed. *Dictionnaire de la musique en France* (Paris: Fayard, 1992), 339. Duron used the term *haute-contre* more generally to refer to the second register of each family of instruments.

[21] Decobert, "La Naissance," 27–28.

[22] For a contemporary engraving by Adam Perelle that shows the large expanse of the pavilion, and especially the high ceilings of its salon, see Christopher Hibbert, *Versailles* (New

more voices, the singers from the latter work could easily have handled the large *Te Deum*.

An instrumental echo in mm. 74–78 makes a gentle transition into section 2, scored for violins, voice, and continuo. Harmonic motion toward G (IV) and A (V) serves to reinforce and confirm this section's D-major tonality by an extended cadential arrival at mm. 86–87. A seamless transition moves this brief *récit* for solo soprano into a three-measure *Ritournelle* for the instrumental trio, in which a second violin enters to play the line previously performed by the voice. This miniature coda elegantly tapers and reinforces the section's key as it derives from the voice's last three notes, d^2–$c\#^2$–d^2, in m. 86. Overlapping imitative entrances cover up the repeated eighth notes (d^2, b^1/g, e^2/a) after the strong beats 1 and 3 in all three parts. The instrumental trio, also abundantly employed in the first two manuscripts, plays as the core group here as well as in many of the other inner sections—5, 8, and 9—even though not always marked as a *Ritournelle*.

The two trios join forces at the outset of the second half of section 2, mm. 91–107. One line of text from the previous solo material restated as a duet between second soprano and bass (mm. 97–101) integrates the composite message: "All the earth worships you, Father everlasting . . . to you Cherubim and Seraphim continually call out." Audibly salient thirds in the upper parts, heard already in Bembo's first *Te Deum,* characterize mm. 97 (the first violin's $c\#^3$), 101 ($g\#^1$), and 107 (b^2). The final two syllables of the word "proclamant" receive both eighth-note and quarter-note settings in m. 107, "call[ing] out" through leaping intervals, rhythmic differentiation, and accentuation. The culmination of section 2 consists of the threefold "Sanctus" in homophonic texture among pairs of instruments and voices. Three statements by full chorus and orchestra, marked *fort,* unite their proclamation in homophonic texture (mm. 108–11, 114–115, and 117–20), with the orchestra echoing the larger group each time (*doux,* mm. 111–114, 116–117, and 120–123). The juxtaposed blocks of full sonorities in the key of E minor hark back to the hymn's modal origin. Apparently, Bembo sought to infuse the section with Italianate features: loud dynamics, prominent thirds, and leaping intervals.

Section 3 returns to the French style with its *récits* for soprano, flute trio, and prominent writing for the inner string parts of the Lully-style orchestra. The poetry's two quatrains essentially dictated their musical setting: the manuscript calls for "flutes" to accompany the first quatrain as well as to play in the instrumental portions framing it, whereas the solo violin appears in the second. In both instances, the solo soprano introduces the vocal trio by singing the first line of the quatrain, after which the remaining two voices

---

York: Newsweek Book Division, 1972), 22. A description and a history of the *Ménagerie* is found in Pierre Verlet, *Le Château de Versailles* (Paris: Fayard, 1985), 55–56.

join her. In the opening six measures of triple meter, mm. 124–129, a pair of *hautes-contre de violon* play the middle parts, whose melody the soprano imitates with "Pleni sunt cæli et terra majestatis gloriæ tuæ," soaring with an ethereal depiction of "heaven" ("cælus") reinforced by the one-octave descent of the b.c. The vocal trio shifts into common time in mm. 136–143 with an obbligato instrumental accompaniment. The *Ritournelle* at mm. 143–146 divides into three parts written in French violin clefs, marked "flutes" in m. 143 on p. 39 of the manuscript (ex. 5.4).

The brief appearance of the flute trio here implies that all three would play the preceding line of accompaniment to the vocal trio (mm. 136–143). Yet, if so, how many would perform the two-part scoring of the previous French violin cleffing at mm. 124–129, and would all three also play in unison the obbligato line at mm. 130–135?[23] Another flute trio appears in the "Sinfonia" from act 5 of *L'Ercole amante,* where Bembo called for an ensemble of two flutes in the alto range with a b.c. part implying the need for a bass flute. At any rate, the present flute trio represents a special texture rarely encountered in other *grands motets*. The violin takes over as the obbligato instrument in mm. 147–156, bringing the section to a bright close in A major.

Highly imitative in nature, the musical setting of section 4 matches the effusive devotion of its textual message: "Tu Rex gloriæ Christe, tu Patris sempiternus es Filius." A lilting triple meter recalls the minuet rhythm of the previous section, with an upbeat on the word "tu" lending it shape (mm. 157 ff.). Conjunct motion on the sixteenth notes following the anacrusis gives a gentle effect to the first line of text. The lack of labeled orchestration suggests that strings alone are to play the accompanying line of the first part (mm. 157–169) as well as the *Ritournelles* of the middle and ending. Points of imitation take place in the ensemble at one-measure intervals throughout mm. 157–162: S^1-B-b.c. / V^1 / S^1-S^2 / V^1 / b.c. The second soprano introduces the second line of text; the gravity of the word "Patris" yields a dotted eighth note at the second beat of m. 162, adding a syncopated touch, subsequently displaced to the downbeat in the first soprano and bass parts. In fairly static harmonic motion, the first two textual statements move toward the dominant, and the remaining two *Ritournelles* frame a repeat of the second line of text with a return to tonic. Full textures impart a jovial quality to the remainder of the section.

Bembo wrote an alternative setting of the first quatrain of section 5 for the *1er dessus* (first soprano) and the three-part string group, which is the one

---

[23] The Fürlinger edition scored the third flute part in the alto clef and transposed most of the music of mm. 142–146 down one octave, perhaps because a flute trio seemed anomalous in featuring a scoring not occurring elsewhere in the manuscript. Yet it must be reckoned with; clearly the third flute here echoes the previous accompanying instrumental part from mm. 140–143, music that should be played by an instrument in the same range.

Example 5.4   F-Pn, Rés. Vm¹114, pp. 39–40, mm. 141–148

noble army of martyrs, praise you! The holy Church throughout all the world

included in Fürlinger's edition (mm. 195–212). She cast the first setting as an elegant trio for two *hautes-contre* and bass, included as example A.8 in appendix 2. The fact that she called for two *hautes-contre* suggests at least two singers per part in the tutti choral numbers; presumably these were drawn from the "chœur de voix." Governed by the quintessentially French rubric, "lentement et tendrement" ("slowly and tenderly"), the trio offers a lovely intimate setting. A gentle descent, A–AA, supports the voices above, all conceived in a slow duple meter (mm. 195 bis–200 bis). Before moving in eighth notes toward GG (mm. 200 bis–201 bis), the descending line pauses on the dominant chord, whose sharps symbolize the "sharpness of death" through text painting reminiscent of the same spot in Bembo's first *Te Deum*. At this point, a lighter mood yields to triple time and the ensemble moves toward D major for the joyful expression of the "opening of the kingdom of heaven" (mm. 201 bis–204 bis).

The soprano solo (the alternative setting) reiterates the trio's statement and then expands into new text. The initial rubric, reduced to "tendrement," implies a quicker tempo for the solo than for the vocal trio. The soprano setting begins in D major, the key in which the trio concluded, but almost immediately introduces a minorization with natural c^2 in m. 196 ("suscepturus"), a tonic chord with a flat seventh that leads to a tonicized subdominant chord (G). This time, at the "aperuisti" section, the bass joins the soprano, essentially doubling the b.c. line (evident only in the manuscript at mm. 200–204).[24] They cadence together in A major at m. 204, with the soprano introducing the final lines "Tu ad dexteram Dei sedes in gloria Patris, judex credderis esse venturus" that initiate an extended fugato (mm. 205–212). The sump-

[24] Fürlinger's edition made tacitly the omission of the ten-measure trio at mm. 195 bis–204

tuous nature of that tutti, with which section 5 concludes (mm. 212–232), lends an appropriately festive character to the midpoint of the *grand motet* that matches the full scoring of its first and last sections. The phrase "in gloria Patris" prompts lengthy sequential melismas from the soprano as she moves from concluding downbeats on e¹ (m. 207), a¹ (m. 208), and b¹ (m. 210) before the cadence in E major in m. 212. These sequences involve the entire "chœur de symphonie" and "chœur de voix," employing split scoring once again. The melismatic, imitative setting of the sequence yields to bold homophony at "judex crederis esse venturus." Perhaps in an overzealous effort to allow all parts to have their moment in the sun, the overabundance of repetitions causes the section to sound somewhat interminable and therefore out of proportion. At m. 221, for example, at the juncture between the violin duet and that for the two *hautes-contre de violon,* the imitative sequence comes to a halt instead of overlapping as it would in proper fugal procedure.

Section 6 begins in the parallel minor mode and again calls for more intimate ensembles. The first such ensemble in mm. 233–238 brings in the violin and continuo to accompany the soprano and, with words describing the "redemption" with "precious blood," literally flows in a sinuous descent from g¹ to e¹, a notable moment of text painting. At "æterna fac," the solo voice moves up to high g²s, echoing the obbligato instrument from m. 238, and next matched by the second soprano soloist at the same pitch in m. 239 in a setting for the core vocal trio. As in section 5, the setting of "Gloria" yields to joyous melismas (mm. 240–244). The concluding *Ritournelle* for the "chœur de symphonie" imitates the vocal sixteenth-note melismas in close imitation and brings the section to a close in G major. At the conclusion of the vocal trio, an exposed b² makes the third emerge from the texture as the highest note, restated again in the final chord (mm. 246, 249). Such exposed, high thirds recall those of the first *Te Deum.*

Section 7, marked "tendrement," again assumes a French character with its ensembles, rubrics, conjunct phrases, and cadential structures. Three pairs present their plea to God: "save your people, o Lord, and bless your heritage" ("salvum fac populum tuum Domine, et benedic hæredidati tuæ"). The first soprano ("1er dessus") and first violin ("1er Viol.") are paired for the first statement, which they deliver in G major with a modulation toward the dominant key area, D, which serves as a IV chord to A (mm. 250–254) for the music of the "2e dessus" and "2e Viol." Where the two treble-range pairs moved largely in thirds, the *haute-contre* and bass voices proceed in sixths (mm. 259–264). The

---

bis and the bass part for the duet at mm. 200–204. While in n. 3 of his foreword he described two "versions" of "Per singulos dies" in section 8—"in Bembos Partitur-Konzept findet sich eine zweite Fassung des 'Per singulos dies' für Sopran-Solo und Streicher . . . diese wurde in unsere Ausgabe nicht aufgenommen"—he did not mention such versions for section 5. Both settings play an integral role in the harmonic motion of the motet.

musical setting shares with the first *Te Deum* a depiction of the diverse people's plea to the divinity. As if to unite the people in this wish, the three groups of paired voices give way to a concluding homophonic setting for the vocal trio (mm. 266–269). The *Ritournelle* for the "chœur de symphonie" that follows in mm. 269–281 resembles the procedure of section 6, but now with an expanded section for the instruments to play. A motive derived from the text "et rege eos" (mm. 264–265) develops as the orchestra moves both homophonically and imitatively to confirm the B minor tonality in which the subsequent section will proceed. The full instrumental tutti closes section 7 in majestic sonority.

Fürlinger omitted the soprano solo in section 8 (mm. 282 bis–332 bis) and provided instead the alternative setting for bass solo (mm. 282–298).[25] The 50-measure soprano solo with string accompaniment (ex. A.9) precedes a far shorter bass solo that leads directly into a passage for the "chœur de voix" (mm. 298–306) followed by a passage for the core vocal trio (mm. 306–320). As in the previous two sections, a lengthy *Ritournelle* for the "chœur de symphonie" confirms the key of arrival, A major (mm. 320–327).

In mm. 282 bis–332 bis, the soprano sings a melodious line well-matched by a complement of four-part strings, whose constituency raises some question regarding orchestration. The lowest part moves down from C3—its clef in the *Ritournelle* passages—to the F4 clef, suggesting that another instrument takes over to accompany her. Given the earlier supposition that the C3 parts went to the *haute-contre de violon*, it may be that this instrument was to play the *Ritournelle* portions and the viola da gamba to accompany the soprano's *récit*. The figures for the b.c. appear in the lowest part regardless of the clef designation. The four-part strings surround the soprano's voice in close harmony, aiding her to amplify the text. The sober key of B minor lends a distinguished character to her solo.

The theme found in both settings of "Per singulos dies" strongly resembles a bass *récit* from Lalande's *Confitebor tibi Domine*, S. 56, with their nearly identical contours in B minor (ex. 5.5). Both modulate to A major: Bembo in mm. 290–298 and mm. 298 bis–303 bis, and Lalande in mm. 41–47 (ex. 5.6). According to the title pages of the manuscripts preserved in the Toulouse-Philidor collection, Lalande wrote the parts for this *grand motet* in the years immediately preceding Bembo's work.[26]

The orchestration and resulting phrase divisions of section 9 represent a slight variation on scoring procedures already observed in earlier sections.

[25] Section 8 presents numerous discrepancies between manuscript and edition. The foreword acknowledges the omission of mm. 282 bis–332 bis, but the edition is even more abridged: no first basso continuo part appears in mm. 282–286; the chorus should not be doubled by instruments at mm. 298–302; mm. 313–314 have been compressed from the original; and the *Ritournelle* omits eight bars from pp. 89–90 of the manuscript.

[26] Philippe Oboussier, ed., preface, *Michel-Richard de La Lande, Confitebor tibi Domine* (Sevenoaks, Kent: Novello, 1982), x.

Example 5.5   Lalande, *Confitebor tibi*, S. 56, "Memoriam fecit," mm. 1–12

He has made his wonderful works,

The first soprano, accompanied by two violins and continuo in mm. 328–332, sings "Dignare Domine die isto, sine peccato nos custodire" ("Deign to keep us without sin this day, o Lord"), which the second soprano repeats. For a special effect, the b.c. at the cadence in m. 335 takes on the syncopated rhythm of the singer's rendition of "custodire." The pivot, m. 336, includes the resolution of this cadence as well as a shift into the parallel minor mode initiated by the first violin's f^1. The rubric "fort lentement et tendrem[en]t"

Example 5.6   Lalande, *Confitebor tibi*, S. 56, "Memoriam fecit," mm. 41–47

es - cam de - dit ti - men - - - - -

ti - bus se.

he has given meat to them that fear him.

("very slowly and tenderly") for the core vocal trio, mm. 336–346, is repeated for the subsequent instrumental conclusion as a literal echo in mm. 346–356.

Section 10 revisits the felicitous procedures found in section 7 whereby three pairs—S[1] and V[1]; S[2] and V[2]; and HC and B—offer a series of presentations whose entries modulate toward the dominant or fifth (table 5.3). The variety of voices suits the nature of this plea for the people: "Fiat misericordia tua Domine super nos, quemadmodum speravimus in te."

The manuscript designates *dessus* for the soprano voices and the treble-range instruments. The range fits the flute, if a softer dynamic level were desired; certainly, the text allows for a more tender moment here, and the flute's timbre would increase the contrast between this section and the boisterous character of the next, the grand tutti finale. The second statement of the theme at m. 363 features the *dessus* instrument above the voice for an unusual effect. The proximity of the *haute-contre* and bass voices at the third entrance, sounding primarily in thirds, contrasts with the sixth sonorities found for the musical setting of these voices in section 7. The narrow range of the *haute-contre*, b–g#[1], bolsters that voice atop the foundation of the b.c. and the bass voice. The tag leading from m. 370 into the final section of the *grand motet* curiously stops short of the a toward which it seemed to be heading; the notation starts only on the second beat in 6/8 meter in m. 371. Reminiscent of the missing

TABLE 5.3 Performers and Modulations in Section 10, *Te Deum*
(F-Pn, Rés. Vm[1]114)

S[1]–V[1]	S[2]–V[2]	HC–B
Measures 357–363	Measures 363–367	Measures 367–370
i (am)–v (em)	v–V/V (BM)	V/V–V (EM)

da capo or dal segno notes of the *petits motets* from *Produzioni armoniche* (nos. 38–39), an eighth-note a should nonetheless be supplied on the downbeat in performance for the impetus required to bring in the "chœur de symphonie."

The final section offers a grand celebration; its major key and large performing forces make it more effusive in mood than its counterpart in Rés. Vm^{1}112. Table 5.4 shows its ABB structure and its layout by measure, performers, and tonal area. Two halves, the second repeated, yield the formal scheme: A(36) / B(24) B (24).[27] Mm. 376 bis–379 bis, missing from the edition, appear in example 5.7.

The abbreviations used in table 5.4 include "Ritt." for the opening ritornello (m. 371–383), "anti." for antiphonal music (such as mm. 392–393), and "sync." in m. 400 to signal a syncopated entrance. Component four-measure periodic statements, such as at mm. 383–387, typify the section. The harmonic scheme, too, exhibits regularity; A major is established in the first half through repetition and modulation toward its dominant E (m. 399), while the second half moves via pedal ds and an E (mm. 403–409) through the subdominant and dominant key areas en route for a conclusive tonic arrival.

The ritornello (mm. 371–383) does not provide the exact material that the voices take up at their entrance in m. 383, unlike in the opening *Symphonie*. Nevertheless, the rhythmic motives present in the opening instrumental music clearly owe their existence to the text. Whether with a dotted or an equal sixteenth-note pickup, the first phrase accentuates "Do-" (motive A). Two sixteenth-note pickups also accentuate the syllable "-fun-" in the second phrase (motive B), with an associated extension in the third phrase, where two accented eighth notes—at times lengthened to quarter notes—signal the syllables "-ter-num" as the goal of the line (mm. 386–387). Mm. 387–390 provide a good example of how motive B serves as material for imitation by itself and in conjunction with the third phrase.

In mm. 392–394, paired instruments echo the voices in the same range, marked *doux*. These witty antiphonal effects might be considered as this motet's counterpart to the play on the meaning of "non confundar" ("I shall not be troubled") examined in the first *Te Deum*, as might the syncopated entrances that surround the dal segno return in mm. 399–400. The displacement of the syncopation, at an offbeat from the downbeat of the b.c., lends a new guise to the repetition of the theme at this point in the music.

Bembo's *Te Deum* testifies to her successful adoption of the French style within the quintessentially Gallic *grand motet*, which she modeled after her contemporary, Lalande. The neutral language of Latin allowed her to cultivate "les goûts réunis" with the flexibility to move between styles, yielding her own particular mixture of vocal and instrumental textures. With the

---

[27] The modern edition omits the four measures that appear on p. 101 of the manuscript, thus the total figure "32" instead of "28" for the A section.

Example 5.7   F-Pn, Rés. Vm¹114, p. 101, mm. 376bis–379bis

completion of the *grand motet*, "Antoinette" could complete her guise in set-ting the seven penitential psalms in French (F-Pn, Rés. Vm¹116). By contrast, the companion piece to the *grand motet*, *Exaudiat te, Dominus*, represents an Italianate conception within which hints of French taste appear. Bembo's wide-ranging palette of styles afforded her the unique opportunity to range from both national extremes to a neutral middle ground, where she united their tastes like a versatile cook.

TABLE 5.4 Analysis of the "Ritt[ornell]o,"
Te Deum (F-Pn, Rés. Vm¹114)

Measures	Texture	Key
371–383	Ritt.	A (I)
383–387	Tutti motive A	A (I)
387–392	Motive B	A (I)
392–394	Anti.	A (I)
394–399	Build-up	E (V)
400–401[a]	Tutti/sync.	A (I)
401–403	Anti.	A (I)
403–406	Tutti/anti.	D (IV)
406–409	Build-up	E (V)
409–412[a]	Conclusion	A (I)

[a]After m. 412, repeat begins at m. 400.

The Concept of the *petit motet*

By a strict definition of the *grand motet,* only the second *Tè Deum* fits the genre with its scoring for full chorus and orchestra. The instrumental and vocal trios constituting the *Exaudiat te, Dominus* and the first *Tè Deum* restrict both to the category of the *petit motet,* even though by their sectional nature they easily exceed the dimensions of those of *Produzioni armoniche.* Those small-scale pieces mostly scored for singer and b.c. suggest possible usage at the Petite Union Chrétienne, where religious ceremonies mirrored the practice of the Chapelle Royale at Versailles and other Parisian venues. The two *petits motets* of the compilation entitled "Domine salvum fac regem," nos. 4 and 40, featured both solo soprano and duo soprano settings with b.c. accompaniment. Fine models of their kind, they employed the final verse of Psalm 20, one of the seeds sown for later expansion here, a decade further on (fig. 3.3). Indeed, *Produzioni armoniche* provided the genesis for the three larger motets; the complete setting of the psalm perhaps serves as the most notable example of that intended link. Two clues mentioned above suggest intentional connections among her works: the complete setting of Psalm 20 grew out of the two *petit motet* settings of its final verse in *Produzioni armoniche* (nos. 4 and 40) and its dedicatory material reused a phrase from its encomiastic cantata (no. 2).

The theme of *Exaudiat te, Dominus* revisits the idea that the unworthy aspirant musician seeks help from a greater power. Here the conjugation of the verbs "exaudire" (to hear) and "invocare" (to call) become the musician's tools for continued attention from the king and from God, and simultaneously a psalm intended for the king, with which he could make a personal plea to God in a time of military defeats and personal loss. The oppositions of voice in the text (you–he–they) reinforce the sense of seeking divine assistance (table 5.5).

Despite its division into ten verse sections, the psalm's through-composed character has more in common with the *petits motets* from *Produzioni armoniche* than with the distinct sections of the *Tè Deum* hymn. Only two rubrics are found here: the Latin "Symphonia" and a "Ritt[ornell]o" marked in section 9 for the concluding "Domine salvum fac regem." Table 5.6 shows the harmonic progression of the work at a glance, with the home key of C minor framing the piece. The key does not reappear at the midpoint of the psalm, as it did in the *Tè Deum;* instead, an arrival at the dominant (G major) via the relative E-flat major from section 5 (outlining the C-minor triad) defines its midpoint in sections 6 and 7. B-flat major acts as the temporary dominant at the end of section 5 until the return to the home key in section 9. Major and minor modes on G, the third in the E-flat triad, define the harmonic excursions of sections 6 and 9. The relative simplicity of this motet in orchestration and harmonic scheme following the complexities of the *grand*

TABLE 5.5 Text and Translation of the *Exaudiat te, Dominus*, Ps. 20
(F-Pn, Rés. Vm¹115)

1. Exaudiat te Dominus in die tribulationis, protegat te nomen Dei Jacob.	1. May the Lord hear you in the day of tribulation: may the name of the God of Jacob protect you.
2. Mittat tibi auxilium de sancto, & de Sion tueatur te.*a*	2. May he send you help from the sanctuary: and defend you out of Sion.
3. Memor sit omnis sacrificii tui, & holocaustum tuum pingue fiat.	3. May he be mindful of all your sacrifices: and may your whole burnt offering be made fat.
4. Tribuat tibi secundum cor tuum, & omne consilium tuum confirmet.	4. May he give you according to your own heart; and confirm all your counsels.
5. Lætabimur in salutari tuo & in nomine Dei nostri magnificabimur.	5. We will rejoice in your salvation; and in the name of our God we shall be exalted.
6. Impleat Dominus omnes petitiones tuas: nunc*b* cognovi quoniam salvum fecit Dominus Christum suum.	6. The Lord fulfill all your petitions: now have I known that the Lord has saved Christ God.
7. Exaudiet illum de cælo sancto suo: in potentatibus salus dexteræ ejus.	7. He will hear him from his holy heaven: the salvation of his right hand is in power.
8. Hi in curribus & hi in equis:*c* nos autem in nomine Domini Dei nostri invocabimus.*d*	8. Some trust in chariots, and some in horses: but we will call upon the name of the Lord our God.
9. Ipsi obligati sunt & ceciderunt: nos autem surreximus & erecti sumus.	9. They are bound and have fallen: but we are risen and are set upright.
10. Domine salvum fac regem: et exaudi nos in die qua invocaverimus te.	10. O Lord, save the king: and hear us in the day that we shall call upon you.

*a*The transcription of the text comes from Louis Ferrand, *Liber psalmorum cum argumentis, paraphrasi et annotationibus* (Paris: André Pralard, 1683), 295–296. Bembo's manuscript, F-Pn, Rés. Vm¹115, has "nos" instead of "te" at this point and still other variants, as noted below. The English translation has been adapted from *The Holy Bible* (New York: Douay Bible House, 1941), 520.

*b*Manuscript reads "non;" probably a scribal error, as the negation does not fit the phrase meaning.

*c*Manuscript reads "et in æquis."

*d*Manuscript reads "invocavimus."

motet offers it as lovely a complement as did the larger *Divertimento* the more intimate first *Te Deum*.

The core vocal trio represents the fullest vocal ensemble in this psalm setting. As established in the previous religious works, accompanying instruments reinforce, embellish, or interject the vocal texture. The instrumental trio here matches the voices in range. A similarly scored setting of *Exaudiat te, Dominus* by Charpentier (H. 165), subtitled "Precatio pro Rege"("Prayer for the King"), suggests one of the models that Bembo may have drawn on for

TABLE 5.6 Analysis of the *Exaudiat te, Dominus*, Ps. 20 (F-Pn, Rés. Vm¹115)

Section	Text/Rubric	Key	Scoring	Measures
1.	*Symphonia*	c	V¹, V², b.c.	1–23
	Exaudiat te Dominus in die tribulationis,			
	protegat te nomen Dei Jacob.		S¹, S², B, b.c.	23–47
2.	Mittat tibi auxilium de sancto, et de Sion			
	tueatur te.	c–Eb	Tutti	48–56
	[Instrumental trio]	Eb	V¹, V², b.c.	57–68
3.	Memor sit omnis sacrificii tui,			
	et holocaustum tuum pingue fiat.	Eb	Tutti	69–87
	[Instrumental trio]		V¹, V², b.c.	88–99
4.	Tribuat tibi secundum cor tuum,			
	et omne consilium tuum confirmet.	Eb	S¹, S², B, b.c.	99–104
5.	Lætabimur in salutari tuo	Eb	S¹, S², B, b.c.	104–113
	et in nomine Dei nostri magnificabimur.	Eb–Bb	Tutti	114–122
6.	Impleat Dominus omnes petitiones tuas:	Bb–G	Tutti	122–131
	nunc cognovi quoniam salvum fecit			
	Dominus Christum suum.			
7.	Exaudiet illum de cælo sancto suo:	G–Bb	Tutti	131–135
	in potentatibus salus dexteræ ejus.	Bb		135–140
8.	Hi in curribus et hi in equis:	Bb	Tutti	140–153
	nos autem in nomine Domini Dei nostri			
	invocabimus.			
9.	Ipsi obligati sunt et ceciderunt:	g–Bb	Tutti	153–159
	nos autem surreximus et erecti sumus.	Bb–c	Tutti	160–212
	Ritt[ornell]o	c	V¹, V², b.c.	212–220
10.	Domine salvum fac regem:	c	Tutti	221–282
	et exaudi nos in die qua invocaverimus te.	c–C	Tutti	283–296

this composition.[28] The subject matter and mood of Bembo's *Exaudiat te, Dominus* foreshadows her penitential psalm settings in French.

The somber key of C minor contrasts with the bright A major of the *grand motet*, perhaps as a reflection of the tone of penitence and tragedy that the final years of Louis's reign witnessed. Indeed, the minor mode of the first *Te Deum* matched more closely the Phrygian mode of the Gregorian hymn, but its contrasting major-mode *Divertimento* brought a happier mood to the occasion; the manuscript for the duchess had a minor/major order. By contrast, these motets occur in major/minor order. Perhaps Bembo had a further link in mind between the two manuscripts when she framed the *Divertimento* and *grand motet* with two religious works scored for vocal and instrumental trio ensembles: the first *Te Deum* and the setting of Psalm 20.

The text and its translation shown in table 5.5 indicate the few variants between Bembo's Latin text and a prominent contemporary source by Louis Ferrand. The numbering of the verses corresponds to the musical sections,

[28] Marc-Antoine Charpentier, "Meslanges autographes," *Œuvres complètes* I, vol. 2. Facsimilé du manuscrit F-Pn, Rés. Vm¹259 (Paris: Minkoff France Éditeur, 1991), 152–165.

most of which flow seamlessly from one to the next. Motive and harmony
link the inner verses in particular; these are much shorter than the first and
the final two sections of the psalm, as if to move the action along toward more
dramatically compelling junctures.

The opening measures encapsulate the entire movement, a kernel out of
which the psalm's setting grows. By mm. 2/24, the C minor triad (c–Eb–G)
provides the notes that will engender the tonalities of the inner sections: E-
flat functions as relative major and G major figures significantly at the midpoint of the psalm in sections 6–7 with a brief allusion to its minor mode at
the outset of section 9. The word "Exaudiat," an invocation to the deity, returns in the middle and end of the psalm as well in the conjugations "exaudiet" and "exaudi" of sections 7 and 10. It is hard to ignore the implication
that Bembo sought redemption via her work, and her plea may well have
been personally intended; it served as her own need to cry out and be heard,
now not just by the king but by invoking the greater power needed by her,
the king, and the kingdom. Via a standard liturgical setting, Psalm 20 held a
twofold function as a means of redemption for herself and for the king.

In comparable fashion to the procedure employed in the *grand motet,* the
opening instrumental "Symphonia" presents two main motives matching the
word rhythms that the singers take up nearly identically at their entrance in
m. 23.[29] Motive A, corresponding to mm. 1–3/23–25, moves slowly and
clearly delineates the common-time meter with dotted quarters on "Exaudiat" on the main beats. Bembo chose a syncopated interjecting rhythm for
motive B, the plea "protegat te," which provides relief when set against the
more placid texture established by motive A. At mm. 32–33, the upper voices
briefly move into the dominant key area of G major, providing a bright affect. Always the last to sing motive B, the bass closes the first part of the section with a solo in the home key (m. 48).

The second part also presents a syncopated rhythm, now augmented with
a dotted quarter-note entry on the second beat of the new triple meter in imitative textures starting at m. 50. At mm. 55–56, the vocal ensemble portion
closes with the second soprano and second violin sounding the highest notes
within the chord. The second soprano's voice soars out of the texture with a
bb^2 on the word "tueatur," coming to rest on a g^2 on "te," which the second
violin doubles. These emphasized high-register thirds recall the quality noted
in the two *Te Deum* settings associated with the Italian style, as do the dotted
rhythms, syncopations, and leaping intervals found throughout section 2.

A short two-measure theme moving down a third characterizes section 3
(mm. 69–71). Midway through, the first soprano and first violin imitate the
theme presented by the second soprano and second violin (m. 78) and initi-

[29] For all references to the music, consult the first modern edition by Conrad Misch, *Exaudiat te, Dominus* (Kassel: Furore Verlag, 2003).

ate a chain of imitative sequences that descends from f^2 (m. 78) to g in the bass (m. 82), where each successive voice takes over the pitch from the previous one (D (S2/S1, m. 79), B-flat (S2/B, m. 81)). Harmonically, the sequences on "Memor sit omnis sacrificii tui" ("May he be mindful of all your sacrifices") involve the b.c. and lower two voices in a descant of six-three chords that lend an archaic quality to the passage at mm. 81–82, reminiscent of the *stile antico* lingering during Monteverdi's generation. The instrumental trio echoes that sonority in mm. 93–94 during the concluding sequence, which recalls section 5 of the *grand motet*.

After a lengthy trill in m. 98 that confirms the relative major of E-flat, the vocal trio enters with homophonic music accompanied only by the b.c. at m. 99, contrasting with the preceding imitative material in a seamless transition to the verse "Tribuat tibi" in section 4. Like "protegat" from section 1, the syncopated entry of "Tribuat" accentuates the word's first syllable.

The first soprano initiates each of the three imitative passages comprising section 5. A quick tempo with one beat per lilting measure, in the bright key of B-flat major, provides an apt madrigalism for rejoicing (mm. 104–113). The second passage begins with an upbeat to m. 114, followed by stretto imitation in the other voices. The violins echo the word settings, after which the two sopranos offer an imitative and melismatic rendition of the verb "magnificabimur" ("shall be exalted") at the upbeat to m. 117 for the third passage, echoed by the violins and the bass to close the verse. A slur between the penultimate and last notes of "magnificabimur," on the syllable "-ca-," indicates retroactively the smooth connection for the entire melisma in mm. 117–118 and 121 (ex. 5.8). Bembo's second and third manuscripts share this scribal shorthand, typical of sacred music manuscripts of the time.

Section 5 displays strongly Italianate features, such as the strong–weak setting in equal note values of "tuo" (m. 107), which recalls the settings of similar two-syllable words from *Produzioni armoniche*: Italian ("tenti," ex. 3.4; "Francia," ex. 3.7; and "fuoco," ex. 3.8) and Latin ("die," ex. 3.6). Lully's French-style setting of "die" instead prolongs the first syllable to make it double the length of the second (ex. 3.15). In effect, Bembo's setting of "tuo" matches quite closely the accent that Couperin injected into his subject for Corelli (ex. A.5), where—in the first two measures of the *Second Air*—a strong first gesture falls on the first beat, followed by a weak dotted quarter note on the second.

In much of her music, Bembo often displaced a theme from one beat in a measure to another within an imitative passage, not just from like beats (strong–strong, or weak–weak), but from a weak beat placement to a strong beat placement. Apparently, it was her intention to employ a species of imitation in which strong and weak beats are exchanged, *per arsin et thesin*. Just as many instances provide points of "correct" imitation. "Mi basta così" (ex. A.1) offers a good example with its displacements of the themes in the voice

Example 5.8   F-Pn, Rés. Vm¹115, p. 27, mm. 116–118

and b.c. At the point of imitation between the first and second sopranos in section 6, "Impleat Dominus omnes petitiones tuas," the entry of the phrase falls on the second beat (m. 122), the second on the first beat (m. 125). The result varies the phrase and the accentual hierarchy of the measure.[30] The accompanying instruments reinforce each initial entry.

The transcription of the psalm text provided in table 5.5 from Louis Ferrand presents some notable discrepancies vis-à-vis that found in the manuscript. In verse 2, "tueatur te" presents no textual difficulties, but in section 6, Bembo's "non cognovi" cannot be correct because it would negate the phrase "now have I known that the Lord has saved Christ God." Probably a scribal error, the edition reads "nunc cognovi." The other two discrepancies involve small variants tacitly corrected by the editor. Section 6 is harmonically dynamic and moves toward the fifth of the c–Eb–G triad introduced in the opening section. A full G-major cadence at m. 131 comes after a passage for the entire ensemble.

The exhortatory subjunctive, "exaudiet," returns at the opening of the section 7, introduced by the first soprano.[31] As if to illustrate "holy heaven," she rises up to the highest pitch of the motet, the bb² in m. 133, heard pre-

---

[30] Ex. 3.6, mm. 27–28; ex. 3.7, mm. 11–12; ex. 3.8, mm. 1–3; and ex. 3.12–3.13 provide further instances of thematic accent displacement.

[31] The edition has "exaudiat," which should be corrected as suggested here.

viously at the conclusion of section 2 (m. 55). She then descends the octave and reaches the tutti cadence in B-flat major at m. 135. The second soprano and bass, too, move upward to sing in the highest parts of their registers for the melodic word painting. Conjunct motion and a smooth articulation in the first violin and the sopranos lend a particularly French sound to this juncture.

An unusually clear break occurs between sections 7 and 8, separated by two beats of rests in m. 140. Quick-paced text setting evokes the very motion of horses and chariots to which the text refers. The imitative musical setting provides a tangible impression of the stampede: one should trust not in the fleeting nature of either horses or chariots but in God's steadfastness. "Invocabimus," the final word of verse 8—"we will call upon the name of the Lord our God"—presages the conjugation of the verb "invocare" in the final section. A prolonged trill through a lengthened syncopated rhythm in the upper voices—a typical feature of Bembo's work—brings the section to a close on a B-flat-major cadence at mm. 152–153. Mm. 152 and 154 use the same syncopated cadential figure in the treble voice parts, the second diminished in value from a quarter-note–half-note pair to an eighth-note–quarter-note pair; this subtle connection contributes to the fluid and imperceptible transition between sections 8 and 9.

The final two sections embody some of the distinctions established above regarding Italian Music and French Music. The boisterous quality of section 9, which concludes with a "Ritt[ornell]o," suggests an Italianate conception. By contrast, the gentleness of the dance-influenced French phrases and the periodic structure of the "Domine salvum fac regem" in section 10, represent a distillation of the French taste.[32] That both sections are of practically the same length lends credence to the idea that Bembo made a concerted effort to give equal weight to both tastes at the conclusion of a manuscript intended to unify them.

Through meter and tonality, the text of section 9 sets up an opposition between a wrongful "they" and a righteous "we": "Ipsi obligati sunt et ceciderunt: nos autem surreximus et erecti sumus" ("They are bound and have fallen: but we are risen and are set upright"). The musical equivalent of the verse's dividing colon consists of a metric shift from duple to triple time dividing the phrases at m. 159 and a tonal scheme that pits G minor (m. 170 ff.) against its relative major, B-flat (m. 159). Textural differences, too, contribute to the sense of opposition as the homophonic setting in mm. 153–158 yields to the imitative procedures in m. 159 that underscore the meaning of "rising up" with decorative melismas on the iterations of "surreximus." Rokseth noted the "return of confidence" represented by the choral passages in section 9, describing them vividly as "long florid passages [that form] garlands

---

[32] An analysis of the dance origins found in several French motets appears in Montagnier, "Modèles chorégraphiques," 141–156.

of thirds and tenths."[33] Such "garlands" grow as an extension of the idea seen for the S¹-B pair at mm. 161–163, as "surreximus" ("we are risen") is expanded into a five-measure-long melisma in the ensuing passages in several other vocal or vocal-instrumental combinations, such as the music from the soprano duet in mm. 182–186 subsequently developed by the violins without the continuo in mm. 186–190. Short, two-measure melismas and still longer garlands characterize the music for the singers up through their cadence in m. 212. The manuscript indicates the "Ritt[ornell]o" at m. 212, but the edition instead calls the juncture a "Tutti." The dotted figures and eighth notes connecting them have a bright, martial quality very Italian in style; that is, they have no hint of *notes inégales*. These sequential passages, along with the extensive devices used to create the madrigalisms depicting the phrase's meaning, cast the motet's penultimate section in an incontrovertibly Italian guise.

The final two sections of the piece were those that attracted Rokseth's attention in her brief survey of the composer's works; she did not specifically mention the other verses. Indeed, the inner verse settings clearly serve to propel the piece forward to its culmination in these ultimate sections. The tonal buildup is clear from table 5.6, which shows the establishment of tonic C minor in the first two sections, relative E-flat major in sections 2–5; a move toward the fifth of the chord, B flat, effected in sections 6–8; while section 9 moves the motet back to the home key via the previous B-flat as well as G minor. The "Domine salvum fac regem" of section 10 hereby received an elegant tonal preparation and lead-in from the previous material, resting firmly in the home key to gently reinforce it for one final time, reconfirmed via the third- and fifth-related tonalities toward which it ebbs and flows. Built upon a descending tetrachord, the opening phrase is beautifully balanced as the bass voice and the b.c. form the foundation on unison sustained pitches, respectively—c¹–b-flat–a-flat–g—with one pitch per measure for each of its four measures (mm. 221–224). The second soprano provides the inner harmony while the first sings the conjunct, symmetrical melody that divides into a pair of two-measure phrases. The instrumental trio imitates the voices exactly, but in the absence of the bass voice the b.c. takes on the rhythmically active bass line instead of the sustained pitches. Jean-Paul Montagnier has noted French national characteristics in several composers' settings of "Domine salvum fac regem" and Bembo mostly adhered to the "accentuation française."[34]

At m. 225, Misch's edition calls for flutes and bassoon to mark the change to the gentler character of section 10. Although Bembo did not specify the orchestration, giving this music to the soft instruments nicely recalls the French-style music for the flute trio found in section 3, as well as other moments marked "doux" in the *grand motet Te Deum*.

[33] Rokseth, "Antonia Bembo," 157.

[34] Montagnier, "Modèles chorégraphiques," 150.

At the second statement for the vocal trio beginning in m. 229, the second soprano takes over the melody, now transposed to fit above the descending tetrachord that continues its trajectory down the C-minor scale in the bass parts: g–f–eb–d. The instrumental trio in mm. 237–243 echoes the singers' two four-measure phrases in antiphonal style. At m. 244, the bass enters on the conclusion of the cadence of the instrumental trio, introducing a fragmented interpretation of the periodic four- and eight-measure phrases that the sopranos and violins will imitate. The performance results in a shimmering effect from the echoing words "Domine" and "salvum." The weight of the words creates a kind of meditative stasis of beseeching prayer to which the periodic phrases lend an aural sheen and calm atmosphere. For the final statement of the phrase (mm. 262–74), the first soprano twice reaches the climax of the section on a sustained g^2. The first violin mirrors that ethereal sustained note (mm. 278–279) in an eight-measure postlude that functions as a *petite reprise.*

The second half of the verse moves into common time for a sprightly rendition of the phrase "et exaudi nos in die qua invocaverimus te" ("and hear us in the day that we shall call upon you"). The dotted notes used to set the text lend it a vigorous character, and they also recall a similar procedure used for the two *petit motet* settings of the "Domine salvum fac regem" in *Produzioni armoniche.* The two halves of no. 40 (ex. 3.14) and Lully's setting of the text (ex. 3.15) reveal the same metric arrangement, with a triple meter first half and a common time second half. No. 4 retains the common time between halves, but moves into a more energetic dotted rhythm for the setting of the second text phrase in both motets. In all cases, the word "exaudi" truly calls attention to itself with its imperative to "hear us!" as the natural complement to the crying out of "invocaverimus." The motet's final invocation, then, begins with music for the first soprano and bass with pointed interjections from the first violin (mm. 283–285). The piece concludes with a bright Picardy third in the final cadence, sounded high—as e^2—in the first violin at m. 296, in a triumphant conversion of C minor into C major.

In F-Pn, Rés. Vm^{1}114–115, Bembo succeeded in providing two motets that united the tastes. She cast the *Te Deum* within the trappings of the quintessential French *grand motet,* but without losing sight of several Italian elements, including strong dynamic contrasts, leaping intervals, and dotted rhythms. By contrast, from within an Italianate conception of the *Exaudiat te, Dominus,* she echoed the developments of the French *petit motet* cultivated along the lines of Lully and Charpentier. Her unification of the styles matches Couperin's later concept of "les goûts réunis": from within a native perspective, difference can safely and tastefully get mixed in. She would further the process of her musical naturalization when she turned to the setting of exclusively French texts: the seven penitential psalms translated from the Hebrew and paraphrased by one of Louis XIV's most accomplished artists, Élisabeth-Sophie Chéron.

Chapter 6

PENITENCE

The manuscript that Bembo called her "third opus" suggests its association with the 1708 Battle of Tortosa (doc. 26), a calculation that squares with an estimate of 1697–1701 for the first manuscript and 1704–1705 for the second. The three remaining manuscripts preserved in the Bibliothèque Nationale do not easily continue the chronology. That all three bear a dedication to Louis XIV provides a *terminus ante quem* of 1715. Even though the year 1707 appears on the title page of the first of two volumes containing *L'Ercole amante* (F-Pn, Rés. Vm⁴9–10), the date cannot be accepted without question, especially as it subverts Bembo's claim that the manuscript containing the Latin motets constitutes her "third opus" (the second Duke of Brittany was not born until early in 1707). Rokseth identified Élisabeth-Sophie Chéron as the author of the book from which Bembo drew the seven penitential psalms for *Les sept Pseaumes, de David* (F-Pn, Rés. Vm¹116).[1] Bembo's dedicatory material begins as usual with an address to her patron, once again useful as a source of biographical information. Strikingly new here is that she wrote it in French and she signed her name with the self-naturalized variants "Ant[oinet]te Bembo" (doc. 27) and "Mme. Bembo N[o]ble Ve[nitien]ne" on the work's title page.

> Sire,
>
> Filled with admiration for your Majesty, and inspired by the purest and most ardent zeal that has ever been felt for an august monarch, I can give no other proof of the feelings that penetrate my heart than by devoting all of my talents and my wishes to your Majesty. I have spent more than half of my life, Sire, praying God that he may unceasingly give glory and hap-

---

[1] Rokseth, "Antonia Bembo," 167. *Essay de pseaumes et cantiques mis en vers, et enrichis de figures.* Par Mademoiselle ★★★ [Élisabeth-Sophie Chéron] (Paris: Michel Brunet, 1694; reprint, Paris: P. F. Giffart, 1715).

piness to your Majesty, of which your admirable piety and your heroic
virtues make you so worthy, and use what is left of my time to work in
music, having in mind in all of the airs that I compose, to produce some that
could be felicitous enough to have the glory to please your Majesty. It is
with this intention, Sire, that I have composed these airs, to the Psalms of
David, which I dare to take the liberty to present to your Majesty. I beg you,
Sire, to deign to look at this composition as a feeble, but sincere mark of
my profound respect for your sacred person, and of my perfect recognition
of your august good deeds, and of the ardent zeal with which I am, Sire,

Your Majesty's very humble and most obliging servant,

Ant[oinet]te Bembo

Following the formulaic prose of the initial sentence, the composer revealed that she had "spent more than half of [her] life" devoted to the glorification of Louis XIV. A similar allusion to elapsed time had appeared in the
dedication to *Produzioni armoniche,* where she stated that she had "admired the
king since infancy" (doc. 1). She probably did not intend to make a strictly
quantitative statement in either case, but by *circa* 1710 she had indeed spent as
many years in Paris as she had in Venice. By assigning that date to her gathered penitential psalms, it is possible to consider that Chéron could have
heard them before she passed away the following year. Moreover, the date fits
well the tone of finality inserted here—"what is left of my time"—as well as
the penitent theme that matched the serious tone at court and in Paris during Louis's own final years. The composer's repentance may have been
prompted by news of the death of her son Andrea in Venice on 14 February
1710; as a committed Catholic, perhaps she regarded the act of setting the poetry to music as a kind of atonement.

In a marked departure from the first three manuscripts, verse follows the
prose dedication here (doc. 28) as it does for *L'Ercole amante* (doc. 30). That
poems accompany the dedications to both works reopens the possibility that
the composer penned at least some of the anonymous texts contained in the
first two manuscripts. Recalling that Antonia's education included tutelage in
letters, it seems quite reasonable to assume that she was capable of extending
her dedicatory skill in her last two works to include verse. With a respectable
nod to French tradition, her dedicatory poem includes a variety of couplet
rhymes, scansion in alexandrines and hemistiches, and a topic emphasizing
her personal investment in the project.

> To the King
> upon the presentation to His Majesty of airs
> composed to the Psalms of David.
>
> 1   A great King filled with pure ardor for heaven,
>   but whom also the Almighty found after his own heart—
>   guided by the beautiful fire of his holy light,
>   proclaimed his fervent prayers to the Lord

5   in the sublime verses of his pious psalms—
David knew well how to praise the sovereign of heaven.
You, who are the living image of such a holy King,
you, Louis, whose faith, candor, and goodness
    are tantamount to justice,
10   you, with whom heaven has shared one hundred virtues,
    deign to accept the deserved homage
my zeal offers you today for your piety.
    To the Canticles of the Prophet King
    I have composed some airs for you:
15   if they make concerts
    that satisfy your soul,
greatest monarch in the universe,
    my glory is assured!

Allusions to the monarch in Bembo's œuvre progress notably from allegorical comparisons to Apollo and Louis IX in *Produzioni armoniche,* to Jupiter in the manuscripts containing the Latin motets, and here to David, the legendary royal biblical psalmist. It is noteworthy that a painting by Domenichino (Domenico Zampieri, 1581–1641) of "King David Playing the Harp"—probably acquired for Louis XIV during the Mazarin period—graced the halls of Versailles.

The tripartite poem divides into *sizains,* each self-contained with a full stop, linking King David, King Louis XIV, and the composer, respectively. The first stanza, presented in the third-person narrative voice, emphasizes the piety and divine inspiration for the psalms' creation. By shifting to the second-person "toy," the second stanza directly addresses Louis in the reflection of his biblical predecessor. The third stanza embodies every possible means for humility: it comes last, it delays the first-person voice until line 12, and it employs shorter lines with only one alexandrine reserved for the dedicatee. In all likelihood Bembo modeled the poem on Chéron's paraphrases; like them, it places the alexandrines flush left and indents the hemistiches (fig. 6.1). This evidence lends credence to the possibility that she also modeled her verse after Romagnesi's.

The Salon of Élisabeth-Sophie Chéron

Chéron's book of psalm paraphrases was first published in 1694. Many copies survive today that attest to its popularity, as did its posthumous reprinting of 1715.[2] The putative completion date of around 1710 for Bembo's settings

[2] Sources listed in Thierry Favier and Jean-Michel Noailly, "Élisabeth-Sophie Chéron et les Psaumes," *Bulletin de la recherche sur le psautier huguenot* 12 (1996): 15–28.

Figure 6.1   Élisabeth-Sophie Chéron, *Essay de pseaumes*, p. 67 [*recte* 85]. *Source*: Typ 615.94.276, Department of Printing and Graphic Arts, Houghton Library of the Harvard College Library.

opens up the possibility for considering that Chéron might have played some role in their creation and that they could have been performed in her salon. Best known for her work in the visual arts, Chéron was also highly regarded for her companion talents in poetry and music during her lifetime.[3] In 1732 Titon du Tillet noted as much:

> Music was also one of the sweetest amusements of this muse; she played the lute and the harpsichord well. All her fine talents made her name well-known even in foreign countries: the Paduan Academy of the Ricovrati sent her letters confirming her as an academician in 1699 and gave her the nickname of Erato.[4]

Chéron received her early training in painting from her father Henry, a Calvinist who had left the family when she was about fifteen—ostensibly because of a religious conflict between him and his Catholic wife, and

[3] See Évrard Titon du Tillet, *Le Parnasse françois* (Paris: J. B. Coignard fils, 1732; reprint, Geneva: Slatkine, 1971), 540.

[4] Titon du Tillet, *Le Parnasse françois*: "La Musique étoit aussi un des plus doux amusemens de cette Muse; elle touchoit agréablement le Luth & le Clavecin. Tous les beaux talens qu'elle possedoit rendirent son nom célèbre jusques dans les Pays étrangers: L'Académie des RICOVRATI de Padoue lui envoya des Lettres d'Académicienne en 1699 & lui donna le surnom d'ERATO" (541).

Figure 6.2 Élisabeth-Sophie Chéron, *Autoportrait. Source*: Chéron, Élisabeth-Sophie (1648–1711). Self-portrait. Oil on canvas, 88 × 73 cm. Inv.: INV 3239. Photo: La-giewski. Copyright Réunion des Musées Nationaux / Art Resource, NY. Louvre, Paris, France.

Élisabeth-Sophie's subsequent conversion to her mother's faith.[5] Elected in 1672 at the age of twenty-four to the Académie Royale de Peinture et de Sculpture, Élisabeth-Sophie presented her self-portrait as her *morceau de réception* at the recommendation of the artist Charles Le Brun (1619–1690), thereby becoming one of the first women to belong to the academy (fig. 6.2).[6]

[5] M. Fermel'huis, *Éloge funebre de Madame le Hay, connuë sous le nom de Mademoiselle Chéron* (Paris: François Fournier, 1712), 9–15.

[6] In *Les Femmes artistes à l'Académie Royale de Peinture et de Sculpture* (Paris: Charavay, 1885), 10–13, Octave Fidière wrote that three other women preceded her: Catherine Duchemin, the wife of sculptor François Girardon (1628–1715), was received on 14 April 1663; as well as Geneviève and Madeleine Boulogne, daughters of Louis (himself made an academician in 1648), who were received in 1669, preceding the entry of their brothers Bon and Louis in 1677 and 1681, respectively.

Titon du Tillet's description mentions Chéron's skills on the lute and the harpsichord; her *inventaire après décès* further testifies to her ownership of several other musical instruments. The inventory reveals an astonishing collection of stringed and percussion instruments: a spinet, two guitars, a lute, two *angéliques,* three theorbos (one small, two large), two treble viols and a bass, a violin, a bass drum, and a two-manual harpsichord.[7] The summation of the collection not only confirms Titon du Tillet's information but also substantially amplifies it.

Whereas the guitar, the lute, and the theorbo represent familiar early-music instruments today, the *angélique* is rare; organologist Emil Vogl based his description of the instrument on just eight extant examples.[8] Strung with single strings and tuned diatonically like a harp, it contrasts with the double strings of the lute.[9] He suggested that the instrument may have been named after *salonnière* Angélique Paulet (c. 1591–1650).[10] The associations of the *angélique* with the *femmes illustres* may explain why Chéron might have had one; they were in use in the salons of the *précieuses* and the *femmes savantes,* groups of learned women to which she belonged.

The presence of Chéron's two guitars suggests another potential link with Corbetta's French activities, but no evidence supports the idea except the following conjectural one regarding their mutual music-making connections within the circle of the Duchess of Orleans. For the oration at Chéron's funeral at the Académie Royale de Peinture et de Sculpture, Monsieur de Fermel'huis named "Monsieur Soleras" as Chéron's "maître de Luth."[11] "Joseph de Soleras," "joueur de luth" had served Henrietta, Duchess of Orleans.[12] His name appears in a *livret* for the 1658 performance of an anonymous mas-

---

[7] F-Pan MC XLIV, 201: "une petite epinette" (f. 4v), "Item deux guitares, un Lut, Deux angeliques un Teorbe un autre petit theorbe un dessus de viol un tambour de base un estuy de guitare et trois estuis de teorbe et angelique le tout prisé ensemble dix livres" (f. 5r), and "Item Un clavesin a deux claviers prisé cent cinquante livres; Item Une epinette sur deux listaux prisé Cinquante livres; Item une basse de viol un dessus de viol['on' added in another hand] un teorbe le dessus de viol dans son estuy de cuir le tout prisé soixante livres" (f. 17r).

[8] Emil Vogl, "Die Angelika und ihre Musik," *Hudební věda* 4 (1974): 356–368.

[9] See Thurston Dart, "Musical Instruments in Diderot's Encyclopedia," *Galpin Society Journal* 6 (1953): "angélique CDEFGAB.c.defgab.c.'d'e': ten frets" (111).

[10] Vogl, "Die Angelika," 356. Paulet was known for her arresting beauty, enchanting voice, and lute playing. For mention of Paulet in the context of salon culture, see Wendy Gibson, *Women in Seventeenth-Century France* (New York: St. Martin's Press, 1989), particularly chapter 11, "Women in the Cultural Sphere."

[11] Fermel'huis, *Éloge funebre,* 16. See also Jean-François Niceron, *Mémoires pour servir à l'histoire des hommes illustres dans la république des lettres* (Paris: Briasson, 1731), 14: 170 and in Émile Bellier de La Chavignerie, *Dictionnaire général des artistes de l'École Française depuis l'origine des arts du dessin jusqu'à l'année 1868 inclusivement* (Paris: Renouard, 1868–1872), 1: 251.

[12] Maurice Barthélemy, *André Campra: Sa vie et son œuvre (1660–1744)* (Paris: Picard, 1957), 20. Barthélemy located the pertinent document in F-Pan *Cour des aides* Z[1a] 522.

querade performed in Blois whose third *entrée* features Jupiter alone on stage, performed "par le Sr. Soleras."[13] It appears that after Henrietta's death, Soleras lost his royal position and became one of numerous urban lutenists who taught and performed in Paris.[14] He figures in two extant enumerations that help to situate such musicians. The first of these lists appears on a letter written on the subject of music by Monsieur le Gallois to Mademoiselle Regnault de Solier in 1680, where he was called "Monsieur de Solera."[15] A decade later, "M. Solerat" was listed among "les principaux . . . maitres [du lut]" in the Milleran Manuscript.[16]

No other source illuminates whether Chéron received further instruction on the other instruments in her collection. One of her contemporaries, however, wrote that it was in her salon that she and her engraving apprentices played music in the evenings after work, following discussions about art and art theory with some of the leading intellectuals of the day.

> One could often hear brother [Louis Chéron], sister [Élisabeth-Sophie], the illustrious [Roger] de Piles and several *savants* of the highest order debating the most interesting points about painting and the fine arts in this salon. Music followed these excellent discussions; at the end of the day when [Élisabeth-Sophie] and her two nieces [Ursule and Jeanne de la Croix] left their palettes, they gave new proof of their skill through the melodious harmonization of different instruments.[17]

[13] *L'Hymen. Mascarade dansée à Blois devant leurs Altesses Royales* (Blois: Jules Hotot, 1658), 3.

[14] Michel Brenet, *Notes sur l'histoire du luth en France* (Turin: Bocca Frères, 1899; reprint, Geneva: Minkoff, 1973): "The growing dispersal of musical culture soon had the effect of spreading very far away from the kernel formed by the royal establishment the number of virtuosi and composers who worked for the public and who sought, either for glory or fortune, a path different from the one that consisted of fulfilling 'domestic' functions for a sovereign. It is from the abundant list of musicians separated in this way from all official attachments that we encounter some of the most brilliant representatives of French lute music in the seventeenth century" ["La diffusion croissante de la culture musicale eut bientôt pour effet d'étendre très loin au delà du noyau formé par la maison du roi, le nombre des virtuoses et des compositeurs qui s'adressaient directement au public, et qui cherchaient, pour atteindre la gloire ou la fortune, une voie différente de celle qui consistait à remplir auprès du souverain des fonctions 'domestiques'. C'est dans la liste abondante des musiciens ainsi dégagés de toute attache officielle, que nous allons rencontrer quelques uns des plus brillants représentants de la musique de luth en France au XVIIe siècle"] (60–61).

[15] Brenet, *Notes*, 62, n. 1: "Lettre de M. Le Gallois à Melle Regnault de Solier touchant la musique, pag. 62. 1680." Parts of this letter appear in David Fuller, "French Harpsichord Playing in the 17th Century—After Le Gallois," *Early Music* 4 (1976): 22–26.

[16] François Lesure, *Manuscrit Milleran: Tablature de luth française c. 1690 (Bibliothèque Nationale, Paris, Rés. 823)* (Geneva: Minkoff, 1976), introduction, f. 2. See also Brenet, *Notes*, 63–64.

[17] Antoine-Joseph Dézallier d'Argentville, *Abrégé de la vie des plus fameux peintres* (Paris: De Bure, 1762): "On a souvent entendu, dans ce salon, le frère, la soeur, l'Illustre de Piles, & plusieurs sçavans du premier ordre discourir sur les parties les plus intéressantes de la peinture &

Chéron's collection apparently served her students and friends as well as herself. The inventory also reveals that she owned cases for several of her instruments: guitar, *angélique,* theorbo, and treble viol. Although these may have been intended primarily for storage purposes in her home, they also could have been used to take the instruments out for performances elsewhere. In any case, they present strong evidence that her salon was an important one for music making, for she had so many instruments on hand.

That more than one writer has suggested that Chéron also composed music may reflect too wide an interpretation of her universal talents;[18] it remains curious, however, that one of these writers also claimed that she set some of her own psalms to music.[19] Musical iconographer Mirimonde's claim for Chéron's compositional skill was based on the evidence of her second self-portrait, now in the Musée Magnin, Dijon, in which she painted herself surrounded by musical instruments (it had been with her first—now in the Louvre—that she had gained acceptance into the Académie). It is tempting to consider the possibility that Bembo's psalm settings of her poetry might be the ones to which he referred. Lacking any explicit contemporary claims to Chéron's compositional skill, this idea must remain in the realm of conjecture.

Not surprisingly, contemporary accounts attest to the aesthetic beauty of the artist's salon as well. Her brother, Louis (1660–1713), painted several *tableaux* that hung on its walls: *The Apotheosis of Hercules, Moses Strewing Water on the Fields,* and *Angélique and Médor.*[20] The artistic collaboration between the siblings extended to his having supplied 23 engravings as illustrations to a second edition of Élisabeth-Sophie's psalms that appeared in the same year as the first edition, all strongly attesting to the popularity of the book (fig. 6.1).[21]

Titon du Tillet also mentioned Chéron's literary skill, which earned her the honor of election on 9 February 1699 to a second academy, the Ricovrati

---

des beaux arts. La musique succédoit à ces excellentes dissertations; elle occupoit cette soeur & ses deux niéces, qui, quittant la palette sur le déclin du jour, donnaient de nouvelles preuves de leur habileté par l'accord mélodieux de différens instrumens" (4: 328).

[18] Albert Pomme de Mirimonde, "Portraits de musiciens et concerts dans l'École Française dans les collections nationales [xve–xvie–xviie siècles]," *La Revue du Louvre et des musées de France* 15e Année, no. 4–5 (1965): 218. Marcelle Benoit also called her a composer, but noted the lack of surviving compositions (*Versailles et les musiciens du roi,* [Paris: Picard, 1971], 262).

[19] G. de Leris, "Les Femmes à l'Académie de Peinture," *L'Art* (1888): 124.

[20] Ulrich Thieme, ed., *Allgemeines Lexikon der bildenden Künstler* (Leipzig: Seemann, 1912), 6: 467.

[21] *Pseaumes de David et Cantiques nouvellement mis en vers françois, enrichis de figures* (Paris: Luyne, Brunet, Robestel, 1694). See A. P.-F. Robert-Dumesnil, *Le Peintre-Graveur français ou Catalogue Raisonné des Estampes, gravées par les peintres et les dessinateurs de l'École Française* (Paris: Warée, 1838), which gives Louis's biography and works list in vol. 3, 285–295, Élisabeth-Sophie's in vol. 3, 239–251. La Bibliothèque Nationale preserves four copies of the 1694 edition and three of the 1715; one of its 1694 copies [F-Pn, A. 6195] belonged to the king's library.

of Padua, once again with the soubriquet of Erato.[22] Established in 1599 as a forum for intellectual exchange among doctors and scientists, one of the founding members of the Ricovrati was Galileo Galilei.[23] The academy's French affiliation began in the 1670s, when the doctor Charles Patin became a member.[24] Youngest son of Guy Patin—a doctor as well as a celebrated writer who had enjoyed popularity under Louis XIII and Anne of Austria— Charles had been banned from the French kingdom for his outspoken opinions during the Fronde. He fled Paris, eventually settling with his German wife, Maddalena Hommetz, in Padua, where their two daughters, Gabriella and Carla Caterina, were born.[25] Not entirely by coincidence, the year after Patin's election as leader of the academy in 1678,[26] seven French women were named to the academy; by 1699 Chéron's nomination along with five other French women brought the total to nearly twenty.[27] Patin's promotion of women's intellectual pursuits—and of French women in particular—seems unusually generous. It must be interpreted, however, in light of his goals: to elevate the status of his own family members (by 1683, all three Patin women had been elected to the academy) as well as a way to curry favor with the French monarch in hopes of returning to France.[28] Whatever good this did for the women involved, he himself was never allowed to return to his homeland; he died in Padua in 1693.

Following Patin's death, Louis XIV's historiographer Claude-Charles

[22] Maggiolo, "Elena," 35.

[23] Valeri, L'Accademia dei Ricovrati, 10. See, too, Mario Biagioli, Galileo Courtier: The Practice of Science in the Culture of Absolutism (Chicago: University of Chicago Press, 1993), 120.

[24] Maylender, Storia delle accademie d'Italia, 4: 443–444.

[25] For the members of the Patin family, see Nouvelle biographie générale (Paris: Firmin Didot Frères, 1863; reprint, Copenhagen: Rosenkilde et Bagger, 1968), 39: 327–333.

[26] Valeri, L'Accademia dei Ricovrati: "1678. 30 giugno. Eletto 'Principe' Charles Patin, già prof. alla Sorbona, di medicina nello Studio padovano, dotto archeologo e particolarmente numismatico; sotto il suo 'principato' vengono aggregati numerosi personaggi stranieri, tra cui molte letterate francesi" ["30 June 1678: Charles Patin, formerly a professor at the Sorbonne and presently professor of medicine in the Paduan studio, highly educated in archeology and in numismatics, was elected leader. Under his leadership, numerous foreign members were named to the academy, among them many French literati"] (20). On Charles Patin, see C. E. Dekesel, Charles Patin: A Man without a Country. An Annotated and Illustrated Bibliography (Ghent: Biblioteca Numismatica Siciliana, 1990).

[27] Valeri, L'Accademia dei Ricovrati, 34–35. In 1679, Anne d'Acier, Madame de Villedieu, Madame Rousseau, la Comtesse de Suse, Louise-Anastasie Serment, Anne de La Vigne, and la Marquise de Rambouillet; in 1685, Madeleine de Scudéry; in 1688, Antoinette Des Houlières; in 1689, Madame Saliez; in 1697, Marie-Jeanne L'Héritier de Villandon; and in 1698, la comtesse d'Aulnoy and Antoinette-Thérèse Des Houlières (ten years after her mother Antoinette). Chéron was elected along with Catherine Bernard, Claude-Elisabeth Brettonvilliers, Charlotte de Camus de Melsons, Charlotte-Rose de Caumont de La Force, and la comtesse de Murat.

[28] Maggiolo, "Elena," 34.

Guyonnet de Vertron (elected to the Ricovrati in 1682) continued the momentum of the doctor's efforts on behalf of women. In the years immediately preceding Chéron's nomination, Vertron had published copious literary exchanges among many of the illustrious women of the Ricovrati in a two-volume compilation, *La Nouvelle Pandore* (*The New Pandora*) followed by a *Seconde Partie de la Pandore*. A retrospective of the glories of Louis XIV's reign, Vertron's work celebrates its "femmes illustres."[29] He intended that the number of women admitted to the Ricovrati match the names of the muses, to whom he alluded in a quatrain applauding Chéron's psalm paraphrases:[30]

> Chéron with her lofty songs surpasses the nine sisters,
> Her subjects are divine and her voice most touching,
> She notes the regrets of a penitent soul,
> She gives spiritual instruction and converts hearts.[31]

The publication of Vertron's books, however, effectively froze further entry into the Ricovrati. The retroactive, historicizing tribute of *La Nouvelle Pandore* assured that no more French women would be nominated to that academy until the mid-eighteenth century.[32] His tribute portrays Chéron's psalms in musical terms, thereby furthering the later implication that she herself had set them. At any rate, her status as academician to the Ricovrati assured her a royal pension for the remainder of her life.[33]

Lacking any evidence testifying to the acquaintance of Chéron, poet, and Bembo, composer, the connection between Paris and Padua merits consideration. Charles Patin could have met Giacomo Padoani during the early 1660s when both resided in Padua. Although Dr. Padoani was never was elected to the Ricovrati, his colleague Conte Girolamo Frigimelica Roberti—medical

---

[29] M. de Vertron, conseiller historiographe du Roy, académicien de l'Académie Royale d'Arles, et de celle des Ricovrati de Padoue [Claude-Charles Guyonnet, seigneur de La Brosse-Paslis et de Vertron], *La Nouvelle Pandore ou les Femmes illustres du siècle de Louis le Grand. Recueil de pièces académiques, en prose et en vers, sur la préférence des sexes. Dédiés aux dames* (Paris: Veuve de Claude Mazuel, 1697) and *Seconde Partie de la Pandore ou la suite des Femmes illustres du siècle de Louis le Grand* (Paris: Veuve de Claude Mazuel, 1698).

[30] Vertron, *La Nouvelle Pandore*, 441–445.

[31] Vertron, *La Nouvelle Pandore:* "CHERON par ses hauts Chants surpasse les Neufs Sœurs, / Ses Sujets sont Divins, & Sa Voix est touchante: / En marquant les Regrets d'une Ame Pénitente, / Elle instruit les Esprits & convertit les Cœurs" (385).

[32] Maggiolo, "Elena," 35: many Italian women were made academicians from 1725 to 1755; the first eighteenth-century French woman to receive the honor was Anne-Marie Duboccage in 1758.

[33] Jules Guiffrey, *Comptes des bâtiments du Roi, sous le règne de Louis XIV.* Collection des documents inédits sur l'histoire de France, troisième série: Archéologie (Paris: Imprimerie Nationale, 1901). Chéron's annual pension amounted to 400 *livres tournois,* noted as such from 9 February 1700 through 11 March 1705 (4: 687, 801, 1021, 1023, 1233) and January 1706 through April 1711 (5: 99, 190, 288, 386, 478, 570).

doctor and, among other distinctions, witness to the birth of Andrea Bembo in 1665—belonged to the academy and was closely associated with Dr. Patin. Frigimelica had served as its leader from 1668 through his death in 1683.[34] If Antonia had maintained contact with Frigimelica, this would have involved her Parisian years as well. Moreover, Louis Chéron had spent his formative years in Italy, where he had studied the work of Raphael and Romano. The strong Franco-Italian links suggested by the evidence offer the possibility of an acquaintance between Bembo and Élisabeth-Sophie Chéron, yet nothing confirms it.

Might the French "muses" have gathered in various members' salons for academic discussions? The nature of the exchanges of letters and debates contained in Vertron's books suggest that live discussions by the French constituents of the academy preceded the printing process. D'Argentville's description of Chéron's salon lends credence to the idea that it provided a venue for the performance of Bembo's penitential psalm settings. The instruments in Chéron's home, with the addition of just two treble instruments, would have made possible such a performance.

Clearly Bembo participated at the turn of the century in the prevalent Parisian vogue for *cantiques spirituels,* paraliturgical pieces in the French vernacular.[35] Whereas her larger motet settings would have suited the large spaces generally employed for the performance of such works, her settings of the French psalm paraphrases suggest a private devotional setting. Beyond the likeliest venue of Chéron's own salon, these pieces also would have been suitable for a parlor of the Petite Union Chrétienne or even for the Duchess of Burgundy's pavilion. Such works were not intended for display or entertainment, but for piety and introspection in an intimate environment.

The Penitential Psalms in Context

Bembo's choice to set all seven penitential psalms may have arisen from her own needs, but these meshed well with the somber mood that prevailed at the end of Louis XIV's reign. While few, if any, other composers chose to set the penitential psalms as a group, settings of the 150 psalms had enjoyed a long and venerable seventeenth-century tradition. As Denise Launay has shown, Catholic writers sought to paraphrase the psalms rather than to make literal translations of them; one of the most prominent was Antoine Godeau—the bishop of Vence who worked for Louis XIII—whose paraphrases of the 150 psalms served as the texts for many composers, including

[34] Valeri, *L'Accademia dei Ricovrati,* 20.

[35] Laurence Boulay, "Les Cantiques spirituels de Racine mis en musique au XVIIe siècle," *XVIIe Siècle* 34 (1957): 79–92.

Philippe Desportes (1546–1604) and Signac (before 1600–before 1630), Michel Lambert (c. 1610–1696), Pierre de Niert (c. 1597–1682), Jean de Cambefort (c. 1605–1661), Denis Caignet (?–1625), Gabriel Bataille (c. 1575–1630), Thomas Gobert (c. 1600–1672), Antoine Lardenois (?–c. 1672), Étienne Moulinié (c. 1600–after 1669), Jacques de Gouy (d. after 1650), Pierre-César Abeille (1674–1733), and others.[36] Many of the composers involved with the origins of the *grand motet* at mid-century, such as Du Mont, also pursued such paraliturgical musical genres as psalm settings. By the late seventeenth century, the influence of Madame de Maintenon on Louis made him seek such devotional music and encourage others to do so as well.

The popularity of the *cantique spirituel* arose at the end of the seventeenth century, in the wake of Maintenon's program for religious education at her school at Saint-Cyr. The *cantiques* of Jean Racine, for instance, were set by composers roughly contemporary with Bembo, such as Collasse, Jean-Baptiste Moreau (1656–1733), and Louis Marchand (1669–1732).[37] These settings feature ensembles similar to those required by Bembo's penitential psalms, never requiring more than four instruments or four voices. Bembo called her pieces "airs," a nomenclature in keeping with similar works by her French contemporaries.

Thierry Favier has noted that, in addition to Bembo's settings, Jean-Baptiste Drouart de Bousset (1662–1725) also set Chéron's paraphrased psalms to music, a further attestation to the popularity of her work. Bousset's music was published in Paris by Ballard in 1701, entitled *Airs spirituels des meilleurs autheurs, livre second*. Favier transcribed the piece in an article that considers the settings of both composers.[38] Bousset's setting of Psalm 68 calls for a simple duet between soprano voice and *basse continue*. Like Bembo, Bousset employed frequent metric changes to suit the setting of the text; Bousset, however, used comparatively little text painting by comparison with Bembo, whose employment of the technique reflects her Italian heritage.

Chéron did not group the penitential psalms together in her 1694 publication; it was Bembo's idea to unite them in her manuscript. The binding of *Les sept Pseaumes, de David* in red morocco leather completed the set of four volumes preserved in the king's library, three of whose covers bear his coat of arms. The oval center of the fleur-de-lys motif here resembles the brass used for *Produzioni armoniche* (fig. 3.1) but without the crowned L motifs at its corners.

Les sept Pseaumes, de David feature a variety of vocal combinations for the psalm settings, as shown in table 6.1. For convenience, the two upper *dessus* parts are called "violins" here; some of these parts fit the range of the flute

---

[36] Denise Launay, "La 'Paraphrase des Pseaumes' de Godeau et les musiciens qui l'ont illustrée," *Antoine Godeau (1605–1672): de la galanterie à la sainteté—Actes des Journées de Grasse (21–24 avril 1972)*: 235–250.

[37] Boulay, "Les Cantiques spirituels," 89–92.

[38] Favier and Noailly, "Élisabeth-Sophie Chéron," 18–19.

TABLE 6.1   Contents of *Les sept Pseaumes, de David* (F-Pn, Rés. Vm¹116)

Psalm	Title	Text incipit	Key	Scoring	Pages
6	Domine ne in furore	Ne me fais point sentir	e	S, T, V¹, V², b.c.	1–17
31	Beati quorum remisse	Heureux celuy	A	2S, HC, B, V¹, V², b.c.	18–93
37	Domine ne in furore	Ne m'examine point	a	2S, V¹, V², b.c.	94–132
50	Miserere mei Deus	Fais moy misericorde	d	S, V¹, V², b.c.	133–170
101	Domine exaudi orationem	Seigneur qui vois	c	S, B, V¹, V², b.c.	171–230
129	De profundis clamavi	Du profond abime	b	HC, V¹, V², b.c.	231–246
142	Domine exaudi orationem	Si je puis esperer	f	2S, V¹, V², b.c.	247–285

and the oboe, which can be employed as well. The instrumental trio represents a familiar entity from Bembo's previous manuscripts. The two psalms for soprano duo, nos. 37 and 142, are the only pieces in the group that share a scoring scheme.

All of the psalms revisit tonalities from previous compositions. Psalm 37, set in A minor, represents the key most frequently chosen, having appeared in nine of the *Produzioni armoniche* pieces, including, perhaps tellingly, the French *Air* (no. 41). Psalm 6, set in E minor, served as the tonality for three pieces from *Produzioni armoniche* (nos. 32, 37, 39) as well as for the first *Te Deum* (Rés. Vm¹112). The keys of B, C, and F minor were each used twice in *Produzioni armoniche* (nos. 5, 24; 8, 26; 6, 16); C minor also served as the central key for *Exaudiat te, Dominus* (Rés. Vm¹115). D minor matches only *Produzioni armoniche*, no. 11.

A close reading of the C-minor setting of Psalm 101, *Domine exaudi orationem meam*—scored for soprano and bass voices with instrumental trio—will serve here as the representative example for the group of penitential psalms that testifies to the felicitous blend of Chéron's verse and Bembo's sensitive, able musical setting. The instrumental trio selected for the recording by La Donna Musicale features a violin and a transverse flute, with a b.c. consisting of viola da gamba, organ, and harpsichord (CD tr. 9).[39] The violin and flute at times double on the obbligato line and play each *Ritournelle* with the entire instrumental ensemble. The recording and edition together facilitate the analysis undertaken here, which demonstrates the composer's application of techniques found in her earlier works now applied to French poetry of the highest order.[40] The resulting music, convincingly French in style, nevertheless retains the composer's Italianate trademark and heritage with its abundant madrigalism.[41]

[39] La Donna Musicale, *Antonia Bembo: The Seven Psalms of David, Vol. I.* CD LA 2004 (Boston, MA, 2004). The CD includes Psalms 6, 101, 129, and 142, as well as a recording of the Violin sonata in A by La Guerre (1707) performed by flute and continuo.

[40] *Les sept Psaumes de David*, vol. 5 (Psalm 101: Domine, exaudi orationem), ed. Conrad Misch (Kassel: Furore Verlag, 2003).

[41] In *Remarques curieuses sur l'art de bien chanter*, 121–122, Bénigne de Bacilly protests the ac-

The phrase "this Psalm was composed during the Babylonian Captivity" appears below the Latin title of Psalm 101 (fig. 6.1).[42] Many of the editions that contain Louis Chéron's engravings also include captions explaining the context of the psalm at hand. In the case of Psalm 101, it reads: "the time having expired for the Jews to be set free, they ask for deliverance from God through the mouth of one of their Prophets, who represents to God the extreme misery they suffer where they are."[43] With few exceptions, the text of Bembo's score matches Chéron's original poem.[44] Only one variant is found in Psalm 101, which appears in italic in the transcription provided for the analysis below; beyond standardizing the spellings of the verb *répandre* throughout this poem, the transcription reflects the typography of the 1694 print.

By comparison with Bembo's setting of Psalm 20 (F-Pn, Rés. Vm^{1}115), set in Latin, Psalm 101 uses one less soprano and restricts the performance of the second *dessus* instrument to the four *Ritournelle* passages. Similar passages for the instrumental trio in Psalm 20 bore the labels *Symphonia* or *Ritt[ornell]o,* or simply appeared unlabelled. In structure and in tonality, however, Psalm 101 shares common ground with Psalm 20 (table 6.2).

The modal layout of the first four sections of the psalm provides meaningful contrasts between major keys corresponding to the brightness of faith and minor keys to the darkness of repentance. The psalm opens with a setting of the initial couplet with a beseeching cry from the soprano, who depicts a call for God's help with rising lines moving toward the dominant (mm. 1–4). The bass echoes her cry and returns to the tonic (mm. 4–7).

| Seigneur qui vois mes pleurs, exauce ma priere, | Lord who sees my tears, hear my prayer, |
| Que mes cris montent jusqu'à toy. | That my cries may climb up to reach you. |

cusation that good musical airs by necessity must express the sense of each particular word. His statement may be understood as a positioning of the nature of the French air in contradistinction to the prevalence of Italian models for music, and as a suggestion that in general the French eschew localized text painting in favor of overall affect. I am grateful to Catherine Gordon-Seifert for bringing to my attention this portion of Bacilly's treatise in the paper that she presented at the 2005 meeting of the Society for Seventeenth-Century Music: "Rhetoric and Expression in the Mid-Seventeenth-Century French Air: A Rationale for Compositional Style and Performance."

[42] *Essay de pseaumes et cantiques:* "Ce Pseaume a esté composé pendant la captivité de Babylone" (67 [*recte* 85]).

[43] Ibid.: "Le tems marqué pour la délivrance des Iuifs étant expiré, ils la demandent à Dieu par la bouche d'un de leurs Prophetes, qui lui represente l'extreme misere où ils sont" (facing p. 67 [85]).

[44] Ibid., 67 [85]–72 [90].

Ne m'oste pas, mon Dieu, ta divine lumiere;	Do not take your divine light away from me, my God;
Dans mes pressans besoins, Seigneur, écoute moy.	In my pressing need, hear me, Lord.
J'implore ton secours, je t'appelle à mon aide,	I implore you for help, I call you to my aid,
Je sçais que de mes maux toy seul es le remede,	I know that you alone are the remedy for my sorrows.
Tu connois les tourmens dont mes sens sont frappez,	You know the torment with which my senses have been struck,
De mes os dessechez l'humeur est consumée	The marrow of my dried bones has been consumed
Et comme se dissipe une foible fumée	And just like feeble smoke,
Mes tristes jours sont dissipez.	My sad days are dissipated.

The rest of the stanza is set as a duet for soprano and bass in which the soprano initiates all of the imitative entries (mm. 7, 11, 15, 20, 23, 26). Displaced initial accents occur with some frequency in this psalm and, just as they

TABLE 6.2 Analysis of *Domine exaudi orationem meam,* Ps. 101 (F-Pn, Rés. Vm^{1}116)

Section	Text/Rubric	Key	Scoring	Measures
1.	Seigneur qui vois mes pleurs, . . .	c	S, V, b.c.	1–4
	Seigneur qui vois mes pleurs, . . .		B, V, b.c.	4–7
	Ne m'oste pas, mon Dieu, . . .		S, B, V, b.c.	7–29
2.	De même qu'l'on voit par le Soleil . . .	Eb	S, V, b.c.	29–43
	Et je n'ay plus que la figure . . .		S, B, V, b.c.	44–47
	Persecuté de tous, faudra-t-il . . .		B, V, b.c.	47–66
3.	De cendre au lieu de pain ma vie . . .	bb	S, B, V, b.c.	67–79
	Dans l'abîme où tu m'as jetté . . .	Ab	S, B, V, b.c.	80–91
4.	*Ritournelle*	f	V^1, V^2, b.c.	92–125
	De toy, Seigneur, il n'est pas . . .		S, B, V, b.c.	125–157
	Ceux qu'un sombre avenir . . .	f–Eb	S, V, b.c.	158–170
5.	Cette pauvre Sion, cette ville . . .	c–G	S, B, V, b.c.	171–188
	On ne reconnoit plus son antique . . .	G–C	S, V, b.c.	189–202
6.	Esperons toutefois que le Dieu . . .	g–Bb	B, V, b.c.	202–209
	Alors pour signaler hautement . . .	Bb–F	S, B, V, b.c.	209–227
7.	Nous feras-tu sentir ces regards . . .	Bb–C	B, V, b.c.	228–232
	A nous dans les fers detenus . . .	C	S, B, V, b.c.	233–235
	Par le fer & le feu . . .	C–g	B, V, b.c.	236–256
	Ritournelle	g	V^1, V^2, b.c.	256–273
8.	Ah! Seigneur, s'il est vray . . .	g–c	S, B, V, b.c.	273–297
9.	*Ritournelle*	C	V^1, V^2, b.c.	298–346
	Pour joüir de ces biens prolonge . . .		S, V, b.c.	347–368
	Pour joüir de ces biens prolonge . . .		S, B, v, b.c.	369–392
	Ritournelle		V^1, V^2, b.c.	393–399
	C'est toy qui fis les Cieux . . .		S, B, V, b.c.	400–415
10.	Pour toy qui remplis tout . . .	c	S, B, V, b.c.	416–442

did in Bembo's earlier works, appear to be intentional (SB, mm. 15–16; voices and obbligato, mm. 18–19). The flute and violin share the obbligato part in the recording by La Donna Musicale; the former's timbre doubling the soprano entry in m. 11 contributes to the imploring sentiment expressed by the poem. Anchored in the common time established by the initial solo passages, lines 3–8 are delivered; after a notable pause, the final couplet moves into triple time with abundant imitation among all four parts, where short phrases depict the smoky wisps of elapsed time (mm. 20–29). In the concluding cadence of the section, the violin plays a Picardy third among octave C's in the other parts, preparing the way for a shift in mode from minor to major carried out via the tag in the b.c. part (m. 29).

The soprano sings most of the second stanza. At the mention of intense sadness, a sixteenth-note melisma on "tristesse" emerges from the texture, sinking briefly into F minor (m. 35).

De même que l'on voit par le Soleil fanée	Just as one sees grass,
L'herbe mourante et sans vertu,	Dying and withered by the sun,
Ainsi je sens mon cœur de tristesse abbatu,	So do I feel that my heart has been beaten down by sadness,
Ainsi de sa vigueur mon ame abandonnée	So my soul, which has lost its strength,
Succombe sous le fais de mes vives douleurs;	Bends under the weight of my burning pains,
Mes immortels regrets, mes sanglots & mes pleurs	Immortal regret, sobbing, and tears feed me
Me tiennent lieu de nourriture;	Instead of food,
Mes os sont collez à ma peau,	My bones stick to my skin,
Et je n'ay plus que la figure	All I have left is a face that looks like
D'une ombre qui sort du tombeau.	A shadow emerging from the grave.

Despite the lamenting nature of the text, Bembo chose not to dwell on the atrocities it describes and used instead quick-paced recitative style to deliver it without any repetition whatsoever. The violin elegantly delineates the main beats of the solo in mm. 30–44 in concert with the b.c. At m. 38, a question arises regarding uniformity between the voice's eighth notes and the dotted-eighth–sixteenth of the instrumental parts; the manuscript poses interpretive puzzles of this nature throughout. The bass voice enters seamlessly, offering an imitation to the soprano's phrase in m. 44. With a sustained highpoint on beat three (m. 46) in all but the violin part, yielding a matter-of-fact cadence (mm. 46–47), madrigalism and homophony help to communicate the meaning of "emerging from the grave."

The next stanza features a bass solo that employs the extreme registers of his range, beginning high on an e-flat[1] and reaching down to an F by m. 59. Bembo's score offers a variant marked in italics here; where Chéron had "oppressez" ("oppressed," which Misch's edition retained), Bembo wanted instead to convey the sense of siege conjured by the battle imagery:

Persecuté de tous, faudra-t-il que je meure?	Persecuted by everyone, must I die?
Semblable au Pelican qui cherche les deserts,	Just like the pelican who searches through the desert,
Ou comme cet oyseau poursuivy dans les airs,	Or like this bird chased through the air,
Qui des plus sombres lieux fait sa triste demeure:	Making his sad nest in the darkest places;
Ainsi qu'un passereau sur un toit gémissant	Just like the sparrow crying plaintively on the rooftop,
Dés les premiers rayons du grand astre naissant,	At the first rays of the rising sun,
Mes lugubres cris se répandent.	My lugubrious cries resound.
Tandis que des cruels nous tiennent *assiegez,*	While our enemies keep us *besieged;*
Et dans leur rage me demandent	In their rage, they ask me for
Les restes malheureux des jours qu'ils m'ont laissez.	The unhappy remainder of the days that they left to me.

This passage compares the loneliness of the penitent soul with the solo flights of the pelican and the sparrow, as if the sad cries of human woe match those of these birds. The relatively low register of the voice effectively conveys the meaning of "darkest places" (m. 52), reinforced by minor chords rooted on B-flat, E-flat, and D-flat (mm. 52–54). The wretched state of affairs and penitential theme of the text called for minor keys and tonal exploration never reached in the setting of the more optimistic Psalm 20.

With an appropriately lamenting affect the prominent organ sonority in the b.c. introduces the duet of the following stanza, which Bembo set in the key of B-flat minor (mm. 66–67):

De cendre au lieu de pain ma vie est soûtenuë,	I am sustained by ashes instead of bread,
Mon breuvage est mêlé de pleurs,	My drink is mixed with tears,
L'accablement de mes malheurs	But the despondency of my grief
N'est pas le seul mal que me tuë;	Is not the only evil that kills me;
C'est ta juste colere, ô grand Dieu d'équité!	It is your righteous anger, o great God of equity!
Dans l'abîme où tu m'as jetté,	In the abyss where you have thrown me,
Je passe comme l'ombre & mon ame oppressée	I pass like a shadow; my oppressed soul

Oste à mes tristes yeux le repos du sommeil,	Even takes away the relaxation of sleep from my sad eyes;
Je suis comme une fleur par le vent terrassée,	I am like a flower beaten down by the wind,
Qui se flétrit & meurt au coucher du Soleil.	Who withers and dies at sunset.

Vocal homophony in mm. 67–74 assists in the clear delivery of the stanza's first four lines and conveys a sense of unanimous resignation to a miserable meal of ashes and tears. Here, again, a question arises as to whether the violin obbligato needs to conform to the vocal parts (mm. 68, 70), or whether the composer wanted it to be offset by its contrasting rhythms. The soprano's pick-up to m. 75 propels the action forward in a fleeting triple-time gesture and brief moment of imitation as both voices sing of God's "righteous anger." Chéron's poem emphasizes this line with an exclamation point, to which Bembo sensitively responded with a pause and a change of time signature. By means of Phrygian motion in the continuo, d-flat–c, the section comes to a halt in C major before the setting of lines 6–10 in common time. Despite descending motion in the three upper parts intended to depict the gravity of "the abyss," the soprano's initial statement in A-flat major conveys a surprisingly optimistic mood (mm. 80–81). A pleasing homophonic passage concludes the section (mm. 86–91); although beaten down by the wind, the flower seems only to encounter a gentle breeze as the voices, reinforced by the b.c., gracefully move upward together (mm. 86–87). The stanza's final couplet features descending lines in all parts to create the image of the withering of the flower in the sunset (mm. 88–89). The stanza concludes with one of Bembo's typical slow-moving cadences, this one particularly beautiful with its sustained minor-seventh chord resolving into an A-flat major cadence in which the violin sounds a prominent third.

At this point the instrumental trio plays its first *Ritournelle*. With their introduction of the music to which the singers will supply the text, the flute and violin give a foretaste (mm. 92–125) of the declamation of lines 1–4 (mm. 125–157). Evidently Bembo worked retroactively in her compositional process, first setting the singers' texts and next writing the instrumental introduction. The unusual key of F minor in moderate triple meter lends a lovely affect to the trio, whose gentle eighth-note *inégales* display quintessential French style. The parts intertwine as they move toward sustained, suspended downbeats at mm. 103–106, as well as at the trio's conclusion, where the b.c. provides the foundation for the build-up of the imitated phrase (mm. 120–121–122) before it moves up chromatically, d–e-flat–e–f, in an approach to the full cadence (mm. 122–125). At m. 125, the singers take over from the treble instruments, which now coalesce into the obbligato line above them. They perform two statements of lines 1–4:

De toy, Seigneur, il n'est pas de même,	There is no equal to you, Lord,
Tu regnes éternellement,	You reign eternally;
Dans les siecles futurs les Cieux	In the centuries to come the
incessamment	heavens will incessantly
Rediront ta grandeur suprême.	Repeat your supreme grandeur.
Ceux qu'un sombre avenir tient à nos	Those whose dark future is hidden
yeux cachez	from our eyes
Au recit de tes faits se sentiront touchez,	Will be touched by the story of
	your deeds,
Ils beniront, Seigneur, tes oracles fidelles,	They will bless your faithful
	oracles, Lord,
Qui nous assurent qu'en ce jour	Which assure us that today
Sion doit éprouver tes bontez paternelles,	Zion experiences your paternal
	goodness,
Et la grandeur de ton amour.	And the greatness of your love.

The conclusion of the vocal duet at mm. 151–157 follows the general outlines of the two *dessus* parts at their corresponding juncture (mm. 118–125) but now displays more melodic action in the bass and moves higher into the treble range with the violin obbligato line. Such sensitivity to variation recalls the embellishment of the *Seconda* phrases in several arias from *Produzioni armoniche*. Because the cadence of m. 124 employed uniform rhythm, in the analogous place at m. 156 the violin should not move to the second beat—which would clash a g^2 against an f^2 in the soprano part—but instead proceed together in thirds.

The soprano begins the second part of the stanza (lines 5–10) with falling octave Fs via the fifth to convey the image of a "hidden . . . dark future" (m. 158), a corroborating echo of the abyss (m. 80). By contrast with the repetition of melodic lines and text in lines 1–4, the soprano delivers this text in quick-paced recitative style. The F-minor cast to the outset of her solo concerns mystery, which C-major and B-flat-major chords subsequently brighten and reassure of God's goodness (mm. 162, 164). The extended E-flat major cadence halts the pace of the textual delivery, as if to allow the psalmist to bask in the abundant love God holds for Zion (mm. 168–170).

By means of a brief linking tag into 3/2 meter the b.c. descends by step from the cadence in E-flat down to C minor (mm. 170–171). The shift to the minor key sets the next scene, which dramatically portrays the destruction of the holy city:

Cette pauvre Sion, cette ville détruite	Poor Zion—destroyed city,
Triste objet du couroux des Cieux	Sad object of heaven's wrath,
En proye au soldat furieux,	The prey of the angry soldier—
Presqu'en cendre se voit réduite.	Sees itself almost reduced to ashes.
On ne reconnoit plus son antique	Its ancient splendor is no longer
splendeur,	recognizable;

Son Temple, ses palais, marques de sa grandeur	Its temple, its palaces, the marks of its greatness
Ne sont plus qu'un monceau de pierres.	Are now nothing more than a heap of stones.
Miserable Sion qui cause nos soûpirs	Miserable Zion, cause of our sighing,
De tes tristes enfans rebuts de tant de guerres	Even though so much warfare has victimized your children,
Tes ruïnes encor font les plus chers desirs.	Still your ruins represent our most cherished desires.

While the drama is inherent in the verse, Bembo's frequent metric shifts significantly heighten its variety of actions and moods: Zion's sadness (3/2), angry battle (3/8), destruction (3/4), and nostalgic remembrance (C). In this way, she showed her profound understanding of the ways in which her French contemporaries expressed the passions in the *airs sérieux* and in opera, such as in Armide's wavering between lust and hatred (love and duty) as she contemplates with dagger in hand the sleeping Renaud.

The soprano and violin obbligato move in mournful parallelism at their entrance in m. 171, sustained in close harmony by the *petite basse,* which sounds in the alto range.[45] At the bass's imitation of the phrase in mm. 173–174, the continuo doubles him by returning to its usual range an octave below. At m. 174, all four parts render homophonically a slurred *seufzer,* the violin in diminution with quarter notes anticipating its d^1 on the first beat. The sixth harmonies of mm. 173–175 recall the descant noted in the "Salvum fac populum" portions of both of Bembo's *Te Deum* settings. No sooner than the listener settles in for a section devoted to mourning (m. 178), but the third line of text yields to a lively madrigalism for the action that caused the destruction—the "angry soldier"—now in 3/8 time with rapid melismatic virtuosity on the word "furieux" (mm. 180–182). An accented second beat in 3/4 meter brings the action to a halt with the smoldering result of his fury: ashes ("cendre," mm. 183–186). The soprano performs the remainder of the stanza as a solo (lines 5–10) and, again, a metric shift effects a response to a dramatic word in the text: the melismatic phrase on "guerres" ("wars," line 9) moves briefly from common time into 3/8 (mm. 197–199). The soprano's motives trace a triad through quick sixteenth notes and recall a similar turn of phrase found in several pieces for solo soprano from *Produzioni armoniche* (such as nos. 2, 5, and 36). After her cadence in C minor at m. 202, the continuo subsides to G for the ensuing bass delivery of the two initial couplets of the next stanza:

---

[45] "La petite basse" apparently originated during Lully's career, a term used to designate a passage where the bass instruments drop out and give the b.c. to the violas, or the violins. See John Spitzer and Neal Zaslaw, *The Birth of the Orchestra—History of an Institution, 1650–1815* (Oxford: Oxford University Press, 2004), 470–471.

Esperons toutefois que le Dieu de nos
    peres
    Nous tirera d'oppression,
Il peut faire cesser nos sanglantes
    miseres,
Et rétablir tes murs, déplorable Sion.

Alors pour signaler hautement sa
    puissance
Le Seigneur répandra la joye &
    l'abondance
    Parmy son peuple fortuné:
Il leur rendra leurs biens avec usure,

Leurs maux ne seront sceus de la race
    future
Que par l'heureux secours qu'il leur
    aura donné.

Let us continue to hope in any case
    that the God of our fathers
    Will remove us from oppression,
That he can put an end to our bloody
    miseries,
And will rebuild your walls,
    deplorable Zion.

So, then, in order to proclaim visibly
    his power,
The Lord will spread joy and
    abundance
    Among his fortunate people:
He will return their goods to them
    with interest,
Their misfortune will be known to
    their progeny
Only by the happy redemption that
    he will have given to them.

An elegantly shaped cadential melody in the bass characterizes the setting
of the stanza's fourth line in mm. 207–209, where the violin and b.c. reinforce
the textual rhythms conveyed by the voice. Text painting depicts the "rebuild[ing of the city's] walls" with ascending notes (m. 207) and falls by leaps
back down to describe its present ruined state (mm. 207–208). The duet setting that concludes the stanza moves into 3/4 time at m. 211 as a sequence of
moderately paced imitative falling thirds depict the Lord's "spread" of "joy
and abundance" to the fortunate people. The violin begins the series of imitations, followed by the soprano, b.c., and bass through m. 214. The dramatic
alternation between such bright phrases, set tellingly in the major mode, contrasts with the dark minor-mode settings for the sentiments of the penitent
psalmist. The stanza concludes with the confidence that misery will be forgotten by future generations, thanks to the lending of divine assistance.

In the next stanza, a series of three questions casts into doubt the hopes
brought on by the faith just professed. The psalmist states the present sufferings in graphic detail (m. 228 ff.):

Nous feras-tu sentir ces regards
    favorables?
Quand seront-ils, Seigneur, jusqu'à
    nous parvenus,
    A nous dans les fers detenus
    Accablez de maux incroyables?

Par le fer & le feu nos païs ravagez,

Will you show us your favorable
    wishes?
When, Lord, when will they reach us,

We who are burdened by chains,
    Overwhelmed by unbelievable
    misfortune?
Our lands are ravaged by iron
    shackles and by fire,

Sous un sanglant couteau nos peres égorgez,	The throats of our fathers cut by a bloody knife.
Nous mêmes destinez à la mort inhumaine,	And we ourselves who are destined to suffer inhuman death,
Pouvons-nous croire encor qu'un jour nous pourions voir	Can we still believe that one day we may see
Finir nôtre cruelle peine	An end to our cruel pain,
Dans ces lieux regrettez qui font tout nôtre espoir?	In the place we miss, which holds all our hopes?

The bass voice declaims this passage mostly as a dramatic solo, with only one interjection from the soprano (lines 3–4; mm. 233–235) after which, in a shift into triple time (mm. 236–245), he describes the horrors that occurred in Zion. The "bloody knife" of the assassin draws out on a sustained a in mm. 243–244. The facsimile of p. 205 (ex. 6.1) shows the necessity of editing Bembo's score prior to performing it: accidentals noticeably missing in mm. 237 and 240 are typical of passages that venture into keys distant from C minor. The vehement phrases of all three parts vividly convey the dramatic scene, coming to a cadence in G minor at m. 256 that leads into the concluding *Ritournelle* (mm. 256–273). By contrast with the anticipatory nature of this psalm's first *Ritournelle,* the second follows the singers as if to reflect upon the questions that they posed.

Example 6.1   F-Pn, Rés. Vm¹116, p. 205, mm. 237–247

The rising minor sixth of the flute in m. 256 opens with its own question, to which two violins, the second *dessus* and the *petite basse,* respond. Their close-knit texture presents a mournful trio set squarely in G minor, a celebrated key for the expression of grief, as if bereft of any support from the accompaniment sounding in the bass register (until m. 263). Here Bembo joined her contemporaries in writing a typically French minor-key trio; such moments throughout all seven penitential psalms sound as Gallic as do the words of their dedicatory material. The moves toward D major at mm. 258, 263, and 269 lend the trio strong anchor points, sifting down to rest on the dominant in preparation for the instrumental trio's definitive close on an authentic cadence at m. 273. The plaintive, off-beat entrances in the upper parts at m. 264 give way to particularly apt suspended seventh chords in the measures that follow. This concluding *Ritournelle* provides a moment of calm reflection and meditation on the very questions just asked. The following section poses two more:

Ah! Seigneur, s'il vray qu'au comble de la joye	Ah, Lord, if it is true that your people will live
Ton peuple habitera nôtre sainte Cité,	In our holy city, which would be the greatest of their joys,
Que ses Princes sortis de la captivité	That their princes—rescued from captivity—
Possederont les biens que ta main leur envoye:	Will possess the goods that your hand sends to them:
Ce malheureux captif qui compose ces vers,	Will this unhappy captive writing this verse
N'aura-t-il point de part à ces bonheurs divers?	Have no part in all of that happiness?
Jusqu'à cet heureux tems étendras-tu sa vie,	Will you extend his life until that happy time,
Du malheur qui le suit objet infortuné,	Or, as the unfortunate object of unhappiness,
Dans ces lieux accablé d'une peine infinie,	Overwhelmed here by infinite pain
Le dernier de ses jours sera-t-il terminé?	Will the last of his days end in that way?

Both voices participate in the setting of this stanza, where modal contrasts pit optimism (lines 1–4) against pessimism (lines 5–10). Tonicizations in mm. 276, 278, and 283 emphasize the bright keys of E-flat major, D major, and F major, respectively, in a harmonic coloration that matches the text, as do the more pessimistic phrases of mm. 287 and 293, which touch upon G minor, and m. 297, which cadences in tonic. In line 8, Bembo's manuscript has "Du malheur qui *me* suit objet infortuné"; "me" represents a scribal error, for no first-person voice appears in the stanza to justify the change.

A joyful *Ritournelle* (mm. 298–346), performed here by two violins and viola da gamba, precedes the penultimate stanza (mm. 347–393) and provides a brief instrumental *petite reprise* for it as well (mm. 393–400 echo mm. 386–393). The louder dynamic of the string trio reinforced by the percussive harpsichord furthers the bright key of C major and beautifully conveys its sense of triumph. The first measure establishes the three strong beats of the triple meter; the b.c. and first violin enter together, the second beat marked by the lower part. The second violin enters in strict imitation of the first, the two parts in thirds emphasizing the C-major triad (mm. 298–99). As in the *Ritournelle* passages of sections 4 and 7, the b.c. takes on the role of a third *dessus* part when it moves up briefly into the treble range to continue the imitative entrances, effectively another *petite basse* (mm. 300–304). The three sixteenth notes in an upward flourish first presented on the third beat of the violin part at m. 299 should match the groups of sixteenth notes in the other parts, rather than being considered as triplets (as in the edition) because the manuscript shows that the dotted quarter approximates a quarter note tied to a sixteenth. As demonstrated by the recorded performance, *notes inégales* mask these details and dispel any further quibbling over the fine points of rhythm.

The dominant key area reinforces the anchoring of tonic in the cadences at mm. 308, 312, and 320, a procedure that leads into a new passage of thematic imitation at m. 312. The noble character of this lengthy *Ritournelle* serves as a fine prelude to the entrance of the soprano (m. 347), who sings the words from lines 1–4 of the next stanza set to the same melodic lines. The two sections of the *Ritournelle*—mm. 298–320 and mm. 321–346—make sense when one sees that the soprano sings a solo passage in the tonic key (mm. 347–368), and the bass joins her—on the same text—for the second half in G major (mm. 369–393). Lovely imitations of the phrase "aux pieds" ("at the foot") occur in the texted passages of mm. 391–392 as well as in the preceding *Ritournelle*, mm. 344–345.

Pour joüir de ces biens prolonge encor mon âge,	Prolong my life, that I might enjoy those good things,
Fais moy participer à tes ans éternels,	Make me participate in your eternity,
Que je puisse revoir encor ton heritage,	That I may see your heritage again, Lord,
Seigneur, pour t'adorer aux pieds de tes Autels.	So as to worship you at the foot of your altars.
C'est toy qui fis les Cieux & qui formas la terre,	It is you who made the heavens and who formed the earth,
L'air, l'humide élement, & tout ce qu'il enserre;	The air, the wet elements, and everything that they enclose;
Mais tant d'ouvrages differens	But so many different works—
Ces astres éclatans, ce Soleil qu'on voit luire,	Those gleaming stars, the sun that we see shining—

Finiront cependant comme les vestemens	Will nevertheless come to a finish, like raiment
Que le tems enfin voit détruire.	That time will destroy in the end.

In mm. 350–352, the soprano coasts on g^2 to depict the wished-for prolongation of the psalmist's life, while the b.c. again moves into *petite basse* range in m. 348 to play imitations in thirds with the violin. At the bass entrance in m. 371, the b.c. mostly doubles his voice, occasionally adding other notes for harmonic, imitative, or rhythmic purposes, such as in mm. 373, 381–382, 384–386, and 391–392. The strongest statement of "prolong" occurs when all parts participate in its depiction in mm. 373–376. To round off the duet, the instruments echo the phrase, "Seigneur, pour t'adorer aux pieds de tes Autels" ("Lord, . . . to worship you at the foot of your altars," mm. 386–393), with particular emphasis on "pieds" in the psalm's final *Ritournelle* (mm. 393–400).

The second part of the penultimate stanza—the setting of lines 5–10 beginning at m. 401—is set imitatively, starting with the violin, the soprano following, with the doubled b.c. and bass entering last. In the text of lines 5 and 6, the elements are described and depicted in their musical setting: the word "earth" ("terre") comes at the end of a descending phrase (m. 403) and the word "air" receives a melismatic setting—with air literally articulated by the singers' throats—in mm. 404–405. In mm. 408–410, all parts perform sixteenth-note melismas on the words for the "exploding stars" ("astres éclatans," line 8). Even if the text discusses the fragility of all mortal accoutrements—with time, the stars will be destroyed, as will our clothes—the major mode is retained and a strong cadence marks the conclusion of the setting of the stanza at m. 415. The exuberance of this passage recalls that of the passage in the *Divertimento*—which, not by coincidence, also depicts the elements (ex. 4.17)—and also foreshadows the setting of the Chorus of Planets in act 5 of *L'Ercole amante*.

The final stanza returns to the tonic key of C minor, closing the psalm with a recapitulation of its solemn penitence:

Pour toy qui remplis tout par ton immensité,	For you, Lord, who fills everything with your immensity,
Les tems n'ont point, Seigneur, ni de momens, ni d'heures,	Time has neither moments nor hours,
Tu ne sçaurois changer, sans cesse tu demeures	You know no change, for you remain forever
Dans le point de l'éternité.	In one eternal place.
Répans sur tes enfans un rayon de ta gloire,	Spread your glorious ray before your children,
Fais en nôtre faveur ce qu'on ne pourra croire,	Turn to our favor that in which we cannot believe,
En brisant nos tristes liens;	By breaking our unhappy chains;

Que la posterité dans l'avenir ressente	That posterity in the future may experience once again
Encore les effets de ces precieux biens	The effects of these precious good things
Qu'aujourd'huy nous tiendrons de ta bonté puissante.	That we have today, thanks to your powerful goodness.

In keeping with the procedure used in setting most of the previous stanzas, lines 1–4 (mm. 416–429) constitute the first part, lines 5–10 the second (mm. 429–442). The largely homophonic setting of lines 1–4 meditates on God's ubiquitous eternity; the flute obbligato for the second couplet provides an intimate context for the voices to reflect on God's dependable and unchanging nature (mm 425–429). The imperative "répans" of line 5 prompts quicker notes in imitations beginning with the *dessus* line, the violin now doubling the flute (m. 429) in a concerted drive toward the phrase's key word, "gloire" (mm. 431–432). The bass line is particularly noteworthy, as his runs take off from and return to g in scalar motion toward the G-major mode arrival point (m. 432). Text painting also makes apparent the "breaking" of "chains" in quick sixteenth-note figures (line 7; mm. 434–435). Even though p. 227 of the manuscript indicates two notes without a slur on the word "liens," it should be pronounced as one syllable (ex. 6.2). In all likelihood, the scribe for the manuscript pushed the text underlay too far to the left; the four syllables

Example 6.2   F-Pn, Rés. Vm^{1}116, p. 229, mm. 432–436

of "nos tristes liens" belong with the last four notes of m. 435. Erasure in the score at this place, as well as in numerous other spots, reveals a degree of editing from the time that often did not resolve the problem at hand.

The psalm concludes firmly with an authentic cadence in C minor, appropriately desolate due to the lone *dessus* sounding the fifth of the final chord otherwise composed only of octave Cs, with no third defining its mode. Nevertheless, Psalm 101 imparts relative optimism, by comparison with the better-known penitential psalm text of Psalm 129, "De profundis clamavi"; Bembo gave a similarly hollow final chord to its setting, but it sounds still more depressing there due to the text of the final couplet: "If they are abandoned by you, Lord, nothing can save them; they will surely be lost."[46]

Bembo's settings of the penitential psalms not only represent a major contribution to the French tradition of *cantiques spirituels* in the twilight years of Louis XIV's reign but they also shed important new light on women's music-making in the Parisian salons during the period.[47] Having looked at Chéron's salon in particular, this study has called attention to the putative connection among the arts of painting, poetry, literature, and music and the central role that women played in French cultural life thanks the extraordinarily supportive urban and court environments fostered by the king.[48] Whether his magnanimity toward female cultural endeavors can be explained by the model offered by his mother Anne of Austria, by his own interests in all things artistic, or by the abundance of wealth garnered during his reign, it appears that the period offered women an unprecedented degree of latitude in the cultural sphere. In all likelihood, it will never be proven whether or not Bembo frequented the salons of Fedeli, La Guerre, the Duchess of Burgundy, or Chéron—her circumstances dictated the extreme discretion to which the lacking paper trail testifies—but her manuscripts all suggest that these were the venues in which her works were conceived and performed.

Bembo's psalm settings in French represent an important ancillary set of compositions comparable to the two books of *Cantates françoises sur des sujets tirez de l'Écriture* published by La Guerre in 1708 and 1711. Because Bembo and La Guerre represent the two most important women composing music during Louis XIV's reign, their works have been paired in the first recordings of Bembo's music, such as in those made by La Donna Musicale and Bizzarrie Armoniche. In the latter's CD, La Guerre's opening *symphonie* to the cantata

---

[46] La Donna Musicale, *Antonia Bembo: The Seven Psalms of David, Vol. I*, tr. 12.

[47] For a discussion of the ways in which the salons of Madame de Scudéry and Madame de Rambouillet fostered music-making at the outset of the reign, see Lisa Perella, "Bénigne de Bacilly and the *Recueil des plus beaux vers, qui ont esté mis en chant* of 1661," in *Music and the Cultures of Print*, ed. Kate van Orden (New York: Garland, 2000), 248.

[48] On this subject, see Erica Harth, *Cartesian Women: Versions and Subversions of Rational Discourse in the Old Regime* (Ithaca, NY: Cornell University Press, 1992), particularly chapter 1, "Gender and Discursive Space(s) in the Seventeenth Century."

Samson appears alongside Bembo's amorous arias from *Produzioni armoniche,* but it could just as easily mesh with her solo psalm settings.[49] Perhaps it was not entirely to confirm her connection to Cavalli that Bembo undertook the composition of an opera, but rather her need to hew closely to the standards already set by her colleague La Guerre.

---

[49] Bizzarrie Armoniche, *La Vendetta* CD (ORF, Austria, 2004). For an explanation of the associations among Strozzi, Bembo, and La Guerre behind the recording, see Claire Fontijn, "Le armoniose relazioni," *Amadeus* 175 (June 2004): 28–30 (www.amadeusonline.net).

Chapter 7

HERCULES IN LOVE

W

hen the Bibliothèque Nationale acquired the two volumes
containing Bembo's opera *L'Ercole amante* in the 1930s, its
collection of her works became complete.[1] Although dedicated to Louis XIV,
the opera had not previously belonged to the royal library as had the four
other manuscripts. Instead of the red morocco leather binding her in-quarto
volumes, these in-folio volumes were bound in brown leather and stamped
with a nineteenth-century owner's coat of arms (F-Pn, Rés. Vm⁴9–10).

What might have drawn the composer to a libretto specifically intended
for the royal wedding and already set to music in the decade prior to her arrival in France? The title page reveals her cognizance of the opera's history,
and the date written there suggests that her new setting may have preceded
the composition of the penitential psalms (doc. 29):

> Hercules in Love / Tragedy / Newly set to music, by / Lady Antonia
> Bembo, Noble Venetian, / And dedicated to His Most Christian Majesty, /
> Louis the Fourteenth. / In the year 1707.

Several compelling reasons may have motivated her choice to set *L'Ercole
amante* once again. First, with it she could emphasize her identity as one of
the Venetian disciples of Francesco Cavalli, who had been summoned to
France in the days of Mazarin to compose music—this opera—for the wedding of Louis XIV to the Spanish Infanta Maria Teresa. Second, the libretto
of Abbé Francesco Buti (1604–1682), published in a bilingual edition at the
time of the opera's premiere, held fertile ground for a composer specializing

---

[1] Rokseth, "Antonia Bembo," 147, 157–166.

in *les goûts réunis*.[2] Third, through the opera's central character, she could present another epic figure for the king's glorification in her pantheon of allegorical representation.

The dedicatory "Madrigal," placed at the outset of the second volume, offers an analog to the French verse extolling the psalms' monarch (Docs. 28 and 30):

> The lofty clemency, o Sire—
> which decorates your valor to the highest degree
> and gives you pride of place among heroes—
> gives me the strength and daring
> to offer to your right hand, to your great heart
> as a gift, indeed as a tribute, a new song;
> hereby Sire, be so kind as to look
> with mercy on [her] who with all zeal
> offers continual vows to heaven for you.

Whereas the French verse had employed alexandrines and hemistiches for the long and short lines, respectively, the *endecasillabi* and *ottonari* of the "Madrigal" assume the same function. The "Madrigal" also mirrors the former's tripartite structure: lines 1–3, in the second-person voice, address the king as the implied heroic figure of Hercules; lines 4–6, shifting into the first-person voice, present the composition; and lines 7–9, in the imperative, petition for temporal and divine protection.

The idea of the French king as "Hercule Gaulois" goes back at least as far as the sixteenth century.[3] At the time of the birth of Louis XIV, a play written by Jean Rotrou—produced at the Hôtel de Bourgogne and dedicated to Cardinal Richelieu—explored the Christian overtones inherent in Hercules's tale.[4] In examining royal imagery, Jean-Pierre Néraudau found abundant Christian interpretations of Hercules's half-divine, half-human nature: "this double postulation, lived through violence and the tragic, made of him a symbol of the human condition and its aspirations. In many regards, he was the incarnation of divinity come to earth, of that which Christianity defines in the person of Christ."[5] Louis XIV's panegyrists customarily

---

[2] Francesco Buti, *Ercole amante. Tragedia representata per le nozze delle Maestà Christianissime* (Paris: Robert Ballard, 1662).

[3] Jean Seznec, *La Survivance des dieux antiques. Essai sur le rôle de la tradition mythologique dans l'humanisme et dans l'art de la Renaissance* (Paris: Flammarion, 1993), 37, n. 2.

[4] See Derek A. Watts, "Introduction," Jean Rotrou, *Hercule mourant (1630–1634)*. Textes littéraires II, ed. Keith Cameron (Exeter, UK: University of Exeter, 1971), v–xxx at xvii ff.

[5] Néraudau, *L'Olympe du Roi-Soleil:* "cette double postulation, vécue dans la violence et la tragique, faisait de lui le symbole de la condition humaine et de ses espérances. Il était une incarnation de la divinité proche, par bien des aspects, de celle que le Christianisme définit en la personne de Christ" (69).

mixed secular and Christian appellations when praising him as their "Hercule très-chrétien."[6]

Comparisons with Hercules were particularly fitting at the time of Louis XIV's wedding. In an ode written in 1660, when France and Spain signed their peace treaty, one poet praised both Mazarin and Louis:[7]

Lui seul des deux états termine la querelle,	Alone, he concludes the quarrel between the two states,
Et répond à l'espoir de notre jeune Hercule.	And responds to the hope of our young Hercules.

As a direct result of the treaty, the Infanta made her solemn arrival into Paris to join her fiancé, "Hercule Gaulois."[8] In the 1662 production of *L'Ercole amante* Louis danced in costume as the sun,[9] promoting his image as the Sun King through a direct allusion to Apollo, who had allegedly ordered the semi-god to change his name from Alcides to Hercules.[10]

In writing the libretto for *L'Ercole amante,* Buti freely adapted from classical sources his tragic drama based on the final years of Hercules's life: Sophocles's *Trachiniae,* Apollodorus's *Library,* Seneca's *Hercules Œtaeus,* and especially Ovid's *Metamorphoses.* The five acts relate the following story:

Act 1. After having conquered the kingdom of Œchalia and slain its ruler King Eutyrus, Hercules falls in love with the king's daughter Iole, who had gone to Thebes as a captured maiden following his demise. Iole loves Hyllus, the son of Hercules and Dejanira, who returns her affections. The goddess Venus, who supports love at all costs, sides with Hercules, while Juno, the goddess of reason and marriage, sides with Hyllus. When Juno discovers that Venus acts to further Hercules's affections for Iole, she flies into a rage and devises a plan to thwart her rival's intentions.

Act 2. In the midst of their declarations of love, Hyllus and Iole learn of Hercules's unwelcome passion. Meanwhile, Juno visits Pasithea's cave in order to borrow Sleep personified, her husband *Sonno,* to lull Hercules and thereby to delay his actions.

Act 3. While Hercules sleeps, Iole tries to kill him to avenge the death of her father, but Hyllus prevents her. Awakening to the impression that his son was trying to kill him, Hercules threatens him; Dejanira

[6] Ferrier-Caverivière, *L'Image de Louis XIV,* 237.

[7] Ibid., 34, citing Esprit's *Ode sur la Paix.*

[8] Ibid., 36, citing stanza 7 from Caignet's *Sur l'entrée de la Reine dans la ville de Paris, le 26 août 1660.*

[9] Charles I. Silin, *Benserade and his Ballets de Cour* (Baltimore: Johns Hopkins University Press, 1940), 307.

[10] Néraudau, *L'Olympe du Roi-Soleil,* 68.

hastens to protect their son. Hercules banishes Dejanira and orders that Hyllus be imprisoned in a tower by the sea.

Act 4. Juno rescues Hyllus from prison unbeknownst to Iole and Dejanira, who believe him dead; they visit the tomb of Iole's father, whose ghost appears and warns her not to marry Hercules. In a subsequent scene, however, Iole is swayed in Hercules's direction after she sits down in a magic chair conjured by Venus to make her reciprocate his affections.

Act 5. The opening scene takes place in Hell among the souls of those whom Hercules has conquered and killed. Dejanira's servant Lychas has contrived a scheme that is to be enacted at the wedding of Hercules to Iole: she must offer him the Centaur's magic robe.[11] When Hercules puts it on, instead of returning to Dejanira as the Centaur had promised, it makes his flesh burn with its poison. When he tries to remove the robe, his flesh adheres to it and he dies. Juno triumphs as Hyllus reappears, reconciled with Iole. In an apotheosis freeing him of his mortal labors, Hercules ascends to Heaven where he marries Beauty.

Robin Linklater, designer for a recent production of Cavalli's opera, has suggested that the tale

> can be seen as an allegorical demonstration both of Louis XIV's virility and of his readiness to put off his carefree bachelor life (mortality) and take on the responsibility of succession and the sacred body of sovereignty (immortality) via elaborately ritualized fictions of divine status.[12]

Linklater's interpretation casts Louis XIV in a positive light and sees the resolution of the opera—where Hercules assumes divine status in heaven—as a parallel to the terrestrial wedding ceremony. Néraudau has suggested that Mazarin's presence "may be sensed behind the character of Eutyrus," although he hastened to add that the parallel could not be made without qualification.[13]

---

[11] Following Dejanira's wedding to Hercules many years before, the Centaur Nessus had ferried her across the River Evenus. Some versions of the myth hold that he raped her during the crossing, and that Hercules slew him in punishment; while dying, the centaur offered Dejanira a philtre containing a mixture of his sperm and blood, claiming that she should use it in the event of her husband's infidelity.

[12] Robin Linklater, "Program Notes for *Ercole Amante*," *Boston Early Music Festival Catalogue* (Cambridge, MA: Boston Early Music Festival, Inc., 1999), 96.

[13] *L'Olympe du Roi-Soleil:* "ils devinaient encore sa présence [celle de Mazarin] derrière Eurytos, même si Marie Mancini était sa nièce et non sa fille, même si Louis XIV ne l'avait pas tué" (151). For a fascinating analysis of the wedding preparations and allegories around it, see Abby E. Zanger, *Scenes from the Marriage of Louis XIV: Nuptial Fictions and the Making of Absolutist Power* (Stanford, CA: Stanford University Press, 1997).

By all accounts, Cavalli resisted coming to Paris. Mazarin and the singer Atto Melani (1626–1714) had to be persistent in devising an offer that could convince him to leave Venice.[14] The composer traveled to France in July 1660, only after suitable arrangements had been made for his fees and the costs of his journey along with those for his retinue, which included four musicians and a copyist. Although Cavalli immediately set to work on Buti's libretto, the production saw delays caused by Mazarin's illness and the ongoing construction of the new theater at the Palais des Tuileries where it would eventually take place. The theater needed to be large enough for the machines being designed by Gaspare Vigarani (1588–1663) and his sons Lodovico and Carlo (1625–1713). Instead of working steadily toward completing the new opera, Cavalli was asked to adapt for a performance at the Louvre his three-act *Xerse,* produced five years before at Venice's Teatro SS. Giovanni e Paolo. In order to conform to French tragic tradition, he had to expand the opera to five acts, insert ballets by Lully between the acts, and scale back some roles and choruses. When *Xerse* premiered on 22 November 1660, the public's preference for the ballets spelled the end of the first phase of Italian opera in France; one critic wrote that nothing of the recitatives could be understood. Furthermore, Mazarin's death on 9 March 1661 meant the loss of the main bridge between the two cultures and a further step toward Lully's monopoly on musical productions at court.

Cavalli's *L'Ercole amante* marks the final Italian opera presented at court during the two decades of the genre's initial appearance. A libretto printed for the long-awaited premiere on 7 February 1662 provides Buti's Italian verse on the left-hand pages, with rhyming French alexandrines by Benserade on the right hand.[15] Once again, ballets by Lully obligatorily accompanied Cavalli's opera.[16] Envious of the attentions and money paid to the Venetian composer, Lully made no effort to promote him to the French public. In addition to the delays in theater construction and the public's mounting dislike of a language that it could not readily understand, the work was deemed

[14] The most comprehensively documented studies of Cavalli's French years remain the two books by Henry Prunières: *L'Opéra italien en France avant Lulli* (Paris: Honoré Champion, 1913), chapters 5 (Les Fêtes du mariage royal) and 6 (L'Ercole amante et la cabale anti-italienne), and *Cavalli et l'opéra vénitien au XVIIe siècle* (Paris: Rieder, 1931), 25–41.

[15] Buti, *Ercole amante,* op. cit.

[16] Francesco Cavalli, *L'Ercole amante,* I-Vnm MS. It. IV, 359 (9883), and Jean-Baptiste Lully, "Ballet Hercule Amoureux, 1662," F-Pa Mus. Mss. Rés. 926 [III]. For a provocative discussion of the alleged conflicts between Cavalli and Lully during the 1662 production, see Michael Turnbull, "Ercole and Hercule: les goûts désunis?" *Musical Times* 121 (1980): 303, 305–307. Benserade's poetry was published concurrently with the libretto: *Vers du ballet royal dansé par Leurs Majestez entre des actes de la grande tragédie de l' "Hercule Amoureux" avec la traduction du prologue et les argumens de chaque acte* (Paris: Robert Ballard, 1662). For more details regarding the French poetry, see Silin, *Benserade,* 296–312.

too long: the prologue, combined ballets, and five-act *tragedia* took six-odd hours to perform. What was worse, the groaning of the stage machinery and the audience's conversations drowned out the music. According to the chronicler Loret, the public loved the spectacle but not the Italian drama and praised Lully above Cavalli.[17] The spurned Venetian composer left the country immediately after the final production in May, as did Gaspare Vigarani, neither with hopes of returning. Later opinions about *L'Ercole amante* hold the work in greater esteem, as they view the quality of its content rather than the unfortunate circumstances under which it was produced.[18]

One wonders how much of the lore surrounding the premiere of *L'Ercole amante* reached Bembo's attention, whether directly from Cavalli after he returned to Venice or from hearsay once she arrived in Paris. In any case, she was not deterred in her pursuit of a new setting. The multivalent symbolism of Hercules in her dedicatory "Madrigal" and in the libretto offered further possibilities for bringing together the secular and the sacred, and she did not miss the opportunity to compare Hercules's sin, punishment, and apotheosis with Christian redemption. She participated in the modes of Louis XIV's representation as Hercules that were in vogue again at the turn of the eighteenth century. Vertron, whose *La Nouvelle Pandore* had extolled the virtues of Chéron along with other illustrious women, penned a tribute to the king that he named *Hercules gallicus—Hercule gaulois,* while Le Noble published *Les Travaux d'Hercule* in 1693.[19] An anonymous writer praised Louis XIV's quasi-divine status in a depiction that resembles Bembo's microcosm:[20]

Est-ce un homme? Il est sans faiblesse.	Is he a man? He is without weakness.
Est-ce un dieu? Mais il est mortel.	Is he a god? But he is mortal.
Si c'est trop de l'appeler dieu,	If it's too much to call him god,
c'est trop peu de l'appeler homme.	it's too little to call him man.

Assuming the accuracy of the 1707 date found on the title page of the opera, with this work Bembo made the most of Hercules's heroic imagery for Louis's retrospective glorification, saving for the penitential psalm settings the older king's mortal concerns in his guise as David. A dramatic rendition of Hercules's final years actually suited better the court of 1707—when Louis's former youthful conquesting character had softened in pious devotion to Madame de Maintenon—than that of the younger "Hercule Gaulois." Where

[17] Silin, *Benserade*, 299–300.

[18] See, for instance, the chapters mentioned above by Prunières in *L'Opéra italien,* as well as Néraudau, *L'Olympe du Roi-Soleil,* "*Ercole amante,* ou l'opéra décrié," 147–154, at 153.

[19] See Néraudau, *L'Olympe du Roi-Soleil,* 67, n. 28. Vertron's work bears no place or date of publication.

[20] Verses from *L'Apothéose d'un nouvel Hercule, ou le théâtre de la gloire de Louis-le-Grand élevé sur la rivière de Seine* (1699) cited in Ferrier-Caverivière, *L'Image de Louis XIV,* 175.

Cavalli had emphasized Dejanira's suffering in act 2, scene 5, Bembo found a new way to pay musical tribute to her patron by placing her dramatic climax on Hercules's plight in act 3, scene 2.

Cavalli's operas spanned the entire period that Antonia lived in Venice, 1640–1676, and his encounter with French music laid the groundwork for her own more lengthy sojourn in Paris, 1677–1720. Undoubtedly his operatic legacy in general and *L'Ercole amante* in particular constituted the backdrop against which she undertook her new setting. She arrived during the decade that saw Lully's creation of the *tragédie en musique*. Ultimately resolving the problems of the 1660–1662 period, that genre united French Classic tragedy—a drama now heightened through singing rather than speaking—with balletic spectacle and a glorious array of orchestral instruments. By the time that she penned *L'Ercole amante,* Bembo had witnessed the last decade of Lully's work, including such *tragédies en musique* as *Atys* (1676) and *Proserpine* (1680), as well as the efforts of those who continued the tradition in the generation following his death. In examining the ways in which Bembo's opera represents a union of Italian and French tastes, *Cephale et Procris* (1694) by La Guerre, *Tancrède* (1702) by André Campra (1660–1744), and *Alcione* (1706) by Marais offer French models for comparison.[21] The dramatic endeavors of other expatriate Italian composers merit consideration alongside Bembo's, even if no evidence confirms their acquaintance. It may be significant that the careers of the two most prominent such contemporaries overlapped with Bembo in Paris; the staged works *Nicandro e Fileno* (1681) of Paolo Lorenzani (1640–1713), and *Coronis* and *Scylla* (1701) of Theobaldo di Gatti (c. 1650–1727) offered a stylistic mixture in the years prior to Bembo's new setting of *L'Ercole amante.* The timing of her arrival in Paris curiously coincided with a notable renewal of interest in Italian music and musicians, much to Lully's chagrin.[22]

Bembo brought a considerable amount of French material to her setting of Buti's libretto. Scored for six-part orchestra, her *Ouverture* replaced the opera's original Prologue and opening five-part *sinfonia*. Where Cavalli placed a *sinfonia* at the outset of each of the five acts, she called for that same six-part

[21] A facsimile of the Paris 1714 edition of *Proserpine* appears in two volumes in the series *Archivum Musicum: Musica Drammatica* II (Florence: Studio per edizioni scelte, 1994). The Société de Musicologie de Languedoc printed a facsimile of André Campra's *Tancrède, tragédie mise en musique* (Paris: Christophe Ballard, 1702), found in the Bibliothèque Municipale de Toulouse, in 1992. Wanda R. Griffiths edited the first modern score of *Cephale et Procris,* Recent Researches in the Music of the Baroque Era 88 (Madison, WI: A-R Editions, 1998).

[22] For a synthesis of Italian activity in secular circles in Paris circa 1678—including Lorenzani's arrival in France to serve the Queen; the publicizing of Charpentier's acquaintance with Carissimi in Rome and Joseph de La Barre's printing of his own Italian arias, both in the *Mercure galant;* the nomination of Nicolas Mathieu as Abbé to Saint-André-des-Arts, which instigated a renowned Italian circle there—see Jean Duron, "Aspects de la présence italienne dans la musique française de la fin du XVIIe siècle," *Les Samedis musicaux du Château de Versailles—Baroque Français, Baroque Italien au XVIIe siècle* (Versailles: Centre de Musique Baroque, 1992), 55.

ensemble to play an *Entrée* at the end of an act, borrowing the term from the instrumental numbers of the *tragédie en musique*.[23]

Except for the expanded orchestra of the *Ouverture* and *Entrée* portions as well as the brilliant final Chorus for the Seven Planets (ex. 7.5), Bembo's prior compositional experience prepared the way for her operatic endeavor. With its basic components consisting of arias, recitatives, ariosos, recitative-ariosos, and ritornellos, most of the textures recur from her earlier compositions. The instrumental trio accompanies the arias and serves as the foundation for the expanded orchestra.

The French overture with which Bembo opened *L'Ercole amante* shares its orchestration with each *Entrée,* such as that presented at the end of act 1 (ex. 7.1). She scored both for two *dessus* instruments (French violin clefs, G1), three *parties de remplissage* (two C3 clefs and a C4 clef), and b.c. (F4 clef). The orchestration resembles that of the "chœur de symphonie" of her *grand motet:* two violins (G1), two *hautes-contre de violon* (C3), and a *basse de violon* (F4), with the sixth part notated on a C4 clef presumably intended for the *taille de violon,* corresponding to the vocal tenor range found in the *Divertimento* (C4).[24] Continuo instruments such as theorbo and harpsichord would realize the harmony of the bass line, and wind instruments—such as transverse flutes, oboes, and bassoon—would double on the upper treble parts and melody of the bass line. Unlike the *grand motet,* the melody and harmony instruments usually double *colla parte* on the b.c. line, as do the instrumental and choral components (ex. 7.5). At only one place does the score specify a particular instrument: "flauti" for act 5's inserted "sinfonia," actually a four-movement trio sonata (ex. 7.3).

Dotted notes characterize Bembo's French overture, embodying Louis XIV's grandeur. In marked contrast with the brief statements and largely homophonic writing of Cavalli's opening *sinfonia,* her overture presents longer phrases with greater gestural sweep and more contrapuntal complexity. She assumed the approach of the post-Lullian generation; as Campra did for *Tancrède,* she set the music in bipartite form in duple meter throughout.[25]

Bembo's opera presents a hybrid not only for the bridging of musical tastes but also of styles spanning two centuries. The libretto lent the work the fluidity of the incipient *tragédie en musique,* yet the zeitgeist moved it toward the characteristic numbers of the opera seria. The following selection of scene analyses illustrate key aspects of the work's dramatic force.

---

[23] I am grateful to the Boston Early Music Festival for the loan of the first modern score of Cavalli's *L'Ercole amante,* edited by Paul O'Dette, Stephen Stubbs, and Robert Schenke for the 1999 production.

[24] Jean Duron associated the *taille* range with the C4 clef in Benoit, ed., *Dictionnaire de la musique en France,* 659.

[25] Campra, *Tancrède,* i–iv.

Example 7.1   F-Pn, Rés. Vm⁴9, pp. 43–44

Juno's Concluding *Scena* for Act 1

Distressed with the way that "Love mocks" him ("come sì beffa Amor"), Hercules bumbles onstage.[26] With angular, halting phrases, his *basso buffo* aria signals from the outset his ill-placed affections (scene 1). Venus's initial appearance with the Chorus of Graces recalls from the *Divertimento* an analogous vocal trio, singing as consorts of Venus and allegorizing the ladies-in-waiting of Marie-Adélaïde (ex. 4.11–4.13). Whereas that earlier scoring included two sopranos and *haute-contre,* here three sopranos constitute the Chorus of Graces, who also interact with Hercules (scene 2). An orchestral ritornello following the trio offers the balance of a third full texture midway between the *Ouverture* and *Entrée* framing the act.

Juno's composite *scena* brings act 1 to an exciting close (scene 3). Bembo retained most of the libretto's staging indications, such as here for the god-

[26] The libretto prepared by Massimo Ossi for the 1999 *Boston Early Music Festival Catalogue* served as the basis of the English translation quoted here.

dess's arrival: "the clouds hide the machine from which Juno descends; she appears seated on a large peacock."[27] In juxtaposition with Venus's previous scene, Buti established the opposition between the two goddesses who manipulate mortal actions on earth. Juno's recitative, aria, and recitative-arioso, all set in G minor (ex. A.10), flow into the stormy *Entrée* that sums up the intensity of her fury: "Juno leaves, and from her machine fall winds and lightning, which join in a dance to close the First Act" (ex. 7.1). Contrasting emotions signal the complexity of Juno's persona.

Juno's recitative divides into two parts, the first of which expresses her anger against Venus and Hercules (lines 1–15):

GIUNONE	JUNO
1 E vuol dunque Ciprigna,	And so, Venus,
per far contro di me gl'ultimi sforzi	to carry her efforts to their end
de' più pungenti oltraggi,	to inflict upon me the most wounding offenses,
favorir chi le voglie hebbe sì intese	wants to favor the one whose intentions
5 ad offendermi ogn'hora,	were so conceived as to offend me always,
che negli impuri suoi principi ancora	and who, from his unholy beginnings
prima d'esser m'offese?	even before being born, was offensive to me?
Chi pria di spirar l'aure	One who, even before drawing his first breath,
spirò desio di danneggiarmi, e dopo	was animated by the desire to hurt me,
10 aver dal petto mio	and who, after drawing from my breast
tratti i primi alimenti al viver suo,	his life's first sustenance,
con ingrata insolenza	with thankless insolence
d'uccidermi tentando osò ferirmi?	dared to wound me as he attempted to kill me?
Ah, ch'intesi i disegni	Ah, having understood the plan,
15 ma non sia ch'a disfarli altri m'insegni.	I will not need to be taught how to undo it.

Through a descending G-minor triad she disdains the goddess of love and snarls out her name on a cadential dissonant leading tone (mm. 1–2). Catapulting up the octave, her fury accelerates to reach the word "sforzi" on g^2

---

[27] F-Pn, Rés. Vm⁴9: "Nel resto de' nuvoli di detta Machina essendo ascosa Giunone. Questa si discuopre assisa in un gran Pavone" (34).

(mm. 2–3). In considering the "wounding offenses" of Venus's darts, she slows and softens on the lowered seventh f^2 (mm. 3–4). The static pedal Gs in the b.c. begin to move more fluidly as she shifts her attention to Hercules; below her insistent a^1-flats, lowered fifth and seventh chords emphasize his "impure beginnings" (mm. 7–8). She dwells on a question and rests momentarily on a C-minor chord midway through the recitative's first part (m. 9, line 7).

Juno explains the circumstances of her wrath against Hercules (mm. 10–18). Of illegitimate birth, he was the child of none other than Juno's own consort, Zeus, with the mortal Alcmena, herself married to Amphitryon. At one point Hercules inadvertently murdered his own wife and children; in order to atone, he had to perform the Twelve Labors devised by Juno with King Eurystheus. Her inability to defy Hercules over the course of his life explains the anger that gushes forth here. In her final couplet (lines 14–15), closing the first part of the recitative on the fifth scale degree, she promises to undo his pernicious plan (m. 21).

The b.c. initiates the second part of the recitative by means of a tag descending into the relative major, the mention of true love prompting the first major mode harmony heard in the *scena* thus far (mm. 21–22). The sweet B-flat-major triad unfolding over pedal BB-flats makes palpable the "affetto" of Hyllus and Iole (mm. 22–24):

Di reciproco affetto	Hyllus and Iole burn
ardon Hyllo, et Iole,	with tenderness for one another,
e sol per mio dispetto	and, solely to spite me,
l'iniqua Dea non vuole	the villainous Goddess does not
20 ch'Imeneo li congiunga? Anzi procura	want Hymen to join them? Rather,
per mio scorno maggiore,	to give me still greater offense,
ch'il nodo maritale ond'è ristretto	she arranges that the marital knot that binds
Ercole a Dejanira alfin si rompa;	Hercules to Dejanira should at last be broken;
a ciò ch'Iole a questi	so that Iole may be taken today,
25 del di lei genitore empio omicida	in monstrous embrace,
con mostruosi amplessi oggi s'innesti.	by the evil murderer of her own father.
E con qual'arte o Dio? Con arti indegne	And by what means, o God? By such as are unworthy of
d'ogni anima più vil, non che divina.	even the vilest of souls, not to mention of a divine one.

At the mention of Venus, "l'iniqua Dea," the initial G-minor harmony returns, thwarting the betrothed lovers' intention to wed (mm. 24–27). Hercules's misguided love threatens all aspects of "Imeneo" and risks the destruction of his own marriage as well as the potential for that of his son (mm. 29–30). Juno's "scorno maggiore," sounding in D minor (mm. 28–29), reinforces the key in which she vowed to prevent him (m. 21). Lines 25–26 heap further insult upon Hercules, who murdered the father of the woman he claims to love. On a wailing g^2, "non" negates the divine status of both Hercules and Venus (m. 40), and Juno brings the recitative full circle on the same pitch with which she had previously condemned the goddess alone (m. 3).

The concept of negation makes a powerful thematic connection between the recitative and the succeeding aria. Hercules's plan to steal Iole's affections nullifies the purpose of love, without which the music cannot continue and falls silent. Following the *perpetuum mobile* of sixteenth notes in the b.c., the ritornello comes to an abrupt, grinding halt and the bass line drops down to D, abandoned (mm. 43–45). This ingenious setting of the text matches the broader implication of Juno's words:

1	Ma in amor ciò ch'altri fura	But in love, that which swindles others
	più d'Amor gioia non è,	is no longer Love's joy,
	è un' insipida ventura	what he did not grant as a gift, or out of pity,
	ciò ch'egli in dono, o ver pietà, non diè.	is just a pointless adventure.
5	In amor ciò ch'altri fura	In love, that which swindles others
	più d'Amor gioia non è.	is no longer Love's joy.
	Se non vien da grata arsura	If it does not come from a true thirst,
	volontaria all'altrui fé;	voluntarily from another's faith,
	cangia a fatto di natura	it changes entirely its nature
10	come d'odio condita ogni mercé.	as if hatred colored all mercy.

As in several of the arias of *Produzioni armoniche,* the ritornello plays the melody for the voice before it enters (ex. 3.4–3.5); the *perpetuum mobile* of the b.c. recalls "Mi basta così" from the same manuscript (ex. A.1).

Bembo's use of near-silence at this juncture, to portray the nullification of love, recalls a central preoccupation in *Produzioni armoniche:* paradoxically, a singer cannot express humility except through sound. The silence of Juno here (m. 45) is comparable to a procedure employed in La Guerre's opera: in the scene where Cephale mistakenly shoots an arrow through his beloved Procris's heart, two instances of "Silence" occur in the score.[28] It is noteworthy that the two most prolific women composers of Louis XIV's reign both grappled with the notion of silence from within their sounding creations, but

---

[28] Griffiths discussed this feature in her introduction to *Cephale et Procris* (xi). The moments of "Silence" occur during Procris's last accompanied recitative, "Non, vivez" (p. 271, m. 24, and p. 272, m. 33).

not surprising, given that both were raised in cultures dictating that girls should exhibit proper modesty and, in general, keep quiet. That Bembo would still be working this out in her late sixties testifies to the tenacity of this ethos during her upbringing—despite her father's apparent intention to promote her as a singer.[29]

Buti's libretto exploits the dual meaning of "Amor" as both Cupid, "Love" (lines 2, 6) and "love," transcribed here as "amor" (lines 1, 5). The A sections of the aria elaborate on the futility and treachery of an amorous "adventure" (mm. 44–49, 56–59), while the B section addresses how an illegitimate union runs counter to nature and ultimately leads to hatred rather than love (mm. 50–55). The pervasive dotted rhythms in the upper parts, along with the longer note values emphasizing naturally weak beats (mm. 44–46, 50, 52–54, 57), intentionally render a gauche and unnatural impression. Three statements of the last line of the A section, "più d'Amor gioia non è," bring the aria to a close, the last prolonged at its final cadence (mm. 58–59). Mm. 57–59 represent the results of the thorough editing needed to remove the extra beats and add a missing barline from the manuscript.

Juno's final "recitative-arioso" mixes characteristics of both types of singing: her initial question in recitative with b.c. accompaniment alone (mm. 60–63) is followed by an arioso passage with the *dessus* and b.c. (mm. 63–79). The opening G-major triad (m. 60) acts as a counterpart to the first recitative's G-minor triad (m. 1) and connotes her strengthened position over the course of the *scena:*

Ma che più con inutili lamenti	But why am I wasting what little time I have
il tempo scarso alla difesa io perdo?	to defend myself in useless complaints?
Su, portatemi o venti	Come, winds, take me
alla grotta del Sonno; e d'aure infeste	to the cave of Sleep; and let my throne,
corteggiato il mio tron, versi per tutto	surrounded by evil gusts, spread all around

pompe del mio furor, fiamme,
    e tempeste.
	heralds of my fury, lightning, and
	    violent winds.

B-flat major, the key of true love, accompanies Juno's decision to use Sleep as a weapon against Hercules (mm. 63–67). Various types of imitation contribute to the vivacity of the arioso: an initial stretto introduces the entrance

[29] Jeanice Brooks explored the paradox of women's silence and song in "Catherine de Médicis, *nouvelle Artémise:* Women's Laments and the Virtue of Grief," *Early Music* 27 (1999): 419–420. See, too, Gordon-Seifert, "Strong Men—Weak Women," 147, and Thomasin LaMay, ed., *Musical Voices of Early Modern Women* (Aldershot, UK: Ashgate, 2005): "countless writers have concurred that the most important *virtù* an early modern woman could embrace was that of silence" (3).

of the *dessus* (m. 63) after which all three parts participate in quasi-fugato passages ("versi," mm. 68–69), some featuring doubled parts imitating the motive ("corteggiato il mio tron," *dessus*/b.c., mm. 68–69). Melismatic passages lengthen throughout the arioso: two measures for "venti" (mm. 64–65), three for "versi" (mm. 68–71), and finally five for "tempeste" (mm. 74–79). The resulting focus on sound rather than text leads the passage seamlessly into the concluding *Entrée* (ex. 7.1). The stage directions note that "Juno leaves and, from her machine in the clouds, storms and lightning descend, which form a dance to end the first act."[30]

Mirroring Juno's three numbers in G minor (recitative, aria, and recitative-arioso), the *Entrée* assumes a ternary form dividing into sections A (pp. 43–44), B (pp. 44–45), and C (pp. 45–46). Where Lully and La Guerre typically employed one meter throughout an *Entrée*, Bembo's C section moves out of common time and into 6/8 meter. Example 7.1 provides enough of the *Entrée* to demonstrate how it continues—in six parts—the vivacious imitative passages of Juno's closing arioso, now interspersed with homophonic dotted gestures (such as in the last measure of p. 43). Although a double bar repeat sign appears on p. 44 at the end of the first system, only the A section is to be repeated. By means of a dominant chord tonicizing B-flat major, the B section leads directly and seamlessly into the new meter of the C section. A *segno* marks the place to repeat the C section (p. 45, not shown), which, naturally, brings the *Entrée* to a close in G minor.

Example 7.1 shows the rather careless manner with which this manuscript was bound, by contrast to the perfection of the Bembo volumes prepared for the king's library. The truncated capitals "A" and "P" of "Atto Primo" show that the top part of the manuscript got cut off during the binding process of the opera's first volume. The manuscript requires a considerable amount of editorial work for any performance endeavor. For instance, on p. 43, second system, m. 2, the *taille* has a marked e^1-flat, from which the same pitch for the b.c. must be inferred and placed retroactively from the subsequent sixteenth-note flourish of the first *dessus*. The b.c. figures are often easily confused with accidentals; on the last beat of the *Entrée*'s first measure, the sharp sign next to the d^1 refers to the need for an f^1-sharp, not for a d^1-sharp. The rhythm of the b.c. also raises editorial questions: should it align with one of the upper parts or is the odd pattern of eighth, dotted-eighth, sixteenth, and eighth notes intentional?

Erasures and rewritten passages here, as in the other manuscripts, suggest that Bembo made some changes after she received the fair copy back from the scribe. In the last measure of the A section, for instance, the second *dessus* and the b.c. parts reveal an erasure and newly added material. The original first

---

[30] F-Pn, Rés. Vm⁴9: "Giunone parte e fà cader dalle nuvole della sua Machine, tempeste e fulmini che formano la danza per fine del Primo Atto" (42).

dessus part had a descending a^2–g^2–f^2-sharp, which a later pen reversed to avoid a doubled f^2-sharp between the two *dessus* parts (a note already doubled at the lower octave by the first *haute-contre*), and to provide the necessary fifth of the D-major chord. An erasure in the *taille* part (p. 44, second system, m. 1, beat 2) appears to have been made so as to remove a clash with the motion of the three sixteenth notes in the first *dessus* and second *haute-contre*. The thematic material of the second *dessus* had to be eliminated (second system, m. 3, beat 1) because it created parallel octaves with the first *dessus*. The solution makes the lovely effect of tenths sounding between the first *dessus* and the b.c. followed by successive imitation in the final measure of p. 44.

The Sleep Scene

Act 2 starts with an extended love duet between Hyllus and Iole (scene 1), an interruption by the Page, who summons Iole to Hercules (scene 2), an aria for the Page, who sings about "this thing called love"—prefiguring Beaumarchais's celebrated Cherubino—that has so affected Iole and now Dejanira as well (scenes 3 and 4). After a discussion with the Page and her servant Lychas, Dejanira sings alone of the pain that Hercules's infidelity has caused her, as well as of the danger that his passion poses for their son (scene 5). Cavalli gave Dejanira a heartrending aria to sing over the emblematic lament of a descending basso ostinato pattern, the climax of his opera; by contrast, Bembo saved the lament for Hercules in the next act.

The most remarkable part of act 2 in Bembo's hands lies in Pasithea's Sleep Scene (scene 6), which was clearly modeled on prototypes in the Lullian repertory, notably that of *Atys*. Rokseth singled out this passage for its beauty, which is borne out in performance (CD tr. 10). The stage directions indicate that "the scene changes to the cave of Sleep."[31] Pasithea, a high soprano, is accompanied by the instrumental trio in her F-minor "Adagio" and "Aria" (ex. A.11), followed by a Chorus of Breezes and Brooks.[32] Even though they share performing forces, the musical means of expressing Juno's wrath and Pasithea's tranquility could not offer more contrast. Juno's *scena* functions in an Italianate way (boisterous character, jagged melodic lines, extended melismas, fugato passages)[33] and the "Adagio" sections of Pasithea's Sleep Scene

---

[31] F-Pn, Rés. Vm⁴9: "la scena si cangia nella grotta del Sonno" (103).

[32] Rokseth provided part of this aria, as well as the ravishing chorus that follows it, in "Antonia Bembo," 161–165. She found that Bembo's setting "surpasses by far the corresponding scene from Cavalli's opera . . . [and] shows that Louis XIV made no mistake in basing on her those hopes of which he gave proof when he pensioned her" (160). For a transcription of Cavalli's setting of Pasithea's aria and the following chorus, see Prunières, *L'Opéra italien*, "Appendice musical," 27–32.

[33] Duron argued that "in the eyes of French contemporaries, the fugue represented an ital-

function in a quintessentially French manner (introspective character, melodic lines inherently smooth or made so through the application of *tierces coulées* and *notes inégales,* the use of the *petite basse*) thanks to the models that Lully and Couperin bring to bear on the present definitions of national style (ex. A.5 and 7). Particularly noteworthy is that, in keeping with the mood at court at the beginning of Louis's reign, Lully's *Ballet de la Raillerie* separates the two national styles, while at its end, the qualities later described by Couperin make every attempt to unify them.[34] Bembo's contributions to "les goûts réunis" belong to the latter effort, as Pasithea's contrasting "Adagio" and "Aria" demonstrate.

The rubric "Adagio" appears above the *dessus* parts at the outset of the initial ritornello and at Pasithea's entry (mm. 1–7). Smooth melodic lines depict the gentle sound of a natural glade. Tenths join the second *dessus* with the b.c. (mm. 2–3) and thirds unite the first and second *dessus* parts (m. 4) in felicitous harmony punctuated by the dissonance among the parts (c–e^1–d^2-flat) just prior to the cadential resolution (mm. 2–3). As in Juno's aria, the first *dessus* part drops out at the vocal entrance, so that the voice can take over the melody that it presented (mm. 7–12). These symmetrical six-bar phrases elegantly convey the peace and serenity of the text:

PASITHEA	PASITHEA
1 Mormorate	Murmur,
o fiumicelli,	o brooks,
sussurate	whisper,
o venticelli,	o gentle breezes,
5 e col vostro sussurro e mormorio,	and with your whispers and murmurs,
dolci incanti dell'oblio	sweet enchantments of oblivion
ch'ogni cura fugar ponno,	that put all cares to flight,
lusingate al sonno il Sonno.	seduce Sleep itself into sleep.

---

ianism little liked in France;" see "Aspects de la présence italienne," 54. Lest one conclude that the French influence did not hold equal sway in Italy, the impact of the *French tragédie en musique* there should not be underestimated. On this subject, see Piero Weiss, "Teorie drammatiche e 'Infranciosamento': Motivi della 'Riforma' melodrammatica nel primo Settecento," in *Antonio Vivaldi, teatro musicale, cultura e società* (Florence: L. S. Olschki, 1982), 1: 273–296.

[34] In *The Origins of Modern Musical Criticism—French and Italian Music, 1600–1750* (Ann Arbor: UMI Research Press, 1981), Georgia Cowart noted this eighteenth-century trend toward "reconciliation," citing the continuation of the debate between Lecerf de La Viéville and François Raguenet with "a lengthy 'Dissertation sur la musique italienne et française par Mr L.T.'" published in the *Mercure galant* in 1713 (89). Cowart used the Lully-Couperin duet to epitomize the period preceding Rameau in her chapter 5, "Les goûts-réunis" (87–113). The Lecerf-Raguenet debate ultimately boiled down to a matter of taste, which Cowart treated in the context of the period's reigning aesthetic issues.

The b.c. moves into *petite basse* range for the next ritornello (mm. 14–18), creating a texture reminiscent of the close-knit French-style passages in Bembo's first *Te Deum* and Ps. 101, as well as in Lalande's *Super flumina Babilonis* (ex. 4.3).[35] An exact repetition of the initial music for Pasithea follows (mm. 19–24) before continuing on to the second couplet (mm. 25–27). Pasithea initiates the passage, and the b.c. imitates her octave climb canonically, at the distance of two quarter notes, evoking a sense of unanimity and utter accord. In the next interjection of the ritornello, the second *dessus* takes over the canon, while the bass offers a new harmonization and descends gently through the tetrachord, f–e-flat–d-flat–c (mm. 28–30).

Nouns replace imperatives to elaborate on the sound effects of "whispers and murmurs" in stanza 2 (mm. 30–38, lines 5–6). The enchanting quality of this music has much to do with its conjunct motion, especially notable here with a slur over the melisma on "mormorio" (mm. 33–34) supported by the smooth chromatic line of the b.c. that slides into E-flat major (mm. 32–35). These procedures accomplish Pasithea's lofty goal: to ravish with enchantment all senses to rest. Susan McClary's identification of chromatic strategies for female characters in seventeenth- and nineteenth-century operas applies well to Bembo's portrayal of Pasithea, whose beguiling music, however, has only positive intentions.[36] It is only what Juno will do with Sleep in act 3, once she "borrows" him from Pasithea, that equates seduction with danger: she will use him to put Hercules into temporary dormant oblivion.

The climax of Pasithea's aria occurs at the setting of the final couplet, where all forces are brought together to "seduce" Sleep—her husband—into sleep (mm. 41–52). On "lusingate," she embarks on a gentle ascent that climbs stepwise and reaches an ethereal a^2-flat with tender sixth harmonies supporting her (mm. 43–48). As her line ebbs, it retraces those steps, continuing to lull the listener into a state of peaceful rest (mm. 48–52). The extraordinarily high register of the *petite basse* presents one last statement of "lusingate" to close the section (mm. 53–58). The effectiveness of the music matches that of the Sleep Scene from Lully's *Atys*, "Dormons, dormons tous" (act 3, scene 4), where the smoothest melodic lines soothe the listener with help from the personifications of Sleep, Morpheus, Phobétor, and Dreams.

The "Aria" section contrasts with the "Adagio" in its C-minor tonality as well as its several metric shifts, which recall many of the sectional pieces by

[35] The manuscript uses the C1 clef for the b.c. at mm. 14–18; at mm. 56–57, a C3 clef. The transcription employs a treble clef to facilitate the reading of the score in both instances.

[36] See the characterizations of Euridice in "Constructions of Gender in Monteverdi's Dramatic Music," *Feminine Endings* (Minneapolis: University of Minnesota Press, 1991), 35–52 at 42–46, and of the *Habañera* in *Georges Bizet, Carmen*. Cambridge Opera Handbooks (Cambridge: Cambridge University Press, 1992), 74–77.

the same name included in *Produzioni armoniche* that also featured irregular scansion (mm. 72–102):

1	Chi daver ama	Those who truly love
	viepiù il diletto	desire more greatly
	del caro oggetto	the pleasure of their beloved
	che 'l proprio brama:	than their own:
5	quind'è ch'io posi	thus is it that I should derive,
	la notte e 'l die	night and day,
	le contentezze mie	my own happiness
	del consorte gentil ne' bei riposi.	from my gentle husband's peaceful rest.

Pasithea describes the very kind of selfless love that Juno sought in act 1 and adopts a moralizing tone. The first stanza begins in triple meter with the voice moving freely, accompanied simply by the b.c., which displaces its initial accent to a weak beat (m. 72). To illustrate Pasithea's constancy, a steady half-note, double-eighth-note rhythmic pattern prevails (mm. 86–90). The ritornello varies her line, adding the second *dessus* to create a lovely trio texture (mm. 90–93). Duple meter accommodates two statements of the final *endecasillabo,* whose setting reaches the same a^2-flat (m. 98) as had the outer vocal reaches of the "Adagio," linking the sections (m. 48). Based on the rhythms and part of her final phrase, the closing ritornello for the instrumental trio brings the "Aria" to a beautiful close (mm. 100–102).

Apart from the omission of mm. 7–18, mm. 103–161 restate the initial "Adagio." Slight rhythmic variations merited the copying out of the measures rather than providing a segno to indicate a repeat at m. 19. The Sleep Scene demonstrates how Bembo combined the best aspects of French and Italian music. With its longer outside "Adagio" portions, she drew on features of Lully's celebrated Sleep Scene. With its disjunct motion and spontaneous character, the shorter middle "Aria" matches the Italian style presented in many of the arias from *Produzioni armoniche*. In this case musical style, rather than language or rubric, reveals the composer's superb accomplishment of "les goûts réunis."

The Royal Centerpiece
for Hercules

Bembo made more of the Sleep Scene in act 2, scene 6, than did Cavalli for the very reason that he had invested the previous scene with his trademark: the lament as operatic centerpiece.[37] For the aria "Ahi ch'amarezza" ("Ah

---

[37] This concept originated in Ellen Rosand, "Aria in the Early Operas of Francesco Cavalli" (Ph.D. diss., New York University, 1971), 83–86, and has spawned a considerable amount

what bitterness"), he provided Dejanira with a moment for intense and sustained dramatic reflection over a descending C-minor tetrachord, an ostinato with full orchestral accompaniment. Because Bembo underplayed Dejanira's music at this juncture, instead moving the action along with recitative, she dwelt on the emulation of Lully's French-style Sleep Scene. By giving the ostinato bass pattern and emphatic solo aria instead to Hercules in act 3, scene 2, she furthered her goal to glorify Louis with a "royal centerpiece."

Act 3, scene 1, finds Hercules in conversation with Venus, who states her philosophy of love: "as long as you take your pleasure, what do you care that it results from fraud or mercy?" ("pur che tu goda, ch'importa a te che sia per froda o per mercé?").[38] Even though buoyed by Venus's cavalier attitude, Hercules is still concerned that Love not only mocks him, as he stated at the outset of the opera, but that he faces an even greater challenge than he had from his most difficult Labors. As he sings to the Page at the opening of scene 2:

ERCOLE	HERCULES
Adagio [recitative-arioso]	Adagio [recitative-arioso]
1 Amor, contar ben puoi	Love, you may well count
fra' tuoi non minor vanti,	among your more important achievements
che dell'ardir, che torre a me non seppe	that you have deprived me of my courage,
co' latrati di Cerbero, et orrendi	something that even the most terrifying abyss,
5 strepiti suoi lo spaventoso abisso;	with Cerberus's bark, and with its other screams,
tu disarmato m'hai, sì ch'io, che colsi	could not take from me; so that I— who picked
ad onta del terribile custode,	with fearless hand the fruit of the Hesperides,
con intrepida man l'Esperia frutta,	offending its terrible guardians—
quasi di sostenere or non ardisco	I am almost afraid to bear
10 l'avicinar del bel per cui languisco.	the approach of the beauty for whom I languish.

For his Twelfth Labor, Hercules had had to seize from the clutches of Hell the dog Cerberus and bring him to Eurystheus, only to find that it was for

of scholarship into Cavalli's work in the Seicento. See, especially, Wendy Heller, *Emblems of Eloquence: Opera and Women's Voices in Seventeenth-Century Venice* (Berkeley: University of California Press, 2003).

[38] For a reproduction of the opening of Venus's aria from F-Pn, Rés. Vm⁴9 (ms. p. 166), see Rokseth, "Antonia Bembo" (opp. 155). The same excerpt can be found in modern notation in Jackson, "Musical Women," 123.

nought but the challenge; when he delivered the dog, Eurystheus required that he return him to Hell (lines 4–5). Prior to this task, Eurystheus demanded the golden apples of the Hesperides, the children of Atlas. Hercules offered to hold the world for Atlas to convince him to deliver the apples and when Atlas returned, he almost succeeded in leaving Hercules with the burden. Hercules, however, asked him to take the world while he readjusted it, and then happily left with his fruit (lines 6–8). Whereas in act 1 Hercules directed his anger at Love and Iole, now in reflection on his Labors he realizes that he has no one to blame but himself. This soliloquy, set in recitative-arioso style, had little to do with the King Louis XIV of 1662, but in 1707, along with the ensuing aria, it represented an apt analog for the monarch's assessment of his reign and his own introspection.

The conclusion of Hercules's recitative-arioso, "Adagio," and the outset of the following "Aria Adagio" share the key of E minor (ex. 7.2). Marked "R[itornel]lo," the instrumental trio accompanies him throughout (p. 182, second system, last measure). Ample use of madrigalism heightens the drama of the text, as does its range.[39] With a leap down to G, Hercules's lowest note embodies the "terrifying abyss" (p. 181, first system, mm. 1–2) on the same pitch that had been doubled by sixteenth-notes pedal GGs in the b.c. for the "screams" of Hell (p. 180, not shown here). Vivid infernal depictions had already found pride of place in settings of the Orpheus myth by Monteverdi and Rossi, which evidently served as models for the Italian-style music here.

Cadential points in the second half of the recitative-arioso (lines 6–10) on p. 181 anchor the main message of the soliloquy: Love has disarmed me ("tu disarmato m'hai," p. 181, first system, mm. 2–3), but recall when I was armed with the Hesperian fruit ("intrepida man," third system), for at the approach of my beloved ("l'avicinar del bel," p. 182, first system, mm. 2–3), I languish ("languisco," p. 182, second system). Hercules expresses here his rising desire with the chromatic tetrachord e–f–f-sharp–g–g-sharp–a, which falls, defeated, back to the tonic note on which he began (second system, penultimate measure). The setting connotes simultaneously his majesty and his waning powers. Cavalli's Hercules also sings an all-but-chromatic line on "languisco" (e-flat–d–d-flat–c–B-flat), but he provided no basso ostinato pattern for him.

The ritornello introduces the basso ostinato on an e^1, one octave above the note on which Hercules's previous music ended, and then glides gently down by half steps to a (p. 182, second-third systems, C4 clef). Where the original pattern moved upward from e, the new chromatic tetrachord in the b.c. descends from e^1 and—with the exception of the omitted pitches c^1 and a-sharp—mirrors in retrograde Hercules's "languisco" (e^1–d^1-sharp–d^1–c^1-sharp–b–a). For its second and only repetition the basso ostinato drops down

---

[39] For a parallel set of text painting interpretations, see Rokseth, "Antonia Bembo," 165–166.

Example 7.2   F-Pn, Rés. Vm⁴9, pp. 181–182

to the range of e–A, allowing Hercules to sing in his range (p. 183, not shown here) the text for the countermelody introduced by the first *dessus* at the outset of the "Aria Adagio" (p. 182, second-third systems):

ERCOLE	HERCULES
O quale instillano	O, what a pair of eyes,
in arso petto	brilliant with
rai, che sfavillano	great beauty, will instill
di gran beltà	in a chest burning with desire
umil rispetto,	humble respect
bassa umiltà!	and low humility!
Il Ciel ben sà	Heaven knows well
a sì suprema	whether it, itself,
adorabil maestà,	would not tremble
s'ei pur non trema?	before such supreme, adorable majesty?

In addition to her choice of a new placement for the lament, Bembo also diverged from Cavalli in her approach to it. Although the laments of both Dejanira and Hercules begin on an outcry of two beats within their triple-meter context ("Ahi" and "O," respectively), Cavalli brought Dejanira in on beat two, with an effective surprise syncopation that sets up a series of sobbing short broken phrases, where Bembo led Hercules in on the downbeat and gave him a continuous phrase. Cavalli repeated three times his defining diatonic ostinato pattern c¹–b-flat–a-flat–g–f, while Bembo repeated only once her chromatic ostinato. She adopted the same approach to structuring the repeating pattern of the centerpiece in the "Lamento della Vergine" (see table 3.2, ex. 3.9, and CD tr. 4).

Hercules's brief but powerfully revealing aria is unusual insofar as it repeats none of the text and no sign indicates a repetition. Nevertheless, the recitative-aria pair comes at a crucial moment in the drama, which the tetrachordal mirroring and the slow tempo both underscore as significant. In employing the lament style for Hercules's "Aria Adagio," Bembo not only cast his situation in the poignant light of a very common Cavalliesque ostinato but also bestowed new organic strength on the royal centerpiece of her tragedy with the identical descending chromatic tetrachord, the "emblem of lament."[40] Cavalli at the same dramatic moment had given Hercules a light, succinct triple-meter passage. Bembo thereby used her teacher's techniques as a means to achieve the new and original ends required of the historical moment at which she and her patron found themselves.

The Dénouement of the Tragedy

The action accelerates in the scenes following Hercules's soliloquy. Juno arrives with Sleep just a moment too late, for Iole already sits in Venus's magic chair and begins to consider a union with Hercules (scene 4), but sleep soon overcomes him (scene 5). Returning to her senses, Iole, in the name of her murdered father, wants to take revenge on Hercules but Hyllus prevents her (scene 6). Driven by Venus, Mercury flies in and wakes up Hercules, who sees the sword in Hyllus's hand and tries to kill him (scene 7). Dejanira enters, declaring that she could bear infidelity but not the murder of her son— in a rage, Hercules banishes both wife and son (scene 8). Hyllus and Dejanira, united in misery, sing an *aria a due* (scene 9). To conclude the act, the Page sings in wonder about the strange things that Love has wrought all around him (scene 10).

The outset of act 4 focuses on Hyllus and his plight: imprisoned in a seaside tower, he feels jealous of the affections that he witnessed between his father and Iole (scenes 1–3). Juno arrives to rescue him with the assistance of

---

[40] For more about this concept, see Rosand, *Opera in Seventeenth-Century Venice*, 369. In Heller, *Emblems of Eloquence*, the musical example of Iarba's lament in Cavalli's *La Didone* reveals the identical initial whole-whole-half step pattern as the ostinato undergirding Dejanira in Cavalli's *L'Ercole amante* (111).

Neptune, whose conch shell rises from the sea (scene 4).[41] Juno returns to Hercules and, with Sleep, puts him out again (scene 5). The final scenes take Iole and Dejanira to a "cypress garden with royal tombs," where Iole converses with the ghost of her father, King Eutyrus (scene 6) and explains that she must marry Hercules in order to save the life of Hyllus, whom both women fear dead (scenes 7–8).

The story holds some parallels with the sixteenth-century tale of Don Juan, memorialized in Mozart's *Il dissoluto punito ovvero Don Giovanni*: retribution for a murdered father (the Commendatore/Eutyrus) of the central female protagonist (Donna Anna/Iole) taken against the licentious murderer (Don Giovanni/Hercules), in a concluding graveyard scene where the murdered father assumes mortal shape so as to wreak vengeance and save his daughter. Following a transitional Ballet for the Ghosts, act 5 opens in Hell with the Ghost of Eutyrus and a Chorus of Infernal Spirits (S–S–HC–T–B) invoking their "vendetta" against Hercules. Other Dead Souls wronged by Hercules rise up to join the cause: Clerica, queen of Cos; Laomedonte, king of Troy; and Bussiride, king of Egypt. The expressive rubrics that designate each of their entrances recall those of the *cantate spirituali* from *Produzioni armoniche*: "aria dispettosa," "aria sdegnosa," "aria à tempo con sdegno," and an "aria à mesura giusta" with an interpolated passage, "con furia." The five-part chorus interjects between the successive arias sung by each character, whose wishes are granted (scene 1). During the wedding ceremony for Iole and Hercules at Juno's Temple, Iole produces the magic robe that has been soaked with poison from the Centaur's philtre; the chorus of temple worshippers interjects (scene 2). While Hercules sings a final recitative as the robe tears at his skin, Hyllus returns, prompting relief and rejoicing (scene 3).

A "Sinfonia" precedes scene 4 (ex. 7.3). By contrast with the *sinfonie* for full orchestra with which Cavalli opened the acts of his opera, this one is scored for the instrumental trio as a dramatic interlude between scenes 3 and 4. Its rubric "Adagio flauti con affetto" signals the continuation of the extensive quartet in A minor sung by Iole, Dejanira, Hyllus, and Lychas, marked "Adagio e con affetto," in scene 3 (pp. 429–434). By means of the usual stepwise tag, the b.c. descends from the quartet's final chord on *A* to an octave transposition for the *sinfonia*'s new key of E major (p. 435, first-second systems). Where Bembo indicated specific instruments in some of her earlier

[41] In preparation for the 1662 production, Lodovico Vigarani sent to the Duchess of Modena a list of the machines that he, his father, and brother had constructed for use in each act. Preserved among the Vigarani papers in the Archivio di Stato of Modena, the list shows that machinery accompanied most of the scenes highlighted in this analysis, including Venus and the Three Graces, the cave of Sleep, Juno's descent with Sleep, Mercury's flight, Royal Tombs, Hell, Juno's Temple, and the final scene of Heaven, Hercules, and the Seven Planets. See Frederick Paul Tollini, *Scene Design at the Court of Louis XIV—The Work of the Vigarani Family and Jean Bérain*. Studies in Theatre Arts, vol. 22 (Lewiston, NY: Edwin Mellen Press, 2003), 26–27.

Example 7.3   F-Pn, Rés. Vm⁴10, p. 435

compositions (such as the flutes, violins, and bassoon of the *grand motet;* see ex. 5.2–5.3), the *sinfonia's* call for "flauti" represents the opera's only such designation. Scored for two treble instruments and b.c. in four movements with tempo and dance-name rubrics, the *sinfonia* looks like a cross between a Corellian *sonata da camera* and a *sonata da chiesa* (table 7.1).

Even if Corelli's trio sonatas represent the benchmark for the period, clearly other models influenced this composition. Recalling Couperin's claim that "the first Italian 'Sonades' appeared in Paris more than thirty years ago,"[42] that is circa 1690, the trio sonatas of La Guerre offer the most likely candidates for Bembo's work. Moreover, the special effect of transverse flutes lends the *sinfonia* a distinctly French sound, despite its Italian rubrics. Once again, Bembo managed to unite the styles in an exemplary manner.

With its leisurely pace and plenty of opportunity for improvised embellishment, the first movement exhibits classic eighteenth-century closed binary form. The parts move together and then sustain a dominant seventh chord (m. 2), resolved on the next downbeat (mm. 1–3). The eighth notes in

---

[42] Couperin, *Les Goûts-réünis,* "Préface."

TABLE 7.1 Movements of the "Sinfonia," *L'Ercole amante* (F-Pn, Rés. Vm⁴10)

Movement	Form	Meter	Location
Adagio	Binary form	3/4 meter	Manuscript pp. 435–436
Allegro	through-composed	3/8 meter	Manuscript pp. 436–437
[Unlabelled]	through-composed	duple meter (2)	Manuscript p. 438
Menuetto Allegro	ternary form	triple meter (3)	Manuscript p. 439

all parts, unmistakably French in style, require interpretation as *notes inégales.* The second *dessus* has the opportunity for a luxurious trill on its dotted-quarter g¹-sharp, imitated by the first *dessus* in m. 4, which propels the ensemble forward to resolution in the dominant (mm. 3–5). Written-out *tierces coulées* in the first *dessus* embellish the cadence in F-sharp major (mm. 7–8), the key that functions as the applied dominant in the move toward the double bar.

The indication of "flauti" is problematic, even if it applies only to the first movement where it appears. There the first *dessus* part lies within the range of the *flûte traversière* (f¹-sharp–c²-sharp), but the second *dessus* goes below the range six measures before the end when it reaches a low c¹-sharp, a note that can be managed by rolling the embouchure inward from the lowest note of the instrument (d¹), but the resulting sound is not ideal. The second and third movements contain two b's in each of the two *dessus* parts—notes that lie too low for standard transverse flutes, but lie in the *taille* range. But what instruments do "flauti" indicate? Were they only to play the first movement? Alto recorders descend only to f¹. The "flauti," then, whether transverse or fipple, must have been *taille*-sized so as to reach the *taille* range notated for the first three movements.[43] The "Menuetto Allegro" lies high enough for *traversières* to perform (but again too low for alto recorders). Bembo's *sinfonia* may be performed as an independent instrumental trio sonata, whether one chooses (1) to use violins throughout, (2) to employ *traversières* for the first and last movements and violins for the inner ones, or (3) to assemble a consort of transverse flutes equivalent to those that Lully, and apparently Bembo, knew.

The second movement's dotted-eighth, sixteenth, eighth rhythms evoke a gigue, even as the barlines break the phrases into 3/8 measures instead of the composite 6/8 more typical of the dance. The indication "Seguita Allegro" ("the Allegro follows") suggests an attacca into the next movement. Following the Allegro, the score, marked "Tornate" ("Turn the page"), implies that the players would have had it before their eyes, as opposed to having the parts that normally would have been distributed for an operatic performance. These indications leave no doubt that the manuscript represents a performing score.

---

[43] Duron, "Aspects de la présence italienne," pointed out that Lully called for a flute quartet in *Le Triomphe de l'Amour* (1680), ranging from the "flûte allemande" that represents the standard *traversière* today, through "taille, quinte, petite basse," to "grande basse de flûtes" (48).

Pervasive dactyls characterize the unlabelled third movement, reminiscent of a bourrée. The tempo of this movement should be quite quick, as the duple meter, "2," dictates that the main beats fall on the first and third quarters of the measure. The indication for a "Segue" after the cadence signals another attacca. All of the score's verbal connectors point to a performance that should be as continuous as possible, presumably to retain the momentum required as the tragedy speeds toward dénouement. Accordingly, the designated rubrics of the final three movements suggest that they are to be played at a fast tempo.

The fourth movement, a "Menuetto Allegro," recalls the rhythm of the Menuet of the *Divertimento* (ex. A.6). Beside the obligatory meter, the two dances share the following features: a rest on the first beat of the first measure followed by a two-beat anacrusis; the first *dessus* starts with an e^1; a brief rest follows the initial four-measure phrase; and a *petite reprise*. A repetition appears for each of the three sections; the harmony is static, however—all final cadences are in E major. The third section of the "Menuetto Allegro" contains eight measures that represent an embellishment of the second of the two eight-measure phrases of the second section; this *petite reprise* shows still greater sophistication than that found in the *Divertimento*. Such transformative embellishment represents the instrumental analog to a procedure already extensively employed in the vocal music of *Produzioni armoniche* (see, for instance, ex. 3.13).

The *sinfonia*'s placement and trio-sonata structure are both anomalous to the practices found in vocal tragedy, whether in Paris or in Venice. Lully and La Guerre would have used a single instrumental air within an act, but not an entire trio sonata; Cavalli called for *sinfonie,* but they were always orchestral. To what degree was Bembo influenced by the assumption or knowledge that her opera would never make it to the stage of the Académie Royale de Musique? She enjoyed greater independence and freedom than any of the king's musicians, who had to follow strict codes and receive approval before publishing their work.

Beside the *sinfonia*'s "Menuetto," two other dances appear in *L'Ercole amante:* a "Danza" (the Italian word for dance, a designation not encountered elsewhere in Bembo's music) in act 4, scene 5, and a Gigue for act 5, scene 5. The "Danza, allegro," scored for instrumental trio, occurs just after Juno rescues Hyllus from the tower prison. The stage directions indicate that they dance along with a Chorus of Zephyrs. Somewhat reminiscent of a quick, through-composed menuet, the "Danza" (D) does not function independently but works in tandem with Juno's aria (A) ($D–A^1–D–A^2$). In pairing an aria with a dance, Bembo followed the Lullian template; at the identical spot in *Atys,* a Menuet introduces two sopranos who repeat its music with their text (act 4, scene 5).

Whereas Bembo's score previously noted all scene changes from the libretto, none is found at the outset of act 5, scene 4, nor is there a demarca-

Example 7.4   F-Pn, Rés. Vm⁴10, pp. 444–445

tion of the exact place where it commences.[44] Instead, the *sinfonia* leads seam-lessly into an aria in triple time for Juno, also in E major. With copious se-quential triadic fanfares, the victorious nature of Juno's music borders on the martial as she sings of the happiness brought about by Hercules's apotheosis and the reunion of the true lovers (ex. 7.4):

GIUNONE		JUNO	
(A)	Su, su allegrezza,	(A)	Come, come: be happy,
	non più lamenti,		and no more lamentations,
	deh, non più, no,		no, no more,
	ch'ogni amarezza		for Heaven has transformed
	il Ciel cangiò		all bitterness
	tutt'in contenti,		into contentment,

[44] Buti's libretto indicates the following stage directions at the outset of act 5, scene 4: "Cala Giunone nell'ultima machina cortegiata dall'armonia de' Cieli, & apparisce nella più alta parte di questi Ercole sposato alla Bellezza" [Juno descends in the last machine, surrounded by the har-mony of the Heavens, and in the highest part of these Hercules appears, married to Beauty] (154).

	tutt'in dolcezza.		into sweetness.
	Non più lamenti,		No more lamentations,
	su, su allegrezza.		come, come: be happy.
(B)	Non morì Alcide,	(B)	Alcides did not die,
	tergete i lumi,		wipe your eyes,
	non morì, no,		no, he did not die,
	su nel Ciel ride,		he laughs up in Heaven,
	che lo sposò		for the King of the Gods
	il Ré de' Numi		married him off
	alla Bellezza.		to Beauty.

Pages 444–445 illustrate the transition between the aria's A section ("Su, su") and its B section ("Non morì Alcide") of Juno's aria (p. 444, third system, b.c. clef change from C3 to F4). In addition to the triadic fanfares, circling sixteenth-note figurations adorn "allegrezza," sometimes in contrary motion between parts (p. 444, mm. 4–12). Bembo created a similar effect in the "Sonetto al Re" opening *Produzioni armoniche* (line 14, "coronarti il Cielo"). In both cases, her goal was similar: to transform the hero into an immortal ruler, "crowning" him in Heaven. Although the score does not indicate a da capo—again, for the purposes of the dénouement—if performed as an opera excerpt, it can be interpreted as such.

With a syncopated entrance and a brief halting moment of duple meter, the B section tastefully captures the interjection of Juno's announcement of the *lieto fine:* "Alcides did not die" (p. 444, third system). Bembo had employed the same idiosyncratic practice of writing a "4" into the score for the temporary shift out of triple meter (p. 445, m. 1) in "Per il Natale" (*Produzioni armoniche,* no. 5). Thirty-second notes offer a madrigalistic setting of laughter on "ride" (p. 445, second system, m. 2). This triumphant music contrasts beautifully with the lugubrious quality of that found in the previous act. Cavalli and Bembo lent equivalent weight to this moment of the tragedy. Instead of a contrasting B section to announce the news of Hercules's apotheosis, he inserted two measures of duple time in an otherwise triple movement—tantamount to Bembo's idea to present the text with a syncopated entrance.

Following Juno's triumphant song, Dejanira, Hyllus, and Iole reflect in a brief ensemble dialogue and the couple sings a love duet to Juno ("Che dolci gioie, o Dea"). Scene 4 concludes with a five-part chorus (S-S-S-HC-T)[45] with the six-part instrumental ensemble, now including a seventh figured b.c. part ("Da lega d'Amore") (ex. 7.5, p. 477). The characters constitute the chorus: Dejanira, Iole, and Juno, sopranos; Hyllus, *haute-contre;* and Lychas, tenor. The singers' clefs appear in their tacit measures on p. 477. The instru-

---

[45] Rokseth, "Antonia Bembo," commended Bembo's five-part choruses, whose "compactness" she found to be "remarkable," and worthy to "herald the century of Bach and Handel" (160).

mental parts correspond to those of the singers: two G1 clefs and a C1 clef (two *dessus de violons* and the first *haute-contre de violon*), a C3 clef (the second *haute-contre de violon*), and a C4 clef (the *taille*).

From Myth to Reality

The opera's largest ensemble graces the outset of its final scene, "Atto Quinto Scena Quinta" (ex. 7.5). The dramatis personae "Ercole, La bellezza, Coro di Pianeti" appear in the staff on p. 478, where Hercules's bass and Beauty's soprano amplify the previous chorus and provide seven lines *colla parte* with a separate figured b.c. below. A seventh string part joins the core six-part ensemble, notated on the third line with a C1 clef. Cavalli's setting had made use of magnificent antiphonal effects between three- and five-part *cori spezzati*.

The text celebrates the apotheosis of the hero:

CORO DI PIANETI	CHORUS OF PLANETS
Quel grand'Eroe, che già	That great Hero, who once
la giù tanto penò,	down there suffered so greatly,
sposo della Beltà	as husband to Beauty
per goder nozze eterne al Ciel volò;	flew to Heaven to enjoy eternal nuptials;
virtù che soffre alfin mercede impetra,	suffering virtue in the end obtains mercy,
e degno campo a' suoi trionfi è l'Etra.	and Ether is the worthy abode of his triumphs.

The *lieto fine* exonerates Hercules, ascribing none of the tragedy's problems to him but emphasizing, instead, the suffering that he endured. Crowning him with eternal life, his apotheosis holds thinly veiled Christian allusions as he inherits Heaven from his Father (Zeus/God) and leaves behind the earthly sufferings from his mortal mother (Alcmena/Mary).

In keeping with the *tragédies en musique* of Lully, Campra, Marais, and La Guerre—and with Cavalli's usual orchestral scoring—Bembo composed a concluding Gigue for two *dessus* (G1 clefs), only one *haute-contre* and one *taille* (C3, C4), and *basse continue* (F4). The dance's rhythmic quality resembles Gigue 1 of the *Divertimento*, with its pair of sixteenths in the first *dessus* part functioning as an anacrusis (ex. 4.14). The whole ensemble participates in the second and third sections only. The Gigue features modulatory passages represented by the following scheme:

||: i–V :||: III–v :||: V^6–i :|| *petite reprise* of final passage in i ||

Like the "Menuetto Allegro" of the *sinfonia*, the present Gigue—with full textures lending it variety in rhythm, melody, imitation, and harmony—pre-

Example 7.5   F-Pn, Rés. Vm⁴10, pp. 477–478

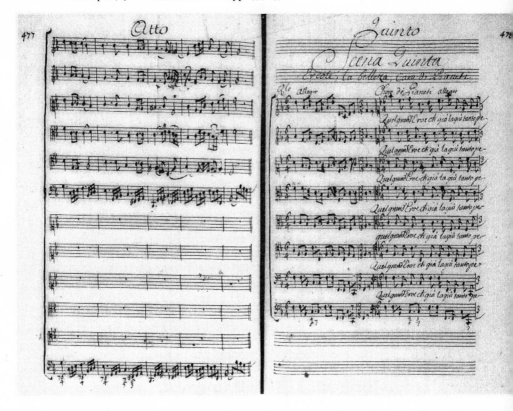

sents a much more elaborate version of the dance than the two appearing in the *Divertimento* of 1704 (see ex. 4.14 and 4.21). It bears some resemblance to Campra's Gigue in the Prologue to *Tancrède*,[46] which sets the first *dessus* apart at the outset. Lully created a large final chorus with numerous *entrées* for *Atys,* and Marais devised the penultimate scene of *Alcione* around a splendid orchestral chaconne.[47]

Making a clean break from the preceding Chorus of the Planets in F major, the G-minor Gigue instead links forward tonally to the duet of Hercules and Beauty. B-flat major, which Juno established as the key of true love in act 1, scene 3, remained the tonal destination for the opera's triumphant resolution. The extended duet for Hercules and Beauty is transformed from relative minor (G) to relative major (B-flat) (pp. 492–503, not shown here).

It is surprising that Bembo needed to make only one major change in the text in adapting a libretto written so many years before. Following the Gigue, she took Buti's verse for the "Gallic Alcides" and "the Iberian Beauty":

[46] Campra, *Tancrède,* Prologue, scene 2, xxxj–xxxij.

[47] Marin Marais, *Alcione, tragédie mise en musique* (Paris: Foucaut, 1706), 238–248.

ERCOLE E LA BELLEZZA	HERCULES AND BEAUTY
Così un giorno avverrà con più diletto,	Thus it will be one day, with greater delight,
che della Senna in sù la riva altera	that from the Seine and upon its high banks
altro Gallico Alcide, arso d'affetto,	another Gallic Alcides, burning with love,
giunga in pace a goder bellezza Ibera;	will arrive in peace to enjoy the Iberian beauty;
ma noi dal Ciel traem viver giocondo	but we in Heaven enjoy our happy life,
e per tal coppia sia beato il mondo.	and let the world be blessed by such a couple.

and replaced it with:

ERCOLE E LA BELLEZZA	HERCULES AND BEAUTY
Così presto avverà ch'il franco Alcide	Thus it will soon happen that the French Alcides
trionferà delle nemiche schiere,	will triumph over the armies of his enemies
e prendendo e squarciando insegne infide	and, taking and destroying false emblems,
de gigli inalzerà l'alme bandiere:	he will hoist up the sacred flags with lilies:
e cangierà così dal Ciel imploro,	and he will change, or so I implore Heaven,
questo secol di ferro in secol d'oro.	this century of iron into a century of gold.

With the removal of the person specifically representing "Beauty," Bembo used her personification to adorn Louis XIV. As in the encomiastic poetry of *Produzioni armoniche,* she depicted the king as the conquering hero capable of transforming military weaponry, "iron," into "lilies" symbolizing the peace and prosperity of France. The final couplet links his terrestrial and sacred powers, suggesting that he was able to transform myth into the proven reality of the "century of gold" that he had abundantly attained.[48] Bembo's duet—an extensive setting for Hercules, Beauty, and the instrumental trio that exhibits tonally that very transformative power—far exceeds Cavalli's relatively straightforward setting of Buti's verse for the same dramatic juncture.

---

[48] On Louis's having put an end to the "iron age," see Marc Fumaroli, "Microcosme comique et macrocosme solaire: Molière, Louis XIV, et 'l'Impromptu de Versailles'," *Revue des Sciences Humaines* 145 (1972): 95–114, at 103, with a passage from an anonymous poem dating from the time of Richelieu: *Imitation et amplification de l'Églogue faite en latin par le Père Campanelle, sur la naissance de Monseigneur le Dauphin.*

One final repetition of the concluding couplet for the Chorus of Planets underscores the tragedy's moral with a tutti for chorus and orchestra. Bembo's straightforward setting counterbalances the lengthy treatment that she gave to the preceding duet. She added her own phrase "Si reprende la Gigue" to Buti's stage directions and removed his statement about a final Chorus of Stars. The Gigue offers music to repeat as needed for the "various influences of the seven planets successively [to] come onstage to dance."[49]

The volumes containing Bembo's opera bear the device "Ardeo, persevero, spero" ("I burn, I persevere, I hope") with peacocks and gold chevrons placed in the quadrants of its coat of arms. This heraldry matches that of the Pavée de Vendeuvre family, known to have lived in the Champagne region and to have been ennobled during the Empire period. *L'Ercole amante* belonged to the family's sizeable collection of operas; indeed, in the two hundred years between its composition and the Bibliothèque Nationale's purchase, it is likely that—unlike the volumes lying dormant in the royal library in Paris—this manuscript did play some role in French musical history prior to the recent wave of interest in early music and in music by women composers. In addition to furthering the Venetian legacy of Cavalli and Strozzi, Bembo's operatic work holds its own among those of her French colleagues Lully, La Guerre, Marais, and Campra, as well as her compatriots in Paris, Lorenzani and Gatti.

---

[49] "Le varie influenze di sette Pianetti scendono sul Palco succeßivamente à danzare, & in fine anche un Choro di Stelle" (160).

POSTSCRIPT:
SUNSET

Following the last measures of the penitential psalms, written around 1710, no more music would be heard from the composer. Yet the Venetian documents still would refer to her as being alive for at least one more decade. Bembo's abundant creative activity coincided with her sunset years, to borrow the phrase used by Peter Burke to describe the end of the Sun King's reign, 1700–1715. As if in fulfillment of her own Ovidian metaphor, when the sunflower was no longer able to cast her eager glances at the sun's rays, she sank back to earth.[1]

Antonia Bembo's prodigious gift of singing sustained her from childhood up to the time that she obtained the king's patronage. After that, she turned to crafting tangible offerings, compositions intended for the highest-ranking members of the royal family. She made the most of her unusual circumstances by cultivating encomiastic song in praise of the French kingdom, by bringing into vital confrontation the Italian and French musical cultures with which she was intimately familiar, and by finding a suitable context in which to convey a particularly feminine perspective and powerful emotion.

Bembo's texts suggest that the "virtù" that her father so treasured—her vocal talent—was somewhat at odds with the usual implication of the term, which connoted proper feminine modesty.[2] Throughout her œuvre, she al-

---

[1] In her book on biographical writing, Hermione Lee grappled with the problem of confronting the death of one's subject, and named her last chapter "How to End it All": "If you are coming to the end of a life you've spent a lot of time with, you will tend to be moved—if only by relief." See *Virginia Woolf's Nose: Essays on Biography* (Princeton: Princeton University Press, 2005), 95.

[2] For a concise examination of the Classical roots informing late Renaissance attitudes toward artistic *virtù*, see Leatrice Mendelsohn, *Paragoni: Benedetto Varchi's Due Lezzioni and Cinquecento Art Theory* (Ann Arbor: UMI Research Press, 1982), 47–52.

luded to that paradox. In a sense, the assurance of the king's pension allowed her to pursue composition, the more modest, "silent" endeavor, by comparison with the earlier act of singing. Indeed, silence, and its corollary, humility, represent such recurrent tropes that they seem to have more to do with working out a personal issue than with customary expressions of obligation. Her corpus of works treats the dangers of flying too high, of overstepping boundaries, of being vainglorious, of succumbing to the allure of song. Echoing the tone of compulsory gratitude found throughout her father's writings, she reused the moralizing couplet set to music in *Produzioni armoniche* at the core of the dedication to her third manuscript: "she who gives what she can, gives what she owes." Silence became an extension of her Venetian penchant for madrigalism when she applied it to the stern aria of the goddess Juno, inveighing against adultery.

As a point of departure for this study, I asked whether Bembo's music represents a significant part of Cavalli's legacy. I did not put forward Barbara Strozzi as a candidate for the distinction, because she and Cavalli died within a year of each other. In any case, the implicit expectation for his legacy was that it would reside in a person who, like himself, would hold a professional title—therefore not in the work of a female composer, who could not obtain a position at places like San Marco or an opera house. Yet it seems quite clear that it was Bembo's very freedom from the obligations of the workaday composer, from specific commissions, that allowed her—like many women composers—the liberty to create vivid expressions of her musical gift. Rather than argue here that the system worked against Bembo's professional success, I suggest the opposite: that she knew how to work the system to optimal result. Such a view espouses Bembo's feminist program, whereby within the confines of allotted space she gave full range to her personal expression, and, moreover, gave voice to countless silenced women. Granted, not having a position means a much smaller repertory; this is apparent when approaching a comparison between Bembo and, say, Marc-Antoine Charpentier.

Another aspect of the legacy resides in what Cavalli encountered when he came to France. Having employed Lully's dialogue between Musique Italienne and Musique Française as an early marker for "les goûts réunis," this study has shown that Cavalli most unfortunately got swept up in the earliest glimmerings of the French cultural monopoly on what constitutes "le bon goût." Already in 1659, Musique Italienne could ask why the French feel compelled to "make the rules" for another's taste, which Musique Française somewhat flippantly dismissed as a simple matter of preferring one's own way to that of another's. Bembo's mixture of the musics of both cultures—whether or not by intention, whether or not she was heard at large—participated in a zeitgeist consumed with how aesthetic judgments were to be made. The legacy of the Sun King itself shaped Enlightenment thinking about taste and etiquette, inevitably leading to the Guerre des Bouffons at mid-century and

Revolution thereafter. While much of the preoccupation with the mixture of styles took place on more neutral ground, for instance with Georg Muffat in Germany, Bembo's was born in the very countries determining those particular tastes. Her contemporary La Guerre also mixed the styles, but not from direct contact with Italy, just second hand. That Bembo was able to establish herself in two radically different cities makes her stand apart from most other women composers, whose movements were more typically restricted to the home or to their places of origin.

Bembo's œuvre is decidedly feminist insofar as she cultivated first her own dramatic singing voice and then, through composition, devoted herself to finding musical expressions for the emotions emanating from selected female characters. In *Produzioni armoniche,* she dramatized the voices of the Virgin Mary (nos. 5–6), Saint Reine (no. 7), a Siren (no. 31), Musica and Virtù (no. 14), as well as an unnamed woman who waits in vain for a distant lover to come (no. 30) or to speak to her (no. 18). Venus, Cupid, and the Chorus of Graces are the heroes of her *Divertimento* for the Duchess of Burgundy— based on a text over which she apparently had some control—whereas they represent a diverting force from good in *L'Ercole amante,* a given with the opera's pre-existent libretto. Even in setting to music liturgical texts, such as the *Te Deum* motets, Bembo managed to bring the feminine into relief by giving her most tender music to the sections treating the annunciation ("non horruisti Virginis uterum"). Her music runs the gamut of feminine expression: from the very dearest, soft caresses of the mother of Christ ("Per il Natale"), to the nagging of a generic wife ("E ch'avete bell'ingrato?"), and from the gently soporific song of Pasithea to the utter ferocity of Juno or of Mary defending her son at the crucifixion scene. These *tours de force* hold strong potential for the claim that Cavalli's legacy has long been concealed inside a Pandora's box. Its contents are golden, astute, humorous, magical, gripping—and no longer possible to ignore.

Appendix 1

DOCUMENTS

1. F-Pn, Rés.Vm^{1}117, *Produzioni armoniche,* Dedication, ff. 4r–5r

Sire

Quella fama immortale, che sino dall'infanzia mi stillò nel Cuore il glo-
riosissimo Nome di Vostra Maestà; Quell'istessa m'indusse ad abandonar Pa-
tria, Parenti, Et Amici per venire ad inchinarmi ad un Monarca Si Eccelso.
Giunsi à questa Real Corte, sono già più anni, dove per mia Sorte, essendo
stato rapresentato à Vostra Maestà, ch'io aveva qualche talento nel Canto, si
compiacque di volermi sentire; E intendendomi abbandonata da chi mi trasse
da Venezia, Vostra Maestà si degnò gratificarmi d'una pensione, colla quale
potessi trattenirmi nella Comunità di Nostra Signora di Buone Novelle, fino
à tanto, che si presentasse occasione di mettermi in qualche altro luogo più
distinto. Ora in questo santo ricovero procuratomi dalla magnificenza della
Maestà Vostra, avendo io fatte alcune Composizioni in Musica, vengo à ras-
segnarle à suoi Reali piedi, come un riverentissimo tributo delle mie immense
Obligazioni. La supplico Umilissimamente di volerle gradire colla solita sua
Reale benignità, e le fò profondissima riverenza.

Di Vostra Maestà
Umilissima et Obedientissima serva Antonia Bembo

2. I-MAa, Archivio Gonzaga, *Carteggi esteri,* Carteggi ad inviati (Venezia), Busta 1571

1654. 14 m[ar]zo
Ser[enissi]ma Altezza

Si compiacque l'A[ltezza] V[ostra] S[erenissima] à mesi passati d['] invitarmi
à quella servitù che per me stesse, haverei già ambita: ne qui terminarono le

sue gratie; p[er]che mene fece ancora dal suo Ministro Bosso esprimermene quo' commodi, che ne haverei ricevuto. Et perche non hò più sentito cosa alcuna in questo particolare, et da altra parte essendo il tempo della ricondotta delli miei più importanti trattenimenti, in questa Città, hò deliberato di spedire à posta il Maestro di Gram[m]atica dell unica mia, costà, per supplicar humilmente l'A[ltezza] V[ostra], come divotamente faccio, à comandarmi, quale più le aggrada, ò'l mio moto, ò lo stato; perche nell'uno m[']istimerei godere felicità, nell'altro haverei il contento d'ubidirla. La Figliuola con felici progressi continova sotto la disciplina del sig[no]r Cavalli, la quale devotissima alla sublimità del merito di V[ostra] A[ltezza] humilissimamente, meco, se le inchina, come che, unitamente con la Madre, nelle profondità degli ossequij, riverisse la Ser[enissi]ma Arciduchessa.

Venetia 14 Marzo 1654
Di V[ostra] A[ltezza] S[ignoria]
Ser[vito]re humilissi[m]o devoti[ssi]mo et osseq[uiossi]mo,
Giacomo Padovani Med[i]co

3. I-MAa, Archivio Gonzaga, *Lettere ai Gonzaga Mantova e Paesi* (1654), Busta 2796/VII, carta 269

Ill[ustrissi]mo et Ecc[ellentissi]mo S[igno]r et P[adro]ne Col[endissi]mo
    Vedo la lettera di V[ostra] E[ccellenza] et quella del Ser[enissi]mo insieme. Delibero d'ubidire p[er]ch[e] lo devo à S[erenissima] A[ltezza] et à V[ostra] E[ccellenza] ma p[er] far mentire ancora quelli, che vantano ch'io cerchi scuse, p[er] no[n] venire. Sò che l'Ecc[ellenz]a V[ost]ra, nella Patente opererà, che siano espresse tutte le cose dette, et con lettere promesse de tratta solam[en]te quella della damigella; come anco la suplico vivam[en]te poiche p[er] il primo anno saranno antecipate le cento doppie, che così nei sussequenti, io no[n] habbia andarle à mendicare, et, come altra volta hò scritto, che no[n] habbia ad arrossire in chiederle; p[er]ch[e] se qui lascio l'emolum[en]to quotidiano, so ch[e] in Mantova no[n] haverò molto che guadagnare, cercando i mali; et questo è la maggior premura che habbia; p[er]ch[e] con questa sola sono stato la più parte spaventato, et da quelli massime che più dovevano inanimarmi.
    Accommodate così le cose, et trasmessami la Patente, co'l denaro, ch[e] e necessario, del primo anno, io m'accingerò alla partenza, et soli 15, ò 20 giorni doppo, potrà venir la barca p[er] levar me, le mie robbe, et la Famiglia. Io credo che trà tutte queste cose passarà il tempo noioso dell'aria di Mantova, et nell'istesso tempo io haverò dato [sesto?] à tutte le mie cose qui, à Dio piacendo. Et ecco tutto quello, ch'io posso dire à V[ostra] E[ccellenza] di quello che à me appartiene, confidando nella magnanimità di S[erenissima] A[ltezza]

il rimanente, che accenna nelle sue lettere, et nella protettione dell'Ecc[el-len]za V[ost]ra, che sarà il mio Protettore. In tanto mi resta di suplicarla à farmi gratia di rivedere la congionta soprascritta, et avisarmi se è quella che era con le lettere ultime trasmessami con quelle di S[erenissima] A[ltezza] del 7 sta[n]te. P[er]ch[e] parmi di credere, che la curiosità maligna faccia qualche moto. Parim[en]te la supplico à far incontinenti sapere à S[erenissima] A[l-tezza] questa mia prontezza di serv[ir]lo acciò che, se volasse qualche spiri-tello p[er] aria, à poner foco et garbuglio, sia conosciuta la frode; et credami V[ostra] E[ccellenza] ch'io no[n] parlo à suon d'acqua p[er]ch[e] parmi di potere sognare, resuscitata la favola d'Esopo della serpe nudrito in seno.

Ho detto troppo ma no[n] sarò mai troppo.

Dell'Ecc[ellenz]a V[ost]ra Ill[ustrissi]ma

Venetia 13 Luglio 1654

Serv[ito]re obligatiss[im]o et devotiss[im]o,

Giac[om]o Padovani

La suplico di [. . .] se le lettere sono capitati et chiuse

4. I-MAa, Archivio Gonzaga, *Lettere ai Gonzaga Mantova e Paesi* (1654), Busta 2796/VII, carta 271

1654. 15.Luglio

Ser[enissi]mo Principe

Ecco il Dottor Padovani Guarito della sua pazzia, e ch[e] mi pare risponda molto a proposito inherendo alle sodisfattioni da V[ostra] A[ltezza] Ser[e-nissi]ma e lasciando ogni altro rispetto da parte; s'assicuri ch[e] ci è persona ch[e] voleva metterci bisbiglio, perch[e] e stato ancora aperta la mia lettera ultima nella quale li scrivevo quello V[ostra] A[ltezza] Ser[enissi]ma mi ha-veva commandato e li havevo inviata inclusa la medema lettera di V[ostra] A[ltezza] p[er]ch[e] più facilmente si disponesse, come ha fatto [di venire a servirla?]; potrà in tanto vedere quello ch[e] il dottore medemo mi scrive, e con rimandarmi la lettera commandarmi quello ch[e] devo risponderli, che io con ogni puntualità obedendola farò adesso e sempre quello ch[e] tocca ad uno.

Di V[ostra] A[ltezza] Ser[enissi]ma

Mantova li 15 Lulio 1654

A hore 19 mi è capitata l'inclusa da Verona per messo a posta

Hum[ilissi]mo div[otissi]mo et obl[igatissi]mo s[ervitor]e

Giulio Cesare Gonzaga

5. I-MAa, Archivio Gonzaga, *Carteggi esteri,* Carteggi ad inviati (Venezia), Busta 1571, Bosso Residente 1654

1654. 14. Luglio

Ser[enissi]mo Sig[no]re mio Sig[no]re Sig[no]re et P[ad]rone Clementiss[im]o

Viene à piedi dell'A[ltezza] V[ostra] Ser[enissi]ma avanti partire per Ale-magna il Sig[no]re Fran[ces]co Corbetta p[er] humilmente riverirla. Dal med[esi]mo V[ostra] A[ltezza] udirà certo particolare in materia del Padre della figlia che canta, è stimo parimente, che l'A[ltezza] V[ostra] à quest'hora ne sarà stata ragguagliata p[er] mio mezo p[er] altra via in tal proposito, ch'io pur scrissi con l'ord[ina]rio passato; ch[e] però sup[li]co riverentem[en]te V[ostra] A[ltezza] Ser[enissi]ma ad à scusarmi del tedio che li porgo, et pro-fondam[en]te m'inchino.

Venetia li 14 luglio 1654

Di V[ostra] A[ltezza] Ser[enissi]ma

Hum[ilissi]mo d[evotissi]mo et rever[itissi]mo ser[vitor]e fed[elissi]mo et ob[ligatissi]mo

Antonio Bosso

6. I-MAa, Archivio Gonzaga, *Carteggi esteri,* Carteggi ad inviati (Venezia), Busta 1571, Bosso Residente 1654

1654. 21 Luglio

Ser[enissi]mo Sig[no]re mio Sig[no]re Sig[no]re et P[ad]rone Clementiss[im]o

Ritorna à piedi dell'A[ltezza] V[ostra] Ser[enissi]ma il Sig[no]re Francesco Corbetta dal quale udirà con la viva voce l'operato da lui in materia della figlia che canta, nel qual interesse non ho io potutto sbraciarmi p[er] esser raggiro adosso tutto à lui, che ne Bartolo, ne Baldo può in ristretto capire gli strattagemi di costoro.

Altro p[er] hora, significo riverentem[en]te all' A[ltezza] V[ostra] sollo che tutti costoro sono una Gabia de Pazzi i quali con suoi fini interessati procurano fini perniciosi. Di più porto alla notitia di V[ostra] A[ltezza] che oltre l'esser il medico caduto in fernesia (bench[e] la voce piu trita, è ch'il Demonio sia di lui in possesato) e la figlia parim[en]te che canta patisse il mal caduco, riportato dalli spaventi frenetici del Padre, il quale hà concesso in matrimonio la d[et]ta figlia al Sig[no]re Corbetta, è con scrittura privata si è sottoscritto restandone al maggior segno invaghito.

Il tutto sia alla confidente notitia p[er] valersene l'A[ltezza] V[ostra] Ser-
[enissi]ma alla quale profondam[en]te m'inchino.

Venetia li 21 Lug[li]o 1654

Di V[ostra] A[ltezza] Ser[enissi]ma

Hum[ilissi]mo d[evotissi]mo et rever[itissi]mo ser[vitor]e fed[elissi]mo
  et ob[ligatissi]mo

Antonio Bosso

7. I-MAa, Archivio Gonzaga, *Carteggi esteri,* Carteggi ad inviati (Venezia), Busta 1571, Diversi 1652

Ser[enissi]mo Mio Sig[no]re

1652. 12. marzo

Il Sig[no]r Cap[itan]o Luca, d'ordine di V[ostra] A[ltezza] Ser[enissi]ma
mi scrise di ritornar al servitio, et io rendo humiliss[im]e gratie à V[ostra]
A[ltezza] Ser[enissi]ma del honore, ma essendo statto nesescitato dalla prece-
dente mia poca fortuna ad impegnarmi con il Sig[no]r prencipe di luneburg,
dal quale hò ricevutto molte gratie tanto à pariggi come qui, suplico V[ostra]
A[ltezza] stante haver tentato molte volte con poca sorte mia il servitio di
V[ostra] A[ltezza] Ser[enissi]ma ad havermi per iscusato, é credere che vivrò
sempre con una Humilissima Divotione a V[ostra] A[ltezza] la cui Ser[enis-
si]ma perssona pregherò sempre Dio che conservi, supplicando V[ostra] A[l-
tezza] no[n] mancarmi della sua benign[issim]a protetione e gratia, che dove
mi sarò, vivrò sempre il solito Humiliss[im]o et fedeliss[im]o, et obligat[is-
sim]o ser[vito]re, à V[ostra] A[ltezza] Ser[enissi]ma à cui con proffond[issim]a
Riverenza saluto.

Di Venetia li 12 Marzo 1652

Devot[issim]o e obligat[issim]o ser[vito]re, a V[ostra] A[ltezza]
  Ser[enissi]ma

Fran[ces]co Corbetta

8. I-MAa, Archivio Gonzaga, *Carteggi esteri,* Carteggi ad inviati (Venezia), Busta 1571, Bosso Residente 1654

1654. 22 Luglio

Ser[enissi]mo Sig[no]re mio Sig[no]re Sig[no]re et P[ad]rone Clementiss[im]o

Doppo scritto la qui inserta p[er] consegnarla in mano del Sig[no]re Fran-
[ces]co Corbetta, il quale non s'è compiaciuto levarla rumpendo l'hora della

partenza, et io ho stimato accertato inviarla all'A[ltezza] V[ostra] Ser[enissi]ma p[er] la via di Verona ch'è la piu breve del corr[ier]o ord[ina]rio di sabbato acciò in qualche parte V[ostra] A[ltezza] resti avvisata del capricioso matrimonio del d[et]to Corbetta e di nuovo profondam[en]te m'inchino.

Venetia li 22 lug[li]o 1654

Di V[ostra] A[ltezza] Ser[enissi]ma

Hum[ilissi]mo d[evotissi]mo et rever[itissi]mo ser[vitor]e fed[elissi]mo
    et ob[ligatissi]mo

Antonio Bosso

9. I-Vas, Notarile, *Atti,* Pietro Bracchi e Girolamo Brinis, Busta 884, ff. 194v–196

Die Venerij 7 men[sis] Junij 1658

L'Ecc[ellentissi]mo S[igno]r Giacomo Padovani suocero da una parte, et il Nob[il] Hu[omo] Lorenzo Bembo del N[obil] H[uomo] Andrea suo genero dall'altra parte hanno concordemente presentato a me Notaro infrascritto l'infrascritta scrittura de 23 maggio scaduto, dissero esser il contratto di nozze dell'Ill[ustrissi]ma S[ignor]a Antonia figliuola del d[ett]o Ecc[ellentissi]mo S[igno]r Giacomo, e moglie di predetto Ill[ustrissi]mo Sig[no]r Lorenzo con la quale ha fatto le parole che presenti il medesimo giorno 23 maggio sottoscritta dalli predetti Sig[no]ri suocero et genero come così affermano, nec non da me Notaro, e dal Sig[no]r Christoforo Brombilla per testimonij come in quella. . . . Et per l'amore che detto N[obil] H[uomo] Lorenzo porta alla predetta Ill[ustrissi]ma sua sposa gli sopragiunge da proprij suoi beni liberam[en]te p[er] controdote, overo doni per le nozze alla dote contenuta nel contratto suddetto ducati tre mille correnti da L. 6.4 per ducato così che la dote predetta compresa la suddetta controdote ascende in tutto la somma de ducati sei mille. Promettendo detto Ill[ustrissi]mo Sig[no]r Lorenzo l'una, et l'altra d'esse dote, et contradote ben regger, et administrar, et quelle / in ogni caso di restitutione dotali restituire in conformità delle leggi di questa Città in tutto, come vien dichiarato nel detto contratto nuptiale sara obligationi delli beni suoi d'ogni sorte presenti e futuri . . .

. . .

Per Dote . . . di detta Sig[no]ra sposa esso Ecc[ellentissi]mo S[igno]r Giacomo / suo Padre promette dar ad esso Ill[ustrissi]mo sposo ducati tremille correnti da L. 6.4 per ducato in questo modo cioè ducati quatrocento in tanti denari contanti, del corpo de quali contenta detto Ill[ustrissi]mo sposo ch'esso

Ecc[ellentissi]mo Sig[no]r Giacomo spendi in habiti noviziali per la sposa p[redet]ta ducati trecento in circa, et il suplimento sborsar ad esso Ill[ustrissi]mo sposo. Item tutti quelli ori che sono di ragione della detta S[ignor]a sposa da esser stimati da p[rese]nti. Item doverà detto Ecc[ellentissi]mo Sig[no]r Giacomo pagar per anni due il nolo delle perle che devono servire per detta S[ignor]a sposa. Item altri mobili per uso della medesima, et di casa per quello sarano stimati da due communi amici. Et per il suplimento di detti ducati tremille sia obligato detto Ecc[ellentissi]mo Giacomo di tener in Casa detti Sig[no]ri sposi, e a quelli far le spese di vita, insieme con una serva, e pagarli anco l'affitto di casa, quali spese, et affitto dette Parti valutano concordemente in ducati trecento all'anno. Con dichiaratione espressa, che se per qual si voglia accidente non potesse, ò, non volesse detto S[igno]r sposo habitare unito et nella casa di detto S[igno]r suo suocero, in questo caso in luoco delle spese di vita et affitto di casa sod[ett]e sia obligato detto S[igno]r Giacomo pagar detto suplimento di dote in ragion de ducati cento / all'anno, e non più . . .

10. I-Vas, Notarile, *Atti*, Camillo Lion, Busta 8022, f. 176

Die p[ri]mo aprilis 1660.
P[rese]ntata per ex. D. Jacobus Padoani ut reg[istris] in actis meis pertinando ut in ea.

Le forme improprie [*crossed out: insopportabile*] con li quali voi N[obil] H[uomo] Lorenzo Bembo fù di Andrea, mio genero andate, continuam[ent]e [*crossed out: incorrigibilmente*] disturbando la quiete mia e della mia casa, mi necessitano à farvi con la presente risolutamente intendere come non posso più tenervi nella detta mia casa, et ciò inere[n]do ad altre proteste più volte à voi privatam[en]te fatte, et fattevi fare. Le mie raggioni sono à voi troppo note ne devo pubblicarle sopra di questa carta, la quale servirà ad effetto, che habbiate nel termine di mesi quattro, à provedervi d'altra habitat[io]ne, essendo io per altro prontiss[i]mo à corrispondervi quanto per le conventioni fatte sono tenuto: Protestandovi, che non facendo voi partenza da detta mia casa, et pretendendo in quella insistere con violenza et autorità come per supponete farò infallibil[men]te ricorso alli Ecc[ellentissi]mi Capi dell'Eccel[s]o Cons[igli]o di X[Diec]i per ripararmi dalle vostre oppressioni pur troppo da me per tanto tempo sofferite, riservandomi anco il poter vi ricorrer prima che passi il prescritto tempo acciò che da quella sublime giustitia sia moderato q[ues]to mio termine et io quanto prima sollevato dalla perseveranti vostra oppressione.

11. I-Vas, Notarile, *Atti,* Camillo Lion,
Busta 8022, f. 178

Die 3. Ap[ri]lis 1660

P[rese]ntata p[er] V[omo] N[obile] Laurentius Bembo ut reg[istris] in actis meis intimanda ut in ea.

Ben forma impropria di trattare é quella che Voi Ecc[ellen]te S[ignor] Giacomo Padoani Medico usate meco con me Lorenzo Bembo, fù de Andrea, mentre senza causa, che p[er] parte mia in sij stata data, havendo io sempre vissuto et trattato con tutti, et con voi in particolare con quelli modi, et costumi, che si ricercano alla mia nascita, mi s[i]ete mosso à impennare nella tal qual scrittura, mi è stata à vostra instanza intimata concetto lontano dalla verità, inventato con artificioso avantaggio, à oggetto che mi possi sortire quel fine ingiustiss[im]o di non darmi il mio, che giamai sara p[er] seguire mediante la giustitia delle mie raggioni, si che poco devono turbarmi la vanità de vostri protessi mentre non vi e alcun mancam[en]to et dalla mia irreverenza sempre avanti qual si sia giudici e tribunale, saro protetto, et diffeso. Sapete qual sia l'obligo nostro, et la maniera con la quale mi havete trattato se adempirete il nostro debito non in sara occasione di contesa, poiche al giusto. Io ho sempre assentito, e sin p[er] assentire; mà quando diverso sia il nostro pensiero dovero diffendermi nella forma ch'à tutti è permesso; tanto ho voluto significarvi p[er] risposta a d[ett]a scrittura, alla quale in tutte le parti protesto di nullità, senza pregiud[izi]o di cad[au]ne mie rag[gio]ni anco con espressa riserva di esse. Et la p[rese]nte sara reg[istra]ta nelli atti di D[omin]o Camillo Leoni Nod[ar]o di questa città.

12. I-Vas, Notarile, *Testamenti,* Camillo
Lion, Busta 591, no. 87 (13 March
1662), ff. 1; 1v–2r; 2r–2v; 3r

Nel Nome della Sant[issi]ma Trinità P[adre] F[iglio] et Sp[iri]to S[an]to In giorno di Lunedi, 13 Marzo 1662, nel mio Studio, camara sop[r]a la fondam[en]ta in casa da me tenuta ad affitto dall'Ill[ustrissi]mo S[igno]r Scipion Boldu, alli Tolentini, contrà della Croce.

Io Giac[om]o Padovani, dottore di Filosofia et Med[ici]na, di natione vicentino, nato dal q[uondam] Bortolamio, q[uondam] Giac[om]o et di Paula, q[uondam] Anto[ni]o [in] Mainenti, sua legitima Consorte, premonito dalla D[ivina] M[aestà] nell'improviso assalimento del mortale et acutiss[i]mo male, da me p[er] la Iddio gratia superato, degli accidenti à quali sottogiace la fragilità della vita dell'huomo, hò voluto hora, sano di mente, corpo et intelletto, senza frapormi altro indugio, deliberare delle cose mie, ciò è nell'infrascritto modo . . .

. . .

Lascio all'Ill[ustrissi]mo S[igno]r Lor[en]zo Bembo mio genero, p[er] hora, et p[er] una volta tanto il mio Redentor, copia di uno di Titiano che sta in Fontego de Todeschi.

Item Lascio ad Anto[ni]a unica mia figliuola il quadro di S[an] Ant[oni]o da Padova / fatto in Casa del S[igno]r Giosef Ens Pittore à S[an] Polo, et questo p[er] quanto posso p[er] hora, et p[er] una volta tanto li lascio

Et mi dicchiaro di altro no[n] lasciare, ne all'uno, ne all'altro p[er] il poco rispetto, se[n]za Carità che hanno l'uno et l'altro portato à me et alla mia S[igno]ra Consorte et Herede, p[er] compensam[en]to di tante fattiche della poverina di mia moglie in allevare detta mia figliuola, et in farla ammaestrare, et à me p[er] guiderdone d'haver (dissi quasi) spesa l'anima, p[er] farla riuscire, in virtù, di meraviglia al mondo, et p[er] accompagnarla come ho fatto, havendoli data quella dote, che, ne l'obligo Paterno m'astringeva, ne le forze delle mie scarse fortune mi permettevano, oltre le gran spese ch[e] ho sostenute dopo di haver saldata la dote; onde merito la scusa appresso Iddio, appr[esso] la Giustitia et il Mondo; et così app[ress]o di loro. F [marginal note: et li prego à perdonarmi et haver compassione dell'anima mia et far pregar per mia salute].

Aggiongo ch[e] il tutto faccio acciò ch[e] la poverina della mia S[igno]ra Consorte da loro no[n] venga vilipesa, ma conosciuta et trattata da Madre, come sono obligati in conscienza et p[er] Leggi di Dio et della Natura. Aggiongo di più che lascio loro quadri di divotione, acciò s'avveggano che il timore di Dio si deve premettere à tutte le cose. In quanto poi al beneficio più profittevole, dalla mia heredità lo riceveranno, come infra, se trattaranno detta mia S[igno]ra Consorte et herede nel modo che gli obliga Iddio, le leggi de Principi et della Natura.

. . .

A Teresa Serva di Casa, lascio, oltre il suo salario, che dalla mia Herede sia data al suo maritar quella Cortesia parerà ad essa mia Herede, appresso ch[e] li siano donate le spese fatte p[er] lei in Medicine di molta rilevanza, p[er] la sua lunghiss[i]ma malatia, intendendo no[n] ostante che li sia corso il salario.

Mia universale herede, donna (come dicesi) Madonna et Padrona assoluta, voglio et intendo che sia La S[igno]ra Diana, figliuola del già S[igno]r Camillo Paresco, mia Cariss[i]ma Consorte, di ogni et qualunque mio bene et havere, mobili, stabili, eredita et altro che a me aspetta, ò p[er] tempo alcuno aspettar potesse, senza che mai da alcuno, sia chi si sia, possi esser molestata, ò necessitata a liquidatione di / stima di dote, à [unir], ò dar conto della robba, à far assicuratione à dar cautione p[er] il diretto. Intendendo che goder debba il pacifico possesso davanti il tempo della sua vita, p[er] goderne ella pacificamente l'usufrutto; et se p[er] mantenersi fosse necessitata à vender anco il diretto tutto; che in tal caso no[n] possi mai da alcuno essere impedita.

. . .

Che la S[igno]ra Ant[oni]a moglie de S[ignor] Lor[en]zo Bembo et li suoi figliuoli sia unica herede universale doppo seguita la morte di detta sua Madre così del mio, come della dote, di detta sua Madre mia C[arissi]ma Consorte, che la prego di tutto cuore à lasciarglila con obligo pero di detta S[igno]ra Ant[oni]a / che dia all'hospitale della Misericordia in Vicenza p[er] una volta tanto ducati cinquanta, acciò, così dagli orfani, come orfane sia detto ogni giorno, nelli suoi Incuratorij? una Salve Regina, un Pater et un'Ave Maria, con un De profundis, rapresentando il tutto p[er] l'anima di Giac[om]o Padovani, et di Diana sua Consorte et suoi Congionti defunti.

13. S. Romanin, *Storia documentata di Venezia* (Venice: Pietro Naratovich, 1858), 7: 453–454

Nei primi giorni di marzo [1668], il vezir meditando togliere ai Veneziani in Candia l'opportunità dei viveri, fece tacitamente uscire una squadra per battere quella con cui Lorenzo Cornaro scorreva le vicine acque, incarcandone Chalil Pascià, e con lui Durac famoso corsaro, coll'ordine di tenersi in agguato, sorprendere le navi veneziane, portarsi poi alla Standia, e occupato uno dei porti, fortificarsi, incendiare e distruggere i legni della Repubblica. Ma penetrato dal Morosini il suo pensiero, uscì prestamente di Candia, e unite venti galee si spinse nella notte del sette di marzo a quella volta, per modo che soprafatti i Turchi, e quali crederono essere il Cornaro con la solita squadra, gli assalì con gran forza e pari coraggio. Riuscì aspro e duro il combattimento, reso più tremendo dall'orror delle tenebre. Due galere nemiche che assalito aveano la Reale della Repubblica vennero in mano dei Veneziani; Durac stava per occupare la galea di Nicolò Polani, quando accorsovi il Morosini a lume di torcia fece nella nemica entrar le sue genti. A quell'improvviso splendore, creduto di fuochi artifiziati, tale fu lo sbigottimento dei Turchi, che caduto estinto Durac, fatto macello della milizia, restò ai Veneziani la vittoria, e con essa vennero in loro potere cinque galere, quattrocento prigioni, più di mille schiavi cristiani che furono liberati, onde fu il Morosini altamente lodato, e dal Senato creato cavaliere.

14. I-Vasp, Curia Patriarcale, *Sezione antica:*
Filciae causarum, Busta 68 (1672–1673), f. 3

Die 12 X[dece]mbris 1672 Venetijs in Pal[azz]o Pa[triar]chale Cor.am comparuit Vir N[obilis] S[ignor] Laurentius Bembo fuit Andrea Patritius Venetus de P[arochi]a S[an] Barnaba . . .

Primo che il N[obil] H[uomo] Lorenzo Bembo hà mal tratata in fatti et in parole più volte la N[obil] D[onna] Antonia sua consorte per fotendola anco più d'una volta essendo gravida.

[*margin:*] Sup[ra] p[rim]a Positione Rog[antes]: non è vero niente

Sec[ond]o che esso N[obil] H[uomo] Lorenzo ha asportata la robba di casa di d[et]ta N[obil] D[onn]a cosi de spesi vestiti ori, come fornimenti per spender ne le sue sodisfattioni.

[*margin:*] Sup[ra] 2[second]a Positione Rog[antes]: non è vero niente

Terzo che habbia hauto comercio carnale con Le Donne di Casa e per ciò sempre vì daneggiata la detta N[obil] D[onn]a Antonia.

[*margin:*] Sup[ra] 3[terz]a Positione Rog[antes]: non è vero niente

Qua[r]to che D[ett]o N[obil] H[uomo] è stato cinqu'anni lontano da d[et]ta sua Consorte, et per la maggior parte del tempo l'ha lasciata priva de i debbiti alimenti, con tre figlioli.

[*margin:*] Sup[ra] 4[quart]a Positione Rog[antes]: non è vero niente

Qui[n]to che in Armata ha hauto comercio carnale continuam[en]te con altre femine, con le quali hà anco procreato figlioli.

[*margin:*] Sup[ra] 5[cinqu]a Positione Rog[antes]: non è vero niente

Lorenzo Bembo

15. I-Vas, Notarile, *Atti,* Giovanni Antonio
Mora, Busta 8651 bis, ff. 208–208v

1678. Die Mercurij 18 Mensis Januarij . . .

Il N[obil] H[uomo] Lorenzo Bembo fu de Andrea spont[aneament]e con ogni miglior modo che ha potuto ha cost[ituit]o et ordinato su legitimo procurator, et commesso Il S[igno]r Domenico Selles qui presente, et accentante a poter a nome ut supra, recuperar dalle mani di qual si voglia persone

qual si voglia sorte de beni mobili di rag[io]ne della N[obil] D[onna] Ant[o]-
ni]a Padoani Cons[ort]e di esso N[obil] H[uomo] Lorenzo Const[ituent]e
per la summa de ducati cento sessanta in c[irc]a delli quali fussero stati lasciati
dalla med[esi]ma N[obil] D[onna] in salvo appresso cadaune persone, et del
ricuperato farne le debite ricevute, et quietationi, si publiche, come private,
et per la causa predetta occorendo, et ivi tutte, et cadaune liti, cause, et dif-
ferenze cosi mosse, et da moversi prò, et contra qualunque p[er]sone active,
et passive p[er] qual si voglia ragion, et causa comparer in ogni giuditio, corte,
off[iti]o, Mag[istra]to Ecc[ellentissi]mi Con세gli, et Colleggi di questa Città.

    . . . di essi ducati 160— in circa, doverà detto S[igno]r suo procurator
rimborsarli quello haverà spesso per il conseguimento come sopra, et di pagar
le spese per anni due finirano ultimo febr[ar]o 1678 venturo della N[obil]
D[onna] Diana Bembo figliola de esso N[obil] H[uomo] Constituente es-
istente a spese nel Mon[aster]o di S[an] Bernardo di Murano alla Rev[eren]-
dissi]ma Madre Abbadessa del d[ett]o Monastero . . .

16. I-Vas, Corporazioni religiose, *San Bernardo di Murano,* Busta 18, Mazzo Q, Plica D

Parigi li 11 Marzo 1682
Ill[ustrissi]ma et Reverendiss[im]a Sig[nor]ia Ch[ristissi]ma
    Son molto tenuta à V[ostra] S[ignoria] Reverend[issi]ma p[er] l'espres-
sioni fattemi del suo cortese affetto, nella sua in data delli venti uno decorso
è conservo distinta è particolar obligattione à gl'avisi che si è compacciuta
darmi, toccante lò stato di mia figlia; rimanga però servita di no[n] turbarsi
punto di ogni qual movimento potesse fare S[ignor]e Ill[ustrissi]mo Lorenzo,
stante che quelle Gioie che V[ostra] Reverend[issi]ma concerva nelle mani,
no[n] l'havendo ricevute da lui può sempre giuridicamente negarle onde si /
compiaccia tutta via di concervarle appresso di lè sino à nuova mia disposi-
tione. per ch[e] intendo assolutamente nel termine di trè Mesi e forse manco
di porre in stato i miei affari à fine che V[ostra] S[ignoria] Reverend[issi]ma
resti sodisfata è l'ultima mia finale intenttione è che mia figlia non esca assolutamente dal convento. et à mio partito prenda rissoluttione che no[n] li sia
suggerita da mè. ne (?) aggionga che col' ringratiarla delle sue gentilissime
testimonianze è li prego dal Cielo ogni bramar contento rendendo affettuosi
saluti à Sior Maria Giordana e ancora / a mia figlia
    di V[ostra] S[ignoria] Ill[ustrissi]ma et Reverend[issi]ma
    devotiss[i]ma et oblig[atissi]ma Serva
    Antonia Bembo

17. I-Vas, Corporazioni religiose, *San Bernardo di Murano,* Busta 18, Mazzo Q, Plica D

Parigi li 10 Giugno [1682]

Ill[ustrissi]ma,

Hò ricevuta l'ultima di V[ostra] S[ignoria] Reverend[issi]ma nella quale mi dimanda le copie delle ricevute che concervo appresso di mè li risponde che nè lasciai due in Mano della Abbadessa defonta, no[n] ostante l'invio acciò resti sodisfata è servita, in tanto di lascia in nisuna forma uscire di Mano le dette robe in sino à novelli avisi ch'io farò ogni possibile acciò V[ostra] S[ignoria] Rev[erendissi]ma resti scarica di questo imbarasso che è quanto mi occore pregandola honorarmi d'un saluto à Sior Maria Giordana mentre per fine resto

Di V[ostra] S[ignoria] Illu[strissi]ma et Reverend[issi]ma

Devotiss[i]ma et Oblig[atissi]ma Serva

Antonia Bembo

18. I-Vas, Corporazioni religiose, *San Bernardo di Murano,* Busta 18, Mazzo Q, Plica D

adi 15 Giugno 1682

R[icev]o io S[uo]r Maria Elena Camerlengha del M[onaste]ro di S[a]n Bernardo di Murano dal N[obil] H[uomo] Lorenzo Benbo ducati quaranta p[er] le spese di m[esi] 6 anticipati della Ill[ustrissi]ma S[igno]ra Diana sua figlia qualli mesi fenirano li decembre pros[si]mo pag[a]to—real d[ucati] 40

Dichiaro pero con questa ricevuta non intendo pregiudicar il Monastero delli ducati duce[n]to che sono Creditor di allimenti passati prima che partise di Monastero es[s]endo andada à casa et hora ritorna ["et il soprad[et]to suo padre," crossed out]

19. I-Vas, Notarile, *Atti,* Vincenzo Vincenti, Busta 13852 (protocollo, 1683), ff. 141 r–v

1683. Die Sabbati, 2 M[ens]is Octobris. In Cancello.

Scr[ittur]a pr[es]entata per N[obil] H[uomo] Gio. Mattio Bembo, intimanda con in[stan]za.

Non sò vedere qual cagione faci dimostrar cose renitente Voi Lorenzo Bembo, amato frattello di mè Z[an] Mattio, mentre a moltiplicate Instanze fattevi che vedeste di metter in salvo in qualche Monast[er]o Diana vostra Figliola, altro non havete risposto, che subterfugi, fino a tanto che mutandovi di Casa procuraste di farmi persuadere, che quella ricevessi in mia Casa, con obligatione di pagarmi le spese a ragione di d[uca]ti 60, fino a tanto di ritrovaste d[ett]o Monastero. Che però piu e piu volte, doppo ricevuta la stessa ricercatori il ritrovar Monastero a d[ett]a vostra Figliola, mi rispondeste, che concordem[en]te si ricevasse, et fu da me ritrovato, et a Voi notificato; Che però mi lasciò intendere e vi sia dette, e protestato, che mentre non levaretete d[ett]a vostra figliola dalla mia Casa nel termine di giorni otto. Io intenderò, che mi paghiate p[er] le sue spese Ducati Cento e Dieci, essendo in età ottima; Che però per vostro avvantaggio, et mio grande solievo, et della mia Casa, sarammi molto piu gratto esser della medema solevatto, per li rispetti a Voi noti; Et ciò vi sia detto in ogni miglior modo et notificato; protestando a qual si sia protesto, che faceste, intendendo esser sempre ultimo a protestare, et / le presente sarà registrata negl'atti del Signor Nodaro Vincenti.

20. I-Vas, Corporazioni religiose, *San Bernardo di Murano*, Busta 18, Mazzo Q, Plica D

Copia tratta dà una simile presentata à gl'Ecc[ellen]ti Cappi dell'Ecc[el]so C[onsiglio de'] X[ie]ci.

Adi *30* Marzo *1685.* in Murano.

Un Zogiello con rubini diversi con due Balassi, et una Perla, che pende	240 d.
Un Fior con Diamanti	80 d.
Un detto con Perle	60 d.
Una Goletta con Perle, e Smeraldi	70 d.
Un Paro Rechini con Smeraldi	15 d.
Un Paro detto con 6 Pari Perla, che pende	20 d.
Un Horologgio con Cassa d'oro fil à grana	40 d.
Un d[ett]o con Cassa d'ambra	15 d.
Bottoni d'ambra negra coperti d'oro no. 7	14 d.
Un Coresin Prasma ligato in Oro, Un Botton, e due capete d'oro	4 d.
Medaglie d'arg[en]to no. 5	1 d.
Quattro Bottoni d'ambra coperti d'oro, un botton con Perletti, e due Graspi Granatine	4 d.
Un paro Manini d'oro à Cordon	16 d.
Una Cadeneletta d'arg[en]to	d. 0.12
14 pezzi con smeraldi	6 d.

Granatine, et un pezzo d'ongia legati in arg[en]to	1 d.
Una Scatoletta con Coraletti, Perlete, e perusini	1 d.
Una Corona de Smeraldo, con sua medaglia compagna	
pur di Smeraldo con figura	60 d.
Una Corona de Perusini con Croce di Cristal	
de Montagna con una medaglia d'oro	15 d.
Bottoni d'arg[en]to no. 12	3 d.
Un Cucchiaio di Madre Perla	d. 0.12
Un Coresin fornito d'oro, Un Boletto di Diaspro,	
Una Vera d'oro, et un Scatolin con Perusini, et altro	4 d.
Una Croce d'arg[ent]o fil à grana	4 d.
Una Scatola d'arg[en]to con due Coperchie	12 d.
Cartoni di Tartaruga forniti d'argento	4 d.
	692 d.

La sud[ett]a stima fatta dà mè Gasparo Romieri	
Gioielier al Lievro d'Oro.	
Un Reliquiario di Cristal di Montagna fornito d'argento	2 d.
Perosini d'oro [crossed out: arg{ent}o] no. 3	1 d.
Una Pistoletta d'arg[en]to dorada con Cadenella d'oro	5 d.
In una Scatola diverse Agate, Corniole, ambre negre,	
et altro	2 d.
	10 d.

1685 a[di] 30 mar[z]o

Invent[ari]o di Biancaria del N[obil] H[uomo] Lor[enz]o Bembo, che si
ritrova esser in Dep[osit]o nel Monast[eri]o di San Bernardo di Murano.

1.	Tovaglioli no. 60	no 60
2.	Mantili	no 4
3.	Mantili di fillo	no 7
4.	Lenzuoli p[ar]o	no 8
5.	Traverse	no 4
6.	Una Coltrina di Cendà Verde	no 1
7.	Camise da' Donna	no 2
8.	fazzoli da' man	no 12
9.	Intimelle p[ar]o	no 8
10.	Traversa con merlo	no 1
11.	Cossini da' letto	no 3
12.	fazzioli Turcheschi con fiori naturali	no 8
13.	Coverte da' Cuna di seda	no 2
14.	Coverte da' Cuna di ponto	no 1
15.	Telletti tessuti di nero	no 3
16.	Canevazze	no 10
17.	Un faciol Turchesco	no 1
18.	2 Vasi di Pezza	no 2
19.	Un sechieletto di Cristal	no 1

Io Pietro Vallotti fante delli Ill[ustrissi]mi, et Ecc[ellentissi]mi S[ignor]i Cappi dell Ecc[el]so C[onsiglio de'] X [Dieci] hò fatto il p[rese]nto Invent[ari]o et haverli commesso alla Mad[r]e Abbad[ess]a di dover lasciar fuor in nota la sop[radet]ta robba con l'ord[in]e di S.S.E.E. [Sue Eccellenze], e parim[en]te le Gioie stimate da D[on] Gasp[ar]o Romieri Orefice al Lievro d'Oro à Rialto per havendo convenuto averzer la Cassetina dalle Gioie, et altre Casse dà Drappi p[er] non esservi trovate le Chiavi.

21. I-Vas, Corporazioni religiose, *San Bernardo di Murano,* Busta 18, Mazzo Q, Plica D

1685. 31 Marzo. Copia.

Udite le riv[eren]te istanza del N[obil] H[uomo] Lorenzo Bembo, e veduta la l[ette]ra scritta dalla N[obil] D[onna] Ant[oni]a Bembo sua Consorta dè *21* 9[novem]bre 1683, e citati p[er] avanti, et uditi li N.N.H.H. [Nobilhuomini] Anz[ol]o Zusto e Vi[cenz]o Vend[rami]n, come Proc[urato]ri del V[eneran]do Mon[aste]rio di S[an] Bernardo de Muran, hanno S.S.E.E. [Sue Eccellenze] terminato, che tutti libri, gioie, et altri mobili essistenti nell'Inventario p[er] ord[in]e di S.S.E.E. [Sue Eccellenze] formato, siano al possibile avantaggio fatti vendere dal N[obil] H[uomo] Anz[ol]o Zusto Proc[urator] del soprad[ett]o Mon[aste]rio, e dà uno de Proc[urato]ri del Mon[aste]rio di S[anta] Maria dell'Oration di Malamocco, e del tutto delli med[esim]i debbano li stessi Proc[urator]i in primo luoco contar' ad Abbadessa del soprad[ett]o Mon[aste]rio di S[an] Bernardo di Muran la summa di d[ucat]i duecento, che erà creditore per sodisfatt[ion]e, e pagam[ent]o delle spese fatte alla N[obil] D[onna] Diana Bembo fig[liuo]la dei pred[ett]i Lor[enz]o e N[obil] D[onna] Ant[oni]a Bembo p[er] il tempo, che s'è trattenuta in d[ett]o Mon[aste]rio, e tutto il restante, che si cavarà debba p[er] essi N.N.H.H. [Nobilhuomini] Proc[urato]ri esser depositato al Trib[unal]e de Capi, p[er]che doppo detta p[rese]ntat[ion]e habbia da esser liberam[ent]e al tempo del suo vestire, che doverà seguir nel termine di mesi quattro senz'alcuna contraditt[ion]e consegnato all'Abb[ades]sa del soprade[ett]o Mon[aste]rio di Malamocco à conto della Robe, e Vestir di d[ett]a figliola in d[ett]o Mon[aste]rio, e non altrimenti, nè ad altri.

Quelli Mobili poi di Biancaria, che servissero p[er] il bisogno di d[ett]a Fig[lio]la nel monacarsi, debbono dà essi Proc[urato]ri esser riservati, e non venduti, p[er] consignarsi con l'Inventario alla med[isim]a Abb[addes]sa, la quale dovrà darli per uso alla med[esim]a figl[io]la, q[ua]ndo sarà stata vestita nel Mon[aste]rio.

Vic[enz]o dà Mula
Zacc[ari]a Salamon   C C x [Capi del Consiglio de' Dieci]
Gio[vanni] Ant[onio] Priuli
Maria Anz[ol]o di Negri, Nod[ai]o D[uca]l

22. I-Vas, Capi del Consiglio de' Dieci,
Notatorio, Filza 38 (1681–1700), ff. 1r–v

1687. 17 Xbre

 . . . c[he] andando la sera di *27* giug[n]o *1683* vagando la città prova sogetto alla giustitia, et altri, che p[er] hora si tacciono, habbiate havuto l'incontro di Antonio Gandiner, che andava con tutta modestia godendo la libertà della città, contro il quale senz'alcun motivo trasportato da' un'impetuoso furore habbiate avventato vigoroso colpo con arma di punta alla mamella sinistra p[er] il quale fù con penetrante ferita ridotto in pericolo della vita, con uscita di molto sangue. Ciò havendo com[m]esso. . . . dolora, deliberatam[en]te e con quelli mali modi, che dal processo sissaltrare, quel termine posesso, e non comparindo si procederà contro di lui la s[ente]nza, è contumatia no[n] ostante.

Adi 18 [dicem]bre 1687
Referi Fra[nces]co Peretti haver intimato il sud[ett]o Mandato
(crossed out: "al Nob[il] H[uom]o s[ignor] Lorenzo") et lasciato
in mano propria di s[ignor] Lorenzo Benbo [*sic*] Suo Padre.

23. I-Vas, Consiglio de' Dieci, *Parti Criminali,* Filza 119, f. 1

Capi: Domenico Mocenigo, Gerolamo Barbigo, Bassadonna
Avogadri: Lunardo Mocenigo, Sebastiano Soranzo, Zuanne Zen
1690. 26 Settembre in Consiglio de' Dieci

Che Lorenzo Bembo fu de Andrea fu Visdomino al Fontego di Todeschi et Bortolo Bortoleti già scontro nell'officio stesso Imputati per quello che scordatisi della fede ch'e dovuta al Principe, e della pontualità che dovevano essercitare nelle loro cariche e stabilito di approfitarsi indebitamente col publico patrimonio habbia esso Bembo con gl'indebiti oggetti sopradetti affettata la permanenza continuata per piu anni successivi, in quell'officio, e il maneggio della cassa per tempo maggiore di quello se le aspettava nell'amministratione della quale habbia in piu tempi riscosse molte summe di denaro da particolari delle quali gli ne ha rilasciate per conto d'affitti di camera di Fontico le ricepute senza far passare il denaro stesso nella publica cassa ne formarsene debitore nei mensuali dell'officio, che servono come di giornali, appropriando a se stesso il publico denaro con intaco patente della cassa medesima passando in cio concerto col detto Bortoleti magistro di dipravata fede, dal quale ad'occultatione della fraude, dell'intaco sono state formate note false sopra libri, e publiche carte, che il denaro predetto fosse entrato nella publica cassa.

Habbia ancora con le predette dannabili formalità e circonstanza riscorso altra rilevante summa di denaro come in processo di ragione de Dacij d'artificiali vivi per conto della camera di Graz, e quello infedelmente convertito in uso proprio con grave mancanza di fede e pregiudicio del Principe e un intaco detestabile della sua cassa.

Habbia esso Bortoleti con dannabile odioza collusione anco con altri ministri dello stesso officio passati di gia ad'altra vita col peso di dover rendere conto delle loro sue letaggini, e particolarmente concesso d'essi al quale non incombeva di erigerirsi nel maneggio del publico denaro lasciato correre e permesso contro le publiche diposizioni, che dallo stesso forse riscosso per lungo tempo somme rilevanti di ragione de Dacij, che dovevano essiggersi dal solo contadore e per facilitarne l'effetto, et il publico discapito siano da lui state girate con diabolica collusione l'essatione medesime nel suo mensuale per le partite di gran parte di esse molto tempo doppo seguiti per esborsi, amenche il denaro non forse passato nelle mani del contadone et entrato in cassa come perscrivono le leggi, cagionando con detta sua infedele, e detestabile collusione assenso e cooperatione gravissimo importante intaco nel denaro del principe e nella publica cassa.

24. I-Vas, Notarile, *Atti,* Pietro Antonio Ciola, Busta 4032 (minute), 20 August 1704

Pardevant les notaires a Paris soussignez fut presente L'Illustrissime Antonia Padovani veuve du feu Illustrissime Lorent bembo noble venetien du feu Illustrissime Andrea, demeurant maintenant en cette Ville De Paris rue de la lune a la Commu[nau]te de l'Union Chrestienne parr[oiss]e de nostre dame de bo[nn]e nouvelle.

Laquelle ajoute a la procuration passée Desja dans notre Etude le quatorze novembre mil sept cent trois dont n[']y est point resté de minutte, en faveur Des Illustrissimes andré et jaques bembo ses enfans aussy nobles venitiens et fils dudit Illustrissime Lorent bembo ausquels elle donne encore pouvoir, faculté, et autorité de se pouvoir Compromettre tant de droit que de faire a la maniere de Venise sans appel dans une ou plusieurs personnes: Cler[c]s, confidents de faire obtenir sentences, et icelles faire executer, compromettre devant tous tribunaux ou magistratures de Venise, Cours, Conseils, Colleges, meme aller aux pieds de sa Séverité de tes excellents Sages, par devant les tres excellents Chefs Du tres excellent Conseil des dix, et pardevant toutte autre representation publique du serenissime Domaine Venitien, et la pouvoir agiter, demander, respondre, contester les proces, elire des avocats ou procurateurs avec la mesme autoritée bornée, faire des offres et recevoir; faire toutte sorte

de constitution ou acte volontaire, conclure dans la cause, obtenir une ou plusieurs sentences et icelles faire executer, ou bien en appeller et faire pour-
suivre les appellations jusqua la fin, tant les depens, et celles reconnues de faire
emprisonner et delivrer des prisons tant debiteur, faire tout serment licite au
nom de ladite Dame Constituante faire toutte sorte de compositions, transactions, et accordes de ratiffier tous ceux que les dits Illustrissimes ses enfans
avoient faits avec l'Illustrissime Bernardo Bembo, fils du feu Illustrissime
Pierre, et enfin faire generallement et agir tout de mesme que si laditte Dame
bembo constituante y estoit presente, sous l'obligation de tous les biens en-
douaires de la Dame Constituante promettant obligeant; fait et passé a Paris
en la demeure de Ladite dame Constituante susdéclarée. L'an mil sept cent
quatre, Dixneuf[iem]e Jour D'aoust et a signé

Antonia Padoani Bembo
Gaillardie
Bailly

Noi Lorenzo Tiepolo p[er] la Ser[enissi]ma Repub[bli]ca di Venetia de
Ambasc[iato]r Ord[ina]rio app[ress]o Sua M[aes]ta Xp[Christissi]ma

Attestiamo a chiunque le p[rese]nti perveniranno qualm[en]te Li Sig[no]ri
Baillij et Gaillardie sono Notari Publici di questa Città di Parigi alli Atti,
Fedi, e Scritture dei quali può darsi una intiera credenza. In fede di che hab-
biamo sigillate le p[rese]nti coll'impronto del glorioso S[an] M[ar]co

Date Parigi li *20* Agosto *1704*
[two seals: French above, Venetian below]
Lorenzo Tiepolo Amb[asciato]re
Gio[vanni] Fran[ces]co Vincenti Seg[reta]rio

25. F-Pn, Rés.Vm¹ 112–113, *Te Deum* and *Divertimento*, Dedication, ff. 3–3v

Te deum per render gratie a Sua Divina Maesta del Glorioso Parto di Vostra
Altezza Reale che a dato al mondo un Principe cosi aggradito a tutto l'Uni-
verso et in particulare a Sua Maesta.

Con l'aggionta d'un picciolo divertimento, per la Nascita del medesimo
Principe.

Music [*sic*]
Musica di Antonia Bembo N[o]b[i]le V[ene]ta

A Madama la Duchessa di Borgogna per la Nascita di Monsig[no]re il Duca
di Bertagna
Madama,

Suplico V[ost]ra Altesza Reale ricever in bun [*sic*] grado Un Te deum per render gratie à Sua Divina Maesta d'haver concesso alla Francia un Principe cosi Caro à Sua Maesta è a tutta la Corte come il Glorioso Duca di Bertagna con l'aggionta d'un divertimento per la Nascita di questo Heröe che riempie le speranze di tutto il mondo. Tutto per rimarca indubitabile del Sommesso zelo con che gli presento i miei profondi rispetti, è raccomandando mi alla Sublime protettione di Vostra Altezza Reale et di tutta la Real familia.

Di V[ost]ra Altezza Reale

Humiliss[im]a div[otissi]ma et fedeliss[im]a Serva

Antonia Bembo N[o]b[i]le V[ene]ta

26. F-Pn, Rés.Vm¹114–115, *Te Deum* and *Exaudiat te, Dominus,* Dedication, ff. 3–3v

Te deum per Impetrar da Sua Divina Maesta la conservatione d'un
Monarcha cosi Grande come Luigi quattordice, è tutta la Sua
Familia Reale.
accompagnato d'un Exaudiat
Compositione di Antonia Bembo N[o]b[i]le V[ene]ta
Sire

Luigi il grande, il Forte, il Saggio, l'Invincibile, Sommo Giove della terra, Monarcha dei Monarchi: ardisco dedicare il terzo laboro di miei deboli fatiche alla Sacra Maesta Vostra. Un Te deum per render gratie a la Maesta Divina (è medesimamente per Impetrar la Conservatione d'un Principe cosi Caro a Vostra Maesta, è a tutta la Corte come il Duca di Bertagna) con l'aggionta d'un Exaudiat.

Sire chi dà quanto può da quanto deve Et le forti passioni più s'esprimonò con un divoto silentio, che con Una faconda Eloquenza. che però ardisco Sottoscrivermi con il più sommesso é profondo rispetto

Di V[ost]ra Maesta xp[christissi]ma

Fedele sommessa et ossequio[sissi]ma Serva

Antonia Bembo N[o]b[i]le V[ene]ta

27. F-Pn, Rés.Vm¹116, *Les sept Pseaumes, de David,* Dedication, ff. 2v–3

Sire,

Toute remplie D'admiration, pour vostre Majesté, et animée pour elle, du zele le plus pur et le plus ardent, qu'on eût jamais ressenti, pour un Auguste Monarque, Je ne puis donner d'autres preuves, des sentimens, dont mon Coeur est penetré, qu'en consacrant A Vostre Majesté, tous mes Voeux, et tous mes talens. Je passe donc, Sire, plus de la moitié de ma vie, a prier le Tres haut, qu'il repande sans cesse, sur Vostre Majesté, La Gloire et les felicitez, dont vostre admirable pieté, et Vos heroiques vertus, vous rendent si digne, et j'employe ce qui me reste de mon tems, a travailler En Musique, N'ayant en Vüe dans tous les airs que je compose, que d'en produire quelques uns qui puissent estre assez heureux pour avoir La gloire de plaire a Vostre Majesté. C'est a cette intention, Sire, Que j'ay composé des airs, sur les Pseaumes de David, que j'ose prendre la liberté, de presenter a Vostre Majesté. Je vous suplie Sire, de daigner me faire la grace de regarder cette composition comme une foible, mais sincere marque, de mon profond respect, pour vostre sacrée Personne, de ma parfaite reconnoissance pour vos augustes bienfaits, et du zele ardent et passionné avec lequel je suis

Sire

De Vostre Majesté

La tres humble et tres obbeissante

Servante

Ant[oinet]te Bembo

28. F-Pn, Rés. Vm^{1}116, *Les sept Pseaumes, de David*, Dedicatory poem, ff. 3v–4

Au Roy

En presentant a sa Majesté des airs

Composez sur les Pseaumes de David

Un grand Roy pour le Ciel plein d'une pure ardeur,
Mais qu'aussi L'Eternel trouva selon son Coeur,
Guidé par le beau feu de ses saintes Lumieres,
Poussoit Vers le Seigneur ses fervantes prieres,
Dans les sublimes vers de ses Pseaumes pieux,
David sçeut bien Loüer Le souverain des Cieux.
Toy, qui d'un Roy si saint est la vivante image,
Toy, Louis, dont la foy, la candeur, la bonté,
    Sont pareilles a l'équité,
Toy, qui receus du Ciel cent vertus en partage,
    Daigne agréer Le juste hommage
Que mon zêle aujoud'huy [*sic*] rend á ta pieté.
    Aux Cantiques du Roy Prophette
    Pour toy j'ay Composé des Airs:
    S'ils pouvoient former des Concerts
    Dont ton ame fut satisfaites,
Monarque Le plus grand qui soit dans L'univers,
    Que ma gloire seroit parfaite!

29. F–Pn, Rés. Vm⁴9, *L'Ercole amante,* Title page, f. 2

LErcole Amante
Tragedia
Nuovamente Posta In Musica, da
Domina Antonia Bembo No[bil]tà Ve[ne]ta
E Consacrata alla Majesta Christ[issi]ma
Di Luigi quarto Decimo
Lanno *1707*

30. F–Pn, Rés. Vm⁴10, *L'Ercole amante,* Dedicatory Madrigal, opp. p. 243

Au Roy
Madrigal

L'alta Clemenza ò Sire
che frezia In Sommo grado il Tuo Valore,
E ti dà frà gl'Eroi Supremo il Vanto;
mi dà forza, et ardire
D'offrir alla tua Destra, al tuo gran Core
In dono, anzi in tributo un nuovo Cantò;
Degnati Sire Intanto
Risguardar Con Pietà chi tutta Zelo
Porge per tè Continui Voti al Cielo.

Appendix 2

LONGER MUSICAL EXAMPLES

Example A.1   F-Pn, Rés. Vm¹117, *Produzioni armoniche*, no. 22, pp. 181–184

Example A.1   *Continued*

I've had enough.
    Disillusioned, mocked,
    I have suffered too much
    for someone who has betrayed me,
    for someone who has wounded me.
I've had enough.
    Through ill-fated temperament,
    embraced by suffering,
    I was like a mole, blind to my well-being,
    I was like a lynx, stalking my destruction,
    night and day.
I've had enough.

Example A.2   F-Pn, Rés. Vm^{1}117, *Produzioni armoniche*, no. 18, pp. 163–165

Example A.2   *Continued*

What's wrong, handsome ungrateful one,
    that you are scornful of me?
What's wrong, o God, what's wrong?
    For pity's sake, answer!
    At least tell me what I have done to you,
    of which crime you hold me guilty.
    Come on, speak; with your silence you are killing me.
What's wrong, o God, what's wrong?
    Since I have already given you my heart,
    since I have consecrated my faith to you,
    since you are my idol:
    at least tell me what I have done to you.
    Ah, cruel one, still you keep silent.
What's wrong, o God, what's wrong?

Example A.3   F–Pn, Rés. Vm^{1}117, *Produzioni armoniche*, no. 19, pp. 166–169

Example A.3 *Continued*

Don't believe those glances, my heart, be careful.
　　Those pitiless eyes
　　are too deceitful;
　　they are beautiful but ungrateful.
　　They promise love,
　　but with all severity
　　they deny mercy.
Don't believe those glances, my heart, be careful.
　　Ah, to its own detriment,
　　faith [in the glances] is always precarious,
　　their deceit certain.

Example A.4. F-Pn, Vm⁷546, Ballard, *Recueil* (1713), p. 215

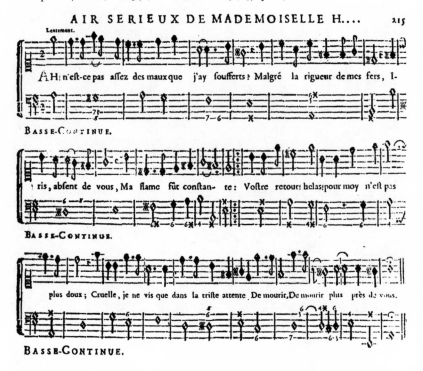

Example A.5. François Couperin, *Concert instrumental sous le Titre d'Apotheose*, p. 15

Example A.6   F-Pn, Rés. Vm¹113, "Menuet," mm. 337–358

Example A.7   Lully, *Ballet de la Raillerie*, LWV 11, "Dialogue de la musique italienne et de la musique française"

Example A.7   *Continued*

mieux tes longs fre - - - - - - dons en - nu-

- yeux, tes longs fre - - - - - - dons en - nu-

Qual ra - gion vuol che tu deg - gi del tuo gus - to al - trui far leg - gi?

- yeux?   Je n'or - don - ne

point_____ du tien, mais je veux chan - ter__ au mien, mais je veux chan - ter au

Io di te can - to più for - te per - chè

mien, mais je veux chan - ter au mien.

Example A.7 *Continued*

Italian Music: Kind French Music, how did my song offend you?
French Music: In so much as your songs often seem dull to me.
Italian Music: You are not capable of making anything but suffering and sad
  lamentations.
French Music: Do you believe that anyone prefers your long, boring humming?
Italian Music: Why should your taste make the rules for another's?
French Music: I'm not commanding your [taste], but I want to sing with mine.
Italian Music: I can sing more loudly than you because I love more than you do;
  he who feels a deathly pain cries out as loudly as he can, "have pity!"
French Music: The way that I sing expresses better my languishing;
  when this pain touches the heart, the voice is less bright.

Example A.8. F-Pn, Rés. Vm¹114, pp. 50–51, mm. 195 bis–204 bis, "Lentement et tendrement"

Example A.8   *Continued*

When it came time for you to deliver man,
you did not abhor the Virgin's womb,
when you overcame the sharpness of death,
you opened the kingdom of heaven to all believers.

Example A.9   F-Pn, Rés. Vm^{1}114, pp. 77–82, mm. 282 bis–332 bis

Example A.9   *Continued*

Example A.9 *Continued*

Day by day we magnify you,
and we praise your name for ever and ever.

Example A.10. F-Pn, Rés. Vm⁴9, pp. 34–42, Juno (I, iii)

Example A.10 *Continued*

Example A.10   *Continued*

Example A.10 *Continued*

Example A.10   *Continued*

JUNO
And so, Venus,
to carry her efforts to their end
to inflict upon me the most wounding offenses,
wants to favor the one whose intentions
were so conceived as to offend me always,
and who, from his unholy beginnings
even before being born, was offensive to me?
One who, even before drawing his first breath,
was animated by the desire to hurt me,
and who, after drawing from my breast
his life's first sustenance,
with thankless insolence
dared to wound me as he attempted to kill me?
Ah, having understood the plan,
I will not need to be taught how to undo it.
    Hyllus and Iole burn
    with tenderness for one another,
    and, solely to spite me,
    the villainous Goddess does not
    want Hymen to join them? Rather,
    to give me still greater offense,
    she arranges that the marital knot that binds
    Hercules to Dejanira should at last be broken,
    so that Iole may be taken today,
    in monstrous embrace,
    by the evil murderer of her own father.
    And by what means, o God? By such as are unworthy
    of even the vilest of souls, not to mention of a divine one.
But in love, that which swindles others
is no longer Love's joy,
what he did not grant as a gift, or out of pity,
is just a pointless adventure.
In love, that which swindles others
is no longer Love's joy.
If it does not come from a true thirst,
voluntarily from another's faith,
it changes entirely its nature
as if hatred colored all mercy.
    But why am I wasting what little time I have
    to defend myself in useless complaints?
    Come, winds, take me
    to the cave of Sleep, and let my throne,
    surrounded by evil gusts, spread all around
    heralds of my fury, lightning, and violent storms.

Example A.11. F-Pn, Rés. Vm⁴9, pp. 103–113, Pasithea (II, vi)

Example A.11. *Continued*

Example A.11. *Continued*

Example A.11. *Continued*

Example A.11. *Continued*

PASITHEA
Murmur,
o brooks,
whisper,
o gentle breezes,
and with your whispers and murmurs,
sweet enchantments of oblivion
that put all cares to flight,
seduce Sleep itself into sleep.
    Those who truly love
    desire more greatly
    the pleasure of their beloved
    than their own:
    thus is it that I should derive,
    night and day,
    my own happiness
    from my gentle husband's peaceful rest.

LIST OF COMPACT DISC TRACKS

Track 1. *Produzioni armoniche,* no. 15, "Clizia amante del sole"
  Adriana Fernandez, soprano; Mathias Spaeter, theorbo; Arno Jochem, viola
  da gamba; Dorota Cybulska, harpsichord
Track 2. *Produzioni armoniche,* no. 16, "Habbi pietà di me"
  Adriana Fernandez, soprano; Mathias Spaeter, theorbo
Track 3. *Produzioni armoniche,* no. 2, "Al Re"
  Adriana Fernandez, soprano; Valérie Winteler, traverso; Hélène Schmitt,
  violin; Arno Jochem, viola da gamba; Mathias Spaeter, theorbo; Dorota
  Cybulska, harpsichord
Track 4. *Produzioni armoniche,* no. 6, "Lamento della Vergine"
  Roberta Invernizzi, soprano; Elena Russo, violoncello; Giangiacomo Pinardi,
  theorbo; Salvatore Carchiolo, harpsichord; Elena Russo, director, Bizzarrie
  Armoniche (Opus 111/Naïve 2001, OP 30341)
Track 5. *Produzioni armoniche,* no. 30 "Passan veloci l'ore"
  Roberta Invernizzi, soprano; Riccardo Masahide Minasi, violin; Elena Russo,
  violoncello; Salvatore Carchiolo, harpsichord; Elena Russo, director, Bizzarrie
  Armoniche (ORF Edition Alte Musik 2004, CD 383)
Track 6. *Produzioni armoniche,* no. 33, "Anima perfida"
  Roberta Invernizzi, soprano; Elena Russo, violoncello; Salvatore Carchiolo,
  harpsichord; Elena Russo, director, Bizzarrie Armoniche (ORF Edition Alte
  Musik 2004, CD 383)
Track 7. *Produzioni armoniche,* no. 27, "Mi consolo, non son solo"
  Maria Jonas, soprano; Markus Märkl, harpsichord
Track 8. *Produzioni armoniche,* no. 32, "M'ingannasti in verità"
  Roberta Invernizzi, soprano; Elena Russo, violoncello; Salvatore Carchiolo,
  harpsichord; Elena Russo, director, Bizzarrie Armoniche (ORF Edition Alte
  Musik 2004, CD 383)

Track 9. *Les sept Pseaumes de David,* Psalm 101, "Seigneur qui voit mes pleurs"
Cristi Catt, soprano; Mark-Andrew Cleveland, baritone; Laura Gulley, violin; Susanna Cortesio, violin; Na'ama Lion, traverso; Laury Gutiérrez, viola da gamba; Noriko Yasuda, harpsichord; Ruth McKay, organ

Track 10. *L'Ercole amante,* II, vi, Pasithea, "Mormorate o fiumicelli"
Magali Dami, soprano; Odile Édouard, violin; Olivia Centurioni, violin; Arno Jochem, viola da gamba; Mathias Spaeter, theorbo; Dorota Cybulska, harpsichord

Track 11. Texts and translations for tracks 1–10

BIBLIOGRAPHY

Manuscript Sources and Rare Prints

CROATIA

Hr-Ppa   Pazin, Povijesni arhiv (Historical Archive)

Battesimi, 1586–1644

Battesimi, 1645–1736

FRANCE

F-Pamae   Paris, Archives du Ministère des Affaires Étrangères

Correspondance politique, Venise, 139

F-Pan   Paris, Archives Nationales

H^5*4168. St. Chaumont, 1690–1694

H^5*4169. St. Chaumont, 1737

H^5*4211. Religieuses de St. Chaumont et de Ste. Aure, Rentes du XVIIIe s. [Activity of notary Bailly for the Union Chrétienne]

L. 1056. Union Chrétienne dite du petit St. Chaumont, 1685–1784

LL. 1667. Filles de St. Chaumont, Registres capitulaires, 1685–1784

LL. 1668. Filles de St. Chaumont, Règle du séminaire de Charonne

LL. 1669. Filles de St. Chaumont, Règles et constitutions

O^1*29 [Naturalization authorization for Brigida Fedeli]

O^1*630 [Pensions, c. 1715]

O^1*656. Pensions, 1687–1780

O^1*2835. Menus plaisirs, 1704

O^1*3715. Maison de la Duchesse de Bourgogne, Household *Abrégé*, 1690–1699

X^{1a}8679. Registration in parliament of Berthelot's house, 1682

341

Z^{1F}607. Registre des lettres patentes et arrêts

Z^{1a}522. Cour des aides [information regarding Joseph de Soleras]

F-Pan MC   Paris, Archives Nationales, Minutier Central

MC XV, 292 [Brigide Fidely]

MC XLIV, 201 [*Inventaire après décès d'Élisabeth-Sophie Chéron*, 1711]

MC LXXIII, 441 [Pension record for Marc'Antoine Bianky, 28 June 1659]

MC LXXVII, 35 [Retirement and pension document for Brigida Fedeli, 1689]

MC XCI, 504 bis [Will of Brigida Fedeli]

MC XCI, 538 [Aurelia Brigida Bianqhi]

MC XCI, 563 [Brigida Fedeli, *inventaire après décès*]

MC CXI, 563 [Notary document for Brigide Fidele, widow of Augustin Romagnesy]

MC CXIII, 129 [Notarized pension payment for Paris *commedia dell'arte* troupe, 1686, rue du Petit Lyon]

F-Pap   Paris, Archives de Paris

5 AZ 1744 [Notary document for Brigide Fidele, widow of Augustin Romagnesy]

F-Pa   Paris, Bibliothèque de l'Arsenal

Mus. Mss. Rés. 926 [111]. Jean-Baptiste Lully. "Ballet Hercule Amoureux," 1662

F-Pbsg   Paris, Bibliothèque de Saint Geneviève

Ms. 3173. "Petites reigles pour l'accompagnement que Monsieur Buterne m'a donné par confiance et dont il fait grant cas et qu'il se réserve"

F-Pm   Paris, Bibliothèque Mazarine

Romagnesi, Marc'Antonio. *Poesie liriche* (Paris: Denys Langlois, 1673) (43892)

Rousseau de La Parisière, Jean-César. *Oraison funèbre* (A. 16.022, 7e pièce)

F-Pn   Paris, Bibliothèque Nationale

Rés. F. 668. Mottets de feu Mr. de Lully

Rés. F. 679. Libretto for Lully, *La Galanterie du temps*, 1656

Rés. L^{36}b3791. Romagnesi, Marc'Antonio [the elder]. *Dichiaratione del Rè Christianissime, publicata nel parlamento, nel quale S.M. si ritrovò il giorno 18 di Gennaro 1634*. Venice: Giacomo Scalia, 1634.

Rés. Vm^{1}112–113. Antonia Bembo. *Te Deum* and *Divertimento*

Rés. Vm^{1}114–115. Antonia Bembo. *Te Deum* and *Exaudiat te, Dominus*

Rés. Vm^1 116. Antonia Bembo. *Les sept Pseaumes, de David*

Rés. Vm^{1}117. Antonia Bembo. *Produzioni armoniche*

Rés. Vm^{4}9. Antonia Bembo. *L'Ercole amante*, volume 1

Rés. Vm^{4}10. Antonia Bembo. *L'Ercole amante*, volume 2

Rés. Vm⁶1. Lully, *Ballet de la Raillerie*

Rés. Vm⁷546. Ballard, *Recueil* (1713)

Rés. Yd. 1232. Romagnesi, Marc'Antonio. *Poesie liriche.* Paris: Denys Langlois, 1673.

F-Po   Paris, Bibliothèque de l'Opéra

Ms. Rés. 625. Thomas-Simon Gueullette, *Histoire du théâtre italien establi en France depuis l'année 1577 jusqu'en l'année 1750 et les années suivantes*

GREAT BRITAIN

Gb-Lbl   London, British Library

Add. MS. 18958. "Establishment of the Duke of York . . . Christmas 1677"

ITALY

I-BRas   Brescia, Archivio antico municipale

Accademia Erranti, Busta 142

I-MAa   Mantua, Archivio di Stato

Archivio Gonzaga, *Carteggi esteri,* Carteggi ad inviati (Venezia), Busta 1571

Archivio Gonzaga, *Carteggi esteri,* Carteggi ad inviati (Venezia), Busta 1574

Archivio Gonzaga, *Lettere ai Gonzaga Mantova e Paesi* (1654), Busta 2796/VII, carte 269 and 271

Archivio Gonzaga, *Mandati,* Busta 52.

Schede Davari, Ms., #14.

I-Paau   Padua, Biblioteca Universitaria, Archivio Antico dell'Università

Codex 275 [Dottori licenziati in chirurgia del 1629 al 1640]

Codex 472 [Notice of the Convocation speech of Giacomo Padoani, 1633]

I-Pas   Padua, Archivio di Stato

Ufficio di Sanità, Busta 482

Ufficio di Sanità, *Registri dei morti,* Registro 479 (1663–1666)

I-Pav   Padua, Archivio Vescovile

S. Georgii, *Battesimi 1643 sino 1687,* Registro 4

S. Georgii, *Mortuorum (1614–1746),* no. 56

S. Laurentij, *Liber Baptizator,* Registro 7

I-Tr   Turin, Biblioteca Reale

Le Esperidi figurate sulle rive del Po per le nozze di Madama Adélaïde [MS.]

I-Tn   Turin, Biblioteca Nazionale dell'Università

Ris. Mus. I/26. *Metodo elementare di musica composta da D. Giuseppe Matteo Vacca in francese* [MS.]

I-Vas   Venice, Archivio di Stato

Avogaria di Comun, *Matrimoni, Sposalici,* Busta 100

Avogaria di Comun, *Nascite,* Registro 59/IX

Avogaria di Comun, *Necrologi dei Nobili,* Busta 159

Avogaria di Comun, *Processi per Nobiltà*, Busta 294/12

Barbaro, Arbori di patrizi veneti

Capi del Consiglio de' Dieci, *Notatorio*, Filza 38

Capi del Consiglio de' Dieci, *Note di prigioni*, Buste 1–2

Cappellari Vivaro, Girolamo Alessandro. *Il campodoglio veneto* (MS.)

Cinque savi alla mercanzia, Busta 74 bis, nuova serie

Consiglio de' Dieci, *Parti Criminali*, Filza 91

Consiglio de' Dieci, *Parti Criminali*, Filza 119

Consiglio de' Dieci, Busta 108

Corporazioni religiose, *San Bernardo di Murano*, Busta 7

Corporazioni religiose, *San Bernardo di Murano*, Busta 18

Corporazioni religiose, *San Bernardo di Murano*, Busta 19

Corporazioni religiose, *Santa Maria dell'Orazione di Malamocco*, Busta 2

Corporazioni religiose, *Santa Maria dell'Orazione di Malamocco*, Busta 7

Corti di Palazzo, *Giudici del Proprio*, Interdetti, Registro 24

Corti di Palazzo, *Giudici del Proprio*, Minutarum, Registro 51

Corti di Palazzo, *Giudici del Proprio*, Successioni, Registro 52

X [Dieci] Savi alle decime, Busta 424

Esaminador, *Interdetti*, Registro 198

Esaminador, *Interdetti*, Registro 206

Giudici del Forestier, *Estraordinario*, Busta 122

Giudici del Forestier, *Estraordinario*, Busta 206

Giudici di Petizion, *Inventari*, Busta 426/91

Libri d'Oro, *Matrimoni*, V/92

Libri d'Oro, *Nascite*, X/60

Libri d'Oro, *Nascite*, XI/61

Miscellanea Codici III, Codici Soranzo 31 (già Miscell. Add. 856), Girolamo Alessandro Cappellari Vivaro, *Il campidoglio veneto*

Notarile, *Atti*, Pietro Antonio Bozini, Busta 1021

Notarile, *Atti*, Pietro Bracchi e Girolamo Brinis, Busta 842

Notarile, *Atti*, Pietro Bracchi e Girolamo Brinis, Busta 871

Notarile, *Atti*, Pietro Bracchi e Girolamo Brinis, Busta 881

Notarile, *Atti*, Pietro Bracchi e Girolamo Brinis, Busta 884

Notarile, *Atti*, Pietro Bracchi e Girolamo Brinis, Busta 885

Notarile, *Atti*, Pietro Bracchi e Girolamo Brinis, Busta 912

Notarile, *Atti*, Girolamo Brinis, Busta 840

Notarile, *Atti*, Pietro Antonio Ciola, Busta 3979

Notarile, *Atti*, Pietro Antonio Ciola, Buste 3984–3985

Notarile, *Atti*, Pietro Antonio Ciola, Busta 4032

Notarile, *Atti*, Giorgio Emo, Busta 5508

Notarile, *Atti*, Giorgio Emo, Busta 5521

Notarile, *Atti*, Battista Ernest, Busta 5487

Notarile, *Atti,* Battista Ernest, Busta 5488

Notarile, *Atti,* Battista Ernest, Busta 5493

Notarile, *Atti,* Battista Ernest, Busta 5494

Notarile, *Atti,* Tadeo Fedrici, Busta 6055

Notarile, *Atti,* Tadeo Fedrici, Busta 6063

Notarile, *Atti,* Giulio Figolin, Busta 5940

Notarile, *Atti,* Camillo Lion, Busta 8022

Notarile, *Atti,* Camillo Lion, Busta 8029

Notarile, *Atti,* Giovanni Antonio Mora, Busta 8629

Notarile, *Atti,* Giovanni Antonio Mora, Busta 8636

Notarile, *Atti,* Giovanni Antonio Mora, Busta 8651 bis

Notarile, *Atti,* Lio Fabio Turighello, Busta 5049

Notarile, *Atti,* Vincenzo Vincenti, Busta 13845

Notarile, *Atti,* Vincenzo Vincenti, Busta 13852

Notarile, *Atti,* Vincenzo Vincenti, Busta 13887

Notarile, *Testamenti,* Tadeo Fedrici, Busta 433

Notarile, *Testamenti,* Camillo Lion, Busta 591

Notarile, *Testamenti,* Pietro Reggia, Busta 831

Notarile, *Testamenti chiusi,* Girolamo Brinis, Busta 642

Ospedali e luoghi pii diversi, Buste 236–239

Provedditori alla sanità, Busta 571

Riformatori allo Studio di Padova, Busta 539

Senato, *Provveditori da terra e da mar,* Armada, Capitano . . . Francesco Morosini, Busta 1114

Signori di Notte al Civil, *Lettere,* Busta 220

Signori di Notte al Civil, *Pagamenti, e assicurazion di dotte,* Busta 46

Signori di Notte al Civil, *Pagamenti, e assicurazion di dotte,* Busta 50

Signori di Notte al Civil, *Pagamenti, e assicurazion di dotte,* Busta 53

Signori di Notte al Civil, *Pagamenti, e assicurazion di dotte,* Busta 54

Signori di Notte al Civil, *Pagamenti, e assicurazion di dotte,* Busta 63

I-Vasp   Venice, Archivio storico del Patriarcato di Venezia

Curia Patriarcale, *Sezione antica: Actorum, mandatorum, et præceptorum,* Busta 116

Curia Patriarcale, *Sezione antica: Filciae causarum,* Busta 68

San Marco, *Registri dei morti,* V

I-Vbc   Venice, Biblioteca del Museo Civico Correr

Ms. P.D.C., Busta 2706/8

Ms. P.D.C., Busta 2714/5

Padovani, Giacomo de' [Padoani, Giacomo]. *Oratione all'illustrissimo Signor Girolamo Bembo nella partenza dal suo reggimento di Podestà a Montona.* Venice: Pietro Miloco, 1640.

I-Vnm   Venice, Biblioteca Nazionale Marciana

MISC. 207/5. Patavinis, Iacobo de [Padoani, Giacomo]. *Oratio Illustrissimo & Excellentissimo Viro Aloysio Valaresso Equiti, cum Præfectura, Patavij summa cum laude, & applausu administrata, abiret, DICTA à Iacobo de Patavinis Vicentino. Anno reparatae Salutis 1632. Die 16. Mensis Decemb.* Padua: Bartholomaei Carectoni, 1632.

MS. It. IV, 359 (9883). Francesco Cavalli. *L'Ercole amante*

MS It. VII, 14 (7418)

MS It. VII, 845 (8924)

MS It. VII, 846 (8925)

MS It. VII, 847 (8926)

MS It. VII, 849 (8928)

MS It. VII, 851 (8930)

MS It. VII, 854 (8933)

I-Vsp   Venice, Parrochia di San Pantalon

Morti dal 1632 al 1652

I-VIbcb   Vicenza, Biblioteca Civica Bertoliana

Cappellari Vivaro Vicentino, Girolamo Alessandro. *Emporio universale delle famiglie.* MS v

Printed Sources (Pre-1800)

Argentville, Antoine-Joseph Dézallier d'. *Abrégé de la vie des plus fameux peintres.* 4 vols. Paris: De Bure, 1762.

Bartoli, Francesco. *Notizie istoriche de' comici italiani che fiorirono intorno all'anno MDL fino a' giorni presenti.* Padua: Conzatti a S. Lorenzo, 1782.

Benserade, Isaac de. *Vers du ballet royal dansé par Leurs Majestez entre des actes de la grande tragédie de l' "Hercule Amoureux" avec la traduction du prologue et les argumens de chaque acte.* Paris: Robert Ballard, 1662.

Bourdelot, Pierre, and Pierre Bonnet. *Histoire de la musique et de ses effets.* Paris: n.p., 1715.

Buti, Francesco. *Ercole amante. Tragedia representata per le nozze delle Maestà Christianissime.* Paris: Robert Ballard, 1662.

[Chéron, Elisabeth-Sophie]. *Essay de pseaumes et cantiques mis en vers, et enrichis de figures.* Par Mademoiselle ★★★. Paris: Michel Brunet, 1694. Reprint, Paris: P. F. Giffart, 1715.

————. *Pseaumes de David et Cantiques nouvellement mis en vers françois, enrichis de figures.* Paris: Luyne, Brunet, Robestel, 1694.

Destouches, André Cardinal. *Issé, pastorale héroïque.* Paris: Christophe Ballard, 1708.

Ebert, Adam. *Anecdota, sive, Historia arcana Europae.* N.p.: Cosmopoli, 1715.

Fedeli, Brigida [Aurelia Fedeli, pseud.]. *I rifiuti di Pindo.* Paris: C. Chenault, 1666.

Fedeli, Brigida [Brigida Bianchi, Comica detta Aurelia, pseud.]. *L'inganno fortunato, overo l'amata aborrita, comedia bellissima, transportata dallo spagnuolo, con alcune poesie musicali composte in diversi tempi.* Paris: Claudio Cramoisy, 1659.

Fermel'huis, Monsieur. *Éloge funebre de Madame le Hay, connuë sous le nom de Mademoiselle Chéron.* Paris: François Fournier, 1712.

Ferrand, Louis. *Liber psalmorum cum argumentis, paraphrasi et annotationibus.* Paris: André Pralard, 1683.

Hamilton, Anthony. *Memoirs of Count Grammont.* New York: Merrill and Baker, n.d.

L'Hymen. Mascarade dansée à Blois devant leurs Altesses Royales. Blois: Jules Hotot, 1658.

Limojon, Alexandre Toussaint de. *La Ville et la République de Venise.* Paris: Louis Billaine, 1680.

Marais, Marin. *Alcione, tragédie mise en musique.* Paris: Foucaut, 1706.

Mercure Galant. Paris, 1679.

———. Paris, 1681.

Niceron, Jean-François. *Mémoires pour servir à l'histoire des hommes illustres dans la république des lettres.* 43 vols. Paris: Briasson, 1731.

Papadopoli, Nicolai Comneni. *Historia Gymnasi Patavinii.* 2 vols. Venice: Sebastian Coleti, 1726.

Patin, Charles. *Lyceum Patavinum.* Padua: Frambotti, 1682.

Rinck, Eucharius Gottlieb. *Bibliotheca Rinckiana.* Leipzig: Widow of B. Casp. Fritschii, [1747?].

Robinet. *Lettres en vers et en prose.* N.p.: Mayolas, 1668.

Romagnesi, Marc'Antonio. *Poesie liriche di Marc-Antonio Romagnesi divise in quattro parti, consecrate all'immortal nome di Luigi XIV.* Paris: Denys Langlois, 1673.

Tarachia, Angiolo. *Feste celebrate in Mantova alla venuta de' Serenissimi Archiduchi Ferdinando Carlo e Sigismundo Francesco d'Austria et Arciduchessa Anna Medici, Il Carnevale dell'Anno 1652.* Mantua: Osanna, 1652.

Valier, Andrea. *Historia della guerra di Candia.* Venice: Paulo Baglioni, 1687.

Vertron, Claude-Charles Guyonnet, seigneur de La Brosse-Paslis et de. *La Nouvelle Pandore ou les Femmes illustres du siècle de Louis le Grand. Recueil de pièces académiques, en prose et en vers, sur la préférence des sexes. Dédiés aux dames.* Paris: Veuve de Claude Mazuel, 1697.

———. *Seconde Partie de la Pandore ou la suite des Femmes illustres du siècle de Louis le Grand.* Paris: Veuve de Claude Mazuel, 1698.

Printed Sources (Post-1800)

Anthony, James R. *French Baroque Music, from Beaujoyeulx to Rameau.* Rev. and expanded ed. Portland, OR: Amadeus Press, 1997.

Apostolidès, Jean-Marie. *Le Roi-Machine: Spectacle et politique au temps de Louis XIV.* Paris: Éditions de minuit, 1981.

Attwater, Donald, and Herbert Thurston, S.J., eds. *Butler's Lives of the Saints.* 4 vols. New York: P. J. Kenedy & Sons, 1956.

Auld, Louis E. *Lyric Theory and Practice.* Part 2 of *The Lyric Art of Pierre Perrin, Founder of French Opera.* Henryville, PA: Institute of Mediæval Music, 1986.

Bacilly, Bénigne de. *Remarques curieuses sur l'art de bien chanter.* Ed. and Trans. Austin B. Caswell. Brooklyn, NY: Institute of Mediæval Music, 1968.

Baldauf-Berdes, Jane L. *Women Musicians of Venice: Musical Foundations 1525–1855*. Ed. Elsie Arnold. Reprint, Oxford: Clarendon Press, 1996.

Baldwin, Olive, and Thelma Wilson. "An English Calisto." *Musical Times* 112 (1971): 651–653.

Barthélemy, Maurice. *André Campra: Sa vie et son œuvre (1660–1744)*. Paris: Picard, 1957.

Bellier de La Chavignerie, Émile. *Dictionnaire général des artistes de l'École Française depuis l'origine des arts du dessin jusqu'à l'année 1868 inclusivement*. 5 vols. Paris: Renouard, 1868–1872.

Bembo, Antonia. *Amor mio*. Ed. Claire Fontijn. Bryn Mawr, PA: Hildegard, 1998.

———. *Exaudiat te Dominus*. Ed. Conrad Misch. Kassel: Furore Verlag, 2003.

———. *Ha, que l'absence*. Ed. Claire Fontijn. Bryn Mawr, PA: Hildegard, 1998.

———. *In amor ci vuol ardir*. Ed. John Glenn Paton. In *Italian Arias of the Baroque and Classical Eras*, ed. John Glenn Paton, 55–59. Van Nuys, CA: Alfred, 1994.

———. *Les Sept Psaumes de David*. Ed. Conrad Misch. 7 vols. Kassel: Furore Verlag, 2003.

———. *Per il Natale*. Ed. Claire Fontijn. Fayetteville, AR: Clar-Nan Editions, 1999.

———. *Te Deum laudamus* [F-Pn, Rés. Vm^{1}112]. Ed. Conrad Misch. Kassel: Furore Verlag, 2003.

———. *Te Deum laudamus* [F-Pn, Rés. Vm^{1}114]. Ed. Wolfgang Fürlinger. Epilogue by Claire Fontijn. *Musik des 17. Jahrhunderts*, vol. 17. Altötting: Musikverlag Coppenrath, 1999.

———. *Tota pulcra es*. Ed. Claire Fontijn. Bryn Mawr, PA: Hildegard, 1998.

Benoit, Marcelle. *Les Musiciens du roi de France (1661–1733)*. Paris: Presses Universitaires de France, 1982.

———. *Versailles et les musiciens du roi*. Paris: Picard, 1971.

———, ed. *Dictionnaire de la musique en France aux XVIIe et XVIIIe siècles*. Paris: Fayard, 1992.

Bernardinello, Silvio. *Le orazioni per l'annuale apertura degli studi nell'Università di Padova (dal 1405 al 1796)—Saggio bibliografico*. Padua: Società cooperativa tipografica, 1984.

Besutti, Paola. "Produzione e trasmissione di cantate romani nel mezzo del Seicento." In *La musica a Roma attraverso le fonti d'archivio*, ed. Bianca Maria Antolini, 137–166. Lucca: Libreria musicale italiana, 1994.

Biagioli, Mario. *Galileo Courtier: The Practice of Science in the Culture of Absolutism*. Chicago: University of Chicago Press, 1993.

Bibliotheca Sanctorum. 13 vols. Rome: Città Nuova Editrice, 1968.

Biver, Paul, and Marie-Louise Biver. *Abbayes, monastères, couvents de femmes à Paris des origines à la fin du XVIIIe siècle*. Vendôme: Presses Universitaires de France, 1975.

Boerio, Giuseppe. *Dizionario del dialetto veneziano*. Venice: Giovanni Cecchini, 1856.

Boston Early Music Festival Catalogue. Cambridge, MA: Boston Early Music Festival, Inc., 1999.

Boulay, Laurence. "Les Cantiques spirituels de Racine mis en musique au XVIIe siècle." *XVIIe Siècle* 34 (1957): 79–92.

Bouquet-Boyer, Marie-Thérèse. "Turin et les musiciens de la Cour 1619–1775: Vie quotidienne et production artistique." Doctoral diss., Université de Paris IV, Sorbonne, 1987.

Brenet, Michel [Marie Bobillier, pseud.]. "Bembo, La signora Antonia." In *Biographisch-Bibliographisches Quellen-Lexikon der Musiker und Musikgelehrten der christlichen Zeitrechnung bis zur Mitte des neunzehnten Jahrhunderts.* 10 vols. Ed. Robert Eitner, 1: 429. Leipzig: Breitkopf und Härtel, 1904.

———. *Notes sur l'histoire du luth en France.* Turin: Bocca Frères, 1899. Reprint, Geneva: Minkoff, 1973.

Brondi, Maria Rita. *Il liuto e la chitarra—Ricerche storiche sulla loro origine e sul loro sviluppo.* Turin: Fratelli Bocca Editori, 1926.

Brooks, Jeanice. "Catherine de Médicis, *nouvelle Artémise:* Women's Laments and the Virtue of Grief." *Early Music* 27 (1999): 419–435.

Brown, Patricia Fortini. *Private Lives in Renaissance Venice: Art, Architecture, and the Family.* New Haven: Yale University Press, 2004.

———. *Venice and Antiquity.* New Haven: Yale University Press, 1996.

Burke, Peter. *The Fabrication of Louis XIV.* New Haven: Yale University Press, 1992.

Calasso, Francesco. "Bartolo da Sassoferrato." In *Dizionario biografico degli italiani.* 35 vols. Ed. Alberto M. Ghisalberti, 6: 640–669. Rome: Istituto della Enciclopedia Italiana, 1968.

Caluori, Eleanor. *The Cantatas of Luigi Rossi.* 2 vols. Ann Arbor: UMI Research Press, 1981.

Calvoli, Giovanni Cinelli. *Biblioteca volante.* 4 vols. Venice: Albrizzi, 1747. Reprint, Bologna: Arnaldo Forni, 1979.

Campra, André. *Tancrède, tragédie mise en musique.* Paris: Christophe Ballard, 1702. Facsimile edition, Béziers: Société de Musicologie de Languedoc, 1992.

Carré, Henri. *La Duchesse de Bourgogne: Une Princesse de Savoie à la cour de Louis XIV, 1685–1712.* Paris: Librairie Hachette, 1934.

Cavalli, Francesco. *Ercole amante.* Ed. Paul O'Dette, Stephen Stubbs, and Robert Schenke. Cambridge, MA: Boston Early Music Festival, Inc., 1999.

———. *Messa concertata.* Ed. Raymond Leppard. London: Faber Music, 1966.

Cessac, Catherine. *Élisabeth Jacquet de la Guerre—Une femme compositeur sous le règne de Louis XIV.* Arles: Actes Sud, 1995.

———. *Marc-Antoine Charpentier.* Paris: Fayard, 1988.

Charpentier, Marc-Antoine. "Meslanges autographes." In *Œuvres complètes.* 2 vols. 1: 152–165. Fac-similé du manuscrit F-Pn, Rés. Vm^{1}259. Paris: Minkoff France Éditeur, 1991.

Chojnacki, Stanley. "Dowries and Kinsmen in Early Renaissance Venice." *Journal of Interdisciplinary History* 5 (1975): 571–600.

Christ, Yvan. *Les Églises parisiennes, actuelles et disparues.* Paris: Éditions "Tel," 1947.

Christout, Marie-Françoise. *Le Ballet de cour de Louis XIV, 1643–1672.* Paris: Picard, 1967.

Cicogna, Emmanuele Antonio. *Delle inscrizioni veneziane.* 7 vols. Venice: Picotti, 1824–1853.

————. *Saggio di Bibliografia veneziana*. Venice: G. B. Merlo, 1847. Reprint, Bologna: Forni Editore, 1967.

Citron, Marcia. *Gender and the Musical Canon*. Cambridge: Cambridge University Press, 1993.

Corbetta, Francesco. *La Guitarre royalle dediée au Roy, composée par Francisque Corbet*. Paris: Bonneüil, 1674. Reprint, Bologna: Forni Editore, 1983.

————. *La Guitarre royalle dediée au Roy de la Grande Bretagne composée par Francisque Corbett*. Paris: Bonneüil, 1671. Reprint, Geneva: Éditions Minkoff, 1993.

————. *Varii capricii per la ghitarra spagnuola*. Introduction by Paolo Paolini. Milan: n.p., 1643. Reprint, Florence: Studio per edizioni scelte, 1980.

Couperin, François. *Concert instrumental sous le Titre d'Apotheose [sic] Composé à la mémoire immortelle de l'incomparable Monsieur de Lully*. Paris: Boivin, 1725. Reprint, New York: Performers' Facsimiles, n.d. [2001?].

————. *Les Goûts-réünis ou Nouveaux Concerts à l'usage de toutes les sortes d'instrumens [sic] de Musique augmentés d'une grande Sonade en Trio. Intitulée Le Parnasse ou l'Apothéose de Corelli*. Paris: Boivin, 1724. Reprint, New York: Performers' Facsimiles, n.d. [2001?].

Cowan, Alexander F. "Love, Honour and the Avogaria di Comun in Early Modern Venice." *Archivio Veneto,* 5th ser., 144 (1995): 5–19.

————. "New Families in the Venetian Patriciate, 1646–1718." *Ateneo Veneto,* n.s. 23 (1985): 55–75.

Cowart, Georgia. *The Origins of Modern Musical Criticism—French and Italian Music, 1600–1750*. Ann Arbor: UMI Research Press, 1981.

Cozzi, Gaetano. *Giustizia 'contaminata'—Vicende giudiziarie di nobili ed ebrei nella Venezia del Seicento*. Venice: Fondazione Giorgio Cini, Marsilio Editori, 1996.

Croce, Benedetto. *Anedotti di varia letteratura*. 2nd ed. Bari: Laterza, 1953.

Cusick, Suzanne. *A Romanesca of One's Own: Voice, Subjectivity, and Power in Francesca Caccini's Florence*. Chicago: University of Chicago Press, forthcoming.

Da Mosto, Andrea. *L'Archivio di Stato di Venezia: Indice generale, storico, descrittivo, ed analitico*. Rome: Biblioteca d'arte editrice, 1940.

Daolmi, Davide, and Emanuele Senici. " 'L'omosessualità è un modo di cantare'— Il contributo *queer* all'indagine sull'opera in musica." *Il saggiatore musicale* 7/1 (2002): 137–178.

Dart, Thurston. "Musical Instruments in Diderot's Encyclopedia." *Galpin Society Journal* 6 (1953): 109–111.

Davis, J. C. *The Decline of the Venetian Nobility as a Ruling Class*. Baltimore: Johns Hopkins University Press, 1962.

Davis, Natalie Zemon. "Beyond the Market: Books as Gifts in Sixteenth-Century France." *Transactions of the Royal Historical Society* 33 (1983): 69–88.

————. *The Gift in Sixteenth-Century France*. Madison: University of Wisconsin Press, 2000.

Decobert, Laurence. "La Naissance du grand motet." In *Henry Du Mont à Versailles*, 21–47. Arles: Actes Sud, 1992.

Dekesel, C. E. *Charles Patin: A Man without a Country. An Annotated and Illustrated Bibliography.* Ghent: Bibliotheca Numismatica Siliciana, 1990.

Dubowy, Norbert. "Ernst August, Giannettini, und die Serenata in Venedig (1685/86)." *Analecta musicologica* 30 (1998): 167–235.

Duchartre, Pierre Louis. *The Italian Comedy.* Trans. Randolph T. Weaver. London: Harrap, 1929.

Dumolin, Maurice, and Georges Outardel. *Les Églises de France: Paris et la Seine.* Paris: Le Touzey et Ané, 1936.

Duron, Jean. "Aspects de la présence italienne dans la musique française de la fin du XVIIe siècle." In *Les Samedis musicaux du Château de Versailles—Baroque Francais, Baroque Italien au XVIIe siècle,* 43–65. Versailles: Centre de Musique Baroque, 1992.

Elliott, Charles. *Princesse of Versailles—The Life of Marie Adelaide of Savoy.* New York: Ticknor and Fields, 1992.

Favier, Thierry, and Jean-Michel Noailly, "Elisabeth-Sophie Chéron et les Psaumes." *Bulletin de la recherche sur le psautier huguenot* 12 (1996): 15–28.

Felici, Lucio, ed. *Poesia italiana del Seicento.* Milan: Aldo Garzanti, 1978.

Ferrier-Caverivière, Nicole. *L'Image de Louis XIV dans la littérature française de 1660 à 1715.* Paris: Presses Universitaires de France, 1981.

Ferro, Marco. *Dizionario del diritto comune e veneto.* 2nd ed. 2 vols. Venice: Andrea Santini e figlio, 1845.

Fidière, Octave. *Les Femmes artistes à l'Académie Royale de Peinture et de Sculpture.* Paris: Charavay, 1885.

Fischer, Axel. "Hannover." In *Die Musik in Geschichte und Gegenwart.* 10 vols. Kassel: Bärenreiter, 1996.

Fontijn, Claire. "Antonia Bembo." In *Women Composers: Music through the Ages.* 7 vols. Ed. Martha Furman Schleifer and Sylvia Glickman, 2: 201–216. New York: G. K. Hall, 1996.

———. "Antonia Bembo: 'Les goûts réunis,' Royal Patronage, and the Role of the Woman Composer during the Reign of Louis XIV." Ph.D. diss., Duke University, 1994.

———. "Antonia Padoani Bembo." Liner notes to La Donna Musicale, *The Seven Psalms of David,* vol. I. CD, 2004.

———. "Le armoniose relazioni." *Amadeus* 175 (June 2004): 28–30.

———. "Baroque Women: Antonia Bembo." *Goldberg Early Music Magazine* 6 (1999): 110–113 [Bilingual article translated into Spanish by José Luis Gil Aristu].

———. "Baroque Women: Brigida Bianchi, Comica detta Aurelia." *Goldberg Early Music Magazine* 9 (1999): 106–109.

———. "Baroque Women: Élisabeth-Sophie Chéron." *Goldberg Early Music Magazine* 13 (2001): 114–117.

———. "Baroque Women Composers." Liner notes to Bizzarrie Armoniche, *La Vendetta* CD (ORF, Austria, 2004).

————. "Epilogue/Nachwort." In Antonia Bembo, *Te Deum laudamus.* Ed. Wolfgang Fürlinger. Altötting: Musikverlag Coppenrath, 1999.

————. "In Honour of the Duchess of Burgundy: Antonia Bembo's Compositions for Marie-Adélaïde of Savoy." *Cahiers de l'Institut de recherches et d'histoire musicale des états de Savoie* 3 (Geneva: Éditions Slatkine, 1995): 45–89.

————. "The Virgin's Voice: Representations of Mary in Seventeenth-Century Italian Song." In *Maternal Measures—Figuring Caregiving in the Early Modern Period.* Ed. Naomi J. Miller and Naomi Yavneh, 135–162. Aldershot, U.K.: Ashgate, 2000.

————. "The Voice of the Virgin: Representations of Mary in Seventeenth-Century Italian Song." In *Divine Mirrors: The Virgin Mary in the Visual Arts.* Ed. Melissa R. Katz and Robert A. Orsi, 139–141. New York: Oxford University Press, 2001.

Fontijn, Claire, ed. Antonia Bembo, *Amor mio.* Bryn Mawr, PA: Hildegard, 1998.

————. Antonia Bembo, *Ha, que l'absence.* Bryn Mawr, PA: Hildegard, 1998.

————. Antonia Bembo, *Per il Natale.* Fayetteville, AR: Clar-Nan Editions, 1999.

————. Antonia Bembo, *Tota pulcra es.* Bryn Mawr, PA: Hildegard, 1998.

Fontijn, Claire, and Marinella Laini. "Bembo, Antonia." In *The New Grove Dictionary of Music and Musicians.* 29 vols. Ed. Stanley Sadie and John Tyrrell, 3: 220–221. 2nd ed. London: Macmillan, 2001.

————. "Bembo, Antonia." In *The Norton/Grove Dictionary of Women Composers.* Ed. Julie Anne Sadie and Rhian Samuel, 56–57. London: Macmillan, 1994.

Fournel, Victor. *Les Contemporains de Molière.* 3 vols. Paris: Firmin Didot, 1863–1875.

Fuller, David. "French Harpsichord Playing in the 17th Century: After Le Gallois." *Early Music* 4 (1976): 22–26.

Fumaroli, Marc. "Microcosme comique et macrocosme solaire: Molière, Louis XIV, et 'l'Impromptu de Versailles.'" *Revue des Sciences Humaines* 145 (1972): 95–114.

Fürlinger, Wolfgang, ed. Antonia Bembo, *Te Deum laudamus.* Altötting: Musikverlag Coppenrath, 1999.

Gianturco, Carolyn. "The Italian Seventeenth-Century Cantata: A Textual Approach." In *The Well-Enchanting Skill: Music, Poetry, and Drama in the Culture of the Renaissance,* Ed. John Caldwell, Edward Olleson, and Susan Wollenberg, 41–51. Oxford: Clarendon Press, 1990.

Gibson, Wendy. *Women in Seventeenth-Century France.* New York: St. Martin's Press, 1989.

Ginzburg, Carlo. *The Cheese and the Worms: The Cosmos of a Sixteenth-Century Miller.* Trans. John Tedeschi and Anne Tedeschi. Harmondsworth: Penguin, 1982. Originally published as *Il formaggio e i vermi: Il cosmo di un mugnaio del '500* (Turin: Giulio Einaudi Editore, 1976).

Glixon, Beth. "New Light on the Life and Career of Barbara Strozzi." *Musical Quarterly* 81 (1997): 311–335.

————. "More on the Life and Death of Barbara Strozzi." *Musical Quarterly* 83 (1999): 134–141.

Glover, Jane. *Cavalli.* New York: St. Martin's Press, 1978.

Gordon-Seifert, Catherine E. "Rhetoric and Expression in the Mid-Seventeenth-

Century French Air: A Rationale for Compositional Style and Performance." Paper given at the Annual Meeting of the Society for Seventeenth-Century Music, Evanston, IL, April 2005.

————. "Strong Men—Weak Women: Gender Representation and the Influence of Lully's 'Operatic Style' on French *Airs Sérieux* (1650–1700)." In *Musical Voices of Early Modern Women—Many-Headed Melodies,* Ed. Thomasin LaMay, 135–167. Aldershot, U.K.: Ashgate, 2005.

Green, M. A. Everett, F. Bickley, and F. H. B. Daniell, eds. *Great Britain, Public Record Office, Calendar of State Papers, Domestic Series.* 28 vols. London: Longmans, Green, Reader, Dyer, and Roberts, 1860–1939. Reprint, Nendeln, Liechtenstein: Kraus, 1968.

Grendler, Paul F. *Schooling in Renaissance Italy: Literacy and Learning, 1300–1600.* Baltimore: Johns Hopkins University Press, 1989.

Griffiths, Wanda, ed. *Cephale et Procris.* Recent Researches in the Music of the Baroque Era 88. Madison, WI: A-R Editions, 1998.

Guiffrey, Jules. *Comptes des bâtiments du Roi, sous le règne de Louis XIV.* Collection des documents inédits sur l'histoire de France, troisième série: Archéologie. 5 vols. Paris: Imprimerie Nationale, 1901.

Guilhermy, M. F. de, and R. de Lasteyrie. *Inscriptions de la France du Ve siècle au XVIIIe: Ancien diocèse de Paris.* 5 vols. Paris: Imprimerie Nationale, 1873–1883.

Harth, Erica. *Cartesian Women: Versions and Subversions of Rational Discourse in the Old Regime.* Ithaca, NY: Cornell University Press, 1992.

Haussonville, Gabriel-Paul-Othenin de Cléron, comte de. *La Duchesse de Bourgogne et l'alliance savoyarde sous Louis XIV.* 4 vols. Paris: Calmann-Lévy, 1898–1908.

Heller, Wendy. *Emblems of Eloquence: Opera and Women's Voices in Seventeenth-Century Venice.* Berkeley: University of California Press, 2003.

Heyer, John Hajdu. "Lully's 'Jubilate Deo,' LWV 77/16: A Stylistic Anomaly." In *Jean Baptiste Lully—Actes du colloque Saint-Germain-en-Laye/Kongreßbericht Heidelberg 1987,* Ed. Jérôme de La Gorce and Herbert Schneider, 145–154. Neue Heidelberger Studien zur Musikwissenschaft, vol. 18. Laaber: Laaber-Verlag, 1990.

Hibbert, Christopher. *Versailles.* New York: Newsweek Book Division, 1972.

Highfill, Jr., Philip H., Kalman A. Burnim, and Edward A. Langhans. *A Biographical Dictionary of Actors, Actresses, Musicians, Dancers, Managers, and Other Stage Personnel in London, 1660–1800.* 14 vols. Carbondale: Southern Illinois University Press, 1975.

Hillairet, Jacques. *Dictionnaire historique des rues de Paris.* 2 vols. Paris: Éditions de minuit, 1964.

Holzer, Robert Rau. "Music and Poetry in Seventeenth-Century Rome: Settings of the Canzonetta and Cantata Texts of Francesco Balducci, Domenico Benigni, Francesco Melosio, and Antonio Abati." Ph.D. diss., University of Pennsylvania, 1990.

Institut de l'Union Chrétienne—Maison séminaire de Poitiers. Poitiers: Chaperon, 1935.

Iversen, Erik. *The Myth of Egypt and its Hieroglyphs in European Tradition.* Copenhagen: Gec Gad, 1961. Reprint: Princeton: Princeton University Press, 1993.

Jackson, Barbara Garvey. "Musical Women of the Seventeenth and Eighteenth Centuries." In *Women and Music—A History*, 2nd ed., ed. Karin Pendle, 97–144. Bloomington: Indiana University Press, 2001.

Jacobs, Fredrika H. *Defining the Renaissance Virtuosa: Women Artists and the Language of Art History and Criticism.* Cambridge: Cambridge University Press, 1997.

Jal, Auguste, ed. *Dictionnaire critique de biographie et d'histoire.* Paris: Plon, 1867.

Jurgens, Madeleine, ed. *Documents du Minutier Central concernant l'histoire littéraire (1650–1700).* Paris: Presses Universitaires de France, 1960.

Keith, Richard. "The Guitar Cult in the Courts of Louis XIV and Charles II." *Guitar Review* 26 (June 1962): 3–9.

———. "'La Guitare Royale'—A Study of the Career and Compositions of Francesco Corbetta." *"Recherches" sur la musique française classique* 6 (1966): 73–93.

Kendrick, Robert L. *Celestial Sirens: Nuns and their Music in Early Modern Milan.* Oxford: Clarendon Press, 1996.

Kettering, Sharon. "Gift-Giving and Patronage in Early Modern France." *French History* 2 (1988): 131–151.

Kuehn, Thomas. "Some Ambiguities of Female Inheritance Ideology in the Renaissance." *Continuity and Change* 2 (1987): 11–36.

Lafontaine, Henry Cart de. *The King's Musick. A Transcript of Records Relating to Music and Musicians (1470–1700).* London: Novello, 1909.

La Fontaine, Jean de. *Œuvres complètes.* 2 vols. Paris: Bibliothèque de la Pléiade, 1958.

La Gorce, Jérôme de, and Herbert Schneider, eds. *Jean-Baptiste Lully—Actes du colloque Saint-Germain-en-Laye/Kongreßbericht Heidelberg 1987.* Neue Heidelberger Studien zur Musikwissenschaft, vol. 18. Laaber: Laaber-Verlag, 1990.

———. *Quellenstudien zu Jean-Baptiste Lully—Hommage à Lionel Sawkins.* Musikwissenschaftliche Publikationen, vol. 13. Hildesheim: Georg Olms, 1999.

Laini, Marinella. "Antonia e le altre: percorsi musicali femminili nella Venezia del Sei- Settecento." In *Ecco mormorar l'onde: la musica nel Barocco,* ed. C. de Incontrera and A. Sanini, 138–169. Monfalcone: n.p., 1995.

———. "La musica di Antonia Bembo: Un significativo apporto femminile alle relazioni musicali tra Venezia e Parigi." *Studi Musicali* 25 (1996): 255–281.

———. *La raccolta zeniana di drammi per musica veneziani della Biblioteca Nazionale Marciana, 1637–1700.* Lucca: Libreria Musicale Italiana, 1995.

———. "Le 'Produzioni Armoniche' di Antonia Bembo." Laureate thesis, Università degli studi di Pavia, 1987.

Lalande, Michel-Richard de. *Confitebor tibi Domine.* Ed. Philippe Oboussier. Sevenoaks, Kent: Novello, 1982.

———. *Super flumina Babilonis,* S. 16. Ed. Philippe Oboussier. London: Novello, 1988.

LaMay, Thomasin, ed. *Musical Voices of Early Modern Women—Many-Headed Melodies.* Aldershot, U.K.: Ashgate, 2005.

Lange, Augusta. "Disegni e documenti di Guarino Guarini." In *Guarino Guarini e l'internazionalità del Barocco.* 2 vols. Turin: Académie des Sciences de Turin, 1970.

Lathuillère, Roger. *La Préciosité: Étude historique et linguistique.* 2 vols. Geneva: Droz, 1966.

Launay, Denise. "La 'Paraphrase des Pseaumes' de Godeau et les musiciens qui l'ont illustrée." *Antoine Godeau (1605–1672): de la galanterie à la sainteté—Actes des Journées de Grasse (21–24 avril 1972):* 235–250.

Lee, Hermione. *Virginia Woolf's Nose: Essays on Biography.* Princeton: Princeton University Press, 2005.

Le Moël, Michel. "Un Foyer d'italianisme à la fin du XVIIe siècle: Nicolas Mathieu, curé de Saint-André-des-Arts." *"Recherches" sur la musique française classique* 3 (1963): 43–48.

Leppard, Raymond, ed. Francesco Cavalli, *Messa concertata.* London: Faber Music, 1966.

Leris, G. de. "Les Femmes à l'Académie de Peinture." *L'Art* (1888): 121–133.

Lesure, François. *Manuscrit Milleran: Tablature de luth française c. 1690 (Bibliothèque Nationale, Paris, Rés. 823).* Geneva: Minkoff, 1976.

Linklater, Robin. "Program Notes for *Ercole Amante.*" In *Boston Early Music Festival Catalogue,* 95–96. Cambridge, MA: Boston Early Music Festival, Inc., 1999.

Litta, Pompeo. *Famiglie celebri italiane.* 10 vols. Milan: Paolo Emilio Giusti, 1819–1883.

Lorenzani, Paolo. *Nicandro e Fileno.* Ed. Albert La France. Versailles: Éditions du Centre de Musique Baroque de Versailles, Société Française de Musicologie, 1999.

Loret, Jean. *La Muze historique.* 4 vols. Ed. Ch.-L. Livet. Paris: Daffis, 1878.

Luin, Elisabeth Jeannette. "Das künstlerische Erbe der Kurfürstin Adelaide in ihren Kindern, Enkeln und Urenkeln." In *Festgabe für seine Königliche Hoheit Kronprinz Rupprecht von Bayern,* 152–179. Munich: Verlag Bayerische Heimatforschung, 1953.

Lully, Jean-Baptiste. "Domine salvum fac regem," LWV 77/iv, in *Mottets de feu Mr. de Lully.* Reprint Edition. Béziers: Société de Musicologie de Languedoc, n.d.

———. *Proserpine.* Archivum Musicum: Musica Drammatica II. 2 vols. Florence: Studio per edizioni scelte, 1994.

Maccà, Gaetano. *Storia del territorio Vicentino.* 5 vols. Caldogno: Gio. Battista Menegatti, 1812–1816.

Maggiolo, Attilio. "Elena Lucrezia Cornaro Piscopia e le altre donne aggregate all'Accademia patavina dei Ricovrati." *Padova e la sua provincia* 24 (n.s., no. 11/12) (November–December 1978): 33–36.

Magne, Émile. *Les Fêtes en Europe au XVIIe siècle.* N.p., 1930.

Marin, Louis. *Portrait of the King.* Trans. Martha M. Houle. Minneapolis: University of Minnesota Press, 1988. Originally published as *Le Portrait du roi* (Paris: Éditions du minuit, 1981).

Mauss, Marcel. *The Gift.* New York: Norton, 1967.

Maylender, Michele. *Storia delle accademie d'Italia.* 5 vols. Bologna: Licinio Cappelli, 1926–1930.

McClary, Susan. *Feminine Endings.* Minneapolis: University of Minnesota Press, 1991.

———. *Georges Bizet, Carmen.* Cambridge Opera Handbooks. Cambridge: Cambridge University Press, 1992.

Mendelsohn, Leatrice. *Paragoni: Benedetto Varchi's Due Lezzioni and Cinquecento Art Theory.* Ann Arbor: UMI Research Press, 1982.

Mirimonde, Albert Pomme de. "Portraits de musiciens et concerts dans l'École

Française dans les collections nationales [xve–xvie–xviie siècles]," *La Revue du Louvre et des musées de France* 15e année, no. 4–5 (1965): 209–228.

Misch, Conrad, ed. Antonia Bembo, *Exaudiat te Dominus*. Kassel: Furore Verlag, 2003.

———. Antonia Bembo, *Les sept Psaumes de David*. 7 vols. Kassel: Furore Verlag, 2003.

———. Antonia Bembo, *Te Deum laudamus*. Kassel: Furore Verlag, 2003.

Mitford, Nancy. *The Sun King*. New York: Harper and Row, 1966.

Molmenti, Pompeo. *La storia di Venezia nella vita privata*. 6th ed. 3 vols. Bergamo: Istituto italiano d'artigrafia, 1925.

Monson, Craig A. *Disembodied Voices: Music and Culture in an Early Modern Italian Convent*. Berkeley: University of California Press, 1995.

Montagnier, Jean-Paul C. "Modèles chorégraphiques dans les grands et petits motets français." In *Le Mouvement en musique à l'époque baroque,* ed. Hervé Lacombe, 141–156. Metz: Éditions Serpenoise, 1996.

———. "Le *Te Deum* en France à l'époque baroque—Un emblème royal." *Revue de Musicologie* 84 (1998): 199–233.

Montagnier, Jean-Paul C., ed. *Charpentier, Te Deum, H. 146*. London: Ernst Eulenburg, 1996.

Morteani, Luigi. *Storia di Montona*. Trieste: Tipo-Litografia Leghissa, 1963.

Néraudau, Jean-Pierre. *L'Olympe du Roi-Soleil—Mythologie et idéologie royale au Grand Siècle*. Paris: Société d'Édition "Les Belles Lettres," 1986.

Noël, Bernard, ed. *Les Souvenirs de Madame de Caylus*. N.p.: Mercure de France, 1965.

Norwich, John Julius. *A History of Venice*. New York: Vintage Books, 1989.

Nouvelle biographie générale. 46 vols. Paris: Firmin Didot Frères, 1863. Reprint, Copenhagen: Rosenkilde et Bagger, 1968.

Ogilby, John. *The Fables of Aesop*. 1668. Introduction by Earl Miner. Reprint, Los Angeles: William Andrews Clark Memorial Library, University of California, 1965.

Olivier, Eugène, Georges Hermal, and Robert de Roton. *Manuel de l'amateur de reliures armoriées françaises*. 29 vols. Paris: Charles Bosse, 1924–1935.

Ossi, Massimo, trans. "Libretto for *Ercole Amante*." *Boston Early Music Festival Catalogue,* 103–149. Cambridge, MA: Boston Early Music Festival, Inc., 1999.

Pancrazi, Pietro. *L'Esopo moderno*. Florence: E. Ariani, 1930.

Pandolfi, Vito. *La commedia dell'arte: storia e testi*. 6 vols. Florence: Sansoni Antiquariato, 1957–1961.

Paolini, Paolo. "Preface." *Francesco Corbetta, Varii capricii per la ghittara spagnuola*. Milan, 1643. Facsimile edition, Florence: Studio per edizioni scelte, 1980.

Park, Katharine, and Lorraine Daston. *Wonders and the Order of Nature, 1150–1750*. New York: Zone Books, 1998.

Pasquale, Marco di. "Corbetta, Francesco." In *Dizionario enciclopedico universale della musica e dei musicisti. Le Biografie,* ed. Alberto Basso, 314. Torino: UTET, 1985.

Paton, John Glenn, ed. *Italian Arias of the Baroque and Classical Eras*. Van Nuys, CA: Alfred, 1994.

Pendle, Karin, ed. *Women in Music—A History*. 2nd ed. Bloomington: Indiana University Press, 2001.

Perella, Lisa. "Bénigne de Bacilly and the *Recueil des plus beaux vers, qui ont esté mis en chant* of 1661." In *Music and the Cultures of Print*, ed. Kate van Orden, 239–270. New York: Garland, 2000.

Perti, Giacomo Antonio. *Cantate morali, e spirituali*. Bologna: Giacomo Monti, 1688. Reprint, Bologna: Arnaldo Forni, 1990.

Petit Larousse illustré. Paris: Larousse, 1976.

Pinnell, Richard T. *Francesco Corbetta and the Baroque Guitar*. 2 vols. Ann Arbor: UMI Research Press, 1980.

Preto, Paolo. *Venezia e i Turchi*. Florence: G. C. Sansoni, 1975.

———. "Venezia e la difesa dei Turchi nel Seicento." *Römische historische Mitteilungen* 26 (1984): 289–302.

———. *Venezia e la difesa del Levante, da Lepanto a Candia 1570–1670*. Venice: Arsenale Editrice, 1986.

Prunières, Henry. *Cavalli et l'opéra vénitien au XVIIe siècle*. Paris: Rieder, 1931.

———. *L'Opéra italien en France avant Lulli*. Paris: Honoré Champion, 1913.

Ranum, Orest. *Artisans of Glory: Writers and Historical Thought in Seventeenth-Century France*. Chapel Hill: University of North Carolina Press, 1980.

Ranum, Patricia M. *Méthode de la prononciation latine dite 'vulgaire' ou 'à la française.'* Arles: Actes Sud, 1991.

Rasi, Luigi. *I comici italiani: Biografia, bibliografia, iconografia*. 3 vols. Florence: Bocca, 1897.

Ravaisson, Felix. *Archives de la Bastille, Règne de Louis XIV*. Paris: A. Durand et Pedone-Lauriel, 1874.

Robert-Dumesnil, A. P.-F. *Le Peintre-Graveur français ou Catalogue Raisonné des Estampes, gravées par les peintres et les dessinateurs de l'École Française*. 11 vols. Paris: Gabriel Warée, 1835–1871.

Rokseth, Yvonne. "Antonia Bembo, Composer to Louis XIV." *Musical Quarterly* 23 (1937): 147–169.

Rollin, Monique. "La Musique de ballet dans les tablatures de luth: Souvenir et source d'inspiration." *Cahiers de l'Institut de recherches et d'histoire musicale des états de Savoie* 1 (1992): 53–75.

Romanin, S. *Storia documentata di Venezia*. 10 vols. Venice: Pietro Naratovich, 1853–1861.

Rosand, Ellen. "Aria in the Early Operas of Francesco Cavalli." Ph.D. diss., New York University, 1971.

———. *Opera in Seventeenth-Century Venice: The Creation of a Genre*. Berkeley: University of California Press, 1991.

Rosand, Ellen, ed. *Cantatas by Barbara Strozzi, 1619–c. 1664*. The Italian Cantata in the Seventeenth Century, vol. 5., ed. Carolyn Gianturco. New York: Garland, 1986.

Rose, Gloria. "The Italian Cantata of the Baroque Period." In *Gattungen der Musik in Einzeldarstellungen, Gedenkschrift Leo Schrade*, ed. Wulf Arlt, Ernst Lichtenhahn, Hans Oesch, and Max Haas, 655–677. Bern: Francke Verlag, 1973.

Rossetti, Lucia. *Acta nationis germanicae artistarum (1616–1636)*. Padua: Editrice Antenore, 1967.

Sadie, Julie Anne. "Paris and Versailles." In *The Late Baroque Era: From the 1680s to 1740*, ed. George J. Buelow, 129–189. Music and Society Series. Englewood Cliffs, NJ: Prentice Hall, 1993.

Saint-Arroman, Jean. *L'Interprétation de la musique française 1661–1789. I. Dictionnaire d'interprétation (Initiation).* Paris: Honoré Champion, 1983.

Sand, Maurice. *Masques et bouffons (Comédie Italienne).* Paris: M. Lévy, 1860.

Sansovino, Francesco. *Venetia città nobilissima et singolare, descritta in XIIII libri, con aggiunta da D. Giustiniano Martinioni.* 14 vols. Venice: Steffano Curti, 1663. Reprint, Venice: Filippi, 1968.

Saunders, Harris. "The Repertoire of a Venetian Opera House (1675–1714): The Teatro Grimani di San Giovanni Grisostomo." Ph.D. diss., Harvard University, 1985.

Sawkins, Lionel H. "Chronology and Evolution of the *grand motet* at the Court of Louis XIV: Evidence from the *Livres du Roi* and the Works of Perrin, the *sous-maîtres* and Lully." In *Jean-Baptiste Lully and the Music of the French Baroque: Essays in Honor of James R. Anthony*, ed. John Hajdu Heyer, 41–79. Cambridge: Cambridge University Press, 1989.

———. "Lully's Motets: Source, Edition and Performance." In *Jean Baptiste Lully—Actes du colloque Saint-Germain-en-Laye/Kongreßbericht Heidelberg 1987*, ed. Jérôme de La Gorce and Herbert Schneider, 145–154. Neue Heidelberger Studien zur Musikwissenschaft, vol. 18. Laaber: Laaber-Verlag, 1990.

Schnapper, Antoine. *Le Géant, la licorne, la tulipe—collections françaises au XVIIe siècle.* Paris: Flammarion, 1988.

Scott, Virginia. *The Commedia dell'Arte in Paris, 1644–1697.* Charlottesville: University of Virginia Press, 1990.

Scribe, G. [Tommaso Belgrano, pseud.]. "Aurelia comica." *Caffaro*, 28 March 1886.

Selfridge-Field, Eleanor. *Pallade Veneta: Writings on Music in Venetian Society, 1650–1750.* Venice: Fondazione Levi, 1985.

Seznec, Jean. *La Survivance des dieux antiques. Essai sur le rôle de la tradition mythologique dans l'humanisme et dans l'art de la Renaissance.* Paris: Flammarion, 1993.

Shepard, Odell. *The Lore of the Unicorn.* Boston: Houghton Mifflin, 1930.

Silin, Charles I. *Benserade and his Ballets de Cour.* Baltimore: Johns Hopkins University Press, 1940.

Spitzer, John, and Neal Zaslaw. *The Birth of the Orchestra—History of an Institution, 1650–1815.* Oxford: Oxford University Press, 2004.

Strozzi, Barbara. *Diporti di Euterpe overo cantate e ariette a voce sola di Barbara Strozzi Opera Settima.* Venice: Francesco Magni, 1659. Reprinted with commentary by Piero Mioli. *Archivum Musicum: La cantata barocca* 3. Florence: Studio per edizioni scelte, 1980.

———. *Diporti di Euterpe overo cantate e ariette a voce sola di Barbara Strozzi Opera Settima.* Venice: Francesco Magni, 1659. Reprint, with introduction by Ellen Rosand, in the series *The Italian Cantata in the Seventeenth Century* 5, ed. Carolyn Gianturco. 16 vols. New York: Garland, 1987.

Symcox, Geoffrey. *Victor Amadeus II: Absolutism in the Savoyard State, 1675–1730.* Berkeley: University of California Press, 1983.

Talbot, Michael. *Benedetto Vinaccesi: A Musician in Brescia and Venice in the Age of Corelli.* Oxford: Clarendon Press, 1994.

———. "The Serenata in Eighteenth-Century Venice." *Research Chronicle of the Royal Musical Association* 18 (1982): 1–50.

———. "Vivaldi and a French Ambassador." *Informazioni e studi vivaldiani* 2 (1981): 31–41.

Thieme, Ulrich, ed. *Allgemeines Lexikon der bildenden Künstler.* 37 vols. Leipzig: Seemann, 1912.

Timms, Colin. "Brigida Bianchi's *Poesie Musicali* and Their Settings." *I quaderni della civica scuola di musica,* numero speciale dedicato a "La cantata da camera nel barocco italiano" 19–20 (December 1990): 19–37.

Titon du Tillet, Évrard. *Le Parnasse françois.* Paris: J. B. Coignard fils, 1732. Reprint, Geneva: Slatkine, 1971.

Tollini, Frederick Paul. *Scene Design at the Court of Louis XIV—The Work of the Vigarani Family and Jean Bérain.* Studies in Theatre Arts, Vol. 22. Lewiston, NY: Edwin Mellen Press, 2003.

Tomlinson, Gary. "Music and the Claims of Text." *Critical Inquiry* 8 (1981–1982): 565–589.

Touring Club Italiano. *Guida d'Italia: Veneto (esclusa Venezia).* 6th ed. Milan: Touring Club Italiano, 1992.

Tramontin, Silvio. "Ordini e congregazioni religiose." In *Storia della cultura veneta: Il Seicento,* ed. Girolamo Arnaldi and Manlio Pastore Stocchi, 23–60. Vicenza: Neri Pozza Editore, 1983–1984.

Turnbull, Michael. "Ercole and Hercule: les goûts désunis?" *Musical Times* 121 (1980): 303, 305–307.

Tyler, James, and Paul Sparks. *The Guitar and its Music: From the Renaissance to the Classical Era.* Oxford: Oxford University Press, 2002.

Valeri, Diego. *L'Accademia dei Ricovrati alias Accademia Patavina di Scienze Lettere ed Arti.* Padua: La sede dell'Accademia, 1987.

Van Orden, Kate, ed. *Music and the Cultures of Print.* New York: Garland, 2000.

Verlet, Pierre. *Le Château de Versailles.* Paris: Fayard, 1985.

Vogl, Emil. "Die Angelika und ihre Musik." *Hudební věda* 4 (1974): 356–368.

Watts, Derek A., ed. *Hercule mourant (1630–1634),* by Jean Rotrou. Textes littéraires II, ed. Keith Cameron. Exeter: University of Exeter, 1971.

Weiss, Piero. "Teorie drammatiche e 'Infranciosamento': Motivi della 'Riforma' melodrammatica nel primo Settecento." In *Antonio Vivaldi, teatro musicale, cultura e società* 1: 273–296. Florence: L. S. Olschki, 1982.

Zanger, Abby E. *Scenes from the Marriage of Louis XIV: Nuptial Fictions and the Making of Absolutist Power.* Stanford, CA: Stanford University Press, 1997.

Zapperi, Ada. "Bianchi, Brigida," In *Dizionario biografico degli Italiani,* ed. Alberto M. Ghisalberti, 10: 71–72. 35 vols. Rome: Istituto della Enciclopedia Italiana, 1968.

INDEX

Abeille, Pierre-César, 224
Académie de Peinture et de Sculpture.
 See Chéron, Élisabeth-Sophie
Académie Royale de Musique, 266
Academy of the Erranti, Brescia. *See*
 Corbetta, Francesco
Academy of the Ricovrati, Padua, 33, 216,
 220–221, 223 n.34
 and Galileo Galilei, 221
 See also Chéron, Élisabeth-Sophie;
 Frigimelica Roberti, Count
 Girolamo (doctor); Patin,
 Charles; Vertron, Claude-
 Charles Guyonnet de
Adélaïde of Bavaria, 135
Aesop, 19
aesthetics. *See goûts réunis* ("the united
 tastes"), *les*
air, 113, 123
 air de cour, 122
 air sérieux, 122, 232
 air sérieux et à boire, 122
Amtman, Franz Christoph, 67
animals
 basilisk, 112–113, 122, 131
 lynx, 113, 131
 mole, 113
 monsters, 97, 131
Anna Medici, Archduchess of Austria, 18
 n.27
Anne, Queen of England, 54
Anne of Austria, 54, 56, 58, 61–64, 77–78,
 186, 221, 239

antiphony, 92, 139, 156, 160, 165, 169, 171,
 173, 175, 202, 212
Apollo, 136, 151. *See also* Louis XIV, as
 Apollo
Apollodorus, 243
Argentville, Antoine-Joseph Dézallier d',
 219 n.17, 223
aria, 109–112, 118–119, 131, 176, 248, 250,
 252–253, 262
 allegra/allegro, 119
 à mesura giusta . . . con furia, 263
 à tempo con sdegno, 263
 binary, 110, 116–117, 119
 da capo, 110, 116–117
 dispettosa, 263
 refrain, 110, 113, 115, 122–123
 sdegnosa, 263
 sectional, 110–111
 spiritosa, 108
 violente, 108
arietta, 110, 113 n.24
arioso, 102, 105, 110, 130, 248, 253–254
Arlequin. *See* Biancolelli, Domenico
Arran, Richard Butler, Earl of, 56
Aurelia. *See* Fedeli, Brigida
autobiography, 3, 13

Bacilly, Bénigne de, 225 n.41, 239 n.47
Bailly, Mathieu, 70–71, 78–79
Balbi, Marcella Bembo, 34
Balbi, Marco, 36
Balbi, Palazzo, 18, 23
Balbi, Zan Francesco, 16, 25

Ballard, Christophe, 122–123, 127, 224
ballet. *See* dance
Banducci, Antonia, 4
baptism, 15–16, 32
Barre, family de La, 62
Bartolo and Baldo, 21
basso buffo, 249
basso continuo (b.c.), 8, 81, 98, 102, 112,
    116–117, 119–121, 125, 127, 129,
    139, 145–146, 158, 160, 168, 183,
    187, 196, 200–202, 204, 224, 229,
    253, 256–258, 267
    basso ostinato and, 105, 111, 113,
      116–117, 255, 259–260, 262
    figured bass and, 181, 191, 197, 199,
      208, 248, 254
    solo music for, 147, 173
    tag, function of, 144, 147, 156, 201, 228,
      231, 251, 263
    walking bass and, 105, 127
    See also *petite basse*
bassoon, 186–191, 211, 248, 264
Bataille, Gabriel, 224
Beauty (allegorical character), 270–271
Bembo, Alvise, 25 n.43
Bembo, Andrea (1593–1658), 24–25, 29,
    34, 35 n.83, 70
Bembo, Andrea Giacomo (1665–1710),
    16 n.18, 32–33, 34 n.79, 36, 52,
    70, 73, 214, 223
Bembo, Angelo Maria, 75 n.106
Bembo, Antonia Padoani
    autobiography of, 3–4, 13, 85, 93, 102,
      182, 213–214
    autograph of, 71
    childhood of, 3, 15–22
    compositions of, 3–6, 8–9, 58, 81 (*see
      also by manuscript name*)
    education of, 16–17, 20, 23, 214, 262
    epilepsy of, 22, 24
    French career of, 7–9, 13, 58, 75
    inheritance and, 31, 40, 44, 70–75, 78
    jewelry of, 29, 37, 39–40, 42–53, 69, 80
    letters of, 3–4, 13, 42–45, 48
    marriage and, 5–6, 22, 24, 27–31,
      36–41, 50–51, 71
    meter, use of
      change of, 113, 120, 126, 147, 156,
        210, 224, 228, 230–234, 254, 257
      displacement of accent within, 227,
        258
      insertion of common time and, 268
      inversion of, 113–114, 119

    as music teacher, 81
    noble status of, 3–4, 13, 27, 31–32
    as poet, 118
    patronage of, 61–62, 76, 96, 102, 176
    pregnancy of, 37
    residences of, 3–4, 13
    rhythmic tendencies of, 230
    spinet of, 40
    stretto procedure of, 144, 147, 149
    style of, 6–7, 9, 258
    voice of, 6, 9, 20–23, 41, 50, 81, 85, 87,
      97–98, 100, 102, 119, 131, 182,
      273–275
    voyage to Paris of, 40–42
Bembo, Antonio, 25, 29, 35, 38, 46
    Nanto and, 73–75
    Saint Anthony of Padua, Nanto, church
      of, 75
Bembo, Bernardo, 33–34, 38, 70, 72–73,
    75, 180
    Ospedale della Pietà and, 52–53
Bembo, Bianca, 25
Bembo, Diana, 32, 36, 39–40, 43–48,
    50–51, 53, 67, 70–71, 75
    marriage of, 69, 73
Bembo, Faustina Briani, 24–25
Bembo, Giacomo, 32, 34–36, 70–71, 73,
    75
Bembo, Girolamo, 14, 25, 27
Bembo, Illuminata, 25–26
Bembo, Isabetta Priuli, 52, 73
Bembo, Laura Querini, 25, 29, 38
Bembo, Leone, 27
Bembo, Lorenzo (1527–1570), 27 n.46
Bembo, Lorenzo (1637–1703), 8, 24–30,
    34–40, 43–44, 46–47, 49–52, 72,
    74–75
    Calle del Forno (Cà Bembo), 53, 72–73
    crime and punishment of, 37, 67–70
    post-traumatic stress and, 39
Bembo, Lorenzo (1687–bef. 1716), 52
Bembo, Marc'Antonio, 28 n.52
Bembo, Nicolo (1658–1683), 25, 29, 35,
    38, 74
Bembo, Nicolo (1689–bef. 1716), 52, 74
Bembo, Orseta Corner, 25, 28, 39
    Nanto (Bosco di Nanto), 28–30, 35,
      72–75
Bembo, Pellegrina Priuli, 73, 75
Bembo, Piero (1603–after 1652), 25, 29, 33
Bembo, Cardinal Pietro (1470–1547),
    25–27
    genealogy and, 26

Bembo, Zan Mattio (1491–1570), 27, 53
Bembo, Zan Mattio (1551–1627), 25 n.42
Bembo, Zan Mattio (?–1668), 25, 28,
    30 n.58, 35
Bembo, Zan Mattio (1653–1740), 25, 29,
    35, 38, 46–47, 53, 74
Bembo-Boldù, Palazzo, 26
Benserade, Isaac de, 94, 245
Bergerotti, Anna, 61–62
Bernabei, Giuseppe Antonio, 64
Bernier, Nicolas, 126
Berry, Charles, Duke of, 167
Berthelot, François, 76–77
Bessi, Diana Bembo. See Bembo, Diana
Bessi, Iseppo, 52, 69
Bessi, Regina, 75
Bianchi, Brigida. See Fedeli, Brigida
Bianchi, Marc'Antonio, 59
Biancolelli, Domenico, 66
Biancolelli, Françoise, 66, 80
Biancolelli, Orsola Cortesi, 66
Bizzarrie Armoniche, 239–240
Boldù, Scipion, 30 n.61
Borromeo, Alessandro, 24 n.40
Bortoleti, Bortolo, 68
Bosso, Antonio, 17, 20–22, 24
Bourgogne, Hôtel de, 242. See also Italian
    Community in Paris
Bourgogne, Théâtre de. See Italian Com-
    munity in Paris
Bousset, Jean-Baptiste Drouart de, 224
Bouzignac, Guillaume, 186
Bovolenta, 72–73
Braunschweig-Lüneburg, Dukes of, 23
Brenet, Michel, 5
Briani, Marina, 29, 39
Briani, Zambattista, 25 n.42
Brittany, Duke of (b. 1704), 9, 133–134,
    137, 150–180, 182
Brittany, Duke of (b. 1707), 181–182, 213
Burgundy, Louis, Duke of, 85, 127–131,
    133–135
    portrait of, 168
Burgundy, Marie-Adélaïde of Savoy,
    Duchess of, 127–131, 133–180,
    249, 275
    agency of, 136, 177–178
    coat of arms of, 138
    as dancer, 136
    as dedicatee, 7, 9, 76, 85, 94, 127–131,
        133
    household of, 179, 239
    as mother, 9, 136, 139, 178

as peace-maker, 9, 128–130, 135, 178
    portraits of, 161, 168
    Turin and, 127, 135
Burke, Peter, 182, 273
Buterne, Jean-Baptiste, 151, 154
Buti, Francesco, 10, 64, 241, 243, 245,
    247, 249–250, 253, 267 n.44,
    270–272

Cà Bembo (Palazzo Bembo-Boldù, Santa
    Maria Nova), 26–27, 38, 46, 53,
    72–73, 75. See also Bembo,
    Lorenzo (1637–1703), Calle del
    Forno (Cà Bembo)
Caccini, Francesca, 7
Caignet, Denis, 224
Calisto, masque, 57
Calvinism. See spirituality, Christianity
    and
Cambefort, Jean de, 224
Campana, Abbess Isabella, 42–45
Campra, André, 136, 247–248, 269–270,
    272
Candia (Crete), War of, 34–39
    Iraklion, 35–36
    See also Greece
Canossa, Luigi and Orazio, 61
cantata, 87, 89, 92–94, 99–102, 110, 118,
    127–131, 135, 139, 182, 204
    cantate spirituali, 81, 103–110, 114, 131
cantiques spirituels, 79, 81, 109, 223–224,
    239
Capona, Lugrezia, 32
Carissimi, Giacomo 142
Cavalli, Francesco, 5–7, 16–18, 64, 142,
    173, 247
    legacy of, 10, 247, 272, 274–275
    L'Ercole amante, 8–9, 64, 184, 244–247,
        255, 258, 260–263, 266, 269–272
    as teacher, 16–17, 20, 21 n.31, 23, 85,
        240–241, 262
    Xerse, 245
Cavalli, Giovanni, 34
Cavalli, Maria, 18
Cavarzere, 72–73
census, 15, 18, 23
Champaigne, Philippe de, 56
Charles II, King of England, 54–56, 62
Charpentier, Marc-Antoine, 9, 127,
    139–140, 142, 212, 274
    Exaudiat te, Dominus, "Precatio pro
        Rege," H. 165, 205–206
    Te Deum, H. 146, 142–150

Chaumont, Saint, Bishop of Lyon, 76
Chéron, Élisabeth-Sophie, 9, 81, 212–240
  and Académie de Peinture et de Sculp-
    ture, 217–218, 220
  and Academy of the Ricovrati, Padua,
    33, 216, 220
  as musician, 216, 218–220, 222
  as poet (Erato), 216–217, 220–221, 225
  portrait of, 217
  Saint Sulpice and, 9
  salon of, 9, 215–223, 239
Chéron, Henry, 216
Chéron, Louis, 216, 219–220, 223, 226
chiaroscuro, 88
Chiesa, Elisabetta Giulia della, 60
chorus, 137, 144, 150–151, 154, 157,
    160–161, 168–169, 175, 181,
    192–193, 204, 210, 248, 263
  chœur de symphonie, 186–191, 198–199,
    202, 248
  chœur de voix, 188–191, 197–199
  Chorus for the Seven Planets, 248
  Chorus of Breezes and Brooks, 255
  Chorus of Graces, 160–161, 163–165,
    249, 275
  Chorus of Infernal Spirits, 263
  Chorus of Planets, 269–272
  Chorus of Stars, 272
  cori spezzati, 269
  grand chœur, 186, 194
  petit chœur, 186
chromaticism, 146–147, 184, 257, 260, 262
Cicogna, Emmanuele Antonio, 14 n.7, 39,
    42, 50–51
Cinelli Calvoli, Giovanni, 14
Cintio. See Romagnesi, Marc'Antonio
cittadino, 6, 13–14, 27, 52, 69
Clytie (Clizia), 87–90, 104, 114, 131
Colbert, Jean-Baptiste, 66 n.77
Collasse, Pascal, 224
Collegio Clementino, Rome, 60
Comédie Italienne. See Italian Community
    in Paris
commedia dell'arte, 56, 58, 62, 65 n.72
Condanati, Jail of the. See Bembo,
    Lorenzo (1637–1703), crime and
    punishment of
convents, 7
Corbetta, Francesco, 5, 7, 13, 16, 21–22,
    39
  Academy of the Erranti, Brescia, and,
    22, 24 n.39
  as guitarist, 22, 24, 40–41, 54, 56–57, 89

"il Capriccioso," 22–24
La Guitarre royalle and, 23 n.35, 54, 56,
    59, 62
London and, 55–57, 62
Mantua and, 24, 61
Paris and, 23, 40–42, 53–54, 57–59,
    88–89, 218
portrait of, 55
as teacher, 54, 154
See also Braunschweig-Lüneburg,
    Dukes of
Corelli, Arcangelo, 124, 127, 185, 208, 264
Corner, Lorenzo, 35
cosmos, 81, 92, 169, 176
  geography and the, 94, 116–117,
    130–131, 246, 269
  solar system and the, 92, 94, 97, 99–100,
    102, 117, 131, 136, 237, 271
Couperin, François, 9, 127, 135–136, 208,
    210, 264
  L'Apotheose . . . de Lully (1725), 183–186,
    256
  Les Goûts-réünis (1724) 124, 183–186,
    256, 264
  See also goûts réunis ("the united tastes"),
    les
Couperin, Louise, 136, 154
Croix, Ursule and Jeanne de la, 219
Cupid (Amor, Amorino), 136, 151, 160,
    167–168, 253, 259–260, 262, 275
custos, 162, 173

dames pensionnaires, 77–81
dance, 168–169, 178, 210, 264, 270, 272
  Académie royale de danse, 165
  ballet, 183–186, 210, 245–246, 256, 274
  bourrée, 266
  danza, 266
  gigue, 164, 173, 175, 266, 269–270, 272
  menuet, 164, 166–168, 196, 266, 269
Dangeau, Philippe de Courcillon, Marquis
    de, 137
Decobert, Laurence, 187
Dedalus, 91
descant, 208, 232
Descosteaux, René Pignon, 154, 175
Desportes, Philippe, 224
dessus, 95, 97, 129, 148, 175, 186, 194, 196,
    198, 201, 224, 226, 231, 235–239,
    248, 253–258, 265–266, 269–270
Destouches, André Cardinal, 136
Divertimento (F-Pn, Rés. Vm¹113), 6, 9,
    128, 133–134, 136, 139, 150–180,

194, 213, 237, 248–249, 266, 269–270, 275
divorce, 37–38, 53
Domenichino, 215
Donghella, Theresia, 32
Donna Musicale, La, 228, 239 n.46
Dornel, Antoine, 173
dowry, 27–30, 38 n.93, 44 n.2, 73–76
drum, 218
Du Mont, Henry, 126, 186–187, 224
Durac, 35–36
Duron, Jean, 139, 265 n.43
durus, 146

Edict of Nantes, 97
education of women, 6, 17, 20, 33 n.72, 51, 69, 75, 77–81
Egypt, 101 n.9, 131, 182, 263
Eick, Giusto van, 37 n.92
emblem of lament. *See* tetrachord, descending, as emblem of lament
encomium, 9, 93–103, 110, 128, 134, 158, 182, 204, 271, 273
epithalamium, 128, 130. See also *Produzioni armoniche*, wedding music of (nos. 13–14, 35)
Erato. *See* Chéron, Élisabeth-Sophie
L'Ercole amante, Cavalli. *See* Cavalli, Francesco
L'Ercole amante (F-Pn, Rés. Vm⁴9–10), Bembo, 5–6, 9, 81, 180, 213–214, 237, 241–272, 275, CD tr. 10
  coat of arms of, 272
Eularia. *See* Biancolelli, Orsola Cortesi
Exaudiat te, Dominus (F-Pn, Rés. Vm¹115), 6, 9, 81, 96, 126, 180–183, 203–213, 225–226
Expilly, Gabriel, 187

Fabris, Tomaso, 178 n.31
Fame (allegorical character), 150, 158
Favier, Thierry, 224
Fedeli, Aurelia. *See* Fedeli, Brigida
Fedeli, Brigida, 54, 56, 58–63, 66, 139, 239
  beauty of, 65 n.74
  musicianship of, 65–66
  poetry of, 63–64, 110, 113, 121–122
  stage career of, 62–64, 121
feminism, 274–275
femmes illustres, 218, 222
femmes savantes, 218
Ferdinand III of Austria, Holy Roman Emperor, 18 n.27

Ferdinand Karl, Archduke of Austria-Tyrol (Ferdinando Carlo d'Austria), 18 n.27
Ferdinand Maria, Elector of Bavaria, 135
Fermel'huis, Jean-Baptiste, 217–218
Ferrand, Louis, 205–206
Ferro, Marc'Antonio, 37
Filles de l'Union Chrétienne. *See* Union Chrétienne ("grand Saint Chaumond")
Fiorilli, Tiberio (Scaramouche), 54, 61, 63
Flora, 136
flute, 104, 175, 186, 190–191, 195, 211, 224–225, 228, 230, 235, 238, 248, 263–265
  flute quartet, 265 n.43
  flute trio, 196, 211, 248, 265
  recorder and, 265
Fontaine, Jean de La. *See* La Fontaine, Jean de
Fontaine, Joseph-Antoine Hennequin de Charmont, French Ambassador, 177
Fonte, Moderata, 17 n.23
Fontego dei Tedeschi, 31, 67–70
Forestier, Barbara Riccioni. *See* Riccioni Forestier, Barbara
Formé, Nicolas, 186
Forqueray, Antoine, 154
French overture, 247–249
Frigimelica Roberti, Count Girolamo (doctor), 14, 24 n.40, 32–33
  and the Academy of the Ricovrati, Padua, 222–223
Frigimelica Roberti, Girolamo (librettist), 33
Fürlinger, Wolfgang, 190, 197–199

Gaillardie, Mathieu-Antoine, 70–71, 80
Galanterie du temps, La. See Lully, Jean-Baptiste
Gandiner, Antonio, 52
Gatti, Theobaldo di, 247, 272
Giacomoni, Isabetta, 15 n.15
Gianturco, Carolyn, 110 n. 19, 121
Glixon, Beth, 5, 15 n.13, 17 n.22, 24 n.38, 35 n.82, 36 n.88, 37 n.92, 40 n.101
Glixon, Jonathan, 37 n.91, 40 n.101
Glory (allegorical character), 150, 157–158
Glover, Jane, 10 n.14, 18 n.26, 21 n.31
Gobert, Thomas, 187, 224
Godeau, Antoine, Bishop of Vence, 223

Gonzaga, Carlo II, Duke of Mantua, 7,
    16–17, 20–21, 24, 61–62
music and, 23
Gonzaga, Ferdinando Carlo, Duke of
    Mantua, 61
Gonzaga, Giulio Cesare, 18–21
Gonzaga, Isabella Clara, Archduchess of
    Austria and of Mantua, 17, 61 n.57
Gonzaga, Maria, 22
goûts réunis ("the united tastes"), les, 9,
    124, 128, 131–132, 136, 183–186,
    202–203, 212, 242, 247, 256, 264,
    273–275
    aesthetics and, 247, 274
    French style, 142, 183–186, 202–203,
        210–212, 224–225, 230, 235,
        256–258, 264–265
    Italian style, 142, 183–186, 191,
        202–203, 207–208, 210–212,
        224–225, 255, 258, 260, 264
Gouy, Jacques de, 224
Gozzi, Maria Giordana, 43, 45–46, 52, 71
Graces, Three, 136, 168–169, 173, 175,
    263. See also chorus, Chorus of
    Graces
Grammont, Count (Anthony Hamilton),
    54, 56, 62
grand motet, 9, 139, 143, 181–204, 206, 208,
    211–212, 224, 248, 264
Greece, 81, 131
    Crete, 34–36
    Delos, 95, 131
    Juno and, 249–255, 262–263, 266–267,
        274–275
    Lorenzo Bembo in, 37, 39
    mythology of, 93–94, 97, 132, 176
    Olympus and, 91
    Venus and, 160–162, 249–252, 259, 262,
        275.
    War of Candia, 34
Grego, Zorzi, 36
Grigis, Cattarina, 15
Grimani, Fiorenza, 20–21
Guerre des Bouffons, 185, 274

H., Mademoiselle, 123–124
Halil, Pasha, 35
haute-contre, 129, 139, 150–151, 160, 173,
    186, 190, 197, 201, 248, 255,
    268–269
Heinz, Joseph, 31
Hell, 259–260, 263
Henri IV, King of France, 135

Henri de Cinq Mars, 105
Henrietta, Duchess of Orleans,
    "Madame," 56, 59, 62, 77, 167,
    218–219
Henry, Duke of Gloucester, 54
Hercules, 135, 241–272. See also Louis
    XIV, as Hercules ("Hercule
    Gaulois")
Hizzel, Anna, 67–68
homophony, 144–145, 195, 198–199, 210,
    228, 230, 232, 238, 248, 254
homosexuality, 105
Horace, 160
Hôtel des Invalides, 76
Hôtel Saint Chaumond. See Notre Dame
    de Bonne Nouvelle
Hotteterre, Jacques Martin, "Le Romain,"
    173
humility, 93, 98, 100, 102, 127, 133–134,
    204, 214–215, 252, 273–274

Iardins, Mademoiselle des. See Villedieu
    (Marie-Catherine Desjardins),
    Madame de
Icarus, 91, 93, 100–101, 131
improvisation, 64, 112, 119, 148, 264
Incogniti, Academy of the, 7, 105
intermarriage, 27, 32
Inverardi, Cattarina, 178 n.31
Isabelle. See Biancolelli, Françoise
Istria
    Capodistria, 15 n.11
    Montona (Motovun), 14–16 (see also
        Padoani, Giacomo)
Italian Community in Paris, 7, 41–42, 58,
    66, 139, 178
    Comédie Italienne (Hôtel de Bour-
        gogne), 42, 57–67, 77, 81
    Théâtre de Bourgogne, 64

Jacquet de La Guerre, Élisabeth-Claude.
    See La Guerre, Élisabeth-Claude
    Jacquet de
James, Duke of York, 56
Jouvin de Rochefort. See Rochefort,
    Albert Jouvin de
Juno. See Greece, Juno and
Jupiter, 219. See also Louis XIV, as Jupiter

keyboard instruments, 33–34, 40, 65–66,
    80–81
    harpsichord, 98, 151, 175, 216, 218, 225,
        236, 248

organ, 98, 151, 191, 225, 229
spinet, 40, 218

La Fontaine, Jean de, 94, 99
La Guerre, Élisabeth-Claude Jacquet de,
      7–8, 81, 94, 109, 127, 186,
      239–240, 275
   Cephale et Procris, 240, 254, 266, 269, 272
   Samson, 240
   trio sonatas, 264
Laini, Marinella, 4–6, 27 n.50, 33 n.73,
      72 n.95, 110
Lalande, Michel-Richard de, 9, 126–127,
      139–140, 183, 187, 202
   Confitebor tibi Domine, S. 56, 199–201
   Super flumina Babilonis, S. 13, 148–149,
      257
Lambert, Michel, 224
lament, 93, 103–106, 229, 253 n.29, 255,
      258, 261–262
Lardenois, Antoine, 224
Launay, Denise, 223
Le Brun, Charles, 217
Le Gallois, Jean, 219
Lemene, Francesco de, 114
Le Noble, 246
Linklater, Robin, 244
Lolli, Ange, 60
Lorenzani, Paolo, 115, 247, 272
Loreo, 72–73
Loret, 246
Louis, the Grand Dauphin, "Mon-
      seigneur," 76, 94, 101–102, 130,
      167
Louis IX, "the Pious," Saint, 97, 215
Louis XIII, 97, 135, 186, 221, 223
Louis XIV, 3, 7, 9, 13, 41–42, 54, 56, 85,
      94, 126, 128, 130, 137, 150,
      154–155, 167–168, 180, 204, 207,
      223–224, 239
   as Apollo, 94, 99, 128–129, 131, 215,
      243
   coat of arms of, 87, 182–183, 224
   as Hercules ("Hercule Gaulois"), 131,
      242–243, 246, 260, 270–271
   as Jupiter, 181–182, 215
   and King David, 9, 131, 214–215, 246
   as patron, 57, 61 n.55, 62–63, 77, 88, 91,
      93–94, 97, 102, 181–182, 204,
      212–214, 221–222, 239, 241, 248,
      262, 273–274
   as Sun King, 8, 87–88, 99, 101, 131
   twilight years and legacy of, 239, 274–275

Louis XV, 167
Ludes, Mademoiselle de, 137
lullaby, 104
Lully, Jean-Baptiste, 62, 124–125, 127,
      139–140, 182, 187, 195, 212, 247,
      254, 266, 269–272
   Armide, 232
   Atys, 247, 255, 257–258, 266, 270
   Ballet Hercule Amoureux, 245–246
   "Dialogue de la musique italienne et
      de la musique française," from
      Ballet de la Raillerie, 183–186, 210,
      256, 274
   La Galanterie du temps, 54, 61–62
   petit motet and, 9, 125–126, 186, 208, 212
   Proserpine, 247
   Triomphe de l'Amour, Le, 265 n.43
   See also dance; tragédie en musique

madness, 21–24
madrigalism, 8, 10, 88–89, 93, 111, 115,
      117, 124, 127, 129–130, 144–145,
      154, 159, 168–169, 171, 173, 176,
      195–198, 208–211, 224–226,
      228–231, 233, 235, 237–238,
      251–253, 256, 260, 268, 274
   definition of, 89
Maintenon, Madame de, 109, 137, 224,
      246
   Saint-Cyr and, 137, 224
Mancini, Philippe-Julien, Duke of
      Nevers, 115
Mantua, Duke of. See Gonzaga, Carlo II,
      Duke of Mantua; Gonzaga, Ferdi-
      nando Carlo, Duke of Mantua
Marais, Marin, 247, 269–270, 272
Marazzoli, Marco, 64
Marcello, Antonia Bembo, 27
Marchand, Louis, 224
Marconi, Corte di, 18
Maria Teresa of Spain, 155, 241, 243,
      270–271
Marie-Adélaïde of Savoy, Duchess of
      Burgundy. See Burgundy, Marie-
      Adélaïde of Savoy, Duchess of
Marie-Anne-Christine-Victoire,
      Dauphine, 76–77, 167
Marie de Médicis, 135
Mars, 136
Mary, Blessed Virgin, 103–108, 122, 146
   as Pietà, 107
Mathieu, Nicolas, 185
Mazarin, Jules, 54, 58, 215, 241, 243–245

McClary, Susan, 257
Medici, Cosimo III de', 18 n.27
Melani, Alessandro, 64
Melani, Atto, 244
Melchiori, Giulia, 39, 42, 45, 49
melisma, 115, 129–130, 157, 171, 184, 198,
    210–211, 228, 232, 237, 254, 257
Ménagerie. *See* Versailles, Ménagerie
Menus Plaisirs, 139
Mercure galant, 89–90
Mercury, 136, 262
Mignard, Pierre, 56
Mirimonde, Albert Pomme de, 220
Misch, Conrad, 143 n.24, 148–149, 207,
    209, 211, 225 n.40, 229
Mitford, Nancy, 168
Mocenigo, Betta, 20, 21 n.31
Molière (Jean-Baptiste Poquelin), 62, 94,
    182
Monseigneur. *See* Louis, the Grand
    Dauphin, "Monseigneur"
Monsieur. *See* Orleans, Philippe, Duke of
    Chartres and, "Monsieur"
Montagnier, Jean-Paul, 126, 143 n.23,
    210 n.32, 211
Monteverdi, Claudio, 8–9, 110, 129, 173,
    208, 260
Montona. *See* Istria
Moreau, Jean-Baptiste, 224
Moreschi, Antonio, 15
Morosini, Francesco, 34–36
motet, 131, 140, 149, 151
    elevation, 126–127
    See also *grand motet; petit motet*
moto perpetuo, 121, 160, 252
motto, 96–97, 113–114, 117, 119–120, 159,
    169, 176
Moulinié, Étienne, 224
Mozart, Wolfgang Amadeus, operas of,
    255, 262–263
Muffat, Georg, 275
Mula, Vicenzo da, 51
Murano, San Bernardo di. *See* San
    Bernardo di Murano, convent of
Music (allegorical character), 151. See also
    Produzioni armoniche, wedding
    music of
Muti, Maria Elena, 45–46
Muze historique, La, 62

Nani, Alvise, 75 n.108
Nanto. *See* Bembo, Antonio; Bembo,
    Orseta Corner

narrative style, 8, 85, 101–102, 104,
    108–109, 131, 176, 215, 242
Negri, Maria Angelo di, 51
Néraudau, Jean-Pierre, 242, 244
Niert, Pierre de, 224
Nivers, Guillaume-Gabriel, 126
nobility, determining status of, 16 n.18
Normand, Marc-Roger, "il Coprino,"
    135–136
notes égales, 185
notes inégales, 211, 230, 236, 256, 265
    definition of, 142
Notre Dame de Bonne Nouvelle, 3, 13,
    42, 66, 70–71, 130
    Anne of Austria and, 78
    church of, 56, 66 n.76, 76–78
    community of (*see* Italian Community
    in Paris)
    See also Union Chrétienne ("grand
    Saint Chaumond")
Nouvelles Catholiques, 77

oboe, 137, 225, 248
Octave. *See* Zanotti
Olympus. *See* Greece, Olympus and
opera, 232, 240–272, 274
Opéra, the Paris, 137
opera seria, 248
Orazio. *See* Bianchi, Marc'Antonio;
    Romagnesi, Augustin
orchestra, 135, 139, 151, 181, 186–204,
    247–249, 261, 269–272
orchestration, 181, 191, 196, 204, 211, 248,
    269, 272
Orleans, Anne-Marie of, Duchess of
    Savoy, 135, 167
Orleans, Henrietta, Duchess of. *See*
    Henrietta, Duchess of Orleans,
    "Madame"
Orleans, Philippe, Duke of Chartres and,
    "Monsieur," 85, 94, 102, 135, 167
ornamentation, 112, 116–120, 123–124,
    127, 145, 148, 157, 164, 185, 208,
    210, 256, 264–265
    of *Seconda* phrase, 106, 117–119, 231
ostinato, 92–93, 105–106, 111, 113, 116–117
Ovid, 87–89, 243, 273

Padoani, Diana Paresco, 6, 15–16, 19–20,
    25, 31, 38–40
Padoani, Giacomo, 13–14, 17–20
    Collegio Veneto and, 14
    employment of, 20 n.29, 23, 61

and madness, 21–24
as orator, 14, 25, 27, 31, 33 (see also
    Padua)
as physician, 13–14, 21, 222
residences of, 16, 25, 27–30, 32, 34,
    37–38, 48 n.6, 222 (see also Istria)
status of, 6, 13–14, 27, 31, 41
Vicenza and, 13
Padua, 14–15
Paganoni, Franco, 69–70
Pallavicino, Carlo, 64
Paolini, Paolo, 22 n.33
Paresco, Camillo, 15
Paresco, Giacomo, 15 n.15
Paris, maps of, 43, 65
parlando, 117
partie de remplissage, 248
Patin, Carla Caterina and Gabriella, 221
Patin, Charles, 33 n.72, 221–223
Patin, Guy, 221
Patin, Maddalena Hommetz, 221
Paton, John Glenn, 6
Paul, Saint Vincent de, 76
Paulet, Angélique, 218
Pavée de Vendeuvre family, 272
per arsin et thesin, 208
Pergolesi, Giovanni Battista, 185
Perrin, Pierre, 187
petite basse, 159, 232, 235–237, 256–257,
    265 n.43
    definition of, 232 n.45
petite reprise, 93, 115, 124, 127, 143–144,
    166, 173, 192, 212, 236, 266, 269
    definition of, 93
Petite Union Chrétienne. See Union
    Chrétienne
petit motet, 9, 81, 122, 125–127, 139, 143,
    204–212. See also Lully, Jean-
    Baptiste
Petrarch, 115
Philidor, André Danican, 137
Phyllis (Filli), 114–115, 118, 131
Piles, Roger de, 219
Pinnell, Richard T., 22 n.33, 54 n.33
Piscopia, Elena Lucrezia Cornaro, 33 n.72
pitch, French vs. Italian, 91
plague, 25
plucked instruments, 98
    angélique, 218
    guitar, 56, 154, 218, 220
    lute, 17, 216, 218–220
    lyre, 168
    theorbo, 151, 175, 191, 218, 220, 248

poesie per musica, 9, 58, 60–64, 109, 114,
    121–122, 176
Polani, Nicolò, 35
Pollalion, Marie, 76
précieuses, 62, 218
Presentadi, Jail of the. See Bembo,
    Lorenzo (1637–1703), crime and
    punishment of
Priuli, Giovanni Antonio, 51
Produzioni armoniche, 3–6, 8–9, 66, 85–132,
    134, 144, 167, 176, 178–180, 183,
    213–215, 230, 240, 258, 271, 274
    "Amanti a costo" (no. 34), 116, 122, 140
    "A Monseigneur" (no. 12), 101, 128
    "Amor mio" (no. 20), 116, 122, 140, 146
    "Anima perfida" (no. 33), 115, 119,
        CD tr. 6
    "Beata sirena, deh, frena" (no. 31), 118,
        275
    cantate spirituali of (sacred cantatas,
        nos. 5–7), 81, 98, 103–109, 114,
        225, 262–263, 268, 275
    "Chiaro esempio di gloria" (no. 2),
        95–98, 104, 118, 126, 129, 139–140,
        182, 232, 252, 274, CD tr. 3
    "Chi desia viver in pace" (no. 36),
        118–120, 130, 148, 209 n.30, 232,
        266
    "Clizia amante del sole" (no. 15),
        87–90, 110, CD tr. 1
    coat of arms of, 224
    "Dal centro della luce" (no. 10), 128,
        182, 208
    "Di bell'ire accesi i sguardi" (no. 25),
        118–119, 209 n.30
    "Domine salvum fac regem" (nos. 4, 40),
        97–99, 122, 124–126
    "Freme Borea" (no. 29), 118
    "Ha, que l'absence" (no. 41), 113,
        122–123, 130, 225
    "Habbi pietà di me" (no. 16), 57,
        89–91, 110, 116, 178–180, 225,
        CD tr. 2
    "Immenso splendore" (no. 9), 98–99,
        128
    "Lamento della Vergine" (no. 6), 85,
        CD tr. 4
    "Mi basta così" (no. 22), 113–114, 119,
        122, 208, 252
    "Mi consolo" (no. 27), 116–117, 130,
        CD tr. 7
    "M'ingannasti in verità" (no. 32),
        118–119, 225, CD tr. 8

Produzioni armoniche (continued)
"Non m'hai voluto credere" (no. 24), 118, 225
"Pace a voi" (no. 11), 128, 225
palette for subsequent work, as, 132
"Panis angelicus" (no. 38), 126–127, 145–146
"Passan veloci l'ore" (no. 30), 111–113, 115, 275, CD tr. 5
"Per Monsieur" (no. 37), 102–103, 130, 135, 208, 225
petits motets of (nos. 3–4, 38–40), 81, 122, 124–127, 129–130, 139–140, 142, 181, 187, 194, 202, 204, 208, 212, 224–225, 232, 275
"Pour Saint Louis." (see *Produzioni armoniche, petits motets of* (nos. 3–4, 38–40); *Produzioni armoniche,* "Triumphet astris Lodovici" (no. 3))
"Prendete la porta" (no. 28), 113, 122
"S'è legge d'amore" (no. 26), 116, 118, 225
settings of Fedeli's poetry (nos. 17–19), 58, 121–122
"E ch'avete bell'ingrato" (no. 18), 58, 121–122, 275
"In amor ci vuol ardir" (no. 17), 58, 121
"Non creder a sguardi" (no. 19), 58, 122, 140, 154
"Sonetto al Re" (no. 1), 94–95, 118, 130, 176, 267
"Son sciolti i miei laci" (no. 21), 118
table of contents of, 59, 86
"Te vider gli avi miei" (no. 8), 91–93, 128, 178–180, 208, 225, 252
"Triumphet astris Lodovici" (no. 3), 97–98, 149, 165, 171
"Volgete altrove il guardo" (no. 23), 112–113
wedding music of (nos. 13–14, 35), 9, 85, 127–131, 133–134, 139–140, 150, 171, 173, 178, 275
Pure, Abbé Le, 62

Racine, Jean, 224
Ramis, Pietro, 40
Ranum, Patricia, 126
Raphael, 223
Raynal, Guillaume, 165
récit, 142, 147–149, 186, 195, 199
recitative, 88–90, 94, 99, 102, 104, 110–111, 128, 130, 158, 167–168, 231, 248, 250–254, 262–263
recitative-arioso, 248, 250, 253–254, 260
recitativo affettuoso, 108
recitativo con forza, 108
Redentore, church of the, 28, 52
Regina (Reine), Saint, 103–104, 108–109, 122
Regnault, Marie, 76
Regnault de Solier, Mademoiselle, 219
Rena, Domenico, 64
retrograde, 260
Riccioni Forestier, Barbara 33, 34 n.75
Richelieu, Armand Jean, 242
ritornello, 106–107, 160, 164, 166, 169, 186, 202, 208, 248–249, 252, 257–258
Ritournelle, 140, 143–144, 147–150, 154, 190, 195–196, 198–199, 225–227, 230, 234–237
Rittornello, 154, 211, 226
Robert, Pierre, 187
Rochefort, Albert Jouvin de, 64–65, 67
Rokseth, Yvonne, 4–6, 103, 180, 191, 210, 241 n.1, 255, 259 n.38, 260 n.39, 268 n.45
Romagnesi, Augusten, 61, 66 n.75
Romagnesi, Augustin, 59–60
Romagnesi, Marc'Antonio, 56, 58–59, 62, 66, 121–122, 182, 215
England and, 62
grandfather of, 61 n.56
Poesie liriche and, 58, 60–61, 87–88, 91, 102, 114, 116–118, 128, 138
as poet, 87–89, 103, 114, 118, 121, 139, 176
Romano, Giulio, 223
Romano, Stefano, 178 n.31
Romieri, Gasparo, 48–49
Rosan, Giulio, 15
Rosan, Isabella, 15
Rosand, Ellen, 110, 258 n.37
Rossi, Giovanni Carlo, 64
Rossi, Giuliano, 63
Rossi, Luigi, 260
Rotrou, Jean, 242

Saint-Chamond, Marquis de, 76
Salamon, Zaccaria, 51
Sales, François de, 56, 77
salon, 9, 137, 215–223, 239. *See also* Chéron, Élisabeth-Sophie, salon of

San Bernardo di Murano, convent of, 4, 39–40, 42–45, 47–49, 51, 69, 71, 178–180
San Cassiano, church of, 16 n.17
San Pantalon, parish of, 18 n.25, 34
    Cavalli's home in the, 18
    church of, 18 n.26
    Dukes of Braunschweig-Lüneburg and, 37
San Pantalon in salizada, Padoani home at, 16, 25, 28–30
Santa Maria dell'Orazione in Malamocco, convent of, 32, 39, 47–48, 51–52, 69, 71, 75
Santa Maria Mater Domini, parish of, 15, 16 n.17
Santerre, Jean-Baptiste, 160–161, 163
savants, 219
Savoy
    Christine Marie of France and, 135
    Treaty of Cherasco and, 134
    Turin and, 134–135, 167
    Victor Amadeus I, Duke of, 135
    Victor Amadeus II, Duke of, 134
    War of the Piedmont and, 134
scansion, 118
    alexandrine, 124, 214–215, 242
    endecasillabo, 94, 113, 118–119, 242, 258
    hemistich, 214–215, 242
    irregular, 119, 258
    ottonario, 242
    quartina, 94
    quinario, 173
    senario, 105, 113
    senario piano, 114
    senario tronco, 114
    settenario, 113
    sizain, 215
    terzina, 94
    tronco, 115, 118
Scaramouche. See Fiorilli, Tiberio (Scaramouche)
scena, 249–255
Selles, Domenico, 40–41, 50
Seneca, 243
sept Pseaumes, de David (F-Pn, Rés. Vm¹116), Les, 6, 9, 81, 149, 180, 203, 206, 212–240, 273
    Domine exaudi orationem meam, Ps. 101, 225–240, 257, CD tr. 9
serenata, 179
serpent, 187

seufzer, 108, 232
sex, 37, 105
shawm, 186
Sigismund Francis, Archduke of Austria (Sigismundo Francesco d'Austria), 18 n.27
Signac, 224
silence, 95, 98, 100, 131, 181–182, 207, 252–253, 274
Soleras, Joseph de, 218–219
Sophocles, 243
Sourches, Louis François du Bouchet, Marquis de, 154, 175
spirituality
    astrology and, 92–93, 131
    Christianity and, 176, 242, 246, 269
        Calvinism and, 95, 97, 216
        Catholicism and, 103, 130–131, 214–216, 223
        God and, 130–131, 134, 204, 207, 233, 242
split scoring, 191, 198
stasis, 111, 116–117, 196, 212, 251
Steffani, Agostino, 64
Strozzi, Barbara, 7–8, 20, 21 n.31, 24, 37 n.92, 85, 104–105, 114, 131, 173, 272, 274
    "Basta così," 85, 113–114
    "Il Lamento," 85, 105
Strozzi, Giulio, 105
syncopation, 146, 184, 196, 200, 202, 207, 210, 262, 268

taille, 194, 248, 254–255, 265, 269
Te Deum, 79
    Te Deum (F-Pn, Rés. Vm¹112; Bembo's first Te Deum), 6, 9, 96, 128, 133–151, 175, 178–181, 187, 191–192, 194–195, 197–199, 202, 204, 206, 213, 225, 257, 275
    Te Deum (F-Pn, Rés. Vm¹114; Bembo's second Te Deum), 6, 139, 175, 180, 181–204, 211–213, 275
terra ferma, Venice and, map of, 74
Test Act, 57
tetrachord, descending, 92, 106, 127, 211–212, 257, 259–260, 262
    as emblem of lament, 106, 258 n. 37, 262
text painting. See madrigalism
Tiepolo, Lorenzo, 71, 80, 165
Titian, 31, 50

Titon du Tillet, Évrard, 216, 218, 220
Toulouse-Philidor collection, 199
tragédie en musique, 81, 186, 247–248, 269
tritone, 147
trumpet, 95, 104, 137
 and brass, 143
turba, 104
Turgot, Michel-Étienne, 66–67

Union Chrétienne ("grand Saint Chaumond"), 65–66, 70, 76 n.113, 77,
 187
 canonical hours and, 79
 Hôtel Saint Chaumond, 65, 67, 76
 La Petite Union Chrétienne des Dames
 de Saint Chaumond ("petit Saint
 Chaumond"), 3–5, 7, 42, 46, 48
 n.7, 57–58, 66, 71, 76–81, 85, 109,
 194, 204, 223
 See also Notre Dame de Bonne Nouvelle
University of Padua, 13–14, 32
University of Venice, 23 n.37

Vacca, Giuseppe Matteo, 135
variation techniques, 112, 119, 122, 154,
 184
Vendramin, Degna Merita, 42, 48
Vendramin, Vincenzo, 51
Ventadour, Duchess of, 168
Verona, 20, 24, 32, 60
Versailles, 81, 94, 137, 151, 187, 215
 Chapelle Royale, 151, 194, 204
 Grand Trianon, 137
 Ménagerie, 137–138, 154, 194, 223, 239
Vertron, Claude-Charles Guyonnet de,
 221–223, 246
Vicenza, 14–15
Vigarani family, 245–246, 263

Villedieu (Marie-Catherine Desjardins),
 Madame de, 56
Vinaccesi, Benedetto, 177, 182
Vincenti, Giovanni Francesco, 71, 80
viola da gamba, 191, 199, 218, 220, 225,
 236
violin, 104, 112, 137, 140, 143, 145–146,
 148–149, 151, 158, 175, 186,
 190–192, 195, 200–201, 207–208,
 212, 218, 224–225, 228, 230–232,
 236, 238, 248, 264
 clefs for, 140, 185, 196, 198
 petits violons, 62
 vingt-quatre violons du Roi, 137, 194
virtù, 20, 31, 253 n.29, 273
Virtue (allegorical character), 151. See also
 Produzioni armoniche, wedding
 music of
virtuosity, 115–116, 119–121, 130, 157
Visée, Robert de, 154
Viviani, Giovanni Buonaventura, 64
voice, 8, 13, 20–21, 80–81, 95, 275

women in music, 5, 7
 child prodigy and, 6, 20–21
 domesticity and, 275
 perspective of, 108, 273
 woman's song and, 122, 146, 273–275
 women composers and, 6–8, 123, 272,
 274

Xerse. See Cavalli, Francesco

Zanforti, Raimondo, 18, 24 n.40, 32–33
Zanotti, 66 n.77
Zeno, Apostolo, 72
Zustiniani, Madalena, 178 n.31
Zusto, Anzolo, 51